Asian Contributions to Cross-Cultural Psychology

EDITORS

JANAK PANDEY
DURGANAND SINHA
DHARM P.S. BHAWUK

SAGE PUBLICATIONS
NEW DELHI/THOUSAND OAKS/LONDON

First published in 1996 by

Sage Publications India Pvt Ltd
M-32 Greater Kailash Market, I
New Delhi 110 048

Sage Publications Inc
2455 Teller Road
Thousand Oaks, California 91320

Sage Publications Ltd
6 Bonhill Street
London EC2A 4PU

Published by Tejeshwar Singh for Sage Publications India Pvt Ltd, phototypeset by Pagewell Photosetters, Pondicherry, and printed at Chaman Enterprises, Delhi.

Library of Congress Cataloging-in-Publication Data

Asian contributions to cross-cultural psychology / editors, Janak Pandey, Durganand Sinha, Dharm P.S. Bhawuk.

    p.   cm.

    Proceedings of the Fourth Asian Regional Conference of the International Association for Cross-Cultural Psychology, held Jan, 3–7, 1992 in Kathmandu, Nepal.

    Includes bibliographical references.

    1. Ethnopsychology—Asia—Congresses. 2. Cognition and culture—Asia—Congresses. 3. Family—Asia—Congresses. I. Pandey, Janak, 1945–   . II. Sinha, Durganand. III. Bhawuk, Dharm P.S. IV. International Association for Cross-Cultural Psychology, Asian Regional Conference (4th: 1992: Kathmandu, Nepal)

GN625.A79   1996   155.8′095—dc20   95–50271 CIP

ISBN   0–8039–9244–0 (US-hb)   81–7036–473–6 (India-hb)
          0–8039–9245–9 (US-pb)   81–7036–474–4 (India-pb)

Sage Production Editor: *Payal Mehta*

Contents

List of Tables

List of Figures

Preface

To facilitate communication among psychologists and other social scientists, the International Association for Cross-Cultural Psychology (IACCP) periodically organises international and regional conferences. Regional conferences enable scholars belonging to a region to interact among themselves and also with psychologists from other parts of the world who share their interests. The Fourth Regional IACCP Congress was held in Kathmandu, Nepal, from 3 to 7 January 1992. The recently formed Nepalese Psychological Association, the Human Resource Development Centre, Kathmandu, and the International Training Institute, Kathmandu, were the local hosts.

Nepal has special significance for cross-cultural psychology in a number of ways. Inhabited by many ethnic groups with their distinctive lifestyles and cultures, it can be regarded as a veritable gold mine for comparative cross-cultural research. With some of the highest and most inaccessible mountains girded by lush and fertile *Terai* and a belt of marshy jungles and rugged foothills, the country provides a unique opportunity to experience cultural and ecological diversities that shape human functioning. One can still find people uncontaminated by modern civilisation along with those displaying all the trappings of modernity. In transportation, the country moves from mountain bridle paths to jet travel. Apart from the rich academic fare that the organisers had arranged, the participants had a chance to experience the grandeur of its snow peaks and the breath-taking beauty of its valleys. Though modern psychology had a somewhat delayed start, the country has within a short time produced scholars whose studies in cross-cultural areas have been remarkable.

This book of proceedings consists of invited addresses delivered by several distinguished cross-cultural psychologists and some selected and edited papers presented during the scientific sessions of the Congress. The volume is organised in four sections: theoretical issues and applications; family experiences and cognitive processes; dimensions of self and the achievement process; and social values and problems of developing societies. Contributions included in the volume highlight some of the psychological concerns that have attracted the attention of cross-cultural psychologists and provide a glimpse of their research perspectives and comparative empirical studies. It is hoped that psychologists, anthropologists, sociologists, educators, and other students of human behaviour interested in understanding the influences exerted by the socio-cultural milieu will find the volume useful.

The IACCP would like to express its gratitude to all the Nepalese colleagues and friends who participated and assisted in various ways in the organisation of the Congress. Special thanks are due to scholars like Dr Trailokya Nath Uprety, Vice-Chairman of the National Education Commission; Mr Kedar Bhakta Mathema, Vice-Chancellor, Tribhuvan University; Professor Dor Bahadur Bista; Professor Pannalal Pradhan, Chief of the Planning Division, Tribhuvan University; Professor Ayan Bahadur Shrestha, President, Nepalese Psychological Association, and Head, Department of Psychology, Tribhuvan University; and Mr Parimal Jha of the Human Resource Development Centre, Kathmandu. Professor Çiğdem Kağitçibaşi, President of the IACCP, encouraged and supported the Kathmandu Congress. We take this opportunity to thank her and the past President, Professor Roy S. Malpass, for supporting the publication of this volume.

We are also grateful to the Department of Psychology, University of Allahabad, the Institute of Industrial and Labour Relations, University of Illinois at Urbana-Champaign, the International Training Institute, Kathmandu, and the Department of Psychology, University of Manitoba, for extending facilities to the editors in the preparation of the volume, and to Ms Geeta Biswas for her editorial assistance.

JANAK PANDEY
DURGANAND SINHA
DHARM P.S. BHAWUK

Section 1

Theoretical Issues and Applications

1

Introduction

This section includes five contributions on cross-cultural psychology: Asian scenario, applications of cross-cultural psychology in development, implications of the indigenous psychology approach, and conceptualisation of the theory of agency, action, and culture. Durganand Sinha has traced the historical development of cross-cultural psychology in Asia. He has presented various dimensions of the contemporary research trends in the Asian context. He has argued that the Asian intellectual traditions have been particularly sensitive to appreciate and understand the behaviour and reactions of people in their cultural context. This orientation is the core of cross-cultural psychology and, therefore, the Asian soil has been the most fertile for the development of this discipline. In addition, diversities in socio-cultural, economic, political, linguistic, religion and other aspects of society and culture in Asia facilitate the growth of cross-cultural psychology. However, a word of caution needs to be added that the Euro–American dominance of the field has acted as a major inhibitor leading to rare instances of research comparing two or more Asian cultures.

Çiğdem Kağitçibaşi has argued that for social scientists including psychologists in developing countries, development is "the number one item on the agenda". While recognising the role of human factors in development, she has strongly advocated that the western assumptions and theories about human nature need to be replaced by sound knowledge based on cross-cultural research which takes into account traditions, values, and the way of life of the people. She has identified a number of socio-cultural variables which are typical characteristics of developing societies and has attempted to relate them to development processes. For example, the prevalent value of family interdependence and family culture of relatedness lead to the socialisation of familistic and communal values of mutual support rather than individualistic achievement. Kağitçibaşi, has strongly argued that a different model is needed to understand the family dynamics and society for effective social engineering to facilitate human development. Models based on the individualistic cultural ethos do not have much significance in developing countries. She has suggested a holistic model of human development focusing on the interaction of the growing child with his/her family and the interaction of the family with its environment (the community).

John G. Adair has examined the growing movement which he has labelled the indigenous psychology bandwagon; he has argued that psychology borrowed from the west needs to be replaced by a discipline that is better suited to the local culture. He has clarified the goal of indigenisation and its function as a process to develop an "appropriate" psychology for the culture. Generally regarded as a positive development, there has been a tendency to confuse indigenisation as a goal. The evidence of this reification is seen in the tendency to equate indigenous with early religious or philosophical writing, with a narrow search for uniquely native traits or concepts, or to define indigenous linguistically. The tendencies to condemn western influence or to call for indigenous developments instead of conducting culturally-appropriate research, or to focus on differences and comparisons with the west, suggest an indigenous psychology may be alternatively regarded as a discipline that has matured to the point where it addresses questions of local behaviour and important social issues.

Ype H. Poortinga has discussed the way in which ethnocentrism has entered cross-cultural psychology at four levels: in the choice of stimuli or items, in the choice of measuring instruments, in the formulation of theories and, most important, in the selection of topics for research. According to Poortinga, the indigenous psychology movement is a welcome development to redress this ethnocentrism. However, he has cautioned that by emphasising local understanding and explanation of behaviour, intercultural differences in psychological functioning tend to be overrated.

Lutz H. Eckensberger has presented an action theoretical approach to cross-cultural research. To understand human activities, Eckensberger has systematically formulated that it is essential to analyse the subjective rule and meaning systems in a certain context and to understand the collective meaning and rule systems of which the individual is a part and makes reference to. In the course of development, cultural and societal rule systems are habituated. These systems define the framework within which the individual's regulations take place and offer possibilities for and limitations to regulatory actions. These papers present the ongoing debates on the nature and applications of psychology in general and cross-cultural psychology in particular.

2

Cross-Cultural Psychology: The Asian Scenario

DURGANAND SINHA

In order to appreciate and understand the behaviour and reactions of people, the cultural context in which they occur is important. This contextual orientation has been accorded special importance since times immemorial in the cultural traditions of India and other Asian countries. According to Indian wisdom, man's reality is inextricably interwoven with the socio-cultural milieu, and to understand and judge his conduct, it is essential to place it in the context of *desh* (place), *kala* (time), and *patra* (individual). This orientation can easily be considered as the core of cross-cultural psychology. With this contextual perspective, it is not surprising that Asia occupies a significant place in the development of cross-cultural psychology. Besides, the continent provides enormous heterogeneity and unlimited diversity in geographical, demographic and socio-cultural characteristics, philosophies, religions, and languages. These diversities exist not only between different countries, but also within the same country. Since one of the main strategies adopted by cross-cultural psychology is to maximise variations among groups by careful sampling of cultures, countries in Asia due to their heterogeneity open up immense possibilities for cross-cultural research. It is, therefore, not surprising that at the turn of the century the first observations on the influence of culture on psychological processes like perception, memory, susceptibility to certain types of geometrical optical illusions were made among the Asian people by W.H.R. Rivers (1901, 1905), the founding father of cross-cultural psychology.

Some of the important studies by cultural anthropologists, which can be regarded as the precursor of cross-cultural psychology, were done in Asia. In most "multinational" cross-cultural studies on social-isation, child development and gender stereotypes, Hong Kong, India, Nepal, the Philippines and other countries in Asia have helped to provide the comparative data. The west "needed" the Asian countries as a crucible to put to rigorous test psychology's tentative theories. The initiative for the studies came from the west and its theoretical needs predominated over the relevance of research to the countries concerned.

The situation has changed and Asia has become the major site outside the English-speaking world where cross-cultural research has been making rapid strides. Dawson organised a strong nucleus in the University of Hong Kong in the 1960s. His Traditional versus Modern-ity Scale (Dawson, 1963) was one of the earliest tools used in cross-cultural psychology for measurement of attitudinal modernity. Further, his work on cultural and physiological influences upon spatial-percep-tual process is an outstanding example of a theoretical model integrating the two factors in the determination of a psychological process (Daw-son, 1967). Subsequently, the Chinese University of Hong Kong has also developed a strong tradition of cross-cultural research. Since ancient times India has a sound base for cross-cultural research in its tradition of viewing behaviour in its contextual aspect. Scholars, there-fore, had no difficulty in adopting the strategy of cross-cultural research. It is indeed noteworthy that even a country like Nepal which has very few psychologists has made a significant contribution to the analysis of map drawing and reading among Nepalese children (Dart and Pradhan, 1967). If one goes merely by the number of papers published in international journals that cater to cross-cultural interests, the contri-bution of Asian scholars has been next only to those from North America and Europe.

Asia's contribution to the development of the field is significant in yet another way. It was in 1972 in the Department of Psychology,

University of Hong Kong that the International Association for Cross-Cultural Psychology (IACCP) was established and the first international Congress was held. The interest of Asian scholars and the contributions on the international plane are reflected by the fact that no less than four regional IACCP conferences, since the inception of the association, have been held in Asian countries. It is also significant that of the 12 presidents of the IACCP elected so far, four have been from Asian countries.

Even before the formal introduction of the subject in the late 1950s, cross-cultural orientation seemed to be at least implicitly at the back of most of the studies. A majority of these studies were replicative of western researches. But the main reason advanced for replication was to find out whether or not the results obtained conformed to the findings of corresponding studies in the west (see D. Sinha, 1986 for details). Though not cross-cultural in the strict sense of the term, their perspective was clearly cross-cultural. The soil was, therefore, ready, and it did not take long for cross-cultural psychology to blossom into a vigorous area of research activity on the continent.

A BRIEF REVIEW OF CROSS-CULTURAL PSYCHOLOGY IN ASIA

It is not possible to provide an exhaustive review of the studies conducted and the trends they reflect. However, some main points are indicated.

The studies conducted display varying levels of scientific sophistication. At one end there are studies where the main thrust has been to obtain differences on certain psychological characteristics by comparing cultural groups that are easily available. No rationale is provided for making the comparison or to examine the relevance of the characteristic in question or the appropriateness of the measure used. On the other hand, there are studies—and their number is fortunately growing—that emanate from a distinct theoretical model, generate specific hypotheses after taking into account the cultural features of the groups, and instead of using "borrowed" tests they suitably modify or develop appropriate tests, and interpret the findings in the light of the ecological and cultural characteristics of the groups. Careful ethnographic analysis often precedes the designing of such studies. Studies of Triandis and his Asian colleagues (Hui, Triandis, and Yee, 1991) on individualism–collectivism, and of DeRidder, Tripathi and their associates (DeRidder and Tripathi, 1992) on intergroup relations in India and the Netherlands, and of Sinha and his colleagues using the eco-cultural model and studying psychosocial concomitants of acculturation on tribes (D. Sinha, 1979, 1980; D. Sinha and Bharat, 1985; D. Sinha and Shrestha, 1992; G. Sinha, 1988) provide appropriate examples of such long-term systematic investigations.

Child Rearing and Socialisation

India has been one of the target countries for providing comparative data. Minturn and Lambert (1964) and Minturn and Hitchcock (1966), as part of the *Six Cultures* studies, have highlighted a large number of behaviours that seem to characterise the Indian child, e.g., sparing use of positive reinforcement, frequent use of "don't" in guiding behaviour, absence of training in self-reliance and responsibility, absence of learning to solve problems, and inculcation of dependency. The findings have influenced the thinking of many developmental psychologists in the country.

Rohner and Rohner (1976) have studied the Indian child in the context of the acceptance–rejection theory. Kakar (1978, p. 33) has pointed to the sudden reversal from unrestricted protective indulgence by the mother during infancy in matters of feeding, sleeping and toilet training to enforcement of strict disciplining later on, which has been regarded as a source of anxiety (D. Sinha, 1962). More recently, patterns of socialisation in India (Orissa) and Sweden have been compared with regard to parental norms and expectations, the former being concrete, unanimous, easy to reinforce and perceive, while the Swedish attitudes were found to be abstract, vague and often contradictory (Ekstrand and Ekstrand, 1985). A significant finding was the cultural difference in conceptualising "independence". While in Orissa it had a social dimension with synonyms like interdependence, independent in one's thought, being able to stand on one's own, the Swedish concept was closer to self-reliance, autonomy, and individualistic independence (Ekstrand, 1990).

Kakar's (1978) researches in this area are outstanding. He has brought to light the significance of elaborate systems of rituals and ceremonies prescribed at various stages in the life of a child in his psychosocial development. He has also highlighted the contrasts between the Indian and western child-rearing practices.

Thai psychologists have done a signal service in emphasising the importance of the Asian cultural context in child development. The volume *Handbook of Asian child development and child rearing practices* (Suvannathat, Bhanthumnavin, Bhuapiron, and Keats, 1985), in spite of its heavy dependence on western theory and orientation, is a significant source of information on the socio-cultural situation of the child in Asia in the context of changing family patterns.

It is admitted that cross-cultural studies on child development in Asia have been heavily influenced by the west and western conceptual framework is still popular. But Asian scholars are increasingly becoming aware of their limited applicability.

Study of Values

Systematic cross-cultural comparison of values goes back to the work of Charles Morris (1956) in the mid-1950s. Impressed by this work, Indian psychologists undertook comparative studies of values and attitudes of Indian, Chinese, British, and American students (Singh, Huang, and Thompson, 1962; Beg, 1966; Bhatnagar, 1967). Following the development of value measures like Rokeach, cross-cultural surveys have become increasingly popular. Ng and his colleagues (Ng et al., 1982) in Bangladesh, India, Hong Kong and six other countries in East Asia and the Pacific slightly modified Rokeach's list to suit the politico-economic changes in the region and analysed the characteristic value differences. The Weberian line of thinking and the monumental study of Hofstede (1980),wherein he identified the value cluster called "dependent collectivism" which characterised many Asian countries was associated closely with the level of economic development, provided impetus for many value studies. This aspect has been of special concern for psychologists in Asia. Seminars have been organised in Hong Kong and Taiwan, and this has led to the publication of two significant volumes: *Social values and development: Asian perspectives* (D. Sinha and Kao, 1988) and the special issue of the *International*

Journal of Psychology entitled "Social Values and Effective Organiz-ations" (Kao, Sung, and D. Sinha, 1990). J.B.P. Sinha (1990) in his *Work culture in the Indian context* has related the findings in India with those obtained by Neville and Super (1986) in their work import-ance study.

Of the many values that have been studied, individualism–collectivism dichotomy is easily the one which has generated the maximum volume of work in Asia. The claim that countries and cultures can be demarcated along this dimension and that economic development and industrial-isation are closely associated with individualistic orientation—the Japanese "miracle" being explained away—have goaded psychologists especially in India and Hong Kong, to develop appropriate measures (Hui, 1988; Hui and Triandis, 1985; J.B.P. Sinha and Verma, 1987) and elaborate and examine the construct critically. Its-dichotomous character has been questioned (Kağitçibaşi, 1987; Kashima, 1987; D. Sinha and Tripathi, 1991). Harry Hui, Leung, Bond, Kashima, J.B.P. Sinha and Verma, among others, have been actively engaged in investi-gating the I–C dimension in a systematic way.

Moral judgment is an important aspect of value, but has not received adequate attention of Asian cross-cultural psychologists despite the claims made about the universality of the Piagetian and Kohlberg models. Some scholars in India and Hong Kong have raised substantial criticism of Kohlberg's model even in its modified form (Shweder, Mahapatra, and Miller, 1990; Miller, Bersoff, and Harwood, 1990). It has been observed that Indians reflect a moral code that accords priority to social duties, while American judgments reflect more of individual rights. In Hong Kong, studies have revealed that the Chinese display not only the prescriptive norm of the "Golden Mean", but compared to the English subjects they also possessed a stronger tendency to perform altruistic acts towards others and abide by law. In general, the Chinese emphasised *Ch'ing* (human affection or senti-ment) more than *li* (reason or rationality), and they valued filial piety, group solidarity, collectivism and humanity (Ma, 1988, 1989).

Social Behaviour

A large number of cross-cultural studies have been conducted on different facets of social behaviour. Among others, leadership, concept of justice and fairness, competitiveness, conformity, attribution, inter-group relations and conflict resolution and gender behaviour have been the favourite topics. In one of the early studies on Indian children, conducted along the lines of Lippitt and White (1958), Mead (1967) observed that unlike the American children, they were more productive under the authoritarian than under the democratic style of leadership. Other investigations conducted in organisational settings, however, have challenged such a sweeping conclusion. In this context, the work that has had the maximum impact is that of J.B.P Sinha (1980) on *nurturant task leader* postulating a third style more suited to the transitional condition of the country. Comparing supervisory orientations in India and Iran, D. Sinha and Saatchi (1977) observed many similarities and differences; the authors attributed the differences to the socio-cultural factors operating in the two countries.

Misumi's (1985, 1992) studies on the TM theory of leadership are noteworthy from a cross-cultural perspective. He concluded that though Japan used the west as its model for development, its management was not necessarily an imitation of the European or American patterns. It is unique and deeply rooted in the tradition of the Japanese society with distinctive work values. Comparisons of two collectivist (Japan and Hong Kong) and two individualist cultures (Britain and the United States) have revealed that in all of them the core of leadership behaviour identified by the subordinates was similar but there were differences in specific actions that were construed as leadership (Smith, Peterson, Bond, and Misumi, 1992).

Exchange and equity theories have stimulated many Asian investigations focusing on cross-cultural comparisons in the interpretation of these concepts. Several Chinese and Indian scholars have made a special study of distributive justice judgment. Orientals as compared with westerners have been found to be generally less inclined to use the proportionality rule (Leung and Bond, 1982, 1984; Mahler, Greenberg, and Hayachi, 1981). Chiu (1991a, 1991b) has observed that the criteria for justice judgment were the Confucian precept *yi* (righteousness) and role expectations, which remained dominant despite modernisation. Others have also observed that Asians favour equality more than the equity rule (Kashima, Siegal, Tanaka, and Isaka, 1988; Leung, 1987). In similar studies conducted in India, reward allocation was found to be according to need rather than merit or equity among Indians than among Australians and Americans (Murphy-Berman, Berman, Singh, Pachauri, and Kumar, 1984; Berman, Murphy-Berman, and Singh, 1985). Krishnan (1992), who has reviewed the traditional Indian views of justice, has rightly pointed to the western orientation of the studies and disregard of the specific aspects that have special relevance to contemporary Indian society.

Co-action and competition, altruistic behaviour, ingratiation and Machiavellianism, risky shifts, conformity, attribution, gender behaviour, intergroup relations and conflict resolution strategies have also been studied cross-culturally. Comparing Australian and Chinese perceptions of social episodes, Forgas and Bond (1985) have observed that while the former emphasised competitiveness, self-confidence and freedom, the Chinese stressed communal feelings, social usefulness and acceptance of authority. Carment's study (1974) revealed that Indians generally were more competitive than Canadians. However, there are only scattered investigations in these areas.

Pandey (1986) has viewed ingratiation as a favourite and ubiquitous manipulative tactic in contemporary India, and has discussed the problem in a cross-cultural perspective and has noted self-degradation, instrumental dependency, name dropping, and changing position with the situation to be the favourite Indian tactics (Pandey, 1980). Some tribal and non-tribal differences have also been noted (Pandey and Kakkar, 1982).

Most studies on prosocial behaviour have been unicultural. However, comparisons between Canadians and Indians revealed no difference in the proportion of offers to help, but Indian males were lower in acceptance of help. Analysing the disbursement of rewards, L'Armand and Pepitone (1975) have observed Indians to reward themselves more while Americans tended to reward their peers more than themselves. Commenting on the studies conducted, D. Sinha (1984) has pleaded for an Indian cultural perspective taking into account the tradition of giving and the social and community orientation.

There have not been many cross-cultural comparative studies of conformity despite the contention often made in the west of Asians being conformists, the existence of strong group influence, and compliance training being an integral part of socialisation. However, Frager's (1970) finding on Asch-type of experiments of Japanese being lower in conformity than Americans was noted to be misleading if one took into account the notions of "proper behaviour" in Japan (Matsuda, 1985). Conformity was determined by the degree of intimacy involved; it was greatest in *seken* (moderately cohesive groups), followed by *uchi* (mutually selected friends), and *soto* (people selected at random). The need for taking into account the cultural expectations and norms is obvious.

Cross-cultural comparisons of attribution have revealed not only differences between Asians and westerners but also among different countries in Asia. Unlike the Whites, Asians tended to attribute success to external causes but assumed responsibility for failure (Fry and Ghosh, 1980). Analysing attributions for doing good to others, Indian subjects were found to make fewer references to disposition and more to situation specific factors than Americans. Conducting a study on intergroup relations, Taylor and Jaggi (1974) observed that Hindu participants made more internal attributions for positive behaviours of Hindus than for negative ones. On the other hand, they tended to make external attributions for positive and internal attributions for negative behaviours of Muslims. In a similar study in Malaysia, Hewstone and Ward (1985) found that the Malays attributed internal factors for positive actions of their own group and external factors for negative ones. The reverse was seen in the case of the Chinese. In a follow-up study in Singapore, while the Malays made internal attributions for the positive behaviours of their own group, there were no significant differences for the positive or negative behaviours of the Chinese, nor did the Chinese attributions favour either group (Hewstone, 1989). Similar results have been obtained in laboratory settings (Hewstone, Bond, and Wan, 1983; Bond, Chiu, and Wan, 1984).

In view of the rapid changes taking place in the Asian countries, cultural factors associated with modernity and its levels have been analysed in different countries. Assisted by Singh, Inkeles and Smith (1974) have made comparisons of different cultures on psychological modernity. The popular image of modernity in India correlated highly with the OM Scale, thereby indicating a close relationship between a cross-cultural measure and "an entirely local, native, culture-based measure of modernity" (Inkeles and Singh, 1975). In this context it should be noted that Dawson (1963), who worked in Hong Kong, analysed the scores obtained by various samples from African countries and observed the interesting phenomenon of "compartmentalization" which characterises persons from countries undergoing rapid social change.

Apart from diversities in culture, religion and ethnicity, countries in Asia often experience tensions and intergroup conflicts. Migrations, international trade and business have brought together groups from very diverse socio-economic and cultural backgrounds. With such cultural interfacings, problems of intergroup differences often arise. Scholars from Hong Kong and Japan have made cross-cultural investigations of the strategies that the Japanese, Malay, Chinese and other groups follow. Their characteristic styles in bargaining, negotiation, arbitration and conflict resolution as distinct from those prevailing in the west have been highlighted (Leung and Wu, 1990). In this context, a long-term systematic study of norm violation and intergroup relations in India and the Netherlands is noteworthy (DeRidder and Tripathi, 1992).

Self, Identity and Personality

Since culture plays an important role in shaping the self, identity and personality, the issue has inevitably attracted the attention of innumerable cross-cultural psychologists in Asia. Doi (1973) has emphasised the concept of *amae* (dependence). Blurring of the distinction between self (person) and social group that the concept implies constitutes a dominant attitude in Japanese society and is said to underlie Japanese personality and many mental health problems. Indian studies have consistently stressed the non-duality between self and non-self, conceptualising the two in a state of symbiotic relationship (D. Sinha, 1990a; D. Sinha and Naidu, 1992). Comparing self in India and America, Ronald (1984) has also emphasised the same point. In a study conducted in Orissa, Shweder and Bourne (1984) have observed that persons were believed to be altered by social relations into which they entered and were described not so much in terms of enduring traits, but in terms of social relationships. While in the west, autonomy and separateness are emphasised and the individual is perceived as comprising a set of separate traits and abilities, in eastern cultures, relatedness and interdependence are sought and are rooted in the concept of self, which is not a discrete entity, but inherently linked to others (Markus and Kitayama, 1991).

Before discussing studies on specific personality traits, it should be noted that Paranjpe (1975), adopting a largely Eriksonian approach, has provided excellent case studies of Indian and Canadian youth. Of particular interest is the manner in which indigenous institutions are utilised in the two cultures for resolving identity crises.

As for specific personality characteristics, in the mid-1950s, Melikian (1956) and Prothro and Melikian (1953) studied the correlates of authoritarianism among Arabs, Egyptians and Americans. Comparisons of six cultural groups on the California F-Scale (Mead and Whittakar, 1967) revealed that the Americans obtained the lowest scores while the Indians had the highest scores. Kureshi and his colleagues have compared Indian students with their Iranian, Palestinian and African counterparts on traits like locus of control, death anxiety and dominance, extrapunitiveness and impunitiveness, and need for achievement and fear of failure (Kureshi and Husain, 1981a, 1981b, 1982; Kureshi, Husain, and Bhatnagar, 1979). Many cross-cultural studies have also been done on anxiety, comparing Indian students with American (D. Sinha, 1962; Spielberger, Sharma, and Singh, 1973) and Iranian students (Sharma, Pranian, and Spielberger, 1983). In all these studies, however, the rationale for making such comparisons are hardly provided.

Stress, Psychopathology and Psychotherapy

Culture makes a difference to the experience of stress, and is an important factor with regard to the kind of social support system available to the individual for coping with it. In spite of the popularity of stress research, not much cross-cultural comparative work has been done by Asian psychologists. The work of Palsane and his associates, however, is significant. They have analysed the concept and factors underlying its generation according to the ancient Indian treatises, and have also compared the Indian and western approaches, especially with regard to the role assigned to the strength of motives and frustrations, and their behavioural consequences (Palsane, Bhavsar, Goswami, and Evans, 1986). In another study, Type A and Type B bus drivers in India and the USA were compared for absenteeism, accidents, reports of occupational stress and on some physiological and behavioural indices (Evans, Palsane, and Carrere, 1987). Further, the interactive effects of an enduring environmental stressor with acute, social stressors on psychological distress were compared using samples from the two countries (Lepore, Evans, and Palsane, 1991). In a different type of study, D. Sinha, Mishra, and Berry (1992a) have compared stress among the nomadic and sedentary tribes undergoing the process of acculturation.

Asian psychologists have made contributions to the area often called "cross-cultural psychopathology": whether symptoms have similar manifestations in all cultures or are culture bound. Taiwanese and Indian scholars have worked on the 9-country WHO project on schizophrenia. Cultural factors were found to play a part. Compared to patients in the west, neurotic patients in India complained more of physical symptoms (Verma and Wig, 1974). Somatisation was observed more in Indian patients than in the west where ailments were more frequently manifested in psychological forms (Rastogi, Jindal, Gupta, Rana, and Singhal, 1976).

Anthropologists for long have been interested in many exotic forms of psychotherapy practised in non-western cultures. Cross-cultural psychologists in Asia have evinced a keen interest in some of the procedures practised in Japan, China, and India. *Amae* (dependency) has been considered vital to Japanese culture (Doi, 1984) and forms the basis of interpersonal relationship during psychotherapy called *Mòrita* (Miura and Usa, 1970). Similarly, *sunao* (obedience) is the core of *Naikan* therapy (Tanaka-Matsumi, 1979). In China, some unique forms of psychotherapies have been investigated utilising modern psychological techniques. The main ones being acupuncture, breathing exercises called *gigong*, and the practise of calligraphy (Kao, 1989). Using the idioms of psychoanalysis and modern psychology, Kakar (1982) has described the traditional healing practises in India, and has highlighted the similarities and differences with western practises. Neki's (1973) *guru-chela* (preceptor-pupil) paradigm is significant from a cross-cultural perspective. It is based on a pattern of inter-personal relationships distinctive of Indian culture, and is considered more appropriate for therapeutic interactions. Changing patterns of socialisation in Turkey (Kağitçibaşi, 1988), and family dynamics in India (D. Sinha, 1988a) against the backdrop of social change and their implications for healthy development have been highlighted. Ward (1989) has discussed altered states of consciousness, traditional health care and mental health from a cross-cultural perspective.

Perceptual and Cognitive Functioning

Owing to their vastly different cultural systems, Asia and Africa have been "targeted" for comparative data by American and European cross-cultural psychologists since the very beginning. Initially, local scholars collaborated only as minor partners in studies on perception and cognition where the main objective was to test theories and paradigms emanating from the west. Sinha has collaborated in a number of such projects: analysis of performance differences on the perception of topological and Euclidean spatial features of children from Hong Kong, India, Scotland, and Zambia (Jahoda, Deregowski, and Sinha, 1974); and analysis of the degree of perceptual difficulty and retention of materials presented only pictorially or in text or both pictorially as well as in text among children from India, Scotland and three African countries (Jahoda, Cheyne, Deregowski, Sinha, and Collingbourne, 1976).

The main impetus for cross-cultural research in this field came from the eco-cultural model of John Berry (1976). Sinha and his associates utilised significant variations in ecological and cultural arrangements that the country provides, and designed a whole programme of studies to analyse the effects of nomadic and sedentary lifestyles of tribal groups (D. Sinha, 1979), family types (D. Sinha and Bharat, 1985), gender differences and economy (D. Sinha, 1980), hill and plains ecology and culture (D. Sinha and Shrestha, 1992), and acculturative influences of exposure to industry, city and formal education (G. Sinha, 1988) on cognitive style. Other aspects of cognitive functioning like intermodal perception and information processing (Sinha, Mishra, and Berry, 1992b, 1992c), and memory processes (Mishra, 1988; Mishra and Singh, 1992) have also been studied within the same framework.

In Piagetian-type conservation research, which is a favourite area, largely sub-cultural differences have been investigated. Cross-cultural data have been provided by Chung (1983) on Korean and British children from contrasting social and cultural backgrounds; and Sinha and Jha (1989) have studied tribals and non-tribals differentially exposed to urban/rural environments and to formal schooling. Matsuda (1992) has made a comparison of Japanese and Australian children on problem solving strategies. By obtaining the conceptions of learning of Nepalese children (Watkins and Regmi, 1992) and comparing the same with those of Australians and Filipinos, the stereotype of Asians being "rote learners" has been examined (Watkins, Regmi, and Astilla, 1991).

Methodological Issues

Most of the tests and instruments for the collection of data in non-western cultures have been developed in western countries, and there is always the problem of equivalence and comparability. Problems of transfer of constructs and tools across cultures have usually been neglected. Pareek and Rao (1980), however, have dealt with some practical aspects of conducting cross-cultural surveys and interviewing. D. Sinha (1983b) has discussed the problems of collecting data on preliterate tribal and rural populations, and has grouped the error factors under two broad categories: *experimental effects* and *demand characteristics of experiment*. Mukherjee (1967) has done cross-cultural analysis of social desirability judgments. The development of culturally appropriate measures has attracted the attention of Sinha who has developed a number of tests like level of aspiration and cognitive style (D. Sinha, 1969, 1978). In these tests, the original paradigm of the measures have been kept constant while indigenous materials and activities have been utilised. Among the cross-cultural psychologists in Hong Kong, Hui and Triandis (1985) have reviewed various strategies of cross-cultural measurement. Leung (1989) has discussed the individual and collective level analyses of cross-cultural differences; and Leung and Bond (1989) have dealt with empirical identification of dimensions of cross-cultural comparison. Problems of validity and equivalence involved in using foreign tests like the EPI in Sri Lanka have been addressed by Perera and Eysenck (1984), and by Watkins, Regmi, and Astilla (1991) for scores on the Learning Process Questionnaire.

General Issues

Many Asian psychologists have evinced a keen interest in important general issues of cross-cultural research. Bond (1988) and D. Sinha (1989) have discussed how the entry of cross-cultural psychology has posed a challenge to the tenets of social psychology which have so far been considered as having universal applicability. "Relational issues" involved in collaborative cross-cultural research with western partners

have been discussed by D. Sinha (1983a). He (1990b) has also emphasised the need for "horizontal collaboration" between psychologists of
developing countries rather than only "vertical collaboration" with
western scholars as has been the case so far.

One remarkable outcome of cross-cultural psychology has been the
generation of interest in indigenous psychologies in various cultures. It
has led to volumes by Bond (1986) on China, on India by D. Sinha
(1986), and Asia and the Oceania by Blowers and Turtle (1987).
Enriquez (1982) has discussed *Sikolohiyang Filipino*. It is not possible
to discuss at length the issues and the processes involved, which have
been dealt by various authors (D. Sinha, 1986, 1988b; Kim, 1990;
Adair, 1992). It should be reiterated (D. Sinha, 1989) that though
indigenous psychologies predate cross-cultural psychology, the former
in many ways can be considered as an out-growth of the latter in its
pursuit of getting the mainstream psychology divest its culture-blind
and culture-bound tendencies. The two have enriched each other and
should be regarded as complementary. As Kao (1989) has observed
"Indigenous psychology based on unique behavioural phenomena
must of necessity be the foundation upon which cross-cultural psychology is built. Only then can cross-cultural psychology become the
ground upon which a true universal psychology is built."

REFERENCES

ADAIR, J.G. (1992). Empirical study of indigenization and development of the discipline
    in developing countries. In S. Iwawaki, Y. Kashima, and K. Leung (Eds.),
    Innovations in cross-cultural psychology. Lisse: Swets and Zeitlinger.

BEG, M.A. (1966). Value orientations of American and Indian students: A cross-cultural
    study. *Psychologia, 9*, 111–119.

BERMAN, J.J., MURPHY-BERMAN, V., and SINGH, P. (1985). Cross-cultural similarities and
    differences in perception of fairness. *Journal of Cross-Cultural Psychology, 16*,
    55–57.

BERRY, JOHN W. (1976). *Human ecology and cognitive style: Comparative studies in
    culture and psychological adaptation*. New York: Sage/Halsted.

BHATNAGAR, J.K. (1967). The values and attitudes of some Indian and British students.
    Race, 9, 27–35.

BLOWERS, G. and TURTLE, A. (Eds.). (1987). *Psychology moving east*. Sydney: Sydney
    University Press.

BOND, M.H. (Ed.). (1986). *Psychology of the Chinese people*. Hong Kong: Oxford
    University Press.

BOND, M.H. (Ed.). (1988). *The cross-cultural challenge to social psychology*. Newbury Park, CA: Sage Publications.

BOND, M.H., CHIU, C.K., and WAN, K.C. (1984). When modesty fails: The social impact of group effacing attributions following success or failure. *European Journal of Social Psychology, 14*, 335–338.

CARMENT, D.W. (1974). Indian and Canadian choice behaviour in a maximizing difference game and in a game of chicken. *International Journal of Psychology, 9*, 213–221.

CHIU, C-Y. (1991a). Role expectation as the principal criterion in justice judgement among Hong Kong Chinese students. *Journal of Psychology, 125*, 557–565.

CHIU, C-Y. (1991b). Response to injustice in popular Chinese sayings and among Hong Kong Chinese students. *Journal of Social Psychology, 131*, 655–665.

CHUNG, M.R. (1983). An examination of conservation performance by children from contrasting social and cultural background. In J.B. Deregowski, S. Dziurawiec, and R.C. Annis (Eds.), *Expiscations in cross-cultural psychology*. Lisse: Swets and Zeitlinger B.V.

DART, F.E. and PRADHAN, P.L. (1967). Cross-cultural teaching of science. *Science, 155*, 650–665.

DAWSON, J.L.M. (1963). Traditional values and work efficiency in West African mine labour force. *Occupational Psychology, 37*, 209–218.

DAWSON, J.L.M. (1967). Cultural and physiological influences upon spatial perceptual processes in West Africa (Part 1 and 2). *International Journal of Psychology, 2*, 115–128, 171–185.

DERIDDER, R. and TRIPATHI, R.C. (Eds.). (1992). *Norm violation and intergroup relations*. London: Clarendon Press.

DOI, T. (1973). *The anatomy of dependence*. Tokyo: Kodansha International.

DOI, T. (1984). Psychotherapy: A cross-cultural perspective from Japan. In P. Pederson, N. Sartorius, and A. Marsella (Eds.), *Mental health services: The cross-cultural context*. London: Sage.

EKSTRAND, G. (1990). *Children of culture*. Malmo: Miniprint No. 701, Department of Educational and Psychological Research, Malmo School of Education, University of Lund.

EKSTRAND, G. and EKSTRAND, L.H. (1985). *Patterns of socialization in different cultures: The case of India and Sweden*. Miniprint No. 513, Malmo: Department of Educational and Psychological Research, Malmo School of Education, University of Lund.

ENRIQUEZ, V.G. (1982). *Towards a Filipino psychology*. Quezon City: Psychology Research & Training House.

EVANS, G.W., PALSANE, M.N., and CARRERE, S. (1987). Type A behaviour and occupational stress: A cross-cultural study of blue collar workers. *Journal of Personality and Social Psychology, 52*, 1002–1007.

FORGAS, J. and BOND, M.H. (1985). Cultural influences on the perception of interaction episodes. *Personality and Social Psychology Bulletin, 11*, 75–88.

FRAGER, R. (1970). Conformity and anti-conformity in Japan. *Journal of Personality and Social Psychology, 15*, 203–210.

FRY, P.S. and GHOSH, R. (1980). Attribution of success and failure: Comparison of cultural differences between Asian and Caucasian children. *Journal of Cross-Cultural Psychology, 11*, 343–346.

HEWSTONE, M. (1989). Intergroup attribution: Some implications for the study of ethnic prejudice. In J.P. Van Oudenhoven and T.M. Willemsen (Eds.), *Ethnic minorities: Social and psychological perspectives*. Lisse: Swets and Zeitlinger.

HEWSTONE, M., BOND, M.H., and WAN, K.C. (1983). Some facts of social attributions: The explanation of intergroup differences in Hong Kong. *Social Cognition, 2*, 142–157.

HEWSTONE, M. and WARD, C. (1985). Ethnocentricism and causal attribution in Southeast Asia. *Journal of Personality and Social Psychology, 48*, 614–623.

HOFSTEDE, G. (1980). *Culture's consequences: International differences in work-related values*. London: Sage.

HUI, H. (1988). Measurement of Individualism-Collectivism. *Journal of Research in Personality, 22*, 17–36.

HUI, H. and TRIANDIS, H.C. (1985). Measurement in cross-cultural psychology: A review and comparison of strategies. *Journal of Cross-Cultural Psychology, 16*, 131–152.

HUI, C.H., TRIANDIS, H.C., and YEE, C. (1991). Cultural differences in reward allocation: Is collectivism the explanation? *British Journal of Social Psychology, 30*, 145–157.

INKELES, A. and SINGH, A.K. (1975). A cross-cultural measure of modernity and some popular Indian images. *Journal of General and Applied Psychology, 1*, 33–43.

INKELES, A. and SMITH, D. (1974). *Becoming modern*. Cambridge, MA: Harvard University Press.

JAHODA, G., DEREGOWSKI, J.B., and SINHA, D. (1974). Topological and Euclidian spatial features noted by children. *International Journal of Psychology, 19*, 159–172.

JAHODA, G., CHEYNE, W.M., DEREGOWSKI, J.B., SINHA, D., and COLLINGBOURNE, R. (1976). Utilization of pictorial information in classroom learning: A cross-cultural study. *AV Communication Review, 24*, 295–315.

KAĞITÇIBAŞI, Ç. (1987). Individual and group loyalties: Are they compatible? In Ç. Kağitçibaşi (Ed.), *Growth and progress in cross-cultural psychology*. Lisse: Swets and Zeitlinger.

KAĞITÇIBAŞI, Ç. (1988). Diversity of socialization and social change. In P.R. Dasen, J.W. Berry, and N. Sartorius (Eds.), *Health and cross-cultural psychology: Towards applications*. Newbury Park, CA: Sage.

KAKAR, S. (1978). *The inner experience*. Bombay: Oxford University Press.

KAKAR, S. (1982). *Shamans, mystics and doctors: A psychological inquiry into India and its healing traditions*. Bombay: Oxford University Press.

KAO, H.S.R. (1989). Insights towards a transcultural psychology: Spotlighting the Middle Kingdom. *Supplement to the Gazette*, University of Hong Kong, *36* (2), 85–92.

KAO, H.S.R., SUNG, K., and SINHA, D. (1990). Social values and effective organizations. *International Journal of Psychology* (Special Issue), *25* (5/6).

KASHIMA, Y. (1987). Conceptions of persons: Implications in individualism-collectivism research. In Ç. Kağitçibaşi (Ed.), *Growth and progress in cross-cultural psychology*. Lisse: Swets and Zeitlinger.

KASHIMA, Y., SIEGAL, M., TANAKA, K., and ISAKA, H. (1988). Universalism in lay conceptions of justice. *International Journal of Psychology, 23*, 51–64.

KIM, U. (1990). Indigenous psychology: Science and application. In R. Brislin (Ed.), *Applied cross-cultural psychology*. Newbury Park, CA: Sage.

KRISHNAN, L. (1992). Justice research: The Indian perspective. *Psychology and Developing Societies, 4*, 39–71.

KURESHI, A. and HUSAIN, A. (1981a). Locus of control among the Indian, Iranian and Palestinian students. *Psychological Studies, 26*, 1–2.

KURESHI, A. and HUSAIN, A. (1981b). Death anxiety and dominance among the Indian and Palestinian students: A cross-cultural comparison. *Japanese Psychological Research, 23*, 55–60.

KURESHI, A. and HUSAIN, A. (1982). Extrapunitiveness, intropunitiveness and dominance among Indian and Palestinian students: A cross-cultural study. *Journal of Psychological Research, 26*, 165–169.

KURESHI, A., HUSAIN, A., and BHATNAGAR, A. (1979). A cross-cultural study of n-Achievement, hope of success and fear of failure among Indian and African students. *Journal of Education Research, 3*, 1–4.

L'ARMAND, K. and PEPITONE, A. (1975). Helping to reward another person: A cross-cultural analysis. *Journal of Personality and Social Psychology, 31*, 189–198.

LEPORE, S.J., EVANS, G.W., and PALSANE, M.N. (1991). Social hassels and psychological health in the context of chronic crowding. *Journal of Health and Social Behaviour, 32*, 357–367.

LEUNG, K. (1987). Some determinants of reactions to procedural model for conflict resolution. *Journal of Personality and Social Psychology, 53*, 898–908.

LEUNG, K. (1989). Cross-cultural difference: Individual-level or culture-level analysis. *International Journal of Psychology, 24*, 703–719.

LEUNG, K. and BOND, M.H. (1982). How Chinese and American reward task-related contributions: A preliminary study. *Psychologia, 25*, 32–39.

LEUNG, K. and BOND, M.H. (1984). Impact of cultural collectivism on reward allocation. *Journal of Personality and Social Psychology, 47*, 793–804.

LEUNG, K. and BOND, M.H. (1989). On the empirical identification of dimensions for cross-cultural comparison. *Journal of Cross-Cultural Psychology, 20*, 133–151.

LEUNG, K. and WU, P-G. (1990). Dispute processing: A cross-cultural analysis. In R.W. Brislin (Ed.), *Applied cross-cultural psychology*. Newbury Park, CA: Sage.

LIPPITT, R. and WHITE, R. (1958). An experimental study of leadership and group life. In E.E. Maccoby, T.M. Newcomb, and E.L. Hastley (Eds.), *Readings in social psychology* (3rd ed.). New York: Holt.

MA, H.K. (1988). The Chinese perspective on moral judgement development. *International Journal of Psychology, 23*, 201–227.

MA, H.K. (1989). Moral orientation and moral judgements in adolescents in Hong Kong, Mainland China and England. *Journal of Cross-Cultural Psychology, 20*, 152–177.

MAHLER, I., GREENBERG, L., and HAYASHI, H. (1981). A comparative study of rules of justice: Japanese versus American. *Psychologia, 24*, 1–8.

MARKUS, H. and KITAYAMA, S. (1991). Culture and self. *Psychological Review, 98*, 224–253.

MATSUDA, N. (1985). Strong, quasi- and weak conformity among Japanese in the modified Asch procedure. *Journal of Cross-Cultural Psychology, 16*, 83–97.

MATSUDA, N. (1992). Problem solving strategies: Comparison between Australian and Japanese children. In S. Iwawaki, Y. Kashima, and K. Leung (Eds.), *Innovations in cross-cultural psychology*. Lisse: Swets and Zeitlinger.

MEAD, R.D. (1967). An experimental study of leadership in India. *Journal of Social Psychology, 72*, 35–43.

MEAD, R.D. and WHITTAKER, J.O. (1967). A cross-cultural study of authoritarianism. *Journal of Social Psychology, 72*, 3–7.

MELIKIAN, L. (1956). Some correlates of authoritarianism in two cultural groups. *Journal of Psychology, 42,* 237–248.

MILLER, J.G., BERSOFF, D.M., and HARWOOD, R.L. (1990). Perception of social responsibilities in India and the United States: Moral imperatives or personal decisions? *Journal of Personality and Social Psychology, 58,* 33–47.

MINTURN, L. and HITCHCOCK, J.T. (1966). *The Rajputs of Khalapur, India.* New York: Wiley.

MINTURN, L. and LAMBERT, W.W. (1964). *Mothers in six cultures.* New York: Wiley.

MISHRA, R.C. (1988). Field dependence-independence as related to face recognition and eye contact among tribal adolescents. *Indian Psychologist, 5,* 21–26.

MISHRA, R.C. and SINGH, T. (1992). Memories of Asur children for locations and pairs of pictures. *Psychological Studies, 37* (1).

MISUMI, J. (1985). *Behavioural science of leadership* (English edition). Ann Arbor, MI: University of Michigan Press.

MISUMI, J. (1992). PM theory of leadership from a cross-cultural perspective. In S. Iwawaki, Y. Kashima, and K. Leung (Eds.), *Innovations in cross-cultural psychology.* Lisse: Swets and Zeitlinger.

MIURA, M. and USA, S. (1970). A psychotherapy of neurosis: Moita therapy. *Psychologia, 13,* 18–34.

MORRIS, C.R. (1956). *Varieties of human values.* Chicago: Chicago University Press.

MUKHERJEE, B.N. (1967). Cross-cultural study of social desirability judgements. *International Journal of Psychology, 2,* 25–32

MURPHY-BERMAN, V., BERMAN, J.J., SINGH, P., PACHAURI, A., and KUMAR, P. (1984). Factors affecting allocation to needy and meritorious recipients: A cross-cultural comparison. *Journal of Personality and Social Psychology, 46,* 1267–1272.

NEKI, J.S. (1973). *Guru-chela* relationship: The possibility of a therapeutic paradigm. *American Journal of Orthopsychiatry, 43,* 755–766.

NEVILLE, D.D. and SUPER, D.E. (1986). *The value scale: Theory, application and research.* Palo Alto, CA: Consulting Psychologists Press.

NG, S.H., AKHTAR HOSSAIN, A.B.M., BALL, P., BOND, M.H., HAYASHI, K., LIM, S.P., O'DRISCOLL, M.P., SINHA, D., and YANG, K.S. (1982). Human values in nine countries. In R. Rath, D. Sinha, H.S. Asthana, and J.B.P. Sinha (Eds.), *Diversity and unity in cross-cultural psychology.* Lisse: Swets and Zeitlinger.

PALSANE, M.N., BHAVSAR, S.N., GOSWAMI, R.P., and EVANS, G.W. (1986). The concept of stress in Indian tradition. *Journal of Indian Psychology, 5,* 1–12.

PANDEY, J. (1980). Ingratiation as expected and manipulative behaviour in Indian society. *Social Change, 10,* 15–17.

PANDEY, J. (1986). Cross-cultural perspective on ingratiation. In B. Mahler and W. Mahler (Eds.), *Progress in experimental personality research.* New York: Academic Press.

PANDEY, J. and KAKKAR, S. (1982). Cross-cultural differences and similarities in ingratiation tactics as social influences and control mechanism. In R. Rath, D. Sinha, H.S. Asthana, and J.B.P. Sinha (Eds.), *Diversity and unity in cross-cultural psychology.* Lisse: Swets and Zeitlinger.

PARANJPE, A.C. (1975). *In search of identity.* New Delhi: Macmillan.

PAREEK, U. and RAO, T.V. (1980). Cross-cultural surveys and interviewing. In H.C. Triandis and J.W. Berry (Eds.), *Handbook of cross-cultural psychology: Vol. 2, Methodology.* Boston: Allyn and Bacon.

PERERA, M. and EYSENCK, S.B.G. (1984). A cross cultural study of personality: Sri Lanka and England. *Journal of Cross-Cultural Psychology, 15*, 353–376.

PROTHRO, E. and MELIKIAN, L. (1953). The California Public Opinion Scale in an authoritarian culture. *Public Opinion Quarterly, 17*, 353–362.

RASTOGI, V.S., JINDAL, R.C., GUPTA, M.P., RANA, S.S., and SINGHAL, S. (1976). Somatic symptoms in neurosis: A cross-cultural study. *Indian Journal of Psychiatry, 18*, 103–108.

RIVERS, W.H.R. (1901). Introduction and vision. In A.C. Haddon (Ed.), *Reports of the Cambridge anthropological expedition to the Toores Straits: Vol. 2, Part 1*. Cambridge: Cambridge University Press.

RIVERS, W.H.R. (1995). Observations on the senses of the Todas. *British Journal of Psychology, 1*, 321–396.

ROHNER, R. and ROHNER, E. (1976). *They love me, they love me not*. New Haven: Human Relations Area Files.

RONALD, A. (1984). The self in India and America. In V. Kavalis (Ed.), *Design of self*. New Jersey: Associated University Press.

SHARMA, S., PRANIAN, S., and SPIELBERGER, C.D. (1983). A cross-cultural study of test anxiety levels in Iranian and Indian students. *Personality and Individual Differences, 4*, 117–120.

SHWEDER, R.A. and BOURNE, E.J. (1984). Does the concept of person vary cross-culturally? In R.A. Shweder and R.A. LeVine (Eds.), *Culture theory*. New York: Cambridge University Press.

SHWEDER, R.A., MAHAPATRA, M., and MILLER, J.G. (1990). Cultural and moral development. In J. Stigler, R.A. Shweder, and G. Herdt (Eds.), *Cultural psychology: Essays in comparative human development*. New York: Cambridge University Press.

SINGH, P.N., HUANG, S.C., and THOMPSON, G.G. (1962). A comparative study of selected attitudes, values and personality characteristics of American, Chinese and Indian students. *Journal of Social Psychology, 57*, 123–138.

SINHA, D. (1962). Cultural factors in the emergence of anxiety. *The Eastern Anthropologist, 15* (1).

SINHA, D. (1969). *Indian villages in transition: A motivational analysis*. New Delhi: Associated Publishing House.

SINHA, D. (1978). Story-Pictorial EFT: A culturally appropriate test for perceptual disembedding. *Indian Journal of Psychology, 53*, 160–171.

SINHA, D. (1979). Perceptual style among nomadic and transitional agroculturist Birhors. In L. Eckensberger, W. Lonner, and Y.H. Poortinga (Eds.), *Cross-cultural contributions to psychology*. Lisse: Swets and Zeitlinger.

SINHA, D. (1980). Sex differences in psychological differentiation among different cultural groups. *International Journal of Behavioural Development, 3*, 455–466.

SINHA, D. (1983a). Cross-cultural psychology: A view from the Third World. In J.B. Deregowski, S.D. Dziurawiec, and R.C. Annis (Eds.), *Expiscations in cross-cultural psychology*. Lisse: Swets and Zeitlinger.

SINHA, D. (1983b). Human assessment in the Indian context. In S.H. Irvine and J.W. Berry (Eds.), *Human assessment and cultural factors*. New York: Plenum Press.

SINHA, D. (1984). Community as the target: A new perspective to research on prosocial behaviour. In E. Staub, D. Bar-Tal, J. Karlowski, and J. Reykowski (Eds.), *Development and maintenance of prosocial behaviour*. New York: Plenum Press.

SINHA, D. (1986). *Psychology in a Third World country: The Indian experience*. New Delhi: Sage.

SINHA, D. (1988a). Changing family scenario in India and its implications for mental health. In P.R. Dasen, J.W. Berry, and N. Sartorius (Eds.), *Health and cross-cultural psychology: Towards applications*. Newbury Park, CA: Sage.

SINHA, D. (1988b). Indigenization of psychology in India and its relevance. *Indian Journal of Social Science, 1*, 77–91.

SINHA, D. (1989). Cross-cultural psychology and the process of indigenization: A second view from the Third World. In D.M. Keats, D. Munro, and L. Mann (Eds.), *Heterogeneity in cross-cultural psychology*. Lisse: Swets and Zeitlinger.

SINHA, D. (1990a). Concept of psychosocial well being: Western and Indian perspectives. *NIMHANS Journal, 8*, 1–11.

SINHA, D. (1990b). Vertical and horizontal collaboration in cross-cultural research. *Cross-Cultural Psychology Bulletin, 24*, 11–12.

SINHA, D. and BHARAT, S. (1985). Three types of family structures and psychological differentiation: A study among the Jaunsar-Bawar society. *International Journal of Psychology, 20*, 693–708.

SINHA, D. and JHA, T. (1989). Invariance of mass and number among tribal and non-tribal children: A study of the influence of age, sex, culture and habitation. *Journal of Personality and Clinical Studies, 5*, 105–114.

SINHA, D. and KAO, H.S.R. (Eds.). (1988). *Social values and development: Asian perspectives*. New Delhi: Sage Publications.

SINHA, D., MISHRA, R.C., and BERRY, J.W. (1992a). Acculturative stress in nomadic and sedentary tribes in Bihar, India. In S. Iwawaki, Y. Kashima, and K. Leung (Eds.), *Innovations in cross-cultural psychology*. Lisse: Swets and Zeitlinger.

SINHA, D., MISHRA, R.C., and BERRY, J.W. (1992b, January 2–7). Some ecological and accultural factors in intermodal perception. Paper presented at the 4th IACCP Regional Congress, Kathmandu.

SINHA, D., MISHRA, R.C., and BERRY, J.W. (1992c, July 14–18). Changes in some aspects of information processing through acculturation. Paper presented at the symposium on Acculturation: Psychological Adaptation, XIth International Congress of IACCP/AIRC, University of Liege, Belgium.

SINHA, D. and NAIDU, R.K. (1992, July 14–18). Multilayered hierarchical structure of self and not-self: The Indian perspective. Paper presented at the symposium on Culture and Self: Theoretical and Philosophical Analysis, 11th International Congress of IACCP/AIRC, University of Liege, Belgium.

SINHA, D. and SAATCHI, M. (1977). A comparative study of supervisory orientation among Indian and Iranian supervisors. *Indian Journal of Psychology, 52*, 228–239.

SINHA, D. and SHRESTHA, A.B. (1992). Ecocultural factors in cognitive style among children from hills and plains of Nepal. *International Journal of Psychology, 27*, 49–59.

SINHA, D. and TRIPATHI, R.C. (1991). Individualism in a collectivist culture: A case of coexistence of opposites. Paper presented at the workshop on Individualism and Collectivism: Psychocultural Perspectives from the East and West, Seoul, 9–13 July 1990.

SINHA, G. (1988). Exposure to industrial and urban environments and formal schooling as factors in psychological differentiation. *International Journal of Psychology, 23*, 707–719.

SINHA, J.B.P. (1980). *Nurturant task leader*. New Delhi: Concept Publishing Company.

SINHA, J.B.P. (1990). *Work culture in the Indian context*. New Delhi: Sage.

SINHA, J.B.P. and VERMA, J. (1987). Structure of collectivism. In Ç. Kağitçibaşi (Ed.), *Growth and progress in cross-cultural psychology*. Lisse: Swets and Zeitlinger.

SMITH, P.B., PETERSON, M.F., BOND, M.H., and MISUMI, J. (1992). Leadership style and leadership behaviour in individualist and collectivist cultures. In S. Iwawaki, Y. Kashima, and K. Leung (Eds.), *Innovations in cross-cultural psychology*. Lisse: Swets and Zeitlinger.

SPIELBERGER, C.D., SHARMA, S., and SINGH, M. (1973). Development of the Hindi edition of State-Trait Anxiety Inventory. *Indian Journal of Psychology, 48*, 11–20.

SUVANNATHAT, C., BHANTHUMNAVIN, D., BHAUPIRON, L., and KEATS, D.M. (1985). *Handbook of Asian child development and child rearing practices*. Bangkok: Behavioural Science Institute, Srinakharinwirot University, Prasanmitr.

TANAKA-MATSUMI, J. (1979). Cultural factors and social influence techniques in Naikan therapy. A Japanese self-observation method. *Psychotherapy: Theory, research and practice, 16*, 385–390.

TAYLOR, D.M. and JAGGI, V. (1974). Ethnocentricism and causal attribution in a South Indian context. *Journal of Cross-Cultural Psychology, 5*, 162–171.

VERMA, S.K. and WIG, N. (1974). A cross cultural comparison of psychiatric patients on some of the parameters of Cornell Medical Index. *Manas, 21*, 17–25.

WARD, C. (Ed.). (1989). *Altered states of consciousness and mental health*. Newbury Park, CA: Sage.

WATKINS, D. and REGMI, M. (1992). How universal are students' conceptions of learning? A Nepalese investigation. *Psychologia, 35*, 101–110.

WATKINS, D., REGMI, M., and ASTILLA, E. (1991). The Asian-learner-as-a-rote-learner stereotype: Myth or reality? *Educational Psychology, 11*, 21–34.

3

Cross-Cultural Psychology and Development

ÇIĞDEM KAĞITÇIBAŞI

For psychologists, as well as for other social scientists in developing countries, *development* is the number one item on the agenda. Psychologists' contribution to development efforts converges on its human aspects. And for this, a central issue is the fit or the compatibility between the prevalent psychological characteristics of the people concerned and the requirements of societal development, in other words, a "human model" for development.

What are the human factors associated with economic development? Is there a pattern of human relations that is optimal for economic growth? These questions are assuming great relevance today, as there is a growing realisation of the importance of non-material aspects of economic development. Much more is known about the technology and economics of development than about its human aspects. Nevertheless, development efforts and models, especially those directed to the developing countries, make assumptions about the underlying human factors; an implicit "human model" is often taken for granted. This "model" is, in turn, commonly based on western experience but is assumed to hold cross-culturally. There is a great need to replace assumptions about human factors with sound knowledge based on cross-cultural research. This is necessary to understand the process of overall economic development and to find satisfactory answers to the two basic questions raised earlier.

Psychology, as the basic discipline focusing on human behaviour, has played a central role in the formation and ready acceptance of this (implicit) model. Psychology as a scientific endeavour, in turn, is a product of western, especially American, scholarship and therefore reflects the values and ideology of the western world. Thus, psychology's construction of the person is in fact a social construction (Gergen and Davis, 1985).

Some concepts, for example, that are basic to developmental psychology, family dynamics and personality theory, which are presumed to have universal validity and relevance may be culture specific. Thus, individual autonomy and independence, personal boundaries as related to separation and individuation (Mahler, 1975) may be western cultural constructs and not universal human phenomena (Kağitçibaşi, 1984, 1990). These concepts indeed constitute the cornerstones of the psychology of the human person or "the human model" in the western world. Accordingly, much emphasis is placed on early independence training, separation and individuation, self-sufficiency, privacy, individual achievement and competition both in theory and practice. Applications are seen, for example, in parent education programme and are well integrated with the western, especially American, individualistic ideology.

A misfit may occur, however, when the western individualistic "human model" is transferred to other cultures or, for that matter, even to ethnic groups and others outside of the dominant middle class culture in the west. Thus, for example, attempts at promoting economic growth through instilling entrepreneurial competitive achievement motivation, based on an individualistic "human model", have failed in collectivistic cultures such as India (Sinha, 1985).

Similarly, expectations of a unidirectional change in human behavioural patterns toward the western model are not actualising. The tacit assumption, based on the modernisation theory, is that whatever is different from the western prototype is transitory and is bound to change through socio-economic development, thus the commonly used term "transitional societies". For instance, interdependent human relational patterns are expected to give way to individualised independence, and closely-knit social–familial structures to undergo a process of nucleation (e.g., Caldwell, 1977; Georgas, 1989).

Yet research evidence (reviewed in Kağitçibaşi, 1990) shows that diversity in human relational patterns and family culture may be enduring, not temporary. Thus, close-knit familial relationships, interdependence and group loyalties are found to persist through social change and development in East Asia as well as in most developing countries (e.g., Hayashi and Suzuki, 1984; Iwawaki, 1986; Bond, 1986; Sinha and Kao, 1988; Phalet and Claeys, 1993). These collectivistic tendencies do not appear to give way to separation, individuation and to individualism. Similarly, numerous cross-cultural studies carried out particularly in East Asia and Latin America (reviewed in Kağitçibaşi and Berry, 1989) provide rich evidence of diversity, as reflected in conflict resolution, distributive justice and cooperative–competitive behaviour. The achievement of high economic technological development in collectivistic cultures, such as Japan and the "four tigers" (Korea, Taiwan, Hong Kong and Singapore) challenge the assumption that collectivism is incompatible with development and that an individualistic "human model" is necessitated by industrialisation. These examples are important and worthy of study, as they are an exception to the generally observed relationship between socio-economic development and individualism (Hofstede, 1980; Triandis, 1985).

However, such evidence is not from the traditional rural areas of developing countries but rather from their urban developed sectors, from students and from educated urban middle classes. Thus, empirical evidence *shows* the direction in which shifts in the human model are in fact occurring in the process of societal development. Our task should, therefore, be to view this evidence seriously with an open-mind rather than interpret it in terms of western social science, such as the modernisation or individual modernity paradigm.

In the face of growing cross-cultural evidence, there is increasing acceptance of the possibility of alternative paths toward development, multidirectional change and multiple end points, depending at least partially on the cultural base from which social change is taking place. Thus new syntheses have been called for (Sinha, 1985; Sampson, 1987; Kağitçibaşi, 1985, 1987, 1990), especially integrating human relatedness with individual autonomy. Some examples are seen in the concepts of nurturant task leader (J.B.P. Sinha, 1980); and social achievement motivation (Phalet and Claeys, 1993). What appears to be needed is an integration of individualistic and group loyalties—a merging of the individual self with the relational self. Only such a synthesis can do justice to the basic human needs for autonomy and relatedness. Models of man which stress one of these needs to the exclusion of the other are bound to be impoverishing and not enriching.

Here is the challenge of an "alternative human model" that is as yet unmet by psychology and social science. Thus, are individual autonomy and group loyalties mutually exclusive concepts as usually assumed, or are they compatible, as suggested elsewhere (Kağitçibaşi, 1987)? What kind of "human model" best fits development efforts in traditional collectivistic societies? Are individualism and collectivism polar opposites of a unidimensional process of change, or do they form independent dimensions (Kağitçibaşi, 1987)? Do they have elements which may coexist? These questions require better conceptualisation and empirical verification which could be achieved by studies examining human relational patterns in diverse socio-cultural contexts and establishing their links with socio-economic development.

A great deal of cross-cultural research, some of which discussed earlier, has indeed attempted to understand different human relational patterns, stressing individualism and collectivism (as reviewed by Kağitçibaşi and Berry, 1989). I have proposed elsewhere that the concept of the "culture of relatedness" characterises human relational patterns in much of the non-western world (Kağitçibaşi, 1990). This view is based on my own research findings of the cross-cultural study on the value of children for parents. Comparing nationally representative samples from Indonesia, Korea, the Philippines, Singapore, Taiwan, Thailand and Turkey, it was observed that the expressed values regarding young children and grown up adult offspring reflected the prevalent value of family interdependence and a family culture of relatedness. This was contrasted by the responses obtained from the US and Germany which rejected dependence and stressed individual autonomy and self-reliance (Kağitçibaşi, 1984).

In the context of material dependence on the primary group, high values are attached to closely-knit interpersonal ties and interdependence, rather than independence. This interdependence first takes the form of the child's dependence on parents and then, in old age, parents' dependence on the grown up children. This type of home environment is conducive to the socialisation of familistic and communal values of mutual support rather than individualistic achievement (Kağitçibaşi, 1984, 1985). Such socialisation values and practices do not fit with a theoretical orientation based on western individualistic ideology, emphasising autonomy and self-reliance in child development. Clearly, different value orientations need to be considered.

Further evidence for the family culture of relatedness comes from a four-year study involving intervention in early childhood enrichment and mother training in the low income areas of Istanbul (Kağitçibaşi, Sunar, and Bekman, 1988; Kağitçibaşi, 1992). In this study both the empirical findings regarding mothers' child rearing attitudes and values, and the general approach used in intervention work reflected close-knit interpersonal/familial human networks, rather than individualistic tendencies. This action research aimed to study the impact of home intervention involving mother training on the overall development of children.

Any applied research involving intervention in such a family context has to be cognisant of and sensitive to this basic culture of relatedness. In fact, such research gains to benefit from capitalising on the existing family culture of relatedness and working through it; otherwise it may be doomed to fail. For example, if in an attempt to develop autonomy in the child, the individualistic model is used and the family culture of relatedness is undermined by encouraging competition and individual loyalties, the intervention may not lend to long lasting results due to the resistance of the indigenous culture.

Both to understand the family dynamics and to work through it for intervention to be effective, a different model is needed than one based on an individualistic cultural ethos. In the study the aim was to foster the overall development of the child working through the mother. Instead of using an individualistic child development model abstracting the child out of context and treating him/her separately as an individual, the closely-knit familial ties were used as support mechanisms for the child. A holistic model of human development was used focusing on the interaction of the growing child with his/her family (especially the mother) and the interaction of the family with its own environment (the community). Thus, interpersonel interactions at different levels were studied and supported within a contextual model.

Specifically, in a mother training programme mothers were encouraged to develop a positive self-concept, feelings of competence, and efficacy as well as specific cognitive skills and positive orientations to provide their children with more cognitive stimulation and enrichment at home. This was done by reinforcing the close mother–child relationship on the one hand, and by capitalising on the existing communal support systems, on the other. The latter were utilised in group meetings of mothers in the community and in paraprofessional home instruction. The impact of intervention on both mothers and children was impressive indeed in the last year of the study (Kağitçibaşi, Sunar, and Bekman, 1988).

A follow-up study done seven years later examined the long-term effects and it was observed that the gains from the intervention were sustained (Kağitçibaşi, 1992). Both after the intervention and in the follow-up, children whose mothers had participated in the mother training programme surpassed the control group in cognitive performance and school achievement. They also showed greater autonomy, more positive self-concept and better family and social adjustment. Trained mothers were found to interact more positively with their children, were pleased with them and had higher educational aspirations for them. These mothers also had higher intra-family status and reported better and closer family relations in general compared with the control group.

This is an illustration of a model of intervention which was successful because it built upon the existing human relational patterns and family culture, instead of ignoring them. As the focus shifted from the individual (child) to interactions between the individual and his/her total environment in a holistic context, multiple and expanding benefits accrued from the intervention. This model has great potential for use in intervention/development programme in developing countries because it works through and builds upon the existing familial/community ties and strengthens them for overall individual–family–community development.

Applied psychological research such as this study has the potential to contribute to development efforts in developing countries for several reasons. First, it serves to build up human potential, which is of key importance in most developing countries where often the most important resources are human resources. Thus, any research designed to promote optimal human development, especially involving higher educational achievement, serves development efforts. Second, the more such applied research is informed by culturally valid theory and utilises culturally appropriate orientations, as exemplified in this study, the more it has a chance to be effective and contribute to development efforts. Third, as such applied research is based upon the existing social structures and human networks and builds upon them, rather than requiring new infra- and superstructures, it tends to be cost-effective and multi-purpose, and it has the potential to expand into large-scale applications. Thus, the same model of family–community involvement could be used for other development related purposes focusing on human behaviour, such as in programmes of family planning, nutrition and public health.

Today, the view that economic growth is the sole indicator of societal development is being questioned and there is a growing recognition of the dynamic link between human and societal development. For example, the World Bank is increasingly focusing on the role of education in improving efficiency and motivation of the labour force and on the well-being of women for child care and lower fertility. With this long overdue recognition of the importance of human factors in development, psychology can assume an important role in development efforts.

Psychologists in developing countries have typically shied away from confronting macro problems of development, such as issues of population, education and migration. This is mainly because of the large-scale proportions of these problems, not amenable to individual level study by psychologists. This attitude must be changed if psychologists, alongside economists and sociologists, are to play a role in development efforts in the world. Often large-scale development issues involve human behavioural problems, which psychologists are best equipped to study. Nevertheless, in order to understand and tackle such problems, psychologists need to confront them *within context* rather than acting on the basis of an imported "human model". This necessitates sensitivity to culture, and cross-cultural psychologists are in a particularly favourable position to play a significant role in this.

It is important to understand how contexts of human development and human behavioural patterns change through socio-economic development. It is also important to establish which human behavioural patterns are compatible with and promote better individual and societal development in diverse cultural contexts. Such knowledge is required for generating culturally relevant psychological theories and applications to contribute to societal development.

REFERENCES

BOND, M.H. (Ed.). (1986). *The psychology of the Chinese people*. New York: Oxford University Press.

CALDWELL, J.C. (1977). Towards a restatement of demographic transition theory. In J.C. Caldwell (Ed.), *The persistence of high fertility* (pp. 25–123). Canberra: The Australian National University.

GEORGAS, J. (1989). Changing family values in Greece: From collectivistic to individualistic. *Journal of Cross-Cultural Psychology, 20,* 80–91.

GERGEN, K. and DAVIS, K. (Eds.). (1985). *The social construction of the person.* New York: Springer.

HAYASHI, C. and SUZUKI, T. (1984). Changes in belief systems, quality of life issues and social conditions over 25 years in post-war Japan. *Ann. Inst. Stat. Math, 36,* 135–161.

HOFSTEDE, G. (1980). *Culture's consequences: International differences in work-related values.* Beverly Hills, CA: Sage.

IWAWAKI, S. (1986). Achievement motivation and socialization. In S.E. Newstead, S.M. Irvine, and P.L. Dann (Eds.), *Human assessment: Cognition and motivation.* Boston: Martinus Nijhoff.

KAĞITÇIBAŞI, Ç. (1984). Socialization in traditional society: A challenge to psychology. *International Journal of Psychology, 19,* 145–157.

KAĞITÇIBAŞI, Ç. (1985). A model of family change through development: The Turkish family in comparative perspective. In I.R. Lagunes and H. Poortinga (Eds.), *From a different perspective: Studies of behaviour across cultures* (pp. 120–135). Lisse: Swets and Zeitlinger.

KAĞITÇIBAŞI, Ç. (1987). Individual and group loyalties: Are they compatible? In Ç. Kağitçibaşi (Ed.), *Growth and progress in cross-cultural psychology.* Lisse: Swets and Zeitlinger.

KAĞITÇIBAŞI, Ç. (1990). Family and socialization in cross-cultural perspective: A model of change. In J. Berman (Ed.), *Nebraska symposium on motivation 1989.* Nebraska: University of Nebraska Press.

KAĞITÇIBAŞI, Ç. (1992, June). Human development and societal development: Linking theory and application. Presidential address at the International Congress of IACCP, Liege, Belgium. Printed in *Cross-Cultural Psychology Bulletin,* June 1992.

KAĞITÇIBAŞI, Ç. and BERRY, J.W. (1989). Cross cultural psychology: Current research and trends. *Annual Review of Psychology, 40,* 493–531.

KAĞITÇIBAŞI, Ç., SUNAR, D., and BEKMAN, S. (1988). Early enrichment project Ottawa: IDRC. Manuscript Report, 209 e.

MAHLER, M.S. (1975). *The psychological birth of the human infant: Symbiosis and individuation.* New York: Basic Books.

PHALET, K. and CLAEYS, W. (1993). A comparative study of achievement motivation in Turkish and Belgian youth. *Journal of Cross-Cultural Psychology, 24,* 319–343.

SAMPSON, E.E. (1987). Individualization and domination: Undermining the social bond. In Ç. Kağitçibaşi (Ed.), *Growth and progress in cross-cultural psychology* (pp. 84–93). Lisse: Swets and Zeitlinger.

SINHA, D. and KAO, H.S.R. (1988). *Social values and development: Asian perspectives.* New Delhi: Sage.

SINHA, J.B.P. (1980). *The nurturant task leader: A model of the effective executive.* New Delhi: Concept Publishing Company.

SINHA, J.B.P. (1985). Collectivism, social energy, and development in India. In I.R. Lagunes and H. Poortinga (Eds.), *From a different perspective: Studies of behaviour across cultures* (pp. 120–135). Lisse: Swets and Zeitlinger.

TRIANDIS, H. (1985). Collectivism vs. individualism: A reconceptualization of a basic concept in cross-cultural social psychology. In C. Bagley and G.K. Verma (Eds.), *Personality, cognition and values.* London: MacMillan.

4

The Indigenous Psychology Bandwagon: Cautions and Considerations*

JOHN G. ADAIR

Criticisms of western psychology and the promotion of indigenous psychology have characterised the discipline in developing countries. Indigenous concepts and approaches have been championed in Mexico (Diaz-Guerrero, 1977), Korea (Kwon, 1979), India (D. Sinha, 1986), the Philippines (Lagmay, 1984), and elsewhere. These developments have been the outcome of insights of key leaders within each country into the deficiencies of the discipline in addressing behaviours in their culture and of their perceptive promotion of indigenous concepts and

* This research has been supported by a Shastri Indo–Canadian Institute Fellowship, and by grants from the University of Manitoba Research Grants Committee, Research Development Fund, and SSHRC Research Fund. The author wishes to acknowledge the assistance of Neharika Vohra, who read and commented on earlier versions of this paper. Correspondence and requests for reprints should be sent to John G. Adair, Department of Psychology, University of Manitoba, Winnipeg, MB, R3T 2N2, Canada.

approaches. Although slow to develop, these pioneering efforts have led to an indigenous psychology movement.

As the movement accelerates in various cultures, however, a broader set of investigators have begun to jump on to the bandwagon. These second stage promoters of indigenous psychology may be distinguished generally by (a) lesser understanding or confusion about what constitutes an indigenous psychology, and (b) uncertainty of how to make one's own research more indigenous. These problems result in more talk than action (Naidu, 1990), the reification of narrow conceptions into definitions of an indigenous approach, and debates over the direction the discipline should take.

Confusions and misconceptions, however, are not exclusive to psychologists of the developing world. At a symposium on the Unity of Psychology at the last International Applied Congress (Kyoto), for example, the APA President expressed the view that all was well within the discipline, except possibly, he said, for the threat from the indigenous psychology movement! Attempts to make the discipline more appropriate to each culture do not threaten the discipline, yet such views reflect the confusion over what is meant by indigenisation of psychology, and the need to reconsider the concept before leaping on to the bandwagon.

INDIGENISATION AND INDIGENOUS PSYCHOLOGY: SOME DEFINITIONS

At the outset, some terms should be clarified. An indigenous psychology has been defined as a discipline that is "culturally appropriate" (Azuma, 1984; Moghaddam and Taylor, 1986). Here it is defined as research that emanates from, adequately represents, and reflects back upon the cultural context in which the behaviour is observed (Adair, 1992). Indigenisation, the process by which an indigenous psychology develops, has been contrasted with endogenisation (Atal, 1981). The latter refers to the process of developing an entirely new or different discipline from within the culture. Indigenisation, on the other hand, takes the methods and discipline of psychology developed elsewhere, and introduces modifications (such as, cultural elements) to make them fit the new culture.

It is also presumed, however, that whereas increased levels of cultural sensitivity, indigenous concepts, and applications of research to the local culture are desirable and necessary in order to develop a culturally appropriate discipline, realistically not all research should be expected to address the local culture. Culture as a variable contributes substantially to the understanding of behaviour, yet it is not the sole determinant. Much research focuses on the basic psychological processes that are perceived by many to be universal and invariant across cultures. As a result there are limits to the level of cultural sensitivity or indigenisation that may be anticipated. Clearly, research in most developing societies is so far short of these limits that a movement toward indigenisation of the discipline is required.

Although examined from a diversity of cultures, the literature on indigenous psychology has consistently suggested that the indigenisation process evolves through a characteristic series of stages (Atal, 1981; Azuma, 1984; D. Sinha, 1984, 1986; J.B.P. Sinha, 1984)—a growing acknowledgement of the limitations of western models, and increasing acceptance of the need for problem-oriented research on national concerns, and a deepening sensitivity to the rich potential that exists in local customs and behaviours peculiarly driven by indigenous traditions. In other words, an indigenous discipline gradually develops as an expanding number of local psychologists engage in blending the imported psychology with increasing attention to unique elements within their culture.

SOCIAL STUDY OF DISCIPLINE DEVELOPMENT AND INDIGENISATION

A study of the indigenisation process from a social studies of science perspective has attracted the attention of several researchers (Adair, 1989). The importation, implantation, maturation, and indigenisation of psychology in developing countries seemed to be suited to the methodologies that social scientists apply to study the evolution of the natural sciences. In the process of operationalising the concepts of discipline development and indigenisation for empirical study, Adair made the assumption that journal articles systematically archive and would adequately reflect changes in the nature of research practices within a country. If there was increasing acceptance, sensitivity, and awareness of the local culture in the research of a widening circle of native researchers, then it should be reflected in changes, it was also fair to assume that journals, as the universally accepted outlet for empirical work in the discipline, provided a uniform database that allowed for comparisons of national differences in discipline development and indigenisation.

Elements within research journal reports were operationalised into specific measures of each of the components of the indigenisation process, that is, the extent to which concepts, problems, hypotheses, methods, and measures (a) emanated from, (b) adequately represented, and (c) reflected back upon the cultural context in which the behaviour was observed. It is important to note that these measures of the indigenisation of the discipline were constructed to be sensitive to changing degrees of general concern with culturally relevant variables and focused on the process rather than on indigenous accomplishments.

For example, one measure could have been a mere count of indigenous contributions—novel, culture-based concepts, methods, or insights. However, such a measure would have focused on achievements rather than on process, and been too infrequent for study of its development. Rather, it was (Adair, Puhan, and Vohra, 1993) decided for such a measure to tally the frequencies of much finer grades of increasingly culturally sensitive research contributions. Empirical research was scaled as making increasingly indigenous contributions if (a) differences between India and the west were identified, (b) differences within India or between India and non-western cultures were identified, (c) the research attempted to explain behaviours observed in the local culture, or (d) an indigenous theory or concept guided the research or its interpretation. Only the latter would be regarded by many as a truly indigenous contribution.

The conception of indigenous psychology developed so far, seems straightforward and appropriate. It has provided a useful framework for studying discipline development and indigenisation, however, Adair has been struck by differences between it and the model consciously practised by the typical psychologist in developing countries.

INDIGENOUS RESEARCH IN DEVELOPING COUNTRIES

The majority of researchers from developing countries have taken up the banner of indigenous psychology, yet confusion and uncertainty persist about indigenisation of the discipline. Although in full agreement with the goal, a majority of the researchers are not clear about how to make their research indigenous. This may mislead some to engage in inadequate attempts that Durganand Sinha (1988) has labelled "cosmetic indigenization". Others, who are prepared to jump on to the bandwagon, look for a model that will be prescriptive for their research practice. This model, usually found in research held in esteem by their peers as examples of indigenous contributions, defines for them the meaning of indigenous and becomes the guide for "culturally-appropriate" research. As a result, some researchers have been led to equate indigenous research with either (a) a narrow search for uniquely native traits or concepts, (b) early religious or philosophical writings, (c) linguistically defined constructs, or less imaginatively, (d) mere identification of differences with western research findings.

A well cited article in indigenisation literature illustrates this process. Sharma (1981) has focused on key social psychological concepts as providing the vehicle through which India's distinctive culture may be researched. He has lamented the lack of work developing "indigenous key concepts . . . to highlight the *emic* aspects of Indian culture" (p. 108), applauded "a small, but growing body of investigators" (p. 107) with that focus, and urged others "to look for key social psychological concepts in the doctrines of classical Hinduism" (p. 108). As a virtual "instruction manual" for the researcher in need of guidance on how to conduct indigenous research, this article defined the search for culturally unique traits or concepts as the goal and means for indigenisation of the discipline.

Through this process a particular approach or source for indigenous achievements may become *the* exclusive definition and mode by which an indigenous discipline develops. For some psychologists in India, for example, indigenous psychology has become synonymous with a cultural psychology derived from ancient writings or scriptures. Problems with attempts to make a revivalist "Indian psychology" derived from these scriptures synonymous with indigenous psychology, have been well articulated (Sinha, 1988). However, it is equally inappropriate to pre-emptively exclude from legitimate status any reference to traditional or religious writings (Sinha, 1988).

The tendency to define indigenous psychology linguistically, the third category, raises special concerns. The widespread use of English as the scientific language, and the native language as the basis for one's feelings and everyday thoughts poses a paradox. In the case of the Indian researcher, facility with English provides access to the majority of the world's literature and a quality foreign peer review system. Yet, it may also promote emulation of the western discipline, insulate investigators from more culturally sensitive topics, and render the development of an indigenous discipline difficult to achieve. In the Philippines, the native languages have played a crucial role in the movement to develop an indigenous psychology (Church, 1987). There is a risk that using native language labels may create a false impression of greater indigenisation than truly exists, divert productive research to less significant definitional arguments, and alienate a national discipline from mainstream discipline developments and interactions. The role of language in the process of indigenisation is one of the most important questions to be addressed; however, it is beyond the scope of this paper.

INDIGENISATION AS A GOAL AND PROCESS

The model of indigenisation in practice creates two major problems. First, it confuses indigenisation as a goal with its function as a process to develop an "appropriate" psychology for the culture. One or more of these categories may become reified as the definition of indigenous research. An investigator, accepting the need to indigenise psychological research using one of these models, may research culturally unique traits or concepts, without regard to how commonly they occur, how they conceptually integrate, or how behaviourally meaningful they are to contemporary society. In other words, indigenisation or indigenous accomplishment replace the development of a culturally appropriate discipline as the goal.

Although it is in many ways different, this reminds one of the problem created by the increased popularity of deception that characterised experimental social psychological research in the 1960s. Social psychologists at that time were so much attracted by experimental manipulation that the cleverness of their deception appeared to be more important to them than the substantive meaning of their research (Ring, 1967). Although indigenous researchers have a more constructive approach, there is a similar risk that research in the developing world will be determined more by its indigenous character— by indigenous or religious concepts, or linguistic distinctions—than by psychological issues. And this diversion may further delay discipline development.

This is another problem that a narrow visioned focus on indigenisation may introduce—to divert researchers' attention from other important factors. Although indigenisation is an important goal, the data from an empirical study of the discipline in India (Adair, 1989; Adair, Puhan, and Vohra, 1993) has indicated that equally important is the general development of the discipline. Although infrequent, there was an increase in the number of articles that were coded as making indigenous contributions across the three time periods. More importantly, the nature of the types of empirical indigenous accomplishments changed over time: a shift from research identifying simple differences between India and the west or within India, to more complex explanations of Indian problems and behaviours. These data coupled with more general indications of discipline development (Adair, 1989), have highlighted the importance of maturation of the discipline to the development of a culturally appropriate psychology. Such research efforts suggest an indigenous psychology may be alternatively regarded as a discipline that has matured to the point where it addresses local behaviours and social issues of importance to national development.

This conceptualisation has important implications for the development of an indigenous psychology. First, there are no short cuts to its development. Rather than a prescriptive model for action, indigenous research developments will come about only from hard investigative work on mature psychological explanations of behaviour that are found to be typical within the country. Second, indigenous research will be promoted by the development of a broader base of young psychologists who have the opportunity to mature as researchers. With poor quality journal editing and reviewing, a lack of professional support from peers, weak or non-existent professional associations, and poorly articulated standards for professional conduct (Adair, Pandey, Begum, Puhan, and Vohra, 1995), this task in itself is as substantial and fundamental as indigenisation of the discipline.

Finally, discipline development provides an answer to a question raised by a member of the audience at the last International Congress of Cross-Cultural Psychology: "Why is it that only psychologists from the developing world feel the need for indigenous psychology?" The answer is to be found in a companion need for maturation and development of the discipline.

In conclusion, these remarks are not intended to in any way diminish the need for indigenisation of the discipline. It is important, necessary, and needs to be promoted. But greater attention to the factors promoting development of the discipline and the professional growth of researchers is also required.

REFERENCES

ADAIR, J.G. (1989, June). *Development of the discipline and its contribution to social development in developing countries*. Invited address to the Interamerican Congress of Psychology, Buenos Aires, Argentina.

ADAIR, J.G. (1992). Empirical study of indigenization and development of the discipline in developing countries. In Saburo Iwawaki et al., *Innovations in cross-cultural psychology* (pp. 62–74). Amsterdam: Swets and Zeitlinger.

ADAIR, J.G., PUHAN, B.N., and VOHRA, N. (1993). Indigenization of psychology: Empirical assessment of progress in Indian research. *International Journal of Psychology, 28*, 149–169.

ADAIR, J.G., PANDEY, J., BEGUM, H.A., PUHAN, B.N., and VOHRA, N. (1995). Indigenization and development of the discipline: Perceptions and opinions of Indian and Bangladeshi psychologists. *Journal of Cross-Cultural Psychology, 26*, 392–407.

ATAL, Y. (1981). Call for indigenization. *International Social Science Journal, 33*, 189–197.

AZUMA, H. (1984). Psychology in a non-western country. *International Journal of Psychology, 19*, 45–56.

CHURCH, A.T. (1987). Personality research in a non-western culture: The Philippines. *Psychological Bulletin, 102*, 272–292.

DIAZ-GUERRERO, R. (1977). A Mexican psychology. *American Psychologist, 32*, 934–944.

KWON, T.H. (1979). Seminar on Koreanizing western approaches to social sciences. *Korea Journal, 19*, 20–25.

LAGMAY, A.V. (1984). Western psychology in the Philippines: Impact and response. *International Journal of Psychology, 19*, 31–44.

MOGHADDAM, F.M. and TAYLOR, D.M. (1986). What constitutes an "appropriate psychology" for the developing world. *International Journal of Psychology, 21*, 253–267.

NAIDU, R.K. (1990). Academic self-respect vs. pseudo universalism: The travails of an Indian psychology teacher. *Indian Journal of Social Science, 3(4)*, 569–575.

RING, K. (1967). Some sober questions about frivolous values. *Journal of Experimental Social Psychology, 3,* 113–123.

SHARMA, S. (1981). Key concepts of social psychology in India. *Psychologia, 24,* 105–114.

SINHA, D. (1984). Psychology in the context of Third World development. *International Journal of Psychology, 19,* 17–30.

SINHA, D. (1986). *Psychology in a Third World country: The Indian experience.* New Delhi: Sage.

SINHA, D. (1988). Indigenisation of psychology in India and its relevance. *The Indian Journal of Social Science, 1,* 77–91.

SINHA, J.B.P. (1984). Towards partnership for relevant research in the Third World. *International Journal of Psychology, 19,* 169–178.

5

Indigenous Psychology: Scientific Ethnocentrism in a New Guise?

YPE H. POORTINGA

The position taken here is that other indigenous conceptualisations are understandable and in many ways welcome reactions to Eurocentric indigenous theories with pretentious claims to universality. The first section summarises what is seen as the main case for the indigenisation movements. In the second section it will be argued that cross-cultural psychologists concerned with indigenisation emphasise differences in behaviour patterns rather than invariance of psychological functioning. The last section presents some experimental evidence from research in Tilburg to support the argument that there are no intrinsic reasons in the relationship between cultural factors and behaviour which make "indigenous psychologies" indispensable.

THE CASE FOR INDIGENISATION

The indigenous development of psychology as a science and as a profession is necessary to the extent to which mainstream theories and applications, which will be referred to as "western psychology", are inadequate for non-western societies. Many arguments have been raised to support the contention that there is indeed such an inadequacy. A majority of these arguments are based on the assumption that the inadequacy of western psychology is unavoidable.

For the purpose of analysis a distinction can be made between four different levels at which western psychological research tends to be ethnocentric (cf. Berry et al., 1992).

1. Selection of items and stimuli in an instrument.
2. Choice of instruments and procedures.
3. Definition of theoretical concepts.
4. Choice of topics for research.

Clear examples of the first level of bias are test items that enquire about factual knowledge of the testee, but that are less familiar to other groups than the one for which the test was originally intended. Usually an item is taken to be biased when relative to other items an unexpectedly low score is found in one of two cultural groups. By and large two findings emerge. For groups at a small cultural distance, only a limited number of items in a test is biased (cf. Berk, 1982). Second, for groups at a great cultural distance, evidence of item bias has been found even in cognitively simple tasks, such as Choice-Reaction Time and curiosity tasks (cf. Poortinga, 1971; Poortinga and Foden, 1975). This level of ethnocentrism lends itself well to empirical scrutiny. It has been extensively studied in traditions of item bias research. Most often item bias is studied with a view to eliminate those items that are biased and to obtain an "unbiased" or psychometrically equivalent assessment instrument. Although item bias may well occur, instruments and procedures should generally yield comparable results after adaptations at the item level have been made, for example, cross-cultural studies with the Eysenck Personality Questionnaire (Eysenck and Eysenck, 1983).

The third general perspective mentioned by Berry and associates is that of universalism, or psychological universalism.[1] Here it is assumed that all psychological processes are universal, but that the manifestations of invariant processes can differ between cultures. In as much as psychological measurements depend on item content and the local understanding of procedural aspects, equivalence of the meaning of scores is unlikely to be realised. This makes the transfer of instruments, and the cross-cultural comparison of data collected with these instruments, highly questionable. It may even be that quite different operationalisations are needed to capture the same psychological traits across cultures. In addition, psychological universalism explicitly recognises the possibility that the formulation of a theory is biased. Most likely it is a conception in which only a limited range of relevant phenomena is incorporated, namely, those found in the researcher's own socio-cultural environment. A telling example is perhaps the low relevance of religion in many western studies of values.

[1] The reader is referred to Van de Vijver and Poortinga (1982; cf. Berry et al., 1992) for further information on the definition and empirical validation of the universality of psychological concepts. "Invariance" is the term used by these authors for empirical relationships which are the same across cultures.

A somewhat more elaborate text would read:

Since the case of universalism is argued in this paper, it is perhaps appropriate to elaborate briefly on the criteria for universality. The term "invariance" is used to indicate that in empirical research identity of specified statistical relationships between variables across cultural populations is the main distinguishing feature for universality. What kinds of relationships should be invariable depends on the rigour or strictness with which such relationships can be defined. Van de Vijver and Poortinga (1982; Berry et al., 1992) have distinguished four categories or levels of universals, which they called, conceptual universals, weak universals, strong universals, and strict universals. Conceptual universals are notions at a high level of abstraction without any implication of measurement. Adaptation would be an example. At the other three levels the question whether a theoretical notion and its operationalisation has universal validity should be empirically testable. Weak universals merely require that the notion under investigation has validity everywhere, or at least that no counterevidence exists. Strong universals are concepts that can be measured on a scale with the same metric units everywhere; for strict universals the scale should not only have same metric, but also the same origin. It is important to note that these requirements impose conditions on the comparability of data. Also, Poortinga and Van de Vijver do not see culture specific versus universal as a dichotomy; rather there are degrees of universality, or in terms of data, degrees of invariance. How these ideas are worked out in actual cross-cultural research will be illustrated later.

As indicated earlier, traditions of indigenisation tend to be relativistic. This implies an emphasis on differences rather than similarities, also at the level of theoretical concepts, and few attempts to find common denominators of behaviour cross-culturally. In recent years, various authors in the field of cross-cultural psychology, who endorse the notion of indigenisation, have avoided a clear choice between relativism and universalism.

For example, according to Sinha (1986), with the indigenisation of psychology in India researchers began to question whether western theories and models were appropriate for the Indian social context. Imported psychology was seen as not "natural" to the Indian situation and it was felt that Indian psychology should have its own distinctive character (1986, p. 63). Such statements may appear to explicitly demand the formulation of a separate psychology for India. At the same time, Sinha has pleaded for the integration of the traditional Indian philosophical literature with western trends, particularly more recent developments like humanistic psychology (pp. 77–78), and he has explicitly mentioned that indigenisation is demonstrated by the choice of topics (for example, economic poverty). In the end Sinha has rejected the notion of separate theory development: ". . . the process of 'indigenisation' is gradually gaining ground in the sense that the phenomenon in question is tried to be viewed in the specific socio-cultural context, and the tools for study are so designed that they are rooted in the specific culture" (p. 103). This conclusion suggests that Sinha sees a need for the reformulation of existing theories in the light of Indian ideas, but that he does not seek a separate psychology for India.

Similarly, Kim (1990) while recommending indigenous description (and rejecting the experimental method) has advocated that "the cross-indigenous approach can lead to the discovery of 'true', empirically based universals" (p. 149). One of the two cases discussed by Kim, namely, the restructuring of the school environment for Hawaiian children, does not presume any non-universal concepts of behaviour, but (merely) a sensitivity to the local conditions. In the second case, on the role of *amae* ("dependence") and *sunao* ("compliance") in Japanese socialisation it is not immediately clear whether these are unique features, which require their own culture specific psychological explanation, or whether they are culture specific conceptualisations of universal psychological principles. Still, it would seem that Kim's advocacy of empirically based universals places him outside the relativists' camp.

When a choice for relativism is made on the basis of a priori metatheoretical arguments it is per definition almost impossible to muster empirical evidence that will be accepted by the adherents of this approach. In the case of authors like Sinha and Kim the emphasis on indigenisation appears to be compatible with the perspective of psychological universalism. The need for a reformulation of concepts and for the use of culturally appropriate instruments is in line with this perspective. However, Sinha and Kim, like the relativists, tend to stress cross-cultural differences in behaviour. The question is whether or not this is done at the cost of cross-cultural invariance in psychological functioning.

BALANCING SIMILARITIES AND DIFFERENCES

It is perhaps surprising that students of culture–behaviour relationships who are usually strong advocates of the notion of "psychic unity of mankind" in their empirical research often look for differences in behaviour across cultures, rather than for similarities. One of the reasons may be the loose usage of the experimental design with insufficient care for the various forms of ethnocentrism discussed earlier. Ethnocentrism will lead to a systematic overemphasis of the size of differences and presumably their importance (cf. Malpass and Poortinga, 1986).

It is also possible to conduct research in which cross-cultural invariance and differences in behaviour repertoire are seen as two sides of the same coin, both requiring equal emphasis. To illustrate such an approach some studies conducted at Tilburg University will be discussed. One has to realise that this approach will work well only if a small proportion of the items is biased.

Stimulus bias tends to operate in one direction, i.e., the same of two groups will almost invariably obtain a lower score on the biased items in a maximum performance test. If more than a small fraction of the items is biased, this will result in systematic differences in score distributions between groups at the level of instruments. In such instances it can be said that the instrument as a whole is biased. Another source of instrument bias has to do with the administration procedures. If groups differ in test sophistication (e.g., speed vs accuracy trade-off) or familiarity with response procedures, such as the multiple choice format, this is likely to affect the performance on all items, again in one and the same direction. Although there are statistical techniques for analysis at this level (e.g., factor analysis), the results are often not clear-cut and it is difficult to identify and eliminate all bias. In general, comparison of psychological data as well as the transfer of methods and procedures from western to non-western settings implies a serious risk of ethnocentrism in the sense of instrument bias.

The third level of ethnocentrism is concerned with theory. When it is difficult to find a procedure that allows a cross-culturally unbiased assessment of a particular theoretical concept the question arises whether the formulation of the theory on which the procedures are based is not itself biased, in the sense of being culturally less appropriate for some populations. Examples are provided by stage theories like those of Piaget and Kohlberg which postulate high stages of development usually not found in non-industrialised village cultures (Piaget, 1966; Kohlberg, 1981, 1984). Two points of view have to be distinguished here. According to the first viewpoint, psychological theories are inherently linked to the cultural context in which they originate. According to the second viewpoint, bias in conceptualisations can be overcome by the reformulation of concepts in the light of insights derived from research in diverse cultures (Berry et al., 1992, ch 10; Poortinga, 1975). Needless to say that the first of these two alternatives leads to culture specific indigenous psychologies, while the second alternative paves the way for a universal psychology, combining western and non-western insights. This issue will be discussed in more detail later. However, it should be noted that the existence of theoretical formulations that are less appropriate for some cultural populations than for others is accepted here.

The fourth and last level of ethnocentrism concerns the topics that are chosen for research and application in current psychology. Taking the world's psychological literature as a whole, there can be no doubt that this choice is heavily biased towards the perceived interests of those living in economically wealthy regions. The needs of the majority of the world population, often living in impoverished circumstances, receives far less emphasis. It is accepted here as a morally legitimate demand that psychological research should be made more relevant to non-western societies (cf. Sinha and Holtzman, 1984).

Indigenous psychology can be justified in two ways. The first is a pragmatic orientation. All four levels of ethnocentrism, but particularly the last one, provide arguments for developing psychology in one's own society. After all, one's own ethnocentrism is likely to be more useful than that which has originated in another cultural context. In as much as indigenisation is an *ad hoc* compensation for existing short-comings rather than a reflection on psychological variations within the human species, it is an understandable reaction to Eurocentric psychology, although its (meta)theoretical basis can be questioned.

The second (and leading) orientation in indigenous psychology is based on a metatheoretical orientation that cultural context affects the structure and organisation of psychological functioning in an essential manner and that a different psychology is needed in each culture (cf. Heelas and Lock, 1981; Enriquez, 1990). From such a perspective, psychological ethnocentrism in the sense discussed here is unavoidable not only in measurement, but also in theoretical conceptualisation.

THEORETICAL RATIONALE

In their recent textbook on cross-cultural psychology, Berry and associates (1992) have drawn a distinction between three basic perspectives on the relationship between culture and behaviour, called relativism, universalism, and absolutism.

Relativism, or cultural relativism, argues that behaviour is only understandable within the cultural context in which it occurs. This also applies to psychological theories which are part of the heritage of the specific cultural population in which they originate. The understanding of behaviour, in this context perhaps more appropriately labelled "human action", is essentially impossible without a detailed knowledge of the historical and socio-cultural factors. Relativists generally refrain from comparisons of cross-cultural data since such comparisons would presume common reference standards (i.e., invariant theoretical concepts and equivalent instruments). Most research in cultural anthropology has a relativistic orientation, but formulations by authors like Valsiner (1987) and Shweder (1990) can also be considered relativistic.

In contrast, the perspective of absolutism, or behavioural universalism, views behaviour as essentially biological; cultural variations are mere ripples on the surface. Psychological principles used in the construction of measurement scales are universally applicable, therefore, instruments should be readily transferable to (all) other cultures. Methodologically, it is typical of this approach that patterns of scores, rather than scores on one or more separate variables, are interpreted. Conceptually, the search for invariance in score patterns is as explicit as the search for differences. The following findings are characteristic.

Similarities in Test Performance Patterns

Van de Vijver (1991) conducted an extensive study of inductive thinking in school children of different grades in four cultural groups, namely, Zambians, Turks, Dutch, and Turkish migrants in the Netherlands. In the construction of each of 8 tests for various aspects of inductive thinking, the author used a facet design to systematically vary item content. Each test was preceded by elaborate instructions in which an example of each facet was given. Despite substantial differences in the levels of scores between the four cultural groups on each of the tests, the correlations between the difficulty levels of the facets were very high. The median value of the correlations over all the tests and the four groups was equal to 0.91. The findings clearly indicated that the same factor made an item of inductive reasoning difficult for a school child in Holland or in Zambia or Turkey, despite the differences in the overall level of performance. The latter differences presumably were due to variables such as school equipment, teaching style, and home background, of which Van de Vijver could show that they were related to test performance.

Limited Generalisation of Cultural Antecedents

Joe (1992) investigated the effects of tonality in language in a wide range of experiments. Various far-reaching effects of this pervasive and life-long linguistic factor have been reported, including effects on brain lateralisation (cf. Fromkin, 1978) and a general facility for the processing of auditory information in tonal language populations (Wober, 1975). Studying groups of children (8 to 12 years of age) from the tonal language island Bonaire and the non-tonal language island Saint Eustatius in the Caribbean, and Dutch control groups, Joe found that the effects of tonality were essentially limited to the recognition of tonal patterns in words. The subjects from Bonaire did better than the other two groups in differentiating phonemically identical words with a different tonal pattern from words with the same tonal pattern. This was the case with words from their own language, Papiamento, as well as with words from Beijing–Chinese, a tonal language unknown to all the subjects. In 12 other experiments, including, among other things, the recognition of emotional tone in verbal utterances, memory for tonal sequences, and brain lateralisation for various kinds of stimuli, no confirmation was found for the suggestion that the effects of tonality could be generalised to broad domains of behaviour. It should be noted that the author included in each experiment stimuli on which tonal language subjects were expected to perform better as well as stimuli on which an equal performance was anticipated for tonal and non-tonal language subjects.

Direct Context Effects

Implicitly or explicitly it is assumed in cross-cultural research that observed behaviour reflects trait-like dispositions acquired earlier in life, rather than a reaction to the prevailing situational context. The study by DeRidder may lead one to question such assumptions. The study, based on an approach to aggression developed by DeRidder (1980), investigated the expected reactions to intergroup norm violations in pairs of contrasting groups in a society. Two such pairs were chosen in each of two countries. In India the groups involved were Muslims versus Hindus, and managers versus workers, in the Netherlands they were Turkish migrants versus autochthonous Dutch, and workers versus managers. Subjects were asked for the expected reactions of their own group to norm violations by members of the other group, as well as for expected reactions of the other group in case of norm violations by their own group. To explain differences in expectations between groups within a pair, four context variables were included in the design, namely: (a) perceived power of one's group, (b) the group's position vis-à-vis the other group measured on a scale of fraternal relative deprivation (cf. Runciman, 1966), (c) attitudes towards the other group, and (d) own-group identity. The main results have been reported by DeRidder and Tripathi (1992). Of interest here are the results of hierarchical regression analyses in which the contribution of the four context variables to the differences in expected reactions between own-group and other group was estimated (cf. Poortinga and Jansen, 1992). A summary of these results is presented in Table 5.1

TABLE 5.1

Effects of Four Context Variables on Expected Reactions to Norm Violations in Four Pairs of Groups

Contrast	R_1^2	Rel. Depr	Rel. Power	Attitude	Soc. Ident	R_2^2
Wo/Ma Ind	.185	(.028)	.236	.046		.014 NS
Wo/Ma Neth	(.118)		.198			.004 NS
Tu/Du Neth	.399	(.015)	.436	.016	.046	.007 NS
Mu/Hi Ind	.015 NS	–	–	–	–	–

Note: Brackets indicate $.01 \leqslant p < .05$.
Source: Poortinga and Jansen, 1992.

The first column of the table shows the difference in reactions to norm violations jointly expected by the subjects of both groups in a contrast pair. This was found to be significant in three of the four contrasts. The other columns indicate how much of the difference can be explained in terms of each of the four context variables. One point, not evident from the table, should be noted, the correlation between the scales for power and relative deprivation was high in all groups. In such cases it is to be expected that only one of these two variables will show a strong effect in hierarchical regression analyses.[2] The last column shows that the difference left to be explained after the effects of the four context variables have been removed is small and insignificant in each of the three relevant contrast pairs. These results indicated that the two context variables reflecting external conditions in which groups of people find themselves (i.e., power and relative deprivation) were considered far more important by the subjects than internalised

[2] Very similar results to those listed in the table for power were found for relative deprivation when the latter score was forcibly entered as the first variable in the regression analyses.

dispositions (represented by own-group identity and attitudes). The prevailing circumstances under which members of a group live rather than cultural variables account for these patterns.

The ethnocentrism of western psychology is undesirable. However, indigenous psychologies can also be ethnocentric, and in fact they are when they make exaggerated claims about the nature and extent of differences in psychological functioning between cultural groups. The examples presented here support an orientation in which universal principles of behaviour are emphasised.

CONCLUSIONS

Within psychological universalism the first three levels of ethnocentrism distinguished earlier can be the subject of empirical analysis. Sophisticated psychometric techniques have been developed to identify item bias. Instrument bias can sometimes be identified through the use of analysis techniques such as LISREL, but it can also be circumvented through the adaptation of measurement procedures, or even the construction of entirely new, culture appropriate instruments. This requires an existing theory that is clearly defined (Poortinga, 1989). If bias in a theory is suspected, a reconceptualisation will be needed to modify and improve the existing notions in order to arrive at formulations that in validation research prove to be less culturally idiosyncratic. This is not only useful for maintaining dialogue between cross-cultural psychology and other fields of psychology, but it is also a necessary condition for decreasing the ethnocentrism in *any* indigenous psychology, be it western or non-western.

Presumably, the choice for or against indigenisation of psychology ultimately should be decided on the basis of considerations related to the fourth level of ethnocentrism. The question is whether an indigenous psychology will meet better the needs of the members of a society than a psychology with claims to universal validity. From psychological universalism as a (meta)theoretical orientation, a definite answer to this question cannot be formally deduced. However, it is possible to derive suggestions and caveats which appear to be fairly plausible. Two such suggestions follow from the arguments presented here. First, the pervasive threat of ethnocentrism in the choice of items and

instruments makes extensive knowledge of the local behaviour repertoire and its context a necessary condition for the application of
psychology across cultural borders. Second, apparent similarities in
psychological functioning increase the possibility that universally valid
theories can be formulated.

Perhaps there is a final consideration that exceeds the level of
discourse presented here. In colonial times "westerners" frequently
argued about other peoples that "they" were different. Those advocat-
ing indigenisation of psychology in non-western countries may also
echo this argument. However, the main message of cross-cultural
psychology is not that "they" are different, but that "we" are the same.

REFERENCES

BERK, R.A. (Ed.). (1982). *Handbook of methods for detecting item bias.* Baltimore, MD:
The Johns Hopkins University Press.

BERRY, J.W., POORTINGA, Y.H., SEGALL, M.H., and DASEN, P.R. (1992). *Cross-cultural
psychology: Research and applications.* Cambridge: Cambridge University Press.

DERIDDER, R. (1980). Agressie in sociale interactie: Waarneming en reactie (Aggression
in social interaction: Perception and reaction). Unpublished doctoral dissertation, Tilburg University, Tilburg.

DERIDDER, R. and TRIPATHI, R.C. (Eds.). (1992). *Norm violations and intergroup relations.*
Oxford: Oxford University Press.

ENRIQUEZ, V.G. (Ed.). (1990). *Indigenous psychology. A book of readings.* Akademya Ng
Sikolohiyang Pilipino. Quezon City: Philippine Psychology Research & Training
House.

EYSENCK, H.J. and EYSENCK, S.B.G. (1983). Recent advances in the cross-cultural study
of personality. In J.N. Butcher and C.D. Spielberger (Eds.), *Advances in personality assessment* (Vol. 2, pp. 41–69). Hillsdale, NJ: Erlbaum.

FROMKIN, V.A. (1978). *Tone: A linguistic survey.* New York: Academic Press.

HEELAS, P. and LOCK, A. (Eds.). (1981). *Indigenous psychologies: The anthropology of
the self.* London: Academic Press.

JOE, R.C. (1992). Cognitive consequences of tonality in language: A cross-cultural
investigation. *Cross-Cultural Psychology Monographs, 2.*

KIM, Y.Y. (1990). Indigenous psychology: Science and applications. In R. Brislin (Ed.),
Applied cross-cultural psychology (pp. 142–160). Newbury Park, CA: Sage.

KOHLBERG, L. (1981). From *is* to *ought*: How to commit the naturalistic fallacy and get
away with it in the study of moral development. In L. Kohlberg (Ed.), *Essays on
moral development: The philosophy of moral development* (Vol. 1, pp. 101–189).
San Francisco: Harper and Row.

KOHLBERG, L. (1984). *Essays on moral development: The psychology of moral development* (Vol. 2). San Francisco: Harper and Row.

MALPASS, R.S. and POORTINGA, Y.H. (1986). Strategies for design and analysis. In W.J. Lonner and J.W. Berry (Eds.), *Field methods in cross-cultural research* (pp. 47–84). Beverly Hills, CA: Sage.

PIAGET, J. (1966). Nécessité et signification des recherches comparatives en psychologie génétique. *Journal International de Psychologie, 1*, 3–13. Published as Need and significance of cross-cultural studies in genetic psychology. In J.W. Berry and P.R. Dasen (Eds.), *Culture and cognition* (pp. 299–309). London: Methuen.

POORTINGA, Y.H. (1971). Cross-cultural comparison of maximum performance tests: Some methodological aspects and some experiments. *Psychologia Africana*, Monograph Supplement, 6.

POORTINGA, Y.H. (1975). Limitations of intercultural comparison of psychological data. *Nederlands Tijdschrift voor de Psychologie, 30*, 23–39.

POORTINGA, Y.H. (1989). Equivalence of cross-cultural data: An overview of basic issues. *International Journal of Psychology, 24*, 737–756.

POORTINGA, Y.H. and FODEN, B.I.M. (1975). A comparative study of curiosity in black and white South African students. *Psychologia Africana*, Monograph Supplement, 8.

POORTINGA, Y.H. and JANSEN, X.H.M. (1992). Cross-cultural equivalence of the data. Results for the separate variables. Hierarchical regression analysis. In R. DeRidder and R.C. Tripathi (Eds.), *Norm violation and intergroup relations* (pp. 137–146). Oxford: Oxford University Press.

RUNCIMAN, W.G. (1966). *Relative deprivation and social justice*. London: Routledge and Kegan Paul.

SHWEDER, R.A. (1990). Cultural psychology—What is it? In J.A. Stigler, R.A. Shweder, and G. Herdt (Eds.), *Cultural psychology: Essays on comparative human development* (pp. 3–43). Cambridge: Cambridge University Press.

SINHA, D. (1986). *Psychology in a Third World country: The Indian experience*. New Delhi: Sage.

SINHA, D. and HOLTZMAN, W. (Eds.). (1984). The impact of psychology on Third World development. *International Journal of Psychology, 19* (1 & 2), (Special issue).

VALSINER, J. (1987). *Culture and the development of children's action*. New York: Wiley.

VAN DE VIJVER, F.J.R. (1991). *Inductive thinking across cultures: An empirical investigation*. Helmond: Wibro.

WOBER, M. (1975). *Psychology in Africa*. London: International African Institute.

6

Agency, Action and Culture: Three Basic Concepts for Cross-Cultural Psychology

LUTZ H. ECKENSBERGER*

More than a decade ago, within the framework of an IACCP Congress in Munich, Eckensberger (1979) insisted that the analysis of cultural rules, their ontogeny, as well as their function and structure should be part of every psychological work. Furthermore, it was elaborated that the inclusion of culture into psychology could probably be realised most conveniently by means of action theories. In this early discussion an argument of Reese and Overton (1970) was extended, and five psychological paradigms and their attached families of theories were distinguished, including action theories. It was argued that the basic metaphor or model of man inherent in any action theory is the potentially self-reflective human being. These arguments have been reviewed by Poortinga and Malpass (1986), thus forming the basis of a critique of (a) Eckensberger's preference for action theories, and (b)

* The author is grateful to Doris Fritzsche for her translation work and the improvements on the style of this paper. He is also indebted to the German Research Foundation for supporting his participation in the conference.

his assertion that cultural rule and meaning systems be essential parts of psychology.

Therefore, this is a welcome occasion not only to carefully examine the state of the art today, but also to take another step in the scientific discourse on the matter, and to further argue in favour of an action theoretical approach, particularly in cross-cultural research.

POORTINGA AND MALPASS' (1986) CRITIQUE OF THE APPLICATION OF ACTION THEORY IN CROSS-CULTURAL PSYCHOLOGY

In the following, the two most important arguments of Poortinga and Malpass (1986) will be discussed: a call for objectivity and causality in cross-cultural research, and a rejection to include the culture concept into psychology.

First, they state that theories which entail teleological elements are only "acceptable as scientific theories . . . to the extent that they can be empirically tested" (pp. 20–21) in the sense of a "neo-Popperian or neo-positivistic framework" (p. 18). Furthermore, they elaborate that teleological relationships "can only be empirically investigated in an indirect way", and thus that "statements have to be formulated in terms of the second model (cause), or the first model (relation between variables)" (p. 46)—the enumeration, here, referring to the models differentiated by Eckensberger in 1979.

In fact, their arguments first and foremost stipulate that action theories be formulated in terms of causality. They can be interpreted as an expression of the assumption that some "paradigms" (especially causal ones) purportedly can (!) be tested in a direct, and hence, more "objective" way.

Second, the authors state that "Culture as a product of human action has not received much attention in cross-cultural psychology" and, in their opinion, " . . . for good reasons. (Because) culture as a human product transcends behaviour as studied in psychology" (p. 20). They, therefore, contend that "Eckensberger has opted for a broader view for which the boundaries of psychological science, as they are usually defined in cross-cultural psychology, have to be extended" (p. 20).

Apparently, the authors assume that laws are ultimately identical in (their causal) nature, and that humans are governed by these (causal) laws. Thus, culture is presumed to have a causal influence on subjects and, for this reason, can be defined as an independent variable.

Clearly, Poortinga and Malpass' (1986) views concur with those held by most of the exponents of mainstream cross-cultural psychology. Usually, for instance, from a technical point of view, in so-called "differentiation studies" (Berry, 1980; Eckensberger, 1969; Strodtbeck, 1964; Whiting, 1954), culture is handled as an independent variable, or as a "bunch" of independent variables (Segall, 1984). As a consequence, this type of approach is factually interested in culture only as far as it represents a possible source of variance or covariance. It is not interested in culture as a subject matter in its own right. On the other hand, in the so-called "generalization studies", culture is treated as altogether irrelevant, as in these cases, only those behavioural aspects are chosen and focused upon, which are culture independent or culturally invariant. Poortinga and associates have poignantly paraphrased the latter as an "onion" which is "peeled" in the process of cross-cultural research "until in the end they (cross-cultural differences) have disappeared and with them the variable culture" (Poortinga et al., 1987, p. 22).

A RESPONSE TO THE CRITICISMS OF POORTINGA AND MALPASS

The Framework: The Relationship between Causal Laws and Cultural Rules in Psychology

Whether or not causal principles are adequate concepts for interpreting psychological processes is a question which has a long history, and led to many systematic debates that cannot possibly be dealt with, in depth, here (cf. Cahan and White, 1992; Eckensberger, 1990a, 1990b; Groeben, 1986; Krewer, 1990). For the present purpose, it will suffice that from a philosophical point of view, this question centres around the dichotomy of "explanation" and "understanding", the former usually being associated with the "causes", the latter with the "reasons" for action. Interestingly enough, and to the best of our knowledge, this discussion has not even been initiated in cross-cultural psychology.

A quotation from the Norwegian psychologist Jan Smedslund (1988) will set the stage on a first general plane. He has elaborated that "two unfortunate circumstances have blocked the development of a generally accepted language in Psychology" which both

> stem from an incompatibility between some features of a scientific ideal inherited from the older physical sciences and the particular characteristics of psychological phenomena . . . : The physical sciences strive to be objective, whereas psychological phenomena are subjective, and the physical sciences involve empirical study of hitherto unknown domains, whereas psychological phenomena are often well known and highly predictable in advance to ordinary people (p. 1).

Since many of the following arguments will be analytical, rather than empirical in nature, a short comment on the relationship between analytically and empirically derived statements in psychology is useful. As a matter of fact, this distinction alone leads directly into the heart of the matter, that is, whether or not psychology merely deals with natural laws, or also with cultural rules.

Again, Smedslund (1988), in his book, *Psycho-logic*, has commented: "A . . . point, not generally recognized by psychologists, is that regularities in data need not necessarily be empirical, that is, need not be knowable only through experience" and, among others, he has referred to the well known case of bachelors. He has elaborated: "The finding that all bachelors are in fact unmarried males cannot be said to be empirical. If the data appear to include a few bachelors who are females, we have to conclude either that these are, after all not bachelors, or that they are not females" (p. 4). He, has added,

> In general, predictions which can be made solely on the basis of one's mastery of the language and membership in a given culture may be characterized as a priori since they neither require empirical support nor are (they) affected by a lack of such support. There are normative correct and incorrect ways of speaking and of behaving nonverbally, and knowledge of these allows one to make extensive and generally correct predictions. When the predictions are falsified, this does not weaken any empirical hypothesis, but simply means

that the assumed antecedent conditions had not been established (p. 4).

In short, Smedslund's position not only underscores the eminent importance of culture in reconstructing human activities, but also elucidates the implications of applying the culture concept in empirical research.

The first aspect is further substantiated by the culture concept used in modern anthropology as, for instance, by Clifford Geertz (1973), or by Goodenough (1981). Geertz has elaborated that culture can be conceptualised in terms of rules, as "a set of control mechanisms—plans recipes, rules, instructions [what computer engineers call 'programs']—for the governing of behavior" (p. 44; cf. also D'Andrade, 1984), Goodenough (1981/1954), on the other hand, has even localised culture "in the heads" of people (cf. § 8).

Although presumably a large part of the psychological profession still has strong reservations against applying philosophical reflections to psychology, in the following, some of the analytical distinctions proposed in modern philosophy will be used (Habermas, 1981; Lenk, 1984; von Wright, 1971). A general acknowledgment of a number of these philosophical distinctions could prevent psychologists from re-inventing the wheel all over again, and above all, could also prevent them from empirically testing analytical sentences.

To treat the two points of criticism of Poortinga and Malpass (1986) on a more specific level, some of the terminology pertaining to action theory will be introduced (cf. also Eckensberger, 1977, 1990a, 1990b; Eckensberger and Emminghaus, 1982; Eckensberger and Meacham, 1984). Incidentally, it deserves to be mentioned that actions are sometimes viewed from a conceptual, and sometimes from a dynamic or processual point of view; that is, in the former case, one is dealing with analytical distinctions, in the latter case, with empirical hypotheses.

Actions are future-oriented, goal directed activities of a potentially self-reflective agency.

Although self-reflectivity is a principle characteristic and an analytical element of any action, it is not assumed to be empirically given in any one human activity; empirically, self-reflection may even be a rare event. Yet, this would not suffice to treat actions as epiphenomena, as any activity, even if it is not self-reflective or "conscious" the very moment it occurs (such as, a habitual activity or an automatism), may easily be subjected to self-reflection and conscious deliberation the very next moment. The possibility of its occurrence is present in virtually any human activity.

Furthermore, not each and every empirically given human activity is preceded by a rational plan or choice. Instead, taking the lead from Piaget (1970) and Hayek (1979), it is assumed that intellectual development is preceded by the development of actions, ontogenetically, and probably, even historically. "Man did not adopt new rules of conduct because he was intelligent. He became intelligent by submitting to new rules of conduct" (Hayek, 1979, p. 163).

Ontologically, there is a clear distinction between actions and behaviour.

Actions comprise the intentional doing of something, the intentional omission of something, as well as the intentional allowance of something to happen. Thus, actions are evidently "interpretive constructs" that hinge upon the interpretation of an event, process or situation as being intended (Lenk, 1984). A description of the instrumental action oriented toward the non-social environment will be presented.

As any structure, the structure of action is defined by elements and their interrelationships.

The elements of an instrumental action are goals, means, results, and consequences.

Action means are applied arbitrarily by a subject in order to attain a goal. "Arbitrariness" implies that, at least in principle, the person has a (subjective) choice. This choice does not necessarily need to be made between action *a* or *b*, but can also be located between doing something, omitting something, or even letting something happen.

Actions ensue results and effects. To this effect, Georg Henrik von Wright (1971) has differentiated:

It is convenient to distinguish between doing things and bringing about things . . . by doing things we bring other things about. For example, by opening a window we let fresh air into the room . . . What we thus bring about are the effects of our action. That what we do is the cause of those effects. The cause I shall also call the result and the effects the consequences of our action (p. 66).

It is necessary to distinguish at least two types of effects of an action: those which are intended, and those which are unintended. The effects of an action can be brought about intentionally, they can simply be accepted, or they can be avoided. From this structure it follows that the actor is responsible for his or her actions, or, at least in principle, can be held responsible for them.

Reflectivity, finality, intentionality, implication, causality and functionality typify the various thought processes pertaining to the relationship between action elements.

The use of the term "cause" in the quotation by von Wright (1971) is an important indication of the fact that within an action schema, all of the "elements" (agency, goals, means) are interrelated by qualitatively different types of "thought processes" or interpretation schemata (Figure 6.1): results and effects, for instance, are interrelated by causality; goals, on the other hand, are reflectively tied to an agency; the chosen means for attaining a goal follow finalistically from the goal; and finally, the results of an action (the open window) are logically implied in the choice of means (opening the window) (Eckensberger, 1977, 1986; Eckensberger and Reinshagen, 1980).

A Contrary Point of View: Teleology as a Precondition for Any Definition of Causality

A clarification of the concept of causality is as yet pending. Although it has been a very popular convention to use the causality principle in psychology, the necessary or even sufficient conditions for its application have not been explicated. Moreover, recent advances in the natural sciences have shown that the "causality principle" is no longer conceivable in terms of nineteenth century physics. Unfortunately, this has hardly been appreciated in the field of psychology. A similar criticism was recently formulated by Jahoda (1990).

As a case in point, the methodological literature provides ample evidence of the fact that causality can neither be derived from, nor identified with prediction or conjunction. "The mere fact that x and y vary together in a predictable way, and that a change in x always precedes the change in y can never assure us that x has produced a change in y" (Blalock, 1964, p. 10). Rather, the causality principle is a (philosophical) issue linking the occurrence of some event/state y to the prior occurrence of some other event/state x, an aspect, which not only makes it difficult to observe empirically, but also to transform it into any formal logical language (Bunge, 1959, pp. 239–245).

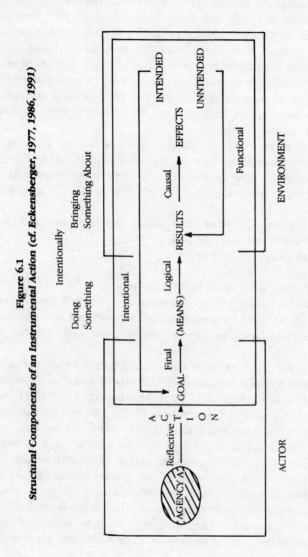

Figure 6.1
Structural Components of an Instrumental Action (cf. Eckensberger, 1977, 1986, 1991)

In turning to the first desideratum of Poortinga and Malpass (1986), it will become clear that Eckensberger disagrees with their position that action theory be reduced to causal processes. Quite to the contrary, it is claimed here that it is neither possible to derive finality or teleology from causality, nor to define teleology in terms of causality; instead, only the reverse is true, that is, it is proposed that the concept of action is presupposed in any scientific effort aiming at an investigation of causal processes. In this respect, the concept of action is always the superordinate structure.

Analytically, these conclusions follow from the above specified types of relationships between the elements of an action (Figure 6.1), and especially from the distinction between "doing things" and "bringing things about". On this basis, von Wright (1971) has proposed

> the following way of distinguishing between cause and effect by means of the notion of action:
> p is a cause relative to q
> if and only if
> by doing p we could bring about q or
> by suppressing p we could remove q or prevent it from happening.
>   In the first case the cause-factor is a sufficient, in the second case the cause-factor is a necessary condition to the effect-factors (p. 72).

It is important to realise that methodologically this "definition" of causality is totally compatible with the general notion of the experiment as the most proper strategy for testing causality (Cook and Campbell, 1979), and it definitively concurs with the methodical preferences set forth by Poortinga and Malpass (1986). What the latter do not take into consideration, however, is that the idea of the experiment, in itself, is only possible within an action theoretical framework: the experiment is but one action in that it is an intentional (systematic) variation of some condition, i.e., independent variable, by which one tries to bring about something else—a variation in a dependent variable. Thus, it is the action—and therefore teleology—which is in fact the precondition for the determination of causality, and not vice versa.

In Defense of "Subjectivity" as an Indispensable Part of Any Scientific Effort

From what has been proposed, and quite opposed to what Poortinga and Malpass have implied, it also follows that no scientific enterprise (whatsoever) can be direct or "objective" in the proper sense of the word. Knowledge about the world and about reality is always (!) indirectly defined:

1. Via actions that constitute the *methods of inquiry*, such as observation, selection or bringing things about.
2. Via actions that represent the *methods of analysis* by which one tries to give a certain order to and an evaluation of the material/findings.

However close these actions may be to the concept of causality, they can never provide thorough empirical evidence to prove its existence, that is, the system on which these actions are based can never be isolated completely. Hence, apart from the variables that are varied systematically, others may well be operating. In course of time this problem was addressed to by philosophers of science, like Russel (1929), Bunge (1959) and Frank (1961), to name but a few.

These deliberations are not only intended to illuminate the empirical limitations to the definitions of causality. They are also intended to clarify the theoretical or epistemological status of the conception that "causal statements or laws are purely hypothetical . . . . they can never be tested empirically in the strictest sense of the word" (Blalock, 1964, p. 13). Thus, their hypothetical status implies that they themselves are "man made" to a certain extent, that is, causal statements are far more "subjective" than Poortinga and Malpass (1986) would concede. Even worse, causal laws are themselves created within a specific scientific culture, and are therefore part of it.

Without discussing the issue in more detail, it is interesting to note that this argument was articulated in the field of physics as early as in 1957 by W. Heisenberg and has been advocated since in psychology by several authors (Valsiner, 1989).

To obviate any misinterpretation, it is not claimed that this process of knowledge construction is totally subjectivistic or completely arbitrary, as may be concluded from the positions held by extreme "social constructivists", such as Gergen (1985). Instead, and concurring with Peeters (1990), it is assumed that any "scientific re-construction of reality" is regulated not only by some "resistance of reality", but also by some "structural factors that impose restrictions on the making of constructs" (Peeters, 1990, p. 80).

What has been achieved so far? The foregoing discussion has indicated that:

1. Teleology is not only the broader concept in that it cannot be reduced to causality.
2. Rather, causality, as well as the notion of "objective knowledge" exclusively controlled by "objective" empirical data, is in itself rather a creed than a scientifically justified ideal. Instead, the whole process of knowledge construction in science is an open process, which is best conceivable within the framework of human actions.

In a way, refutation of the first desideratum of Poortinga and Malpass (1986) was easy, as the preliminary work had already been done by von Wright. One only had to refer to it. What about their second argument, purporting that the culture concept as a product of human actions transcends the behaviour studied in psychology?

Another Contrary Point of View: The Culture Concept is a Necessary Precondition for Reconstructing and Predicting Human Activities

Even if it were accepted that causality can only be determined within an action psychological approach, it could be argued that this does not automatically preclude causality altogether in regard to human activities and achievements. Why not interpret psychological phenomena in terms of the earlier mentioned causality concept? An attempt will be made in the following to define and explicate the specific limitations to applying this causality principle to psychology.

The Reconstruction of Action is Something Other than a Causal Explanation

For the purpose of illustration, for a moment, imagine a person wants to cross a street, but a policeman asks him or her to stop. And imagine also, the person then does in fact stop. One could now be tempted to interpret the utterance of the policeman as a cause for the person to stop. The person's halt could be viewed as representing the effect brought about by the cause. This, however, would obviously be far too simple a story and above all, misleading, as it was not the objective features of what the policeman said that made the person stop. Rather, it is the meaning that the person attached to the policeman's request that made him or her comply with it. "The typical specimen of contemporary psychological research manages to look like a study of causal relationships between objective events, while it actually depends on subtle interpretations of meaning in a complex context in order to maintain contact with what actually goes on psychologically, that is for the participants" (Smedslund, 1988, p. 1).

What does this mean methodologically in terms of the definition of causality developed earlier?

It was again von Wright who pointed out the decisive distinctions between teleological and causal processes. Even though he spoke of "bringing something about" in the case of individuals who were induced to do something, he explained, "this *is not, I maintain, a causal or nomic connection . . . It is a motivational mechanism and, as such not causal but teleological*" (p. 69, italics mine).

Hence, the phrase "to bring about" a consequence in another person, in fact, does not mean to cause some action in that person, but, at best, "to occasion somebody for something".

This is to say that an agency's action is induced by some kind of "social influence" or interaction of another person; for instance, by means of "coercion", "persuasion" or simply by "motivating" the interaction partner to act in one way or another. This also implies that under any circumstances the respective interaction partners must have a similar interpretation of the ongoing situation, and must be interested in exerting mutual influence on each other. Therefore, the meaning of a situation is the common background against which mutual interpretations take place which govern the interplaying actions and reactions of the partners involved.

In Figure 6.2 the distinctions are illustrated. In the upper part, Figure 6.1 is summarised, and the process of "explanation" is introduced: to explain something simply means to interpret something

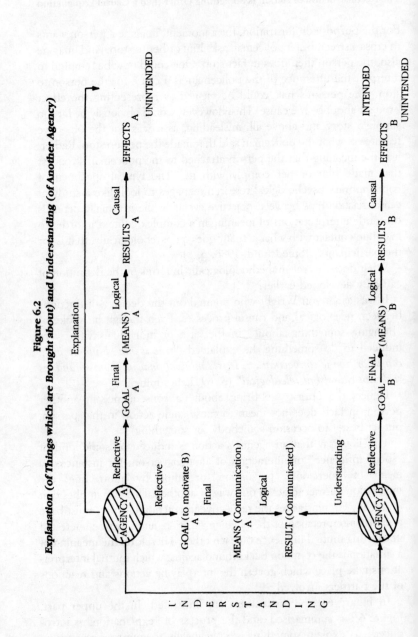

Figure 6.2
Explanation (of Things which are Brought about) and Understanding (of Another Agency)

which has been brought about or which has happened in terms of causation in the material world. On the left hand side of the figure, the interaction with, or the influence upon another agency is illustrated. Here, the goal of agency A is to "induce" another agency B to do something, or to allow something to happen, that is, to act. The kind of interpretation applied to this type of reality is not an "explanation". In as far as teleology or finality is involved in the interpretation of a process or an event, "understanding" is a more appropriate term. This process involves agency A, who uses a means of communication, and agency B, who subsequently needs to interpret the communication of A (Result, A). It is then that B will or will not respond to or comply with agency A's initiative. Hence, the ensuing action elements on B's part (goals, means, results and consequences of B) will follow in part from A's initiative, but cannot be said to have been "caused" by A.

From a psychological and from a constructivist point of view, the interpretive schemata of both explanation (causality) and understanding (teleology/finality) are preconditions for treating the world in varying ways. Psychologically, these schemata first form the basis for distinguishing different domains of thinking constitutive of different aspects of the world, or of what we call "reality".

If some process or event is interpreted as being part of a final action, and not of some natural (causal) process, it is, by definition, part of the social world: Any one agency B is presumed to have initiated that event or process.

However, if some process or event is interpreted as being part of a causal process, it is, by definition, part of the "natural (physical/biological/material) world".

Reality in itself cannot possibly be objectively defined in terms of a causal or final entity. Instead, the varying types of thought processes are constitutive of different aspects of reality (cf. Eckensberger, 1977; Eckensberger and Reinshagen, 1980).[1]

---

[1] I concur with a dualistic position although I am well aware that many philosophers of today hold monistic views. Schurz, for instance, has stated: "the previous confrontation of the natural sciences, explaining objective phenomena, as opposed to the human sciences, explaining human actions, has been surmounted"(Schurz,1988, p. 251). In my opinion, however, these attempts to overcome dualism are unsatisfactory, as in these cases, from a psychological point of view (a) action motives are posed as causal elements (Davidson, 1963), which fail to account for intersubjective experiences; (b) the general concept of causality is used in the Aristotelian tradition as a superordinate category, encompassing a variety of subordinate types of causality (cf. Overton, personal communication); or (c) the concept of causality is fictitiously abandoned or reduced to formal—rather than ontological structures (cf. Schurz, 1988).

From this perspective it is evident that ontology no longer "guides" epistemology (as posited in various forms of realism), but is in itself framed by the epistemology of human individuals. On might even argue that the classic distinction between ontology and epistemology breaks down considerably.

In addition, at least two types of evaluative action orientations can be distinguished: control of the environment and harmonisation between the agency and the environment by means of action. Sinha (1992) has used these two action orientations to characterise "Western" and "Eastern" thought.

If these two general orientations are connected to the two types of reality construction distinguished above, then a 2 × 2 table of four action types emerges, three of which can also be found in western terminology (cf. Table 6.1).

TABLE 6.1

Four Types of Action Resulting from Attempts Either to Control or to Harmonise the Physical/Material/Biological or the Social World

Reality is Interpreted as Being	Action Orientation	
	To Control	To Harmonise
Physical/Material/Biological	Instrumental	Adaptive
Social	Strategic	Communicative

Control of the environment implies the evaluation of an action in terms of its instrumental or functional adequacy. This means that the agency analyses whether the chosen means are instrumentally appropriate for realising a certain end or goal. In the case of the physical/material/biological environment, the resulting action type is called an "instrumental action"; in the case of the social world, it is called a "strategic action". A harmonising orientation of one's action towards the social world clearly resembles the notion of "communicative action", which has been extensively discussed by Habermas (1981). By definition, it involves a moral orientation towards another agency: it presupposes both that another agency has been understood, and also that his/her point of view has been considered and respected. This means that different aspects or elements of an action (goals, means, or, various consequences) are analysed as to whether they possibly could, or in fact, do interfere with the interests or goals of other actors, actions, groups, or even norms or principles. In the case of the physical environment, this orientation would involve what Sinha has called "adaptive" behaviour, which, in our own theoretical framework, we would prefer to call "adaptive actions".

In summary, it is contended that the mere fact that human activities show a considerable amount of regularity does not automatically imply that they follow natural or causal laws. Regularities in human interactions are neither exclusively based on biological functions, nor on causal physical laws, but on the processes of mutual understanding, communication and agreement. Smedslund has convincingly argued: "Human beings have made themselves describable and predictable to each other and to themselves. (And therefore) the social order within which we exist makes us describable, explainable and predictable" (Smedslund, 1984, p. 449). So there is far more to human beings than causal laws. This simple and unpretentious insight is clearly an initial step in rejecting the criticism of Poortinga and Malpass (1986).

In order not only to reject the criticism of Poortinga and Malpass (1986), but also to develop a constructive idea as to how culture can be a part of psychology, two further tasks need to be accomplished. First, a number of additional interpretation schemata besides those of "causality" and "understanding" need to be distinguished and inter-related; and second, the relationship between individual interpretation schemata and cultural rule systems calls for clarification.

Towards Differentiating Interpretive Schemata

In developmental psychology, several "domains of thinking" besides physical (causal) and social cognitions have been discriminated (Shweder, 1980), especially in the field of social cognitions, and more so in the field of prescriptive social cognitions, some differentiations are pertinent. Turiel (1983) has distinguished between "conventions" and "morality", which are complemented by the concept of "personal concerns" (Smetana, 1982). All these rule systems represent interpretive schemata which are applied to various situations. In the following, these and other rule systems will be discussed, and an attempt will be made to elucidate their interrelationships. The action scheme will serve as a frame of reference for this. This is illustrated in Figures 6.3 and 6.4.

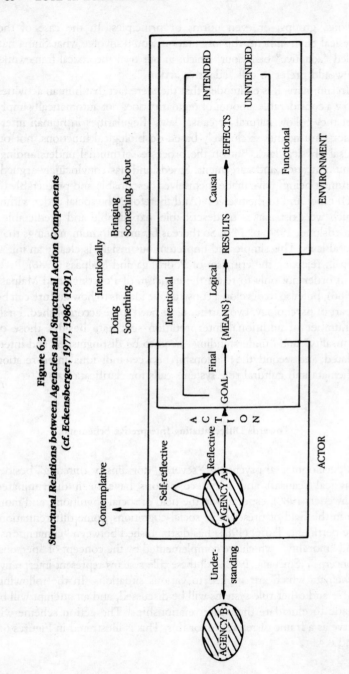

Figure 6.3
Structural Relations between Agencies and Structural Action Components
(cf. Eckensberger, 1977, 1986, 1991)

Figure 6.4
The Interrelationship between Action Barriers and Interpretative Schemata Within the Context of the Agency's Meaning Rule System

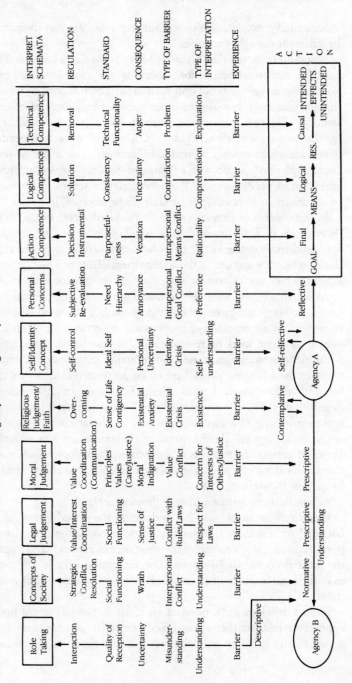

Structurally, actions, agency and other persons are also distinguished by different thought processes.

It should be noted that Figure 6.1 is now used as a basis for Figure 6.3. The earlier defined action scheme is now complemented by the notion that an agency is not only related to its own actions by reflective thought processes, but also to other agencies by processes of understanding (Figure 6.2). First and foremost, the agency is linked to itself by the process of self-reflection. It is related to a transcendental dimension which reaches beyond self-reflectivity. This might be termed "contemplation", indicating a "thought process" which relates the agency to its very existence. This interpretation scheme is involved in religiousness or deliberations of faith (Eckensberger, in press).

In the context of previous research (Eckensberger, 1990a, 1990b), three levels of action were distinguished: *primary actions*, which are applied directly to the world; *secondary actions* (reflections and regulations), which are applied to the actions themselves; and finally, *tertiary actions*, which are self-oriented (self-reflection and contemplation).

Although all these levels are activated to varying degrees within any human activity, in the present context, secondary actions are especially relevant: they are regulatory processes and reflections within an action aiming at some kind of re-orientation of the action. This type of adjustment presupposes some kind of action disturbance or impediment. In the following, actions are no longer treated as analytical units, but rather as empirical units. Here, Eckensberger disagrees with Smedslund (1988) who has argued that "one's mastery of the language and membership of a given culture may be characterized as *a priori*" (p. 4, italics mine). To the contrary, Eckensberger has adopted a Piagetian perspective in terms of a genetic epistemology, which implies that the meaning of a phenomenon is empirically reconstructed within its genesis (Kesselring, 1981).

Action barriers instigate human development.

Empirically, actions may be, and often are impeded by "action barriers" (cf. Figure 6.4). Analytically, an action barrier is a relational term. Empirically, it represents the resistance of certain "facts" against the natural course of an action. The red traffic light in the earlier example is an instance of a possible barrier in the action of crossing a street.

From a developmental point of view, action barriers are of utmost importance because they are assumed to instigate developmental processes. Regrettably, the genuine process of how cognitive schemata are constructed has not yet been clarified (Boom, 1991; Grüter, 1990). Nonetheless, there is consensus that some kind of impediment is essential. Perhaps development can even be reconstructed as a function of contradictions or barriers. In particular, it is assumed that the experience of an action barrier produces

1. An increase of consciousness or reflective activity on the part of the agency.
2. Emotional consequences.
3. Some regulatory adjustment to a given standard of some kind.
4. Leads to differentiation and integration of cognitive and affective schemata.

These aspects will be dealt with individually in their given order, which is not to imply that they inevitably occur in this sequence; to a large extent, they occur simultaneously.

Not only actions (Lenk, 1984) and causality (Blalock, 1964) are conceived as "interpretive schemata"; the experienced action barrier or impediment is in itself qualified as such by interpretation, that is, the action barriers, themselves, to a certain extent, are constructions of the respective agency. Ultimately, this tantamounts to saying that the barriers receive their meaning from interpretation processes. This was demonstrated by the earlier example of the traffic light.

Inevitably the question arises: what do impediments comprise? It is proposed that impediments are first and foremost construed by the very same interpretation processes within which they appear as barriers. Second, the relationship between these interpretations—thought processes—is influenced by the pertinent cultural meaning system within which the interpretation processes occur. In Figure 6.4, the basic scheme of the structure of the action is used to differentiate analytically and to interrelate the most important "domains of thinking".

Take, for example, a barrier which the agency attributes to causal processes. Say, a person travelling in the mountains comes across a landslip or rocks that block his path and interrupt his journey. The agency interprets this impediment as a cause only as long as it interprets the situation in terms of explanation (that is, in terms of a natural phenomenon) (cf. Figure 6.2). Then, a specific quality is attributed to the barrier, thus rendering it what would be called a *problem* in order to denote its causal quality. On the other hand, if the person were suddenly assaulted by a gang of robbers, the interpretation of the barrier would be qualified by a process of understanding, in that the barrier would also be attributed to some kind of teleological/final process (cf. Figure 6.2). For instance, the person might immediately conclude that he will have to hand over all his money to the robbers. The case differs from a problem in that it is part of a *conflict* between contending interests.

Similarly, all other types of barriers encountered in legal conflicts, in conflicting values, in identity or existential crises, in intrapersonal conflicts of goals and/or means, or in what we call contradictions are contained in Figure 6.4. Barriers are thus constituted by different attributional schemata, namely, by processes of respect for the law or for persons and principles, by existential experiences, by self-understanding and self-reflection, by preferential awareness of need, and finally, by goal rationality and processes of cognitive comprehension.

Barriers also lead to different types of consequences. These may be internal (affects) or external (sanctions) in nature, and they may be rather stenic or asthenic (Eckensberger and Emminghaus, 1982).

In the present context, only negative internal and stenic consequences are considered, in order to keep the argument as simple as possible. These negative internal consequences can and need to be differentiated according to the agency's interpretation of the respective barrier: although, in principle, all consequences are emotions that represent the negative experience of the (frustrating) barrier, these emotions assume different qualities or "shades". It is proposed that these shades are determined or defined by the specific type of interpretation of the experience. Thus, in the case of a "natural landslip"—which appears to the agency as a problem caused by nature (explanation), the negative emotion may be "anger". In the case of an interpersonal conflict with a gang of robbers, which presupposes some kind of understanding of the situation, the negative affect may be called "wrath". In Figure 6.4, different terms have been identified to denote the emotional qualities pertaining to the multifarious interpretations of impediments.

Both the experience of a barrier, and the regulatory and reflective processes presuppose some kind of subjective standard.

Unless there is some kind of implicit or explicit anticipation of the course and the results of an action, no barrier can be defined or experienced. However, it is necessary to distinguish different types of regulations, which are intrinsically related to the type of barrier. *Causal problems*, defined by and oriented towards some standard of technical functionality, are *removed* by regulations involving causal processes, or they are simply circumvented. In the case of the landslip, two types of solution are possible: either to remove the rocks, or to use another path. *Social conflicts*, on the other hand, which are defined by and oriented towards some ideal or standard of "social functioning", are not removed, but are resolved by means of some type of *interpersonal conflict resolution*; the traveller, for instance, could argue, negotiate, or even decide to suffer his fate.

The construction of different cognitive interpretive schemata or "domains of thinking", as a final step.

Clearly, here, all three basic conditions explicated by Piaget in his reconstruction of development are relevant (Kesselring, 1981): the process of equilibration, the concept of reflective abstraction, and the process of decentration. In the case of an action barrier, it is consciousness that serves to focus attention (Boesch, 1991, p. 128) because (*a*) it usually increases during the experience of an impediment, and (*b*) because it results in "conceptualization" (Piaget, 1974, p. 261, quoted after Boesch, 1991, p. 129). However, in the case of pleasurable actions (which include successful regulations), consciousness also has the function of checking and confirming (somehow) the action potential of the actor (Boesch, 1991, p. 130). Therefore, generally speaking, consciousness "establishes situations" (Boesch, 1991, p. 131), while affects serve to structure the individual action potential (Boesch, 1984).

The same logic holds for all other types of barriers and attached emotions, types of standards, and kinds of regulation which form the various "domains of thinking". The establishment of their distinctive qualities, the construction of technical and social competence, the domains of moral and legal judgment, of religious thinking, of self-concepts and identity, of personal taste and esthetic preferences, action competence or logical competence are all assumed to follow the same formal line of development.

Not only the differentiation of barriers, but also their interrelationship can be systematised this way. For instance, if the traveller had attributed the landslip or the rocks blocking the path to be the work of the members of the gang, then these rocks would certainly have retained their quality of being a problem, but would have also remained part of the interpersonal conflict.

Individual and Cultural Interpretive Schemata and Rule Systems

In attempting to reconstruct human activities, it is not only essential to analyse the subjective rule and meaning systems applied to a certain context, but it is also necessary to know the collective meaning and rule systems the agency is part of and makes reference to.

It would be highly artificial to assume that the diversity of interpretive individual schemata can develop independently of other people or one's native culture. To the contrary, the analysis presented here reveals an intrinsic interrelationship between the individual's actions, experienced barriers and respective interpretations, and the affective and cognitive schemata underlying the construction of the broader individual meaning and rule systems. Finally, it intends to reflect the internal relationship between an action and the context within which it occurs. This conclusion converges with the position of Rosnow and Georgudi (1986) who have argued that "an act or event cannot be said to have an identity apart from the context that constitutes it; neither can a context be said to exist independently of the act or event to which it refers" (p. 6). A traffic light, for instance, has meaning because of the idiosyncratic interpretations of individuals, and also because of its embodiment into a rule system regulating the traffic in a certain social setting. Imagine an even more complicated case: suppose the traveller interpreted the existing landslip as part of his *karma*, or *kismet*, or fate, then this impediment would be considered both a part of his existential concepts and a part of the religious system pertinent to his culture. Consequently, any individual's rule system is complemented by a cultural pendent. To elaborate on the internal relationship between individuals' and cultural interpretation, on the one hand, and rule schemata, on the other, the framework of human action is used.

Although actions are executed by subjects in real life situations, the action itself can be seen as the dynamic interface between the individual and the situational context (Eckensberger, 1979, 1990a, 1990b).

It can be seen from Figure 6.1 that any action forms the overlap between the internal (agency/goal) and external action fields (results/intended, non-intended consequences). This unit of analysis affords, first, to interrelate the interpretation schemata of any agency with the meaning and rule systems of the respective culture, and second, to interrelate the changes in both domains. By acting, the agency constructs, co-constructs or reconstructs his/her own interpretation schemata, which constitute what is termed the individual internal action field, and by doing so, the person transforms himself or herself in the Piagetian sense. However, the person does this in a material, social and ideatoric cultural setting. On the one hand, it defines the limitations to and the possibilities of experience (Boesch, 1991; Eckensberger, 1979, 1990a, 1990b; Valsiner, 1989); on the other hand, the person himself/herself is changed and recreated within this very same process. Thus, culture is conceived as a meaning and rule system which is a precondition for, and at the same time, a result of actions. Elsewhere, it was argued that "here precisely is the (theoretically located) dynamic interface between individual and cultural rule systems which Shweder (1980) points to' (Eckensberger, 1990b, p. 174).

This interrelationship is illustrated in Figure 6.5. As it is regulations and/or reflections, in particular, which serve as a basis for forming these meaning and rule systems, it is not primary actions, but secondary actions which serve to link individual and collective interpretive systems. Any particular type of regulation is affiliated to a specific type of barrier and interpretation schema within a subject (cf. Figure 6.3), and to the specific external (pre)existing cultural meaning and rule systems. In the course of development, cultural and societal rule systems are habituated. They are common standards for overcoming different types of barriers (regulations). These systems define the framework within which individuals' regulations take place. They offer possibilities for, and limitations to regulatory actions. They exert forms of selective pressure, or impose canalising constraints on regulations (Eckensberger, 1990a, 1990b). In fact, they represent beliefs and normative frameworks, knowledge and rule systems, which refer to the individual (personal concerns), to nature (technology, science), as well as to culture itself (laws, conventions, ethics). At the same time, however, all of them, to a certain degree (Ingleby, 1990), are cultural constructs.

In conclusion, two things have been evidenced so far: culture as a meaning and rule system is obviously an essential part of any psychology, not only of cross-cultural psychology. Moreover, culture cannot simply be handled as an independent variable, as it cannot be interpreted in terms of a single or a multiplicity of causal factors alone. This would be a categorical mistake.

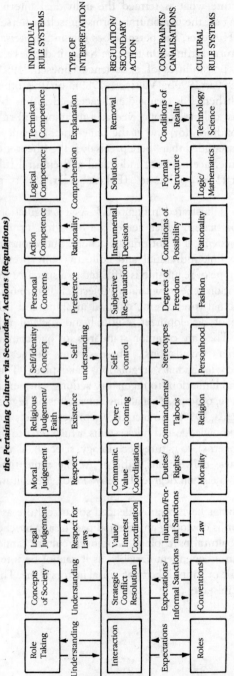

Figure 6.5
Mutual Reference of Interpretative Schemata of an Agency with the Meaning and Rule Systems of the Pertaining Culture via Secondary Actions (Regulations)

A NUMBER OF CONSEQUENCES FOR DESIGNING A CULTURAL PSYCHOLOGY

This concluding section is intended to give only a very brief enumeration of some of the contents and methodological aspects of a cross-cultural psychology (provided it is taken to be part of cultural psychology).

The following contents will be the key targets of future research:

1. First, the most *important goals* in cultural psychology, today, are both *differentiation and analysis of individual and cultural interpretation schemes and rule systems.*

2. Furthermore, *research on emotions* and what they mean to the individual is highly relevant. But in this field, emotions should primarily be conceived as summarised indicators of the meanings that subjects attribute to situations. For this reason, it is easier to analyse meanings by analysing emotions, rather than through cognitive methods (Eckensberger and Emminghaus, 1982).

3. Future research efforts will inevitably focus *on the nature of agency.* Empirically, it is an open question what exactly constitutes an agency. From a psychological point of view, the concept of agency is a rather flexible phenomenon—it might prove beneficial, for instance, to subsume the modern dichotomy of "individualism and collectivism" (Triandis, 1988) under what is called the "boundary" of the agency. This can be defined both in terms of the acting subject, and in terms of the collectively acting or co-acting members of a group. However, processes of self-reflectivity are highly important at various levels of human development. On the level of (a) the current genesis of the single act, (b) ontogeny, (c) pathogenesis, and (d) phylogeny.

From a methodological point of view, the following aspects require attendance:

4. More generally, it is assumed that the fundamental distinction between *emic* and *etic* variables or measurements in cross-cultural psychology will lose its established import. Although this dichotomy has been seriously criticised by Jahoda (1983), it is still commonly applied (Berry, 1989). Unfortunately, the whole strategy of emic, imposed etic and derived etic deduced from this dichotomy represents a kind of scientific imperialism. If,

however, one begins with the notion of culture as a meaning and rule system, an initial attempt should encompass defining "*consensual etic*" concepts, pieces of content, as well as methods that form the basis of cross-cultural research.

5. In the process of what is called "data gathering", that is, in the *methods of inquiry*, it is imperative to consider *the "object" of research at all times, also a subject in its own right*. The interpersonal processes between the researcher and the subject can no longer be reduced to conceptualisations of cause–effect relations between the individual and nature. In other words, Heisenberg's insight that the natural sciences "are no longer conceivable as a reproduction of nature, but rather as a reproduction of our relationship to nature" (1957, p. 31) is more applicable to the social sciences, and to psychology, in particular. Here, the reproduction of any human ability or feature is not merely grounded in "our relationship to another subject", but also in the "subject's relationship to us". For this reason, Habermas (1983, p. 31) called for a "bifocal attitude" which the social scientist should assume towards the object/subject; a mental bearing which is "performatory" as well as "objective" at the same time.

6. *Undoubtedly, the methods of analysis are on the verge of changing*: by no means, of course, should the ideal of exactness be abandoned. Nevertheless it should be kept in mind that it was Albert Einstein who explicitly formulated the limitations of mathematical language for systematising the phenomena of "reality". He stated: "Insofar as mathematical principles refer to reality, they are not certain, and insofar as they are certain, they do not apply to reality" (Einstein, 1956, p. 119). (Would not it be a good idea to print this as an admonition on to the front page of any introductory textbook of statistics of test theory?) Admittedly, Einstein's evaluation referred to the domain of natural sciences. But obviously it is even more true when applied to the social and/or cultural sciences. Psychology is likely to develop greater methodical tolerance in reconstructing and systematising human activities and achievements. The formal languages developed in analytical philosophy (Meggle, 1990), the field of hermeneutic methods (Serpell, 1990), or the scientific developments in type-construction (Werbik, 1985) are only a few examples of the domains psychology can draw on today. Thus, prediction, the "holy cow" among the scientific ideals of

psychologists, will not be totally abandoned. True enough, it will no longer be based on the inevitable principle of causality alone; instead, for the most part, it will be embodied in the serviceable notion of common rule and meaning systems.

REFERENCES

BERRY, J.W. (1980). Introduction to methodology. In H.C. Triandis and J.W. Berry (Eds.), *Handbook of cross-cultural psychology: Vol. 2* (pp. 1–28). Boston: Allyn and Bacon.

BERRY, J.W. (1989). Imposed etics-emics-derived etics: The operationalization of a compelling idea. *International Journal of Psychology, 24,* 721–736.

BLALOCK, A.M., JR. (1964). *Causal inferences in nonexperimental research.* New York: The Norton Library.

BOESCH, E.E. (1984). The development of affective schemata. *Human Development, 27,* 173–183.

BOESCH, E.E. (1991). *Symbolic action theory and cultural psychology.* Berlin: Springer.

BOOM, J. (1991). Collective development and the learning paradox. *Human Development, 34* (5), 273–287.

BUNGE, M. (1959). *Causality.* Cambridge: Harvard University Press.

CAHAN, E. and WHITE, S.H. (1992). Proposals for a second psychology. *American Psychologist, 47,* 224–233.

COOK, T.D. and CAMPBELL, D.T. (1979). *Quasi-experimentation: Design and analysis issues for field settings.* Chicago: Rand McNally.

D'ANDRADE, R. (1984). Cultural meaning systems. In R.A. Shweder and R. LeVine (Eds.), *Culture theory* (pp. 88–119). Cambridge: University Press.

DAVIDSON, D. (1963). Actions, reasons and causes. *Journal of Philosophy, 60,* 685–700.

ECKENSBERGER, L.H. (1969). *Methodenprobleme der kulturvergleichenden Psycholgie.* Saarbrücken: SSIP-Verlag.

ECKENSBERGER, L.H. (1977). "Soziale Kognitionen" und "Sozial–orientiertes Verhalten"— der Versuch einer Interpretation durch das Konzept "Handlung". *Newsletter Soziale Kognition, 1,* 68–90.

ECKENSBERGER, L.H. (1979). A metamethodological evaluation of psychological theories from a cross-cultural perspective. In L.H. Eckensberger, W.J. Lonner, and Y.H. Poortinga (Eds.), *Cross-cultural contributions to psychology* (pp. 255–275). Lisse: Swets and Zeitlinger.

ECKENSBERGER, L.H. (1986). Handlung, Konflikt und Reflexion: Zur Dialektik von Struktur und Inhalt im moralischen Urteil. In W. Edelstein and G. Nunner-Winkler (Eds.), *Zur Bestimmung der Moral. Philosophische und sozialwissenschaftliche Beiträge zur Moralforschung* (pp. 409–441). Frankfurt am Main: Suhrkamp.

ECKENSBERGER, L.H. (1990a). From cross-cultural psychology to cultural psychology. *The Quarterly Newsletter of the Laboratory of Comparative Human Cognition, 12* (1), 37–52.

ECKENSBERGER, L.H. (1990b). On the necessity of the culture concept in psychology: A view from cross-cultural psychology. In F.J.R. van de Vijver and G.J.M. Hutsche-maekers (Eds.), *The investigation of culture. Current issues in cultural psychology* (pp. 153–183). Tilburg: Tilburg University Press.

ECKENSBERGER, L.H. (in press). Zur Beziehung zwischen den Kategorien des Glaubens und der Religion in der Psychologie. In T.V. Gamkrelidze (Ed.), *Brücken: Beiträge zum Dialog der Wissenschaften aus den Partneruniversitäten Praha, Saarbrücken, Sofia, Tbilissi und Warzawa.* Tbilissi.

ECKENSBERGER, L.H. and REINSHAGEN, H. (1980). Kohlbergs Stufentheorie der Entwick-lung des moralischen Urteils: Ein Versuch ihrer Reinterpretation im Bezugsrah-men handlungstheoretischer Konzepte. In L.H. Eckensberger and R.K. Silbereisen (Eds.), *Entwicklung sozialer Kognitionen: Modelle, Theorien, Methoden, Anwendungen* (pp. 65–131). Stuttgart: Klett-Cotta.

ECKENSBERGER, L.H. and EMMINGHAUS, W.B. (1982). Moralisches Urteil und Aggression: Zur Systematisierung und Präzisierung des Aggressionskonzeptes sowie einiger empirischer Befunde. In R. Hilke and W. Kempf (Eds.), *Aggression: Naturwis-senschaftliche und kulturwissenschaftliche Perspektiven der Aggressionsforschung* (pp. 208–280). Bern: Huber.

ECKENSBERGER, L.H. and MEACHAM, J. (1984). The essentials of action theory. A framework for discussion. *Human Development, 27,* 166–172.

EINSTEIN, A. (1956). *Mein Weltbild.* Frankfurt: Ullstein.

FRANK, P. (1961). *Modern science and its philosophy.* New York: Collier Books.

GEERTZ, C. (1973). *The interpretation of culture.* New York: Basic Books.

GERGEN, K. (1985). The social constructionist movement in modern psychology. *American Psychologist, 40,* 266–275.

GOODENOUGH, W.H. (1981). *Culture, language and society.* Menlo Park/Cal.

GROEBEN, N. (1986). *Handeln, Tun, Verhalten als Einheiten einer verstehend-erklärenden Psychologie.* Tübingen: Francke.

GRÜTER, B. (1990). *Widerspruch. Individuelle Entwicklung als Systemsteuerung.* Heidel-berg: Ansger.

HABERMAS, J. (1981). *Theorie des kommunikativen Handelns. Bd. 1: Handlungsrational-ität und gesellschaftliche Rationalisierung.* Frankfurt: Suhrkamp.

HABERMAS, J. (1983). *Moralbewuβtsein und kommunikatives Handeln.* Frankfurt: Suhr-kamp.

HAYEK, F.A. (1979). The three sources of human values. In F.A. Hayek (Ed.), *Law, legislation and liberty* (Vol. 3, pp. 153–173). Chicago: University of Chicago Press.

HEISENBERG, W. (1957). *Das Naturbild der heutigen Physik.* Hamburg: Rowohlt.

INGLEBY, D. (1990). Problems in the study of the interplay between science and culture. In F.J.R. van de Vijver and G.J.M. Hutschemaekers (Eds.), *The investigation of culture. Current issues in cultural psychology* (pp. 59–73). Tilburg: University Press.

JAHODA, G. (1983). The cross-cultural emperors' conceptual clothes: The emic-etic issue revisited. In J.B. Deregowski, S. Dziurawiec, and R.G. Annis (Eds.), *Explications in cross-cultural psychology* (pp. 19–49). Lisse: Swets and Zeitlinger.

JAHODA, G. (1990). Variables, systems and the problem of explanation. In F.J.R. van de Vijver and G.J.M. Hutschemaekers (Eds.), *The investigation of culture. Current issues in cultural psychology* (pp. 115–130). Tilburg: University Press.

KESSELRING, T. (1981). *Entwicklung und Widerspruch. Ein Vergleich zwischen Piagets genetischer Entwicklungstheorie und Hegels Dialektik.* Frankfurt: Suhrkamp.

KREWER, B. (1990). Psyche and culture—Can a culture-free psychology take into account the essential features of the species "homo sapiens"? *The Quarterly Newsletter of the Laboratory of Comparative Human Cognition, 12,* 24–37.

LENK. H. (1984). *Handlungstheorien interdisziplinär. Bd III, 2.* München: Fink.

MEGGLE, G. (1990). Intention, Kommunikation und Bedeutung. Eine Skizze. In Forum der Philosophie (Ed.), *Intentionalität und Verstehen* (pp. 88–108). Frankfurt: Suhrkamp.

PEETERS, H.F.M. (1990). Limits of social constructivism. Beyond objectivism and relativism. In F.J.R. van de Vijver and G.J.M. Hutschemaekers (Eds.), *The investigation of culture. Current issues in cultural psychology* (pp. 77–90). Tilburg: University Press.

PIAGET, J. (1970). Piaget's theory. In P.H. Mussen (Ed.), *Carmichael's manual of child psychology, Vol. 1* (pp. 703–732). New York: Wiley.

PIAGET, J. (1974). *La prise de conscience.* Paris: Presses Universitaires de France.

POORTINGA, Y.H. and MALPASS, R.S. (1986). Making inferences from cross-cultural data. In W.J. Lonner and J.W. Berry (Eds.), *Field methods in cross-cultural research* (pp. 17–46). Beverly Hills, CA: Sage.

POORTINGA, Y.H., VAN DE VIJVER, F.J.R., and VAN DE KOPPEL, J.M.H. (1987). Peeling the onion called culture: A synopsis. In Ç. Kağitçibaşi (Ed.), *Growth and progress in cross-cultural psychology* (pp. 22–34). Lisse: Swets and Zeitlinger.

REESE, H.W. and OVERTON, W.F. (1970). Models of development and theories of development. In L.R. Goulet and P.B. Baltes (Eds.), *Life-span developmental psychology* (pp. 116–145). New York/London: Academic Press.

ROSNOW, R.L. and GEORGUDI, M. (1986). The spirit of contextualism. In R.L. Rosnow and M. Georgudi (Eds.), *Contextualism and understanding in social sciences* (pp. 3–22). New York: Praeger Publishers.

RUSSEL, B. (1929). *Mysticism and logic and other essays.* New York: Norton and Company.

SCHURZ, G. (1988). Was ist wissenschaftliches Verstehen? Eine Theorie verstehens-bewirkender Erklärungsepisoden. In G. Schurz (Ed.), *Erklären und Verstehen in der Wissenschaft* (pp. 233–298). München: Oldenburgverlag.

SEGALL, M.H. (1984). More than we need to know about culture, but are afraid not to ask. *Journal of Cross-Cultural Psychology, 15,* 153–162.

SERPELL, R. (1990). Audience, culture and psychological explanation. A reformulation of the emic-etic problem in cross-cultural psychology. *The Quarterly Newsletter of the Laboratory of Comparative Human Cognition, 12,* 99–132.

SHWEDER, R. (1980). Rethinking culture and personality theory, Part III: From genesis and typology to hermeneutics and dynamics. *Ethos, 8* (1), 60–94.

SINHA, D. (1992, January, 3–7). Indigenous psychology: Need and potentiality. Paper presented at the Fourth Asian Regional Congress on the IACCP, Kathmandu.

SMEDSLUND, J. (1984). The invisible obvious: Culture in psychology. In K.M.J. Lagerpelz and P. Niemi (Eds.), *Psychology in the 1990s.* Amsterdam: Elsevier Science Publisher.

SMEDSLUND, J. (1988). *Psycho-logic.* Berlin: Springer.

SMETANA, J.G. (1982). *Concepts of self and morality: Women's reasoning about abortion.* New York: Praeger Publishers.

STRODTBECK, F.L. (1964). Considerations of meta-method in cross-cultural studies. In A.K. Romney and R.C. D'Andrade (Eds.), *Transcultural studies in cognition* (pp. 223–229). Washington: American Authropological Association.

TRIANDIS, H.C. (1988). Collectivism versus individualism: A reconceptualization of a basic concept in cross-cultural social psychology. In G.K. Verma and C. Bradley (Eds.), *Cross-cultural studies of personality, attitudes, and cognition* (pp. 60–95). London: Macmillan Press.

TURIEL, E. (1983). *The development of social knowledge. Morality and convention.* Cambridge: Cambridge University Press.

VALSINER, J. (1989). *Human development and culture: The social nature of personality and its study.* Toronto, MA: Lexington Books.

VON WRIGHT, G.H. (1971). *Explanation and understanding.* New York: Cornell University Press.

WERBIK, H. (1985). *Psychonomie und Psychologie.* Internal Report No. 8. Nürnberg.

WHITING, J.W.M. (1954). The cross-cultural method. In G. Lindzey (Ed.), *Handbook of social psychology* (Vol. 1, pp. 523–531). Cambridge, MA: Addison/Wesley.

Section 2

Family Experiences and Cognitive Processes

7

Introduction

This section on family experiences and cognitive processes comprises five papers. Gülerce from Turkey has conceptualised family in a way that links the individual with society and culture. Her paper summarises the conceptual framework, construction, and psychometric features of the family assessment scale developed and widely used in Turkey.

The comparative study of East Asian and Euro–American cultures by Boehnke, Scott, and Scott examines the influence of family climate on academic performance. The central hypothesis developed by the authors is that a warm, egalitarian and mutually satisfying family climate would foster certain personality features of the child, namely, high interpersonal competence and low manifest anxiety which in turn are the key prerequisites for high self-esteem. High self-esteem is assumed to be the most important prerequisite for good academic performance. Samples of students, one of their parents, and one of their teachers were surveyed in 7 countries: Hong Kong, Taiwan (Taipei), Canada (Winnipeg), the USA (Phoenix), Japan (Osaka), Australia (Canberra), and Germany (West Berlin). The authors have noted that self-esteem universally was a strong predictor of academic performance with family climate as the decisive background variable for this. Differences between Euro–American and East Asian cultures were found in terms of student aggressiveness which has negative effects on academic performance in East Asian cultures, whereas its influence varied from mildly negative to neutral in Euro–American cultures. Conclusions with regard to school counselling have been drawn by the authors.

Mishra and Tripathi present a study confirming the role of eco-cultural factors in the development of a number of psychological processes among individuals. This has also been confirmed by cross-cultural research conducted during the last two decades. The authors have argued that the culture prescribes what one learns as an individual in that culture. Effective adjustment in any cultural environment demands a set of skills which are often acquired by individuals in informal settings. The most distinctive feature of this type of learning is its embeddedness in a person's daily life activities. These tend to have important psychological consequences for the growth of the individual. However, their transfer to performance in psychological test situations continues to be a major issue of debate. In two fairly matched samples of 9–10-year-olds the effect of "cloth weaving" experiences on the reproduction of a set of patterns using pencil-paper, sand drawing, wire modelling and hand positioning tasks was examined. The findings revealed that children with weaving experiences performed better than those without weaving experiences on all the tasks. However, differences between the two groups were far greater on wire modelling and hand positioning tasks than on pencil-paper and sand drawing tasks. The authors have concluded that experiences embedded in children's daily life activities play an important role in their performance on psychological tasks, which draw upon those experiences.

Sinha, Mishra, and Berry have reported the findings of their larger research project on the role of some eco-cultural and acculturational factors in intermodal perception of stimuli which vary on the dimensions of size, shape, height, and texture, using Birhor (largely nomadic), Asur (recently sedentary) and Oraon (fully sedentary) cultural groups as samples. Their findings revealed that the eco-cultural characteristics of groups and the level of individuals' acculturation are important factors in producing differences in intermodal perception of different type of stimuli.

In their paper, Shrestha and Mishra have examined sex differences in the cognitive style of Brahmin and Gurung children inhabiting the hills and plains of Nepal. The overall comparison of cognitive scores of boys and girls revealed no significant difference either due to gender or due to hill or plains dwelling. However, Brahmin girls and boys differed in their cognitive scores. This difference was not found in the Gurungs. Using the theoretical framework of John Berry (1966), the authors have argued that adherence to authority, conformity and social sensitivity are more strongly inculcated in girls than in boys in the course of socialisation during childhood in "tight" societies like the one of Brahmins of Nepal. Therefore, the lower level of field independence among girls than boys in the Brahmin group as compared to the Gurung group may be attributed to these influences. This section covers a wide spectrum of cross-cultural research involving diverse family experiences and their impact on cognitive skills.

8

A Family Structure Assessment Device for Turkey

AYDAN GÜLERCE

Towards the end of the twentieth century, it has been accepted that human behaviours cannot be studied apart from their contexts. Large human structures such as societies and cultures, on the other hand, do not seem to be homogeneous, stable or sufficiently integrated to allow scientific research easily. However, the family, where the individual meets society and culture, is one system that transcends the limits of the individual, yet is bounded enough to serve as a unit of study. Thus, through an understanding of the family context as the first and most significant socialisation agent, one can take an important step towards understanding society and culture.

Although the importance of family relations has always been emphasised in psychology in general, and in clinical psychology in particular, family became the unit of study following the family/systems movement. Leaving a single person, and surveying the family as a systemic entity which is embedded in even larger systems, family therapists began to see clear redundancies and distinct patterns

(Hoffman, 1981) in family interactions. Of course, studying the family as a whole, instead of its components which may influence the individual's behaviours, and studying the relations called for a significant change in "paradigm" (Kuhn, 1970). Indeed, in psychology, the family/systems approach took a step towards modern scientific epistemology through the adoption of general systems paradigm. As a result, psychological study and assessment of the family context needed a new methodology, which an evaluation of the functioning as a system which is open to the socio-cultural environment, and yet as a structure which has boundaries with society and internal boundaries such as parental, sibling, gender, generation subsystems, as well as the information flow, feedback loops and communication patterns in the family system.

FAMILY ASSESSMENT MEASURES

There are numerous ways of assessing families which may fall into three general categories: (a) holistic, yet nonstandard methods; (b) family component measures; and (c) standard measures of the total family functioning (Forman and Hagan, 1984). The first group includes clinical interview techniques which lack or have problems of validity and reliability. Although the second group of techniques generally have paid attention to psychometric issues, they are not by design suitable to the complex and multidimensional nature of the family context (e.g., Haley, 1964; Guttman et al., 1971; Steinglass, 1980). Thus, what we are actually interested in is the third group.

An examination of the third group measures cited in literature in English reveals 10 major techniques of which conceptual and psychometric considerations have taken place elsewhere (Gülerce, in press). Thus, only their acronyms and names will be mentioned here: (a) BTFES: Beavers–Timberlawn Family Evaluation Scales (Beavers et al., 1985), (b) FACES: Family Adaptability and Cohesion Evaluation Scales (Olson et al., 1978), (c) FAD: Family Assessment Device (Epstein et al., 1983), (d) FAM: Family Assessment Measure (Toronto Foundation of Addiction Research, 1984), (e) FCAM: Family Concept Assessment Method (von der Veen and Novak, 1974), (f) FEF: Family Evaluation

Form (Emery, Weintraub, and Neale, 1980), (g) FES: Family Environment Scale (Moos, 1974), (h) FFI: Family Function Index (Pless and Satterwhite, 1973); (i) SFES: Structural Family Evaluation Scale (Perosa et al., 1981), and (j) SIMFAM: Simulated Family Activity Measure (Straus and Tallman, 1971).

THE NEED FOR A NEW MEASURE

Earlier no suitable technique was available to evaluate Turkish family system and structure. A usual practice, perhaps, was to choose one of these techniques, follow the back-translation method, and conduct a pilot study to demonstrate its psychometric features. In fact, two of the above mentioned measures, FES (Usluer, 1989) and FACES (Fişek, 1990), have been adapted in Turkish while the norm study of the present technique was in process. It is very important, however, to remain loyal to the conceptual base of any technique, and to manipulate the behavioural correlates only for the necessary adaptations to a culture. In addition to this very difficult task, which requires further research by itself, the issue of introduction of new concepts and terminology by family/systems approach, at times meaning different things in different family models, alone may limit a good adaptation.

A careful examination of the conceptual underpinnings of the known measures further led to the construction of a new device for structural/systemic assessment of families in Turkey. Because, either the theoretical models which these measures rely on fall short of studying the family system in the new paradigm, or their dimensions do not exhaust the family context fully.

CONCEPTUAL FRAMEWORK OF THE AYDA

Transformational epistemology (Gülerce, 1987) and the transformational model of family system and structure serve as the conceptual framework for the AYDA (Turkish acronyms for Family Structure

Assessment Device). Detailed discussions of this approach can be found elsewhere (Gülerce, 1987, 1988, 1991). Operationalisation of the transformational model yields various variables which are in continuous interaction. These are: (a) context variables, (b) transformation variables, helping with further transformations, and (c) family structural/systemic variables (see Figure 8.1).

Figure 8.1
Transformational Family Model (I: Communication, II: Unity, III: Management, IV: Competency, V: Emotional Context and VI: Transformational Indices)

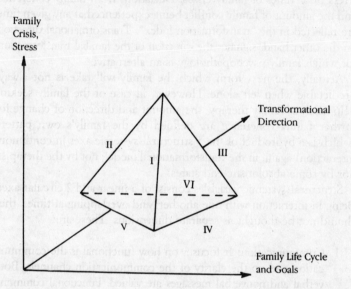

Context variables help to place the individuals in the larger context of the family, yet take their uniqueness into account. They also help to identify the larger context variables with which the family, and thus the individuals, are in continuous exchange. The so-called "inner-context" variables include age, gender, role, employment, meaning, value, health, education, beliefs, phenomenological world of the individual, and so on. The so-called "outer-context" variables include economic status, demographic variables, values, beliefs, attitudes, cultural representations, political situation, group norms, societal change, families of origin, and so on. The distinction between "inner" and "outer" is an arbitrary one, adopted for the sake of discussion here, otherwise the model conceptualises them in coevolution, comprising one "indispensible context".

Transformation variables include family life cycle, family crisis or stress, and the transformational direction. The age of the family and its position in the family life cycle also seem to be relevant factors in studying the family's behaviour. Another common observation is that families move towards new organisations bringing their solutions under stress or at times of family crises. Deviations from family coherence, and the amount of family conflict being experienced, at any given time, are reflected in the "transformation index". Transformational direction, on the other hand, signifies the direction of the familial transformation, for which family psychopathology is an alternative.

Actually, the next form which the family will take is not always predictable when left alone. However, in case of the family seeking help, such as family therapy, the amount and direction of change for further family coherence are defined by the family's own pattern (which is a byproduct of the 5 structural/systemic axes in continuous interaction) again, in the transformational model, not by the therapist, nor by some absolutistic end states.

Structural/systemic variables consist of 3 linear and 2 circular axes. Being in interaction with one another, and overlapping at times, they should not be thought as separate dimensions. These are:

1. Communication: It focuses on how functional is the communication and on the clarity of the communication channels. Both verbal and nonverbal messages are valued. Functional communication is understood as consistency of received and sent messages, and the clarity of the communication, more than the western notion of self-disclosure and assertiveness. It is observed and assumed in the model that family well-being increases as the functionality of communication increases. Thus, this is a linear variable in the model.

2. Emotional context: It concerns marital or familial conflicts (tension, satisfaction, feelings of safety) and security in the family (support, family spirit, self-concept, etc.). This is a linear variable since enhanced emotionally supportive atmosphere in the family leads to an increase in family adjustment.

3. Family competency: Issues involving problem solving skills, sufficiency of the family resources, family health, actualisation of family goals, etc., determine this linear variable which is positively correlated with family psychological functioning.
4. Family unity: It involves the internal and external boundaries of the family system, togetherness in time and space, connectedness of the members, dependency, attachment, intimacy, cohesion, etc. It is a circular axis, hence too much or too little unity in the family is negatively correlated with family well-being.
5. Family management and control: It is concerned with organisation, decision-making, behavioural control and discipline, leadership, family rules, norms, roles and structural flexibility, etc. It is a circular axis; too much or too little of this dimensiôn is negatively correlated with family adjustment.

These axes are depicted as 5 edges of a triangular prism, which appears as an equilateral when reflecting maximum family harmony, in the model (see Figure 8.1). The 6th (and loose) edge represents the transformational index which changes as a function of the continuous interaction of these 5 axes.

While information about contextual and transformational variables can be obtained through various assessment methods, the AYDA addresses itself to the structural/systemic variables of the family.

CONSTRUCTION OF THE AYDA

The initial item pool of the AYDA consisted of items derived from four major sources: (a) items of the present family measures; (b) behavioural objectives for the 5 axes of the transformational model of family structure/system; (c) clinical and ethnographic observations of Turkish families; and (d) everyday mentality, media, idioms, proverbs, cultural symbols and representations, myths, including folk songs and folk tales about the family.

Validity

For *content validity*, the judges (7 social and clinical psychologists) were asked to categorise and rate the degree of representation of each item according to the 5 axes. The median interjudge reliability coefficient was .73 for categorisation, and .58 for rating. Although none of the original 60 items were dropped at this stage, some items were rewritten to increase *face validity*.

The items were analysed in accordance with the obtained responses of 100 participants in the pilot reliability study. Using the extreme groups comparison procedure, it was found that 7 items had no statistical function. These items were either omitted or were combined with other items during the first revision, and a total number of 54 items were obtained. Then, 36 items of the final version of the device were selected in the light of item-to-total correlation coefficients of all family members' responses in a larger and more heterogeneous sample.

The final form of AYDA and the Turkish version of the Family Environment Questionnaire (Usluer, 1989) were administered to 50 female and 50 male participants between 16 to 60 years of age. These participants were the members of "normal" and "intact" families. The scores obtained on the two scales gave a significant ($p < .001$) correlation coefficient of .53.

For the purpose of another *criterion related validity* study, the Beavers–Timberlawn Family Evaluation Scale (Beavers et al., 1985) was administered to 12 families. The semi-structured clinical interviews with the families were video-recorded, and the video tapes were analysed in terms of the BTFES by an expert clinical psychologist who was "blind" to these families' AYDA scores. Families' scores on the two measures gave a meaningful ($p < .001$) correlation coefficient of .78. In addition, the correlation coefficient of family AYDA scores and Minnesota Counseling Inventory Family Relations subscale scores (Ozdemir, 1985) was considerably high and significant (r: .78, $p < .001$).

A study of *construct validity* of the measure is in process in terms of testing whether the AYDA meaningfully differentiates the "clinical" from the "nonclinical" families. AYDA protocols of 23 families a member of which is seeking psychiatric treatment have been collected so far. Other research have also provided some information about construct validity through hypothesis testing.

For instance, Idig (1990) reported that the total AYDA scores of 105 adolescents had a positive correlation (r: .51, p < .001) with the Turkish version of the Piers-Harris Self Concept Inventory (Catakli, 1985) and a negative correlation (r: −.46, p < .001) with the Turkish version of Beck Depression Inventory (Tegin, 1980). In the same study, the parents' total AYDA scores showed low but significant negative correlations with their marital conflict scores, as obtained on the Turkish version of the Parental Attitudes of Child Rearing Questionnaire (LeCompte et al., 1978), Marital Conflict subscale (mothers r: −.26, p < .005, fathers r: −.20, p < .01). Another study (Ward, 1991) reported significant correlations between the AYDA, the Body Image Satisfaction Questionnaire (Gökdoğan, 1989), and the Eating Attitude Test (Savasir and Erol, 1989) scores of 9th graders. Thus, all these findings provided support for the hypotheses in the expected directions.

Reliability

The AYDA was administered to 100 university students twice after an interval of one month, and its *stability coefficient* was found to be .79. *Split halves method* gave a Stanley coefficient of .85, and a Pearson coefficient of .72 for the halves, and an estimate of .83 for the total scale. The internal consistency of the AYDA was also calculated, and Cronbach alpha coefficient of .70 was found satisfactory for the *homogeneity* of the device.

Item-to-total correlation coefficients of the items were calculated on the basis of the responses of 300 families. Items with highest values for both parents and children were retained only for practical reasons, such as obtaining a shorter and more effective scale. Thus, the final version comprised 36 items (9 communication, 9 unity, 8 management, 5 competency, and 5 emotional context).

Application

The AYDA is a self-report measure which can be used with a literate population above the age of 12. Because of the various definitions of the family and rapid social change in Turkey, this technique was used with people who have been living together for a long period of time, and consider themselves as a unit. Systems other than nuclear families can also be evaluated with the AYDA.

The scale includes some items which have separate versions for children and parents. Responses are given on a 10-point scale ranging from "just like us" to "just the opposite". Participants can be asked to evaluate their actual families (AYDA–Real), as well as their ideal family concept (AYDA–Ideal).

Scoring and Interpretation

Linear or circular, the maximum score which can be obtained on each item is 5 and the minimum is 1. Hence, the maximum AYDA total score is 180 which indicates the highest level of perceived family functioning. One blank or invalid response is allowed in each subscale, but is *prorated*. In addition to individual, marital and family AYDA total scores, there are other indices including communication, family competence, management, emotional context, family unity, and also others which have clinical utility such as family satisfaction, resistance to change, and family conflict. All these raw scores are marked on the profile forms, designed separately for mothers, fathers, children and families on the basis of the responses of the normative sample and their T-scores, for easy interpretation.

Norms

Norm tables of various AYDA scores for several groups and a discussion of the family system and structure in Turkish society are being prepared for publication (Gülerce, in press). Validity and reliability study of its English version on an American sample is also in process.

REFERENCES

BEAVERS, W.R., HAMPSON, R.B., and VE HULGUS, Y.F. (1985). Commentary: The Beavers systems approach to family assessment. *Family Process, 24*, 398–405.

CATAKLI, M. (1985). Transliteral equivalence and reliability of the Turkish version of the Piers-Harris Children's Self-Concept Scale. Unpublished Master's dissertation, Boğaziçi University, Istanbul.

EMERY, R.E., WEINTRAUB, S., and NEALE, J.M. (1980) The Family Evaluation Form: Construction and normative data. Manuscript of a presentation made at the annual APA meeting, Montreal.

EPSTEIN, N.B., BALDWIN, L.M., and BISHOP, D.S. (1983). The McMaster family assessment device. *Journal of Marital and Family Therapy, 9*, 171–180.

FIŞEK, G. (1990). Family interconnectedness. Graduate seminar, Boğaziçi University, Istanbul.

FORMAN, B.D. and HAGAN, B.J. (1984). Measures for evaluating total family functioning. *Family Therapy, 1*, 1–35.

GÖKDOĞAN, F. (1989). Beden İmgesi Doyum Anketinin Türkçe versiyonu (Turkish version of the Body Image Satisfaction Questionnaire). Unpublished Master's dissertation, Ankara University, Ankara.

GÜLERCE, A. (1987). Transformational epistemology: A methodological synthesis of psychoanalysis and family systems thinking. Unpublished doctoral dissertation, University of Denver, Denver.

GÜLERCE, A. (1988). Dönüşümsel Model (Transformational Model). In N. Bilgin (Ed.), V. Ulusal Psikoloji Kongresi. Özel sayı. *Psikoloji-Seminer Dergisi, 8*, 323–332. İzmir: Ege University Press.

GÜLERCE, A. (1991). The transformational approach: Basic assumptions of an alternative model for human sciences. *Boğaziçi University Journal, XIV*, 47–59.

GÜLERCE, A. (in press). *Aile Yapısını Değerlendirme Aracı.*

GUTTMANN, H.A., SPECTOR, R.M., SIGAL, J.J., RAKOFF, V., and EPSTEIN, N.B. (1971). Reliability of coding affective communication in family therapy sessions. *Journal of Consulting and Clinical Psychology, 37*, 397–402.

HALEY, J. (1964). Research on family patterns: An instrument measurement. *Family Process, 3*, 41–65.

HOFFMAN, L. (1981). *Foundations of family therapy.* New York: Basic Books.

IDIG, M. (1990). Adolescents' evaluation of their families' psychological well-being in relation with the parents' marital satisfaction, adolescents' self-concept and depression. Unpublished Master's dissertation, Boğaziçi University, Istanbul.

KUHN, T. (1970). *The structure of scientific revolution* (2nd ed.). Chicago: University of Chicago Press.

LECOMPTE, G.K., LECOMPTE, W.A., and OZER, S.A. (1978). Uc sosyo-ekenomik duzeyde Ankarali annelerin cocuk yetistirme tutumları: bir ölcek uyarlaması (Child rearing attitudes of the mothers from the three socioeconomic level in Ankara: A scale adaptation). *Psikoloji Dergisi, 1*, 5–8.

MOOS, R.H. (1974). *The social climate scales: An overview.* Palo Alto: Consulting Psychologists Press.

OLSON, D.H., BELL, R., and PARTNER, J. (1978). *FACES: Family Adaptability and Cohesion Evaluation Scales*. St. Paul, MN: Family Social Science, University of Minnesota.

OZDEMIR, N.P. (1985). A study of the validity of the shortened form of Minnesota Counseling Inventory in Turkish. Unpublished Master's dissertation, Boğaziçi University, Istanbul.

PEROSA, L., HANSEN, J., and PEROSA, S. (1981). Development of the StructuralFamily Interaction Scale. *Family Therapy, 8*, 77–90.

PLESS, I.B. and SATTERWHITE, B.B. (1973). Measure of family functioning and its application. *Social Science and Medicine, 7*, 613–621.

SAVASIR, I. and EROL, N. (1989). Yeme Tutumu Testi (Eating Attitude Test). *Psikoloji Dergisi, 23*, 19–25.

STEINGLASS, P. (1980). Assessing families in their own homes. *American Journal of Psychiatry, 137*, 1523–1529.

STRAUS, M.A. and TALLMAN, I. (1971). SIMFAM. A technique for observational measurement and experimental studies of families. In J. Aldous (Ed.), *Family problem solving* (pp. 381–438). Hinesdale, Il: Dryden Press.

TEGIN, B. (1980). Depresyonda bilissel bozukluklar: Beck modeline gore bir inceleme (Cognitive disturbances in depression: A study of Beck's model). Unpublished doctoral dissertation, Hacettepe University, Ankara.

USLUER, S. (1989). The reliability and the validity of the Turkish family environment questionnaire. Unpublished Master's dissertation, Boğaziçi University, Istanbul.

VON DER VEEN, F. and NOVAK, A.L. (1974). The family of the disturbed child: A replication study. *American Journal of Orthopsychiatry, 44*, 763–772.

WARD, M. (1991). Perceived familial psychological functioning as an antecedent factor of body image satisfaction and eating attitudes among Turkish adolescents. Unpublished Master's thesis, Boğaziçi University, Istanbul.

9

Family Climate as a Determinant of Academic Performance: East Asian and Euro–American Cultures Compared

KLAUS BOEHNKE •
WILLIAM A. SCOTT* • RUTH SCOTT

Academic performance is usually perceived as a behavioural consequence of the ways and means of school teaching (in a wider sense) and/or of the individual intellectual capacity. Neither of these influences can be denied, but conceptually, an attempt is made to analyse academic performance from a different perspective, namely, a system-theoretical, socio-ecological point of view.

Such a view acknowledges that school is a *social system* bringing together members of other systems, for example, members of different

*William A. Scott died on 8 November 1991.

family systems. School, and therefore academic performance, does not start with a *tabula rasa* on the side of its students. Pedagogical literature from the behaviourist paradigm sometimes seems to suggest just that. Its inclination to constantly attempt to reach technical improvements of the learning process are well known. The other extreme is found when biology-minded pedagogues suggest that academic performance is more or less determined by intelligence, thereby implying that academic performance is a question of heredity. Neither the effects of techniques of the learning process nor of genetic predispositions on the actual academic performance of students are denied here. It is the narrowness and person-centredness of the two approaches which is criticised.

Learning in schools is not so much an individual process, but a social phenomenon, and social phenomena can best be understood if one looks at the systems in which they occur and at lower order, higher order and parallel systems with which these systems interact. Such an approach takes into account that the evaluation of academic performance is always comparative, never absolute. Grading may be based on more or less objectivated measurement, but it is always comparative in the sense that what is judged as good or bad is determined by either the individual teacher, the school boards, state authorities, or society as a whole comparing one student with another. Not even in physical education "academic" performance is judged in an absolute manner. For an 8-year-old 14.0 sec in the 100-metre dash will probably be judged as excellent in relation to expectations of an abstract 8-year-old, whereas for an 18-year-old it is quite mediocre.

The conviction that academic performance is one measure of social competence which is strongly influenced by the individual's personality, allows one to focus on the formation process of the student personality in order to understand his or her academic performance. Expressed in system-theoretical terms proposed by Bronfenbrenner (1986) or by Beckmann, Krohns, and Schneewind (1982) this means that properties of the micro-system family, as they influence the personality of the individual student, are analysed in order to understand a certain behaviour of the student (his or her academic performance) in the meso-system school. The general model of influence used for this study is presented in Figure 9.1.

It assumes that certain "blocks" have to be distinguished in the functioning of the family system. More basic is the structure of the family (two-generation vs three-generation, one-parent vs two-parent,

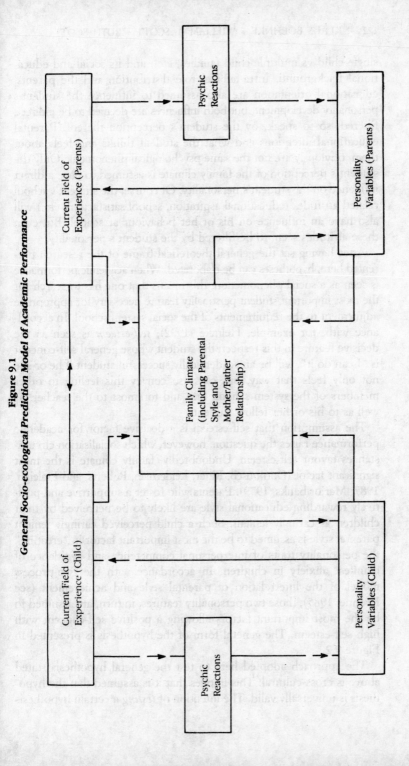

Figure 9.1

General Socio-ecological Prediction Model of Academic Performance

single-child vs multiple-child families, etc.) and its social and educational background. Intra-familial role distribution and the parents' educational orientation are also assumed to influence the student's personality development, but both influences are deemed to be indirect, filtered, so to speak, by the student's perception thereof. Parental educational intentions and what the student thinks and feels about them, obviously are not the same psychological phenomena. Only the student's perception of the family climate is assumed to have a direct influence on the student's personality. Of course, the student's school related attitudes (educational aspiration, school satisfaction, etc.) will also have an influence on his or her behaviour at school. But even these attitudes seem to be filtered by the student's personality.

After having set the general theoretical frame of the research presented here, hypotheses can be elaborated. When academic performance is seen as a social phenomenon, this means that one has to search for the most important student personality feature necessary for appropriate adjustment to the requirements of the social system school. In accordance with, for example, Helmke (1992), *self-esteem* is seen as the decisive feature in this respect: the student whose general self-concept is "I can do it", will be an academically successful student if he or she not only feels that way, but can also convey this feeling to other members of the system school, first and foremost to the teacher, as well as to his or her fellow students.

The assumption that self-esteem is a decisive factor for academic performance raises the question, however, which socialisation circumstances favour self-esteem. Undoubtedly, family climate is the most significant factor (Dornbusch, Ritter, Leiderman, Roberts, and Fraleigh, 1987; Marjoribanks, 1979). Parents who foster a supportive and positively rewarding educational style are likely to be perceived by their children as caringly lenient. Such a child perceived caringly lenient parental style is assumed to be the most important factor in "creating" the personality traits of interpersonal competence and avoidance of manifest anxiety in children. In accordance with the two-process model of the interrelation of parental style and achievement (see Krohne, 1985), those two personality features, in turn, are assumed to be the most important factors allowing a positive self-concept with high self-esteem. The general form of the hypothesis is presented in Figure 9.2.

The approach adopted here to test the general hypothesis stated above is cross-cultural. This implies that it is assumed that the hypothesis is universally valid. The intention of *testing* a certain hypothesis

Figure 9.2
Modified Two-process Prediction Model of Academic Performance

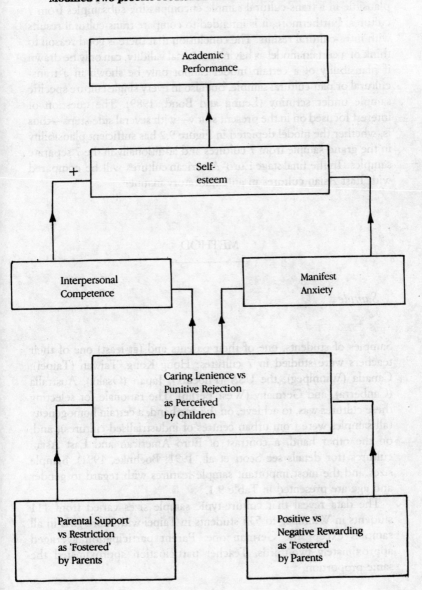

across cultures should not be understood in a rigid methodological manner. The intention is to "see" if the model presented here is plausible in a trans-cultural sample encompassing subsamples from 7 cultures. Furthermore, it is intended to compare trans-cultural results with intra-cultural results. The conclusion that there is good reason to think of a certain model as having universal validity, can only be drawn if plausibility of a certain model cannot only be shown in a trans-cultural or pan-cultural sample, but also in every single culture specific sample under scrutiny (Leung and Bond, 1989). The question of interest focused on in the present study—with several side-steps—thus is, whether the model depicted in Figure 9.2 has sufficient plausibility in the grand sample from 7 cultures and additionally in the 7 separate samples. In the final stage Euro–American cultures will be compared with East Asian cultures in an exploratory manner.

METHOD

Sample

Samples of students, one of their parents and (at least) one of their teachers were studied in 7 cultures: Hong Kong, Taiwan (Taipei), Canada (Winnipeg), the USA (Phoenix), Japan (Osaka), Australia (Canberra), and Germany (West Berlin). The rationale for selecting these cultures was, to achieve, on the one hand, a certain homogeneity (all samples were from urban centres of industrialised cultures), and, on the other hand, a contrast of Euro–American and East Asian cultures (for details see Scott et al., 1991; Boehnke, 1991). Sample sizes and the most important sample features with regard to gender and age are presented in Table 9.1.

The data reveal that culture-typic sample sizes varied from 111 students in Winnipeg to 535 students in Taipei with more girls in all samples except the German one. Parent participation averaged approximately two-thirds. Teacher participation approximated the same proportion.

TABLE 9.1
Sample Characteristics

Characteristic	City						
	Hong Kong	Taipei	Winnipeg	Phoenix	Osaka	Canberra	Berlin
Students							
Total N	498	535	111	399	355	386	248
N of Girls	271	268	69	292	221	234	106
Girls in %	54	50	62	73	62	61	43
N of Boys	227	267	42	107	134	152	142
Boys in %	46	50	38	27	38	39	57
Average Age	16.0	15.5	14.6	15.7	15.1	14.1	15.4
Parents							
Total N	123	500	82	276	281	274	128
N of Mothers	64	164	67	230	229	194	95
Mothers in %	52	33	82	83	81	71	74
N of Fathers	59	336	15	46	52	80	33
Fathers in %	48	67	18	17	19	29	26
Average Age	46.5	45.4	41.5	40.8	44.5	43.9	43.2
% of Students	25	93	74	69	79	71	52
Teachers							
Total N	336	533	125	395	355	315	257
N 1st Teachers	180	531	110	395	355	315	224
% of Students	36	>99	99	99	100	82	90
N 2nd Teachers	156	—	15	—	—	—	33
% of Students	31	—	14	—	—	—	13

Instrument

Students, parents, and teachers were given a lengthy questionnaire. Scales used in the questionnaire were pre-tested in a pilot study in Brisbane. More than 90 per cent of the items included in the questionnaires were "borrowed" from the literature (see Table 9.2 for exact sources), (for details, see Boehnke, 1991). Cross-cultural metric equivalence was attained by discarding items which did not reach a corrected item total correlation of $r \geq .10$ in the a priori scales (formulated on the grounds of the pilot study results) in every culture. Wherever scale analyses showed that source specific indicators, that is, measures from the student, the parent, and the teacher questionnaires intended to measure the same construct, could be collapsed into one second order indicator on the grounds of the same threshold value, this was done. For example, information pertaining to academic performance was sought from students, parents, and teachers. Students were asked, "How do you feel about your ability to do academic work (school work)?" Two items correlated to a median of r: .31 in the 7 cultures. Parents were asked, "How satisfied are you with this child's educational progress at the moment?" Four items had a median internal consistency of α: .64. Teachers were asked: "How well does this student perform in classwork?" Three items achieved a median internal consistency of α: .76. If the three source specific scale means together formed a second order ("across-source") scale (demanding that every scale mean has a corrected item total correlation of $r \geq .10$ with the sum score of the new second order scale in every culture) then it was analysed. The analysis showed that the three source specific scale means could indeed be collapsed into a new across-source second order indicator of academic performance. A selection of indicators relevant to the study is given in Table 9.2 along with scale-typic items. In the table the constructs marked by "AS" are across-source scales. Constructs marked by S, P, or T are source-pure measures including items exclusively from the student, parent, or teacher questionnaires. The indicator "Caring Lenience of Parents" consists of scores on 5 separate scales, namely, the student scales for Nurturant Father, Nurturant Mother, Permissive Parents, and the reversed student scales for Punitive Parents, and Restrictively Protective Parents. These 5 scales have 8, 8, 8, 9, and 6 items, respectively. Their median alpha consistencies are .78, .81, .76, .72, and .70, respectively. The "Family

TABLE 9.2
Scales and Indicators

Construct (Source)	Number of Items	Median α or r
Academic Performance (AS) *How well does this student perform in classwork?* (Taft and Cahill, 1981)	3*	.62
Caring Lenience of Parents (S) *My father could make me feel better when I was upset.* (Parker, Tupling, and Brown, 1979)	5*	.73
Family Satisfaction (AS) *How do you feel about your family members' relations with each other?* (Andrews and Withey, 1976)	2*	.25
Aggressiveness—Parents (P) *This child talks back to its parents.*	12	.75
Aggressiveness—Teachers (T) *[This student] Provokes other students.* (McCabe, 1983)	5	.78
Importance of Friends (S) *[Reversed rank of friends important in life]* (Jessor and Jessor, 1984)	6	.55
Interpersonal Competence—Parents (P) *How would you describe this child's attitudes and behavior at home: cooperative?*	1	—
Interpersonal Competence—Students (S) *How easy is it for you to make new friends?* (Bradburn, 1969)	6	.69
Interpersonal Competence—Teachers (T) *Do you get the impression that this student feels quite at ease with others . . . is unable to relate to other people at all?*	7	.83
Manifest Anxiety—Students (S) *I certainly feel useless at times.* (Taylor, 1953)	9	.65
Manifest Anxiety—Teachers (T) *[This student] Rarely is upset.*	2	.38
Obedience (T) *When this student is told to do something by a teacher, what is the usual response?*	5	.83
Parents' Tendency toward Punishment (P) *How often does this child get a good thrashing?*	4	.49

Table 9.2 (Continued)

Construct (Source)	Number of Items	Median α or r
Rejection by Teacher (S) *My teacher makes me feel I'm not good enough.* (Coopersmith, 1967)	1	—
School Satisfaction (S) *I hate this school ... this school is great, I'd rather be here than anywhere else.*	2*	.32
Self-esteem—Student (S) *How do you feel about yourself?* (Andrews and Withey, 1976)	3	.73
Self-esteem—Teachers (T) *[This student] Is self-confident.* (Ross, Lacey, and Parton, 1965)	6	.79

* Reference to item numbers is to number of scale scores forming the second order scale.

Satisfaction" scale consists of a secondary indicator on "Contentment with Family" (from the student questionnaire) and the parent scale on "Family Harmony". The secondary "Contentment with Family" indicator itself consists of 2 scale scores from the student questionnaire, namely, "Family Harmony" and "Family Solidarity". The original scales have the following numbers of items and median alpha consistencies: Family Harmony (S)—6/.74; Family Solidarity (S)—5/.57; Family Harmony (P)—8/.80. The "School Satisfaction" indicator consists of 2 scales from the student questionnaire, namely, "Contentment with Friends at School" and "Contentment with School" which have 3 and 6 items, respectively; and their median alpha consistencies are .50 and .72. Scale-typic items for which no source is given, were developed. This does not necessarily mean, however, that all items of the respective scale were self-developed. Due to constraints of space it is not possible to cite references for all items used in the study (for further details, see Boehnke, 1991).

The table shows that the typical scale used for analyses has 4 items with an internal consistency of α ≈ .65.

RESULTS

Trans-cultural (Grand Sample) Analyses

In the first step multiple regression analyses (SPSS^x Regression Method Stepwise) were performed on the grand sample data with academic performance as the criterion and all other 36 available indicators as predictor variables (including some which were of lesser importance and, thus, are not documented in this paper). Only those predictors were accepted as substantial which showed a β-coefficient larger than .20 *and* a probability of p < .001. This analysis showed that teacher perceived self-esteem of the student, self-perceived self-esteem of the student, and teacher perceived obedience of the student sufficed that threshold criterion with β = .35, .37, and .30, respectively.

In the second stage, these three substantial predictors were used as (separate) criterion variables in analogous multiple regression analyses. It could be shown that academic performance was a poor predictor of the two self-esteem variables and of obedience than vice versa (β = .32, .22, and .26, respectively). It was therefore decided to run successive *unidirectional* path analyses. This means that a variable which was a criterion variable once, was eliminated from the analyses in calculations where its original predictors now were the criterion variables: academic performance was no longer included in the equations when its substantial predictors, the two self-esteem variables and obedience were the criterion variables. These latter variables were no longer in the equation when their substantial predictors became the criterion variables, and so on.

The described path analyses revealed teacher perceived self-esteem to be best predicted by the teacher's perceptions of the student's interpersonal competence and manifest anxiety. Analogously, student perceived self-esteem was also predicted best by the students' self-reported interpersonal competence and manifest anxiety. In addition, it was well predicted by school satisfaction. Exact β-coefficients are omitted here. Teacher perceived obedience was best predicted by student aggressiveness as perceived by the teacher.

The next level of path analyses revealed that several of the predictors mentioned above were interrelated. As new predictors, family satisfaction (as a predictor of school satisfaction), student perceived rejection by the teacher and student perceived parental caring lenience (as predictors of self-reported manifest anxiety of students), and importance of friends (as reported by the students as a predictor of self-reported interpersonal competence) came into play. No further substantial predictors of teacher perceived student personality features were found. It can be seen from Figure 9.3 how these variables are interrelated.

Intra-cultural Analyses

The next step of analyses focused on testing the validity of the model depicted in Figure 9.3 in the 7 separate samples. Again, multiple regression analyses were run in the unidirectional path-analytic style. This time, however, the ENTER method was used in order to ensure that the variables included in the trans-cultural model would definitely be included in the culture specific model. Standardised regression coefficients per variable interrelation for the 7 cultures are documented in Table 9.3 along with their medians. Using Fisher's (1932) probability agglomeration method it was then meta-analytically tested if one can assume that the null hypothesis of no relation between two variables can be rejected for the 7 samples. An asterisk after the β-coefficient marks a probability level of $p < .01$ per culture, an asterisk after the median score indicates that the agglomerated null hypothesis could be rejected on that probability level. The single letters used as headings for the columns refer to the 7 cities included in the study.

The table shows that in all cases, the agglomerated null hypothesis could be rejected for the levels of prediction reported in this paper. This means that it is sufficiently safe to assume that the model depicted in Figure 9.3 is a cross-culturally valid model. Not in all cultures, however, can all interrelations of variables be shown to be significant. This means that, although valid in all cultures in principle, the model needs culture specific modifications. One important possible amendment is foreshadowed in the last row of Table 9.3. The data in this row indicate that it might be of interest to delve more deeply into a comparison of East Asian and Euro–American cultures: in all Euro–American cultures the teacher's impression of the student's manifest anxiety was a good predictor of his or her aggressiveness, while this interrelation did not exist in any of the East Asian cultures. Aggressiveness appeared to play a different rôle in the two types of cultural backgrounds.

Figure 9.3
Empirical Trans-cultural Prediction Model of Academic Performance

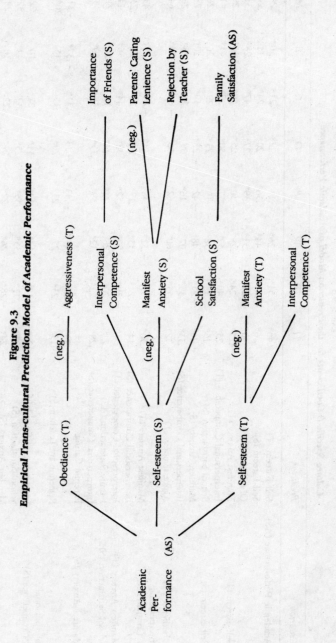

TABLE 9.3

Culture Specific β-Coefficients for the Prediction Model of Academic Performance

Criterion	Predictor	H	T	W	P	O	C	B	Md
Academic Performance (AS)	Self-Esteem (T)	.46*	.51*	.26*	.11	.22*	.21*	.30*	.26*
	Self-Esteem (S)	.26*	.22*	.44*	.36*	.20*	.24*	.11	.24*
	Obedience (T)	.40*	.27*	.31*	.39*	.27*	.47*	.28*	.31*
	Manifest Anxiety (T)	−.25*	−.24*	−.29*	−.30*	−.25*	−.30*	−.35*	−.29*
	Interpersonal Competence (T)	.25*	.40*	.52*	.57*	.30*	.39*	.41*	.41*
	School Satisfaction (S)	.15*	.13*	.38*	.19*	.23*	.29*	.26*	.26*
	Manifest Anxiety (S)	−.26*	−.25*	−.48*	−.42*	−.28*	−.39*	−.20*	−.28*
	Interpersonal Competence (S)	.33*	.35*	.07	.16*	.09	.26*	.28*	.26*
Obedience (T)	Aggressiveness (T)	−.72*	−.55*	−.60*	−.62*	−.66*	−.64*	−.74*	−.64*
Interpersonal Competence (T)	Manifest Anxiety (T)	−.50*	−.37*	−.52*	−.48*	−.34*	−.43*	−.36*	−.43*
	Interpersonal Competence (S)	.14	.24*	.33*	.19*	.24*	.26*	.14	.23*
Manifest Anxiety (T)	Interpersonal Competence (T)	−.53*	−.39*	−.57*	−.52*	−.38*	−.44*	−.36*	−.44*
School Satisfaction (S)	Family Satisfaction (AS)	.21	.20*	.26	.24*	.24*	.15	.20	.21*
	Interpersonal Competence (S)	.28*	.22*	.32*	.39*	.35*	.35*	.50*	.35*
Manifest Anxiety (S)	Parental Caring Lenience (S)	−.23*	−.28*	−.37*	−.33*	−.13	−.31*	−.37*	−.31*
	Rejection by Teacher (S)	.19*	.23*	.25	.23*	.20*	.15	.15	.20*
Interpersonal Competence (S)	Importance of Friends (S)	.26*	.18*	.34*	.19*	.31*	.22*	.10	.22*
	School Satisfaction (S)	.23*	.17*	.35*	.35*	.25*	.32*	.44*	.32*
	Manifest Anxiety (S)	−.24*	−.28*	−.26*	−.22*	−.27*	−.22*	−.10	−.24*
Aggressiveness (T)	Manifest Anxiety (T)	.07	.07	.46*	.25*	.14	.19*	.39*	.19*

East Asian vs Euro–American Cultures

In order to focus more specifically on this assumption, a final round of analyses was done. For purposes of analyses, the grand sample was divided into East Asian (Hong Kong, Taipei, Osaka) and Euro–American subsamples (Winnipeg, Phoenix, Canberra, Berlin) and Stepwise multiple regression analyses of the unidirectional path-analytic kind done for the trans-cultural results were performed (this time only the first two prediction levels are reported). The comparative models for the two cultural backgrounds are depicted in Figure 9.4.

The figure indicates two substantial differences in the prediction of academic performance between Euro–American and East Asian cultures: (a) What the student thinks of himself or herself does not seem to be so important in East Asian when compared to Euro–American cultures. In East Asian cultures, the parents' and the teachers' impressions of the student seem to be of even more significance than in other cultures. (b) Student aggressiveness (as perceived by either parents or teachers) seems to have a substantially more important negative influence on academic performance in East Asian than in Euro–American cultures.

DISCUSSION

The analyses reported here can be subsumed under 7 central points:

1. Self-esteem universally is a very strong predictor of academic performance.
2. High interpersonal competence and low manifest anxiety are the immediate causes of high self-esteem.
3. A family climate which is perceived by children as caringly lenient as well as a perceived similar atmosphere in school are central to the development of low manifest anxiety.
4. Interpersonal competence is closely related to the quality and diversity of peer relations.
5. School satisfaction is rooted in family satisfaction.

Figure 9.4
Empirical Euro—American vs East Asian
Prediction Models of Academic Performance

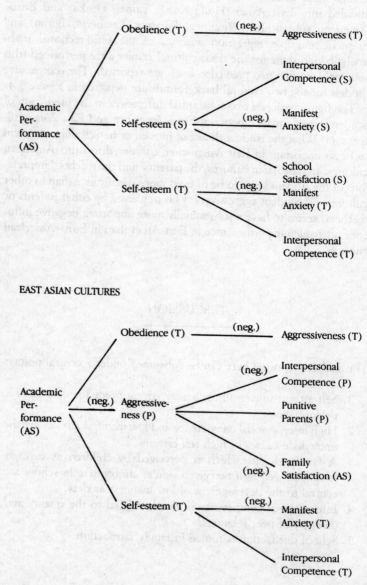

6. Student adherence to school rules ("obedience") is more important for academic performance than originally hypothesised in the present study.
7. The role of aggressiveness in academic performance differs between East Asian and Euro–American cultures. It has stronger and more direct negative effects on academic performance in East Asian than in Euro–American cultures.

All in all, these findings support the conviction that academic performance in school should predominantly be seen as a social skill. A measure of verbal intelligence also included in the student instrument, but not documented here, was not substantially related to academic performance. Although significant at the $p \leq .001$ level in the grand sample analyses, its β-coefficient was about .12 only.

The fact that the teacher's impression of the student's personality and adherence to school rules is so important for academic performance, indicates that school achievement is, in a large measure, a systemic skill: it is not only and not even predominantly a personal skill of the student, or, in a broader sense, his or her personality which matters. It is the perception of that personality by the teacher which influences academic performance.

The so-called two-process model of parental style which links two elements of parental educational orientation with anxiety and (interpersonal) competence and through them to achievement (see Kohlmann and Krohne, 1988) finds some support as long as the theory is stripped of its deterministic elements: it is important whether parents foster a positively or negatively rewarding educational style and also whether they are supporting or rejecting. The influence, however, should not be conceptualised as direct, but as indirect—through "the eyes" of the children: only what is perceived as positively rewarding and supportive (or caringly lenient, the term used here) tends to reduce manifest anxiety. The parents' intentions and behaviours are virtually unrelated to anxiety and competence directly.

Not hypothesised in either Figures 9.1 or 9.2, general satisfaction with one's own family has strong indirect importance for school success; it lays the fundamental for school satisfaction which in turn fosters self-esteem. The quality and diversity of peer relations, also not specifically hypothesised in Figures 9.1 or 9.2, seems to be important for the development of academic performance as well, by fostering interpersonal competence, the other standing leg of self-esteem (besides manifest anxiety as a negative predictor).

All findings discussed so far could be shown to be universally valid (across the universe of 7 haphazard samples from 7 cultures). One substantial cross-cultural difference should, however, be stressed: aggressive students, when perceived as such by their teachers and/or parents, have less of a chance to be evaluated positively with regard to their academic performance in East Asian cultures than in Euro–American cultures.

What do these results mean for school counselling? Any counselling concerned with problems in academic performance should take a systemic approach. Teachers, parents, and students have to be an integrated part of the counselling process, preferably in "joint sittings". Training intellectual capacities or improving teaching techniques are of lesser importance: the two self-esteem variables and the obedience variable accounted for 50 per cent of the variation in the academic performance of the grand sample.

REFERENCES

ANDREWS, F.M. and WITHEY, S.B. (1976). *Social indicators of well-being: Americans' perceptions of life quality.* New York: Plenum.

BECKMANN, M., KROHNS, H.-C., and SCHNEEWIND, K.A. (1982). Ökologische Belastungsfaktoren, Persönlichkeitsvariablen und Erziehungsstil als Determinanten sozialer Scheu bei Kindern (Ecological strain factors, personality variables, and parental style as determinants of social shyness in children). In L.A. Vaskovics (Ed.), *Umweltbedingungen familialer Sozialisation* (The ecology of family socialization) (pp. 143–167). Stuttgart: Enke.

BOEHNKE, K. (1991). The relationship of family climate and school behavior in a cross-cultural perspective. Unpublished habilitation thesis, Free University of Berlin, Berlin.

BRADBURN, N.M. (1969). *The structure of psychological well-being.* Chicago: Aldine.

BRONFENBRENNER, U. (1986). Recent advances in research on the ecology of human development. In R.K. Silbereisen, K. Eyferth, and G. Rudinger (Eds.), *Development as action in context* (pp. 287–309). Berlin: Springer.

COOPERSMITH, S. (1967). *Antecedents of self-esteem.* San Francisco: Fremont.

DORNBUSCH, S.M., RITTER, P.L., LEIDERMAN, P.H., ROBERTS, D.F., and FRALEIGH, M.J. (1987). The relation of parenting styles to adolescent school performance. *Child Development, 58,* 1244–1257.

FISHER, R.A. (1932). On a property connecting chi^2 measure of discrepancy with the method of maximum likelihood. *Atti Congresso Internationale Matematica, Bologna, 6,* 94–100.

HELMKE, A. (1992). *Selbstvertrauen und Schulleistung* (Self-esteem and academic performance). Göttingen: Hogrefe.

JESSOR, R. and JESSOR, S.L. (1984). Adolescence to young adulthood: A twelve-year prospective study of problem behavior and psycho-social development. In S.B. Mednick, M. Harway, and K.M. Pinello (Eds.), *Handbook of longitudinal research, Vol. 2: Teenage and adult cohorts* (pp. 34–61). New York: Praeger.

KOHLMANN, C.-W. and KROHNE, H.W. (1988). Erziehungsstildeterminanten schulischer Leistungsängstlichkeit (Parental style as a determinant of test anxiety in school). *Zeitschrift für Pädagogische Psychologie, 2,* 271–279.

KROHNE, H.W. (1985). Entwicklungsbedingungen von Ängstlichkeit und Angstbewältigung: Ein Zweiproze β-Modell elterlicher Erziehungs wirkung (Developmental conditions of anxiety and coping with anxiety: A two-process model of effects of parental education). In H.W. Krohne (Ed.), *Angstbewältigung in Leistungssituationen* (Coping with anxiety in achievement situations) (pp. 136–160). Weinheim: Edition Psychologie.

LEUNG, K. and BOND, M.H. (1989). On the empirical identification of dimensions for cross-cultural comparisons. *Journal of Cross-Cultural Psychology, 20,* 133–151.

McCABE, M. (1983). Personality and family background of high school counselees. Unpublished honours dissertation, Department of Psychology, The Australian National University, Canberra.

MARJORIBANKS, K. (1979). *Families and their learning environments.* London: Routledge and Kegan Paul.

PARKER, G., TUPLING, H., and BROWN, L.B. (1979). A parental bonding instrument. *British Journal of Medical Psychology, 52,* 1–10.

ROSS, A.O., LACEY, H.M., and PARTON, D.A. (1965). The development of a behaviour checklist for boys. *Child Development, 36,* 1013–1027.

SCOTT, W.A., SCOTT, R., BOEHNKE, K., CHENG, S.-W., LEUNG, K., and SASAKI, M. (1991). Children's personality as a function of family relations within and between cultures. *Journal of Cross-Cultural Psychology, 22,* 182–208.

TAFT, R. and CAHILL, D. (1981). Education of immigrants in Australia. In J. Bhatnagar (Ed.), *Educating immigrants* (pp. 16–46). New York: St. Martin's Press.

TAYLOR, J.A. (1953). A personality scale of manifest anxiety. *Journal of Abnormal and Social Psychology, 48,* 285–290.

10

Reproduction of Patterns in Relation to Children's Weaving Experiences

R.C. MISHRA •
NISHAMANI TRIPATHI

One of the popular paradigms to emerge in psychology in recent years is the "eco-cultural perspective" in which the culture of groups and behaviour of individuals are considered as adaptations to the ecological settings in which people carry out their day-to-day activities. The manner in which people interact with these settings has a considerable influence on their psychological development. An eco-cultural model (Berry, 1976) was developed to comprehend these influences. The revised version of this model (Berry, 1987) comprises two components: an ecological component (which is concerned with the interactions of individuals with their habitat), and a socio-political component (which deals with the effects of such external influences as education, urbanisation and industrialisation often deliberately brought on people by design). Nested in these components are a number of variables that tend to be systematically related to behavioural differences of groups

(Berry, 1976, 1981; Berry et al., 1986; Irvine and Berry, 1988). Studies carried out in the Indian setting using the eco-cultural framework (Mishra and Sinha, 1991; Sinha, 1979; Sinha and Mishra, 1988; G. Sinha, 1989) have provided strong evidence for the predictions of both the components of the eco-cultural model.

A major proposition of the eco-cultural model is that successful adaptation of individuals demands a set of skills which develop either automatically through the individuals' interactional experiences with the ecological setting, or are acquired through the process of learning that often takes place in informal settings. The most distinctive feature of this learning is its embeddedness in peoples' daily life activities (Greenfield and Lave, 1982). There is nothing like a clearly defined curriculum, parents and relatives act as teachers, teaching is generally demonstrational and learning is largely based on observation and imitation. Social contributions of the learner serve as motivation, and maintenance and continuity of tradition are highly valued goals of this kind of education (Greenfield and Lave, 1982).

In psychological literature there is some evidence to suggest that informal learning may be associated with people's performance on a wide variety of tasks (Adjei, 1977; Greenfield and Child, 1977; Harkness and Super, 1977; Price-Williams, Gordon, and Ramirez, 1969). In these studies generally a specific experience (such as, tailoring) has been identified, and its positive relationship with some specific psychological operation (for instance, size judgment) has been demonstrated. Over the years evidence for the relationship between specific experiences and specific performance has been accumulated, and a theory of "specific skills" has been proposed (Cole, Gay, Glick, and Sharp, 1971).

As far as the drawing or reproduction of patterns or pictures is concerned, earlier studies have tended to concentrate largely on the representation of the human figure, and the bulk of literature has been mainly descriptive (Jahoda, 1981). More analytical and experimental approaches have developed during the last two decades (Freeman, 1980). Willats' (1977) work is regarded as outstanding in the sense that he devised a scheme for categorising drawing styles in terms of the type of projection employed. Developmentally, he has postulated not only a regular progression from the absence of any projection to the use of full perspective, but has also implied the development of at least the earlier stages of drawing to be independent of cultural influences.

Using reproduction of patterns, Deregowski (1972), Serpell (1969), Serpell and Deregowski (1971) have observed striking differences in pattern copying skills of children of African and western cultural groups. It was argued that African (Zambian) subjects adopted "strategies" or "programmes" for response organisation different from those of children in the west. Goodnow and Levine (1973) have presented evidence for the existence of certain "starting rules" and "progression rules" which American children followed rather strictly. On the other hand, Greenfield (1978) has emphasised the mode and medium related properties of the task in comprehending differences of cultural groups, and has argued that the rate of structural development in a particular medium may vary as a function of experience with its particular features. In a study (Serpell, 1979) boys and girls in their second year of school were asked to reproduce patterns using different medium: pencil–paper, clay, wire, and hand positions. When the task was to copy the patterns by drawing with a pencil, the British children, who had more experience with this medium in school, showed considerably greater skill. When the same patterns were copied by creating wire models the Zambian boys, who often used this medium while playing, were at an advantage. When the tasks included clay modelling and mimicry, areas in which all the groups had relevant experiences, no differences were found in the skill displayed. In general, the study revealed manifestation of cultural (and sex) differences relative to the medium through which the reproduction skills were assessed, and these confirmed the theory of "specific skills".

An examination of the findings of such studies reveals that relevant experience is a crucial factor in determining the level of pattern reproduction skill as measured by the performance on different tasks. What is less convincing is the extreme specificity of skill deployment in the performance of tasks. One may ask what will happen if there is some correspondence, but not a perfect match, between the experiences that children are exposed to and the operations that are required for psychological tests/tasks. There is some likelihood that the skill acquired with one task (embedded in daily life activity) will be transferred to the other task (the experimental one) depending on the degree to which the experimental task represents the natural context of performance, i.e., it has ecological validity (Berry, 1987).

A pattern is generally formed of horizontal, vertical, oblique, and curved lines. Each requires a particular type of movement and their sequencing if the pattern involves more than one or all of these line components. Studies have indicated that horizontal and vertical lines and patterns containing them are produced more accurately than oblique lines and figures by European children (Freeman, 1980) as well as adults (Laszlo and Bairstow, 1985; Laszlo and Broderick, 1985). Recognisable circles have been reported to be copied by 3-year-olds, whereas squares, triangles, and diamonds have been copied by 4, 5, and 7-year-olds respectively. Studying the copying of upright and tilted squares by Swazi children (5–12 years) and adults, Broderick and Laszlo (1989) have observed that although children and adults were able to perceive the shapes and programme the required movements, the process of planning the movement for drawing was learned, improved with age, and practice was necessary. The results also indicated difficulties in the production and combination of oblique lines due to an increase in the demand for planning.

This study attempts to examine the effect of habitual working with patterns on children's performance on pattern reproduction tasks in two groups of "weaver" and "nonweaver" children. Materials used for reproduction were pencil–paper, sand, wire, and hand positioning. It was hypothesised that:

1. Weaver children, who have habitual experience of working with patterns in cloth weaving and embroidery, would perform better on pattern reproduction tasks than nonweaver children.
2. Differences between weaver and nonweaver children would be less evident on pencil–paper and sand drawings tasks (familiar to both groups) than on wire modelling and hand positioning tasks (more familiar to weaver children alone).

METHOD

Design

The sample comprised two groups of children. One group included children who were regularly involved in cloth weaving and embroidery work. This provided children with ample experience of working with patterns and reproducing them in cloth. The other group served as the control group; it did not engage in cloth weaving and embroidery work at all, and had no direct experience of working with patterns. It was against the performance of the control group that the effect of weaving experiences on pattern reproduction was evaluated.

Sample

The sample comprised 40 male children (11–12 years of age), fairly matched on years of schooling, economic conditions, father's education and some other background variables (Table 10.1). Half of these children regularly worked with their parents in weaving and embroidery activities. They were called "weavers". The remaining children had no such experience of working with patterns; they were called "non-weavers". Both the groups belonged to the Sunni Muslim community. Weaving and embroidery have been the traditional occupations of the families of weaver children for generations. On the other hand, the nonweaver children came from households in which the parents were engaged in some small-scale business or in semi-skilled or skilled jobs.

The study was conducted in Mobarakpur town which is situated about 18 km from Azamgarh city in the eastern part of Uttar Pradesh in India. The town is connected with the main city by a paved road, and has regular bus and taxi service. The town has a heavy concentration of Muslim population.

The traditional occupation of Muslims of this town has been the weaving of cotton and silk *sarees* and other clothes. After calendering these are called "Banarasi sarees". In majority of the Muslim families, children often worked alongside their parents in weaving and embroidery activities, and thus contributed to the family income. The children included in this study were attending a traditional school (Maqtab). They did weaving and embroidery work for a few hours, specially in the mornings and evenings when they were free from school, and also during the day on holidays. The control group also attended the same schools. Instead of working, these children spent their free time playing.

Observations of the weaver families revealed that before these children actually participated in the main weaving activity, they were given some basic training on small looms usually set up outside the house. Spreading threads on the loom and making various kinds of

TABLE 10.1
Sample Characteristics

	Weaver Sample	Nonweaver Sample
N	20	20
Mean Age of Children (in years)	11.70	11.60
Mean Years of Schooling of Children	5.50	5.50
Mean Years of Father's Education	4.60	5.80
Per Capita Family Income per Month (in Rupees)	205.00	190.00
Mean Number of Children in a Family	4.60	4.50
Weaving/Embroidering Experience of Children (Mean Years)	4.85	Nil
Occupation Status of Parents		
Full-time Weaving	20	Nil
Part-time Weaving	Nil	Nil
Self-employment	20	18
Government Employment	Nil	02

loops were tasks which had to be mastered before any weaving could be done. Often the patterns were demonstrated by the parents through certain stereotyped finger movements in space which the children would copy. Sometimes this was practiced for hours. The beginners would initially weave patterns in cloth using threads of different colours, however, once the skill had been mastered to an optimal level, fine golden and silver threads (called *jari*) would be brought into use for weaving or embroidery work.

For each weaver child a nonweaver child, fairly matched in terms of age, years of schooling and other family background variables was selected (see Table 10.1). This sampling procedure was purposive in nature. A home visit was also made to study the economic conditions, lifestyle, and other support systems of the child.

Tasks

Five geometrical designs and five line drawings of objects were presented to the groups for reproduction. These were selected on the basis of a pilot study on the criteria of reflecting developmental changes, internal consistency and level of difficulty. Each design was presented for 10 seconds, after this each child had to reproduce the pattern using pencil–paper or sand or wire or hand configuration. On the pencil–paper drawing task the child had to reproduce the patterns on a sheet of paper with a pencil. In the case of sand drawing task, the patterns had to be reproduced on sand sprinkled on a slate, using the forefinger of the preferred hand (right hand in all cases). The wire modelling task required reproduction of the same patterns using pieces of fine aluminium wire. On the hand positioning task the patterns had to be reproduced by a configuration of the hand.

The reproduced patterns were rated by two judges (school teachers) on a 5-point scale ranging from "dissimilar" (0) to "identical" (4). The interrater reliabilities on these tasks were found to be .72 (wire modelling), .81 (pencil–paper), .78 (hand positioning), and .79 (sand drawing), indicating a satisfactory level of agreement. The order of presentation of the tasks was counterbalanced across subjects in both the groups.

ANALYSIS OF RESULTS

The mean scores of weaver and nonweaver groups on various tasks are given in Table 10.2. It is clear that on all the tasks the weaver group had higher mean scores than the nonweaver group.

Differences between the two groups appeared to be larger on wire modelling and hand positioning than on pencil–paper and sand drawing tasks.

TABLE 10.2
Mean Scores of Groups on Various Tasks

Tasks	Weavers		Nonweavers		Mean Difference
	Mean	S.D.	Mean	S.D.	
Pencil–Paper Drawing	28.80	4.80	17.70	4.71	3.10**
Sand Drawing	23.55	2.14	21.05	4.82	2.50**
Wire Modelling	18.85	3.74	12.10	4.43	6.75**
Hand Positioning	22.60	2.23	16.95	5.22	5.65**

** $p < .01$.

To examine the significance of differences between the performance of weaver and nonweaver children in the context of various tasks, a 2 × 4 factorial ANOVA with repeated measure on the second factor was performed. Besides the significant effects of experience (F (1, 38): 70.87, $p<.01$) and task (F (3, 114): 27, 78, $p<.01$), there was a significant interaction between these factors (F (3, 114): 3.60, $p<.05$). Although weaver children as a group had significantly higher mean scores ($\bar{X}$: 21.45) than the nonweaver children ($\bar{X}$: 16.95), the differences were relative to the nature of the task. This relationship is presented in Figure 10.1. Mean comparisons using the t test revealed that although the weaver group performed significantly better than the nonweaver group on all the tasks, differences between the groups on wire modelling and hand positioning tasks were of a greater magnitude than those on pencil–paper and sand drawing tasks.

Multiple comparison of means on the Newman Keuls test revealed 18 out of 28 comparisons to be significant. Differences between the

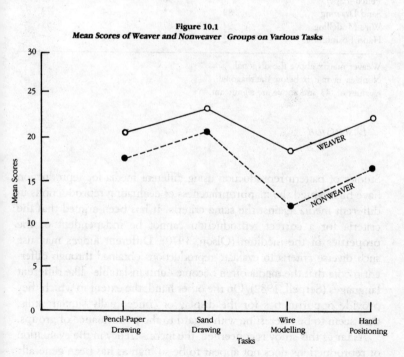

Figure 10.1
Mean Scores of Weaver and Nonweaver Groups on Various Tasks

groups tended to be significant when wire modelling and hand positioning levels of the task variable were involved in the comparison.

Intercorrelations among the scores on various tasks were computed separately for the weaver and nonweaver samples (Table 10.3). While all the correlations were positive and generally significant, their strength across the tasks varied substantially (from .39 to .94). The correlations were a little higher in the nonweaver than in the weaver group, particularly in the case of pencil–paper with wire modelling and hand positioning tasks, and in the case of wire modelling with sand drawing task. The correlation between wire modelling and hand positioning tasks was low, particularly in the nonweaver group.

TABLE 10.3
Correlation Matrix for Various Tasks

	Pencil–Paper	Sand Drawing	Wire Modelling	Hand Positioning
Pencil–Paper	**	.90	.77	.72
Sand Drawing	.89	**	.64	.79
Wire Modelling	.94	.87	**	.53
Hand Positioning	.92	.76	.39	**

Weaver matrix above the diagonal.
Nonweaver matrix below the diagonal.
r values of .43 and above are significant.

Discussion

Studies of pattern reproduction using different media for reproduction have highlighted the inappropriateness of evaluating reproductions in different media against the same criteria. It has been argued that the criteria for a correct reproduction cannot be independent of the properties of the medium (Olson, 1970). Different judges may use such diverse criteria to evaluate reproductions obtained through different media that the media often become "untranslatable" like different languages (Serpell, 1982). On the other hand, the extent to which they provide opportunities for the display of conceptually similar skills, they seem to be interesting with regard to the performance of groups.

As far as this study is concerned, the inconsistency in the evaluation of reproductions does not appear to be so high as has been generally reported. The interrater reliabilities were found to range between .72 and .81. A close scrutiny of the nature of judgments and the educational background of the judges, revealed that the reliabilities were satisfactory, and they permitted an examination of the reproductions of the two groups in a comparative manner.

The findings indicated a distinct superiority in performance of the weaver sample over the nonweaver sample, the nature of task being an equally important variable in the level of performance of the groups. When the media were relatively familiar to both the groups (such as, pencil–paper and sand drawing), the differences in performance of the groups were of a small magnitude than when the groups had differential familiarity with them (for instance, wire modelling or hand positioning). In view of the fact that the reproduction of patterns through hand positioning or wire modelling calls for perceptual–motor skills just as pencil–paper or sand drawing does, it may be argued that the differences between the two groups reflected the effect of different demands of media in the visual–spatial domain relative to the experiences of the groups. An observation of errors made by the nonweaver group, particularly on the wire modelling task, indicated that most of these were of a strategic nature. Their inefficient strategies resulted in manipulation of the wire which, from a motor developmental point of view, appeared highly complex in comparison to those of the weaver group. In their day-to-day weaving activities, the weaver children were exposed to such performatory attempts, and were well versed in the alternative manipulations. These functions (performatory attempts and alternative manipulations) are the essential prerequisites of any skill acquisition including weaving of patterns or embroidery of patterns. The superior performance of weaver children on wire modelling and hand positioning tasks may be attributed to these factors.

Differential cognitive demands introduced as a result of the incongruence between stimulus presentation and its subsequent reproduction may provide another explanation for differences in performance of weaver and nonweaver groups on various tasks. The pencil–paper and sand drawing tasks required reproduction of two-dimensional patterns on a two-dimensional surface; thus, they involved a lower degree of "image transformation" (Goodnow, 1969) for the reproduction of patterns. The cognitive demands of the wire modelling and hand positioning tasks, on the other hand, were relatively greater since these tasks required the reproduction of two-dimensional patterns as three-dimensional objects (for example, making wire models of patterns or copying them in a three-dimensional space through hand configurations). Having faced such transformational demands in their day-to-day life, the weaver children had already acquired some degree of competence in the use of transformational rules. Hence in comparison to other tasks, their performance was superior on these tasks than that of the nonweaver children. Conversely, the pencil–paper and sand drawing activities were more generic in the sense that both groups of children had ample exposure to them in school or play (drawing patterns on the earth with their fingers).

There has been an ongoing debate on the "generality" versus "specificity" of cognitive abilities (Berland, 1983; Berry, 1983). While psychometric theorists have supported the generality of abilities, anthropologically-oriented psychologists (Cole, Gay, Glick, and Sharp, 1971; Serpell, 1979) have argued in favour of specificity of abilities acquired as a function of specific cultural experiences. On the other hand, the cognitive style approach (Witkin, 1978) advocates neither the universality nor the specificity of cognitive abilities; rather abilities are considered as adaptive to the demands placed on individuals by their eco-cultural environment. The findings of the present study, particularly the correlational analyses, confirm the cognitive style viewpoint. There appears a definite patterning of performance in terms of the experiences of groups, but the effect is not confined to a particular task. On the contrary, the evidence suggests that the skills acquired through certain specific experiences, such as weaving or embroidery, are transferred to and reflected in performance on a number of tasks that call for similar operations.

REFERENCES

ADJEI, K. (1977). Influence of specific maternal occupation and behavior on Piagetian cognitive development. In P.R. Dasen (Ed.), *Piagetian psychology: Cross-cultural contributions*. New York: Gardner.

BERLAND, J. (1983). Dress rehearsal for psychological performance. In S.H. Irvine and J.W. Berry (Eds.), *Human assessment and cultural factors*. New York: Plenum.

BERRY, J.W. (1976). *Human ecology and cognitive style*. New York: Sage/Halsted.

BERRY, J.W. (1981). Developmental issues in comparative study of psychological differentiation. In R.H. Munroe, R.L. Munroe, and B.B. Whiting (Eds.), *Handbook of cross-cultural human development*. New York: Garland.

BERRY, J.W. (1983). Textured context: Systems and situations in cross-cultural psychology. In S.H. Irvine and J.W. Berry (Eds.), *Human assessment and cultural factors*. New York: Plenum.

BERRY, J.W. (1987). The comparative study of cognitive abilities. In S.H. Irvine and S. Newstead (Eds.), *Intelligence and cognition: Contemporary frames of reference*. Dordrecht: Nijhoff.

BERRY, J.W., VAN DE KOPPEL, J.M.H., SENECHAL, C., ANNIS, R.C., BAHUCHET, S., CAVALLI-SFORZA, L.L., and WITKIN, H.A. (1986). *On the edge of the forest: Cultural adaptation and cognitive development in Central Africa*. Lisse:Swets and Zeitlinger.

BRODERICK, P. and LASZLO, J.I. (1989). The copying of upright and tilted squares by Swazi children and adults. *International Journal of Psychology, 24*, 333–354.

COLE, M., GAY, J., GLICK, J., and SHARP, D. (1971). *The cultural context of learning and thinking*. New York: Academic.

DEREGOWSKI, J.B. (1972). Reproduction of orientation of Kohs type figures: A cross-cultural study. *British Journal of Psychology, 63*, 283–296.

DEREGOWSKI, J.B. and SERPELL, R. (1971). Performance on a sorting task. *International Journal of Psychology, 6*, 273–281.

FREEMAN, N.H. (1980). *Strategies of representation in young children: Analysis of spatial skills and drawing processes*. London: Academic.

GOODNOW, J.J. (1969). Cultural variations in cognitive skills. In D.R. Price-Williams (Ed.), *Cross-cultural studies*. Harmondsworth: Penguin.

GOODNOW, J.J. and LEVINE, R.A. (1973). The grammar of action: Sequence and syntax in children's copying of simple shapes. *Cognitive Psychology, 4*, 82–98.

GREENFIELD, P.M. (1978). Structural parallels between language and action in development. In A. Lock (Ed.), *Action, symbol and gesture: The emergence of language*. London: Academic.

GREENFIELD, P.M. and CHILD, C.P. (1977). Weaving, color terms and pattern representation: Cultural influences and cognitive development among the Zenacantecos of Southern Mexico. *Intra-American Journal of Psychology, 11*, 23–48.

GREENFIELD, P.M. and LAVE, J. (1982). Cognitive aspects of informal education. In D.A. Wagner and H.W. Stevenson (Eds.), *Cultural perspectives on child development*. San Francisco: Freeman.

HARKNESS, S. and SUPER, C.M. (1977). Why African children are so hard to test. *Annals of New York Academy of Sciences, 285*, 326–331.

IRVINE, S.H. and BERRY, J.W. (1988). The abilities of mankind: A revaluation. In S.H. Irvine and J.W. Berry (Eds.), *Human abilities in cultural context*. New York: Cambridge University Press.

JAHODA, G. (1981). Drawing styles of schooled and unschooled adults: A study in Ghana. *Quarterly Journal of Experimental Psychology, 33*, 133–143.

LASZLO, J.I. and BAIRSTOW, P.J. (1985). *Perceptual-motor behaviour: Developmental assessment and therapy*. London: Holt Saunders.

LASZLO, J.I. and BRODERICK, P. (1985). The perceptual-motor development of drawing. In N.H. Freeman and M.V. Cox (Eds.), *Visual order: The nature and development of pictorial representation*. Cambridge: Cambridge University Press.

MISHRA, R.C. and SINHA, D. (1991). Acculturation, cognitive changes and interpersonal adjustment: A study of some changing tribes in Bihar. *ICSSR Project Report*, New Delhi.

OLSON, D.R. (1970). *Cognitive development: The child's acquisition of diagonality*. New York: Academic.

PRICE-WILLIAMS, D.R., GORDON, W., and RAMIREZ, M. (1969). Skill and conservation: Study of pottery making children. *Developmental Psychology, 1,* 789.

SERPELL, R. (1969). Cross-cultural differences in the difficulty of copying orientation: A response organization hypothesis. Report 12, Human Development Research Unit, University of Zambia.

SERPELL, R. (1979). How specific are perceptual skills? A cross-cultural study of pattern reproduction. *British Journal of Psychology, 70,* 365–380.

SERPELL, R. (1982). Measures of perception, skill and intelligence: The growth of a new perspective on children in a Third World country. In W.W. Hartup (Ed.), *Review of child development research.* Chicago: University of Chicago Press.

SERPELL, R. and DEREGOWSKI, J.B. (1971). Frames of reference for copying orientation: A cross-cultural study. Report 19, Human Development Research Unit, University of Zambia.

SINHA, D. (1979). Perceptual style among nomadic and transitional agriculturist Birhors. In L. Eckensberger, W. Lonner, and Y. Poortinga (Eds.), *Cross-cultural contributions to psychology.* Lisse: Swets and Zeitlinger.

SINHA, D. and MISHRA, R.C. (1988). A developmental study of psychological differentiation among rural and urban tribal children in relation to quality of schooling and religion. *The Creative Psychologist, 1,* 17–25.

SINHA, G. (1989). *Acculturation and psychological differentiation.* Agra: National Psychological Corporation.

WILLATS, J. (1977). How children learn to draw realistic pictures. *Quarterly Journal of Experimental Psychology, 29,* 367–382.

WITKIN, H.A. (1978). *Cognitive styles in personal and cultural adaptation: Heinz Werner lecture series.* New York: Clark University Press.

11

Some Eco-Cultural and Acculturational Factors in Intermodal Perception

**DURGANAND SINHA •
R.C. MISHRA • J.W. BERRY**

Transfer of certain sensory experiences from one modality to another is generally referred to as intermodal or cross-modal transfer. Evidence for this phenomenon can be found in the writings of James (1890), and the same has served as the cornerstone of the earlier theories of perceptual learning (such as Hebb, 1949). Much of the evidence for intermodal transfer has been accumulated using tactual and visual sense modalities. It is argued that there are some common features for tactual and visual experiences (for instance, corners, curves, straight lines, and angles) which are easily accessible and useful for discrimination by touch as well as vision (Gregory and Wallace, 1963).

In early developmental studies it was demonstrated that touch served to control the development of vision (Piaget and Inhelder, 1969). On the other hand, empirical work with children and adults revealed better performance with visual than tactual experiences of stimuli (Cairns and Coll, 1977; Cashdan and Zung, 1970; Jain and Sinha, 1978; Siegal and Barber, 1973; Walsh, 1973). While this finding has been accepted as a general conclusion, it has been argued that the critical variable in intermodal perception tasks is not the modality involved, but the extent to which the concerned modality is utilised by the people in dealing with their environment (Goodnow, 1971). Tactile memory of stimuli appears to be weaker than visual memory not because it is intrinsically so, but because of the relatively lesser use of tactual modality by sighted subjects. Thus, when the accuracy of tactile size and form perception is compared between blind and normal sighted subjects, the difference is significant in favour of blind subjects (Ittyerah and Gupta, 1981).

A good deal of literature on cross-cultural differences in performance on a variety of perceptual–cognitive tasks indicates that cultural differences are rooted to a large extent in experiential differences. Studies of perceptual and cognitive functioning within an eco-cultural framework (comparing nomadic hunting and gathering peoples with sedentary agricultural peoples) have generally revealed that the former are more differentiated (that is, analytic) in their approach to perceptual and cognitive tasks. It is argued that a nomadic life with its mode of subsistence based on locating animals for hunting and forest products such as fruits, nuts, and mushrooms, for gathering demands a higher level of spatial analysis since the objects must be viewed and extracted from the camouflaging surrounding environment (Berry, 1966, 1976; Berry et al., 1986; Mishra, 1990; Sinha, 1979).

Research on Arctic and African groups (Berry, 1966, 1976; Berry et al., 1986) have also revealed that those who are more acculturated (generally those with more contact and experience with other cultures and their institutions) have a more differentiated approach to these tasks (Witkin and Berry, 1975). The ecological and cultural conditions provide groups with such diverse opportunities for the use of different sense modalities and influence their salience that people in different cultures may develop as different "sensotypes" (Wober, 1966), that is, assign varying weights to information coming from different sense modalities. For example, Igbo and Edo cultures of southern Nigeria have been reported to place greater emphasis than western cultures on proprioceptive and aural cues through reliance on tone and rhythm in their languages, and the customs of carrying young infants on the mother's back, and encouraging walking and dancing at early ages (Wober, 1966). The extent to which such variations across groups can be identified, differences in the accuracy of recognition between tactual–visual and visual–tactual conditions of intermodal transfer tasks can be predicted for groups.

Comparisons of inter- and intramodal matching of specific forms and sizes have revealed intramodal matching to be faster than intermodal matching (Ittyerah, 1979). Visual recognition has been found to be faster and more successful than tactual recognition (Ittyerah, Broota, and Gupta, 1981; Rudel and Teuber, 1964). Other studies (for instance, Klatzky, Lederman, and Reed, 1987) have revealed that modality effect is relative to the dimension of the stimulus being investigated. It has been reported that haptic and visual systems have distinct encoding pathways, with the haptic system oriented toward the encoding of substance (such as, texture, hardness), and the visual system oriented toward the encoding of shape and size. It has also been argued that encoding processes and pathways of the haptic and visual systems may or may not be shared (Lederman and Klatzky, 1990). Thus, even when the representations achieved visually or tactually are held common, the two domains are likely to assign different weights to such codes (Lederman, Thorne, and Jones, 1986; Welch and Warren, 1981). This viewpoint leads one to examine the attributes which are considered perceptually and cognitively more important when an object is encoded by tactual and visual systems.

The present study, which is part of a larger research project (Mishra and Sinha, 1991), examines the role of some eco-cultural and acculturational factors in intermodal perception of stimuli which vary on the dimensions of size, shape, height, and texture, using Birhor (largely nomadic), Asur (recently sedentary), and Oraon (fully sedentary) groups as samples. Since nothing is known about cross-cultural differences in intermodal perception, it is difficult to propose specific hypotheses. However, drawing upon the eco-cultural approach adopted here, some hypotheses have been proposed:

1. Due to greater opportunities of differentiation of structural properties of stimuli in their nomadic life, the Birhors as compared to the Asurs and Oraons, are likely to be more successful on tasks involving the perception of shape, size and height of stimuli than those involving texture.
2. High acculturated individuals in general would show greater accuracy in intermodal perception than low acculturated individuals.

3. Differences in intermodal perception of groups would be more evident in visual–tactual than in tactual–visual condition of perception.

SAMPLE AND DESIGN

The study was conducted in Gumla and Hazaribagh districts of Chotanagpur region of Bihar. The sample comprised 210 male and female adults belonging to Birhor (mean age: 39.67 years), Asur (mean age: 41.36 years), and Oraon (mean age: 38.81 years) cultural groups. The level of acculturation of the groups was assessed using a "contact acculturation" (Mishra and Sinha, 1991) measure which included such objective indicators of acculturation as knowledge of tribal languages, knowledge of Hindi and other languages (for example, English), household items (for instance, ornaments, utensils, clothes and furniture), means of livelihood, use of modern technology, religion, dressing style, travel experience, and exposure to movies. It was intended to examine the extent to which an individual of a particular cultural group had experience of participating with other cultures and their institutions. The contact indices were obtained locally, and appeared to be quite useful in understanding the acculturation features of each cultural group examined in the study. Each participant was rated for the degree of change in his/her traditional lifestyle in terms of these objective indices of contact, and was classified as being high or low on acculturation using the median score on the contact measure as the cut off point. There were 35 high and 35 low acculturated individuals of the Birhor, Asur and Oraon tribes, characterising a 3 (tribe) × 2 (acculturation) distribution of the sample.

THE SETTING AND THE CULTURAL GROUPS

The Chotanagpur region of Bihar comprises a large number of valleys and hills (between 600 to 900 metres above sea level). These valleys and hill tops are inhabited by some 29 tribes of distinct origins. These tribals are regarded as the earliest inhabitants of the country, and are called "Adivasi" (original inhabitants) in the official language. Their lifestyles, languages, customs, belief systems, socio-economic and political organisations accord them the status of distinct cultural groups.

According to the 1981 Census, there were some 51 million tribals in India, constituting 7.76 per cent of the total population. They numbered nearly 6 million in the state of Bihar (8.31 per cent); in the Chotanagpur region, they comprised 28.51 per cent of the population. In Gumla and Hazaribagh districts, they accounted for approximately 75 per cent of the total population of the districts.

Among these tribes, the Birhors are the least acculturated as a group. They are largely a nomadic tribe. The word "Birhor" in the local language means "The king of the forest". Thus, the forest was their kingdom, and moving in the forest in small bands in search of game (e.g., monkeys, hare, and porcupines), fruits, roots, honey, wax and fibres was their traditional lifestyle. Exploitation of the forest through hunting and gathering constitutes their main source of livelihood (Vidyarthi and Sahay, 1976). These people have little contact with other tribes of the same area or with the outside world. Many of them do not have a permanent dwelling even today.

The Birhors are generally divided into two groups: the Uthlus (wanderers) and the Jaghis (settlers). The Uthlus are always on the move, camping and hunting in forests. The Jaghis have almost a fixed residence, but make frequent forays into the forest for varying lengths of time. However, this distinction is not very rigid; there is evidence of the Uthlus settling down and of the Jaghis abandoning their fixed settlements.

Having pursued this kind of a lifestyle, the Birhors live in a "transitional" state today. Although their economy is almost entirely dependent on forest produce, they are being "forced" to settle down in colonies built by the tribal welfare department because of the need to conserve forests, the legislation regarding wildlife protection, and the resultant government policy. They are also being offered various incentives to adopt agriculture; however, the sedentary existence has not been fully adopted. Despite adopting a kind of rudimentary agriculture, they continue to pursue a nomadic lifestyle, and are largely dependent on forest resources for their subsistence. The variegated environment of the forest demands a differentiated judgment of things of various sizes and shapes in their day-to-day living.

The Asur tribe represents one of the minor tribes of Bihar. The word "Asur" means "forest people". The earliest account of this tribe (Forbes, 1969) indicates that forest was their abode, and their subsistence economy was largely based on forest resources. With the gradual increase in their population and laws regarding the conservation of forests, they have turned to settled agriculture, and have founded their villages on the hill tops. As the land is harsh, and there are no facilities for irrigation of crops, the agricultural yield is barely sufficient to meet their needs for 3–4 months a year. For the rest of the year, they depend on forest resources. Thus, hunting and gathering activities form a major part of their economy even today; but these activities are not pursued with such regularity as is the case with the Birhors. Cattle rearing, fishing and occasional wage employment are other means of livelihood.

Till a few years ago, the Asur settlements were not easily accessible as there were no roads. Hence their contact with the outside world was minimal. With the establishment of two residential schools for Asur children and of industries for the extraction of aluminium and iron rocks in the Netanhar region of Gumla, the whole area has been exposed to the outside world, and this has led to a change in the traditional lifestyle of the Asurs. The government has also initiated some training programmes in blacksmithy and carpentry for the employment of educated Asur youth, but these have not been sufficiently successful to constitute a full time profession for them. The Asurs have their own rules of marriage, divorce, transfer of property and authority. While the majority practices its own religion, some families have embraced Christianity.

The Oraons were among the first few to settle at the foothills of Chotanagpur region some 1,800 years ago. The word "Oraon" in Mundari language means "hardworking" or "unwearied", and is used to refer to a person who keeps on digging earth throughout the night and does not know when the dawn has set in. They cleared the forests extensively for cultivation and became the rulers of the land, and a dominant tribe of the region. Although they are mainly an agricultural community, fishing, cattle rearing and crafts (e.g., mat making) are practised as subsidiary activities to agriculture. They have a good knowledge of the qualities of the soil and of the crops that may be best grown on them. Besides cultivating rice, millets, pulses and oil-seeds, they also grow vegetables for consumption as well as sale. They follow a system of crop rotation and use indigenous manures and chemical fertilisers to increase the yield of crops, and for irrigation wherever possible.

The Oraons live in large villages inhabited by a number of families. They have a definite lineage, social structure and authority system representing a "tight" (Pelto, 1968) society. They have well developed norms guiding the behaviour of group members, and well articulated rules with regard to marriage, divorce and distribution or transfer of property. Exposure to education has brought them close to the outside world. Many educated Oraons have migrated to the nearby towns or cities where they work in offices, schools, hospitals or industrial organisations. They use a variety of household goods of different textures, including those of wood, cloth, glass, metal, and plastic.

PROCEDURE

A devise for studying intermodal perception was designed along the lines of Rudel and Teuber (1964); and modelled on the work of Jain and Sinha (1978). It consisted of 10 sets of stimuli which varied in shape, size, height, and texture. Two sets of stimuli were used for practice; the remaining 8 sets constituted the test series, 2 for each stimulus dimension. In each series, 2 stimuli, which were more or less similar to the "target" stimuli, served as "distractors" for those series.

The participants were shown the sets of stimuli practice and were allowed to pick them up and feel them. After this initial familiarity with the objects, the stimuli were removed, and the following instructions were given.

The participants were presented one stimulus of the first practice set for inspection. After 10 seconds it was removed, and presented again with two other stimuli of that set. The subjects were asked to identify the stimulus which was shown earlier. This procedure was repeated with the other practice set. Practice for the visual condition was followed by practice for the tactual condition.

One of the stimuli of the first practice set was hidden behind a screen and the participants were asked to pick up the stimulus and get a feel of it (for example, how it looks like, how big it is) for about 10 seconds. The stimulus was then presented with the other 2 stimuli of the set. The subjects were asked to feel and identify the stimulus presented earlier. This procedure was repeated for the second practice trial. Care was taken to ensure that the participants did not see the stimuli.

This initial familiarity with the visual and tactual modes was followed by practice for the intermodal condition. Here the stimuli were sometimes presented visually and recognised tactually; sometimes they were presented tactually and recognised visually. This exercise was followed for both the practice sets.

One stimulus from each set was used as the "target", and was presented visually or tactually for 10 seconds. Then it was presented with the other 2 stimuli of the series, and the participants were asked to identify the stimulus presented earlier either visually or tactually. The sequence of presentation and recognition (visual or tactual) was counterbalanced. Responses were recorded as "correct" or "incorrect"; and 1 point was given for each correct judgment. This is the *recognition score* which varied between 0 and 8. Scores were also obtained separately for shape, size, height, and texture; they ranged between 0 and 2. Failure to recognise the target stimuli was counted as *error*; errors were estimated for the tactual–visual and visual–tactual conditions separately. The time taken on the task constituted the *time score*.

ANALYSIS OF RESULTS

Treatment-wise mean scores of the groups on various measures of the task and the *F* ratios are presented in Table 11.1. Recognition scores of the Oraons and Birhors were higher than those of the Asurs; and the effect of tribe was significant. The effect of acculturation was also significant in favour of highly acculturated individuals.

The effect of tribe appeared to be significant for all the series of stimuli. The Oraons scored significantly higher than the Birhors and the Asurs on the height dimension. In the size series, the Birhors scored significantly higher than the Asurs and the Oraons. The Birhors scored higher than the Asurs, and the Asurs scored higher than the Oraons on the shape dimension. In the texture series, on the other hand, the Oraons scored higher than both the Asurs and the Birhors.

The acculturation effect was significant for all the series of stimuli with the exception of size; highly acculturated individuals obtained

TABLE 11.1
Treatment-wise Mean Scores and F Ratios on Different Measures

Measures	Tribe			F (df)	Acculturation		F (df)	F (Tribe x Acculturation)
	Birbor	Asur	Oraon		HA	LA		
Recognition	6.10	5.57	6.25	5.51**	6.32	5.63	15.49**	1.59
Height	1.52	1.37	1.67	4.24*	1.68	1.37	13.13**	0.78
Size	1.70	1.43	1.56	3.44**	1.56	1.56	0.00	0.80
Shape	1.77	1.59	1.46	5.67**	1.70	1.51	6.81*	2.83
Texture	1.11	1.19	1.59	10.50**	1.39	1.20	4.43*	1.14
Time (Seconds)	248.79	220.10	269.80	18.96**	256.28	260.17	0.19	11.40**
Error	1.90	2.43	1.75	6.09*	1.68	2.37	15.19**	1.03
Tactual–Visual	0.94	1.30	0.89	1.93	0.83	1.27	3.39	3.02
Visual–Tactual	0.96	1.13	0.85	5.57*	0.85	1.10	16.57**	0.19

** $p < .01$.
* $p < .05$.
HA: High Acculturation.
LA: Low Acculturation.

higher scores. None of the interaction effects were found to be signi-ficant. The analysis of time scores revealed acculturation × tribe effect to be significant, besides the main effect of tribe. On the whole, the Birhors took more time than the Oraons, who in turn took more time than the Asurs in making judgments. On the other hand, while low acculturated Birhors (mean: 267.83) and Asurs (mean: 210.97) took lesser time than high acculturated individuals of the same groups (mean: 301.74 and 299.22 respectively), the pattern was reversed in the case of the Oraons; low acculturated Oraons (mean: 301.74) took significantly more time than high acculturated Oraons (mean: 237.89).

On the measure of *errors*, there was a significant effect of accultur-ation indicating a larger number of errors for the low acculturated group. The tribe effect was also significant (Asur>Birhor>Oraon), but the interaction effect was not significant.

Further analysis of errors revealed no reliable differences in the scores of the groups for *tactual–visual* mode either due to tribe or acculturation. In the *visual–tactual* mode, the main effects of tribe as well as acculturation were significant. The low acculturated individuals made more errors than the high acculturated subjects. As for tribe differences, the errors were significantly greater in the Asur than in the Birhor and Oraon samples.

DISCUSSION

The findings of the study are largely in the expected direction. It is apparent that the eco-cultural characteristics of the groups and the level of individuals' acculturation are important factors in producing differences in intermodal perception of different types of stimuli. Differences among cultural groups seem to be clearly linked with the characteristics of the task, hence they are not always in one direction or in favour of a particular group.

The Birhors' better judgment of shape, size, and height on the intermodal perception task may be attributed to their marked analytic abilities, developed during the course of their hunting and gathering activities in the forest. Comparing the salience of visual and tactual modalities for stimulus discriminability, researchers have argued that shape and size are global structural properties of stimuli, whereas texture is a substance related attribute which can be extracted locally (Klatzky et al., 1987). Cross-cultural studies have indicated that a nomadic life characterised by hunting and gathering activities demands analytic skills for successful adaptation to the environment. The routine use of the visual sense modality in attending to objects in the forests is likely to increase the individual's sensitivity to structural properties (such as, shape, size, and height) of objects, and lead to the acquisition of a higher level of differentiation (Tighe and Tighe, 1966) of stimuli characterised by those properties. Greater attention to structural features of objects appears to be an adaptational demand of the Birhor lifestyle. Thus, the present findings largely fit into the eco-cultural framework (Berry, 1976) of perceptual–cognitive development.

A similar argument may be presented for the higher scores of the Oraons with regard to texture judgment. Developmental studies have pointed out that texture based discriminations are achieved earlier than those based on size and shape; they are used as a cue to depth perception even by infants (Walk, 1966). However, when the problem is one of discrimination of texture varying in terms of surface densities (coarse to fine) in an intermodal paradigm, the groups do not show similar proficiency. The findings reported here reveal that agrarian communities acquire greater proficiency in making surface discriminations than hunting and gathering groups. Using the eco-cultural approach it may be argued that while spatial analysis is a part of the routine activity of hunting–gathering people, the demand for surface analysis is a common characteristic of an agrarian lifestyle. A variety of household objects made of different kinds of materials—cloth, wood, glass, metal, and plastic—which are widely used in agricultural families, enable such families to be familiar with varying texture gradients. The greater proficiency of the Oraons in the intermodal perception of texture may be attributed to these eco-cultural demands placed on them in their day-to-day activities.

The effect of acculturation was found to be significant on all the measures except on the judgment of size. There is ample evidence in literature indicating an increase in the scores on perceptual–cognitive tasks with increased acculturation (Berry et al., 1986; Berry, 1990; Witkin and Berry, 1975). A distinction has often been made between "contact-acculturation" and "test-acculturation" in examining the effect of acculturation on the performance of perceptual–cognitive tasks. The effect of contact-acculturation has been observed even after partialling out the test-acculturation effects (Berry et al., 1986). In view of these evidences and the findings of the present study, it may be argued that contact-acculturation is an important factor in the inter-modal perception of stimuli.

There is an ongoing debate on the relative salience of vision and touch with regard to the encoding of information. Earlier studies have assigned greater value to touch than vision in the acquisition of knowledge about objects, but later research has revealed the dominance of vision over touch. Recently (Kaltzky et al., 1987) their salience has been discussed in the context of the properties of stimuli used in the study of intermodal perception. Visual encoding is considered to be more effective for the perception of shape and size, whereas the tactual mode is more effective for the encoding of textural information (Klatzky et al., 1987). The data presented here have not been analysed in the context of these properties. However, the analysis of errors has indicated differences according to tribe and acculturation in the visual–tactual mode of perception but not in the tactual–visual mode. Although the Asurs committed more errors than either the Birhors or the Oraons under both the conditions, the difference was significant only under the visual–tactual condition. A similar pattern was evident for the effect of acculturation, low acculturated individuals committed more errors than high acculturated individuals. It appears that haptic perception develops in a more uniform manner than visual perception, and eco-cultural and acculturational influences are greater on visual encoding.

REFERENCES

BERRY, J.W. (1966). Temne and Eskimo perceptual skills. *International Journal of Psychology, 1,* 207–229.

BERRY, J.W.. (1976). *Human ecology and cognitive style: Comparative studies in cultural and psychological adaptation.* New York: John Wiley.

BERRY, J.W. (1990). Psychology of acculturation: Understanding individual moving between cultures. In R.W. Brislin (Ed.), *Applied cross-cultural psychology.* Newbury Park: Sage.

BERRY, J.W., VAN DE KOPPEL, J.M.H., SENECHAL, C., ANNIS, R.C., BAHUCHET, S., CAVALLI-SFORZA, L.L., and WITKIN, H.A. (1986). *On the edge of the forest: Cultural adaptation and cognitive development in Central Africa.* Lisse: Swets and Zeitlinger.

CAIRNS, E. and COLL, P. (1977). The role of visual imagery in visual–tactual and cross-modal matching. *British Journal of Psychology, 69*, 213–214.

CASHDAN, S. and ZUNG, G. (1970). Effect of sensory modality on form recognition. *Journal of Experimental Psychology, 86*, 458–460.

FORBES, L.R. (1969). *Report on the Ryotwaree settlement of the government farms in Palamau*. Calcutta: Government.

GREGORY, R.L. and WALLACE, J.G. (1963). Recovery from early blindness: A case study. *Experimental Psychological Society Monograph, 2*.

GOODNOW, J.J. (1971). The role of modalities in perceptual and cognitive development. In J.P. Hill (Ed.), *Minnesota symposium on child psychology* (Vol. 5). Minneapolis: University of Minnesota Press.

HEBB, D.O. (1949). *The organization of behavior: A neuropsychological theory*. New York: Wiley.

ITTYERAH, M.C. (1979). A chronometric study of inter- and intramodal matching of form and size. Unpublished doctoral dissertation, University of Delhi, Delhi.

ITTYERAH, M.C., BROOTA, K.D., and GUPTA, G.C. (1981). Inter- and intramodal processing of linear extents. *University Psychology Research Journal, 2*, 15–20.

ITTYERAH, M.C. and GUPTA, V.R. (1981). A comparative study on the congenitally blind and the sighted on tactile size and form perception and handedness. *Indian Journal of Public Administration, 27*, 735–745.

JAIN, R. and SINHA, D. (1978). Intermodality transfer and kinesthetic figure aftereffect. *Journal of Psychological Researches, 22*, 72–76.

JAMES, W. (1890). *Principles of psychology*. New York: Holt.

KLATZKY, R.L., LEDERMAN, S.J., and REED, C. (1987). There's more to touch than meets the eye: The salience of object attributes for haptics with and without vision. *Journal of Experimental Psychology: General, 116*, 356–369.

LEDERMAN, S.J., THORNE, G., and JONES, B. (1986). Perception of texture by vision and touch: Dimensionality and intersensory integration. *Journal of Experimental Psychology: Human Perception and Performance, 12*, 169–180.

LEDERMAN, S.J. and KLATZKY, R.L. (1990). Haptic classification of common objects: Knowledge-driven exploration. *Cognitive Psychology, 22*, 421–459.

MISHRA, R.C. (1990, January 7–12). Perceptual differentiation in relation to children's daily life activities. *Proceedings of the 77th session of the Indian Science Congress*, Cochin.

MISHRA, R.C. and SINHA, D. (1991). Acculturation, cognitive changes and interpersonal adjustment: A study of some changing tribes in Bihar. *ICSSR Project Report*, New Delhi.

PELTO, P.J. (1969, April). The difference between "tight" and "loose" societies. *Transaction*, 37–40.

PIAGET, J. and INHELDER, B. (1969). *The psychology of the child*. New York: Basic Books.

RUDEL, R.G. and TEUBER, H.L. (1964). Crossmodal transfer of shape discrimination by children. *Neuropsychologia, 2*, 1–8

SIEGEL, A.W. and BARBER, J.C. (1973). Visual and haptic dimensional preference for planometric stimuli. *Perceptual and Motor Skills, 36*, 383–390.

SINHA, D. (1979). Perceptual style among nomadic and transitional agriculturist Birhor. In L. Eckensberger, W. Lonner, and Y.H. Poortinga (Eds.), *Cross-cultural contributions to psychology*. Lisse: Swets and Zeitlinger.

TIGHE, L.S. and TIGHE, T.J. (1966). Discrimination learning: Two views in historical perspective. *Psychological Bulletin, 66,* 353–370

VIDYARTHI, L.P. and SAHAY, K.N. (1976). *The dynamics of tribal leadership in Bihar.* Allahabad: Kitab Mahal.

WALK, R.D. (1966). The development of depth perception in animals and human infants. *Monograph of the Society for Research in Child Development, 31,* 82–108.

WALSH, J.K. (1973). Effect of visual and tactual stimulation on learning abstract forms. *Bulletin of the Psychonomic Society, 2,* 357–359.

WELCH, R.B. and WARNER, D.H. (1981). Immediate perceptual response to intersensory discordance. *Psychological Bulletin, 88,* 638–667.

WITKIN, H.A. and BERRY, J.W. (1975). Psychological differentiation in cross-cultural perspective. *Journal of Cross-Cultural Psychology, 6,* 4–87.

WOBER, M. (1966). Sensotypes. *Journal of Social Psychology, 70,* 181–189.

12

Sex Differences in Cognitive Style of Brahmin and Gurung Children from the Hills and Plains of Nepal

AYAN BAHADUR SHRESTHA • R.C. MISHRA

Among the various theories of cognitive development the theory of psychological differentiation has been most widely used in cross-cultural research. It was first advanced as a general theory of human behaviour (Witkin, Dyk, Faterson, Goodenough, and Karp, 1962), later its scope was broadened (Witkin and Goodenough, 1981), it proposes that the organism as a whole may be characterised by reference to a dimension of differentiation. Segregation of self from nonself is one of the main features of psychological differentiation which means that boundaries have been formed between the inner and the outer world. Differences in the degree of self–nonself segregation lead to the differences in the extent to which the self or the field outside is likely to be used as a referent for behaviour. The tendencies to rely on the self or the field outside as primary referents for behaviour are referred to as field-independent or field-dependent (FI-FD) cognitive styles.

Research on the development of these cognitive styles has demonstrated their relationship with certain ecological, cultural, acculturational, and organismic factors. The variable of sex or gender difference has received considerable attention in research among the many other organismic variables influencing the degree of field independence–dependence of individuals. Van Leeuwen (1978) has referred to approximately 500 studies which directly or indirectly deal with sex differences in cognitive style. Generally speaking, studies conducted in North America have revealed that males tended to be more field independent than females. Witkin, Goodenough, and Karp (1967) have reported sex differences in psychological differentiation to be fairly stable from early childhood to adulthood, but later studies indicated that sex differences did not become consistent until early adolescence (Witkin and Berry, 1975).

Cross-cultural research on sex differences in cognitive styles has largely been pursued in an eco-cultural framework proposed by Berry (1976). There seems to be less consistent evidence of sex differences in non-western than in western samples. In general, research has indicated the patterning of sex difference according to the ecological engagements of the groups and individuals: it is relatively uncommon and nonexistent in groups which are largely nomadic than in those which lead a sedentary agricultural lifestyle. Cultural factors like socialisation, social stratification and sex role differentiation, which are often used as mechanisms of sex differences in cognitive style, are adaptive to ecological pressures operating on hunting–gathering and agricultural populations (Berry, 1981).

Conclusions about the pattern of sex differences have been primarily based on the findings of the studies carried out in African countries (Berry, 1966, 1976; Dawson, 1967a, 1967b). In the case of Nepal, only one study has so far been reported on the development of cognitive style (Sinha and Shrestha, 1992) using Berry's (1976) eco-cultural framework. Whether there are sex differences in the cognitive style of Nepalese children during the period of childhood (and beyond) is not known. However, some formulations may be attempted in this respect drawing upon the evidence provided by cross-cultural studies in general, and studies of cognitive style carried out in India (which is geographically and culturally very similar to Nepal) in particular.

Studies with undergraduate students in India (Pande, 1970a, 1970b) and cross-cultural comparisons of American and Indian college students (Parlee and Rajagopal, 1974) have observed greater differentiation on the EFT for males than females. Using Berry's (1976) eco-cultural framework, Sinha (1980) has examined sex differences in 4 cultural groups in India, namely, nomadic Birhors, transitional Birhors, sedentary Oraons, and sedentarised urban school children on the Story–Pictorial EFT (Sinha, 1978). Findings indicated that sex differences in cognitive style were not consistent either in the Birhor group or in the transitional Birhor and agricultural Oraon group. On the other hand, urban boys were significantly more field-independent than girls.

Hills and plains living offers some important contrasts in the ecological features of the groups (Sinha and Shrestha, 1992). The patterns of life in the hill ecology not only generated pressures for autonomy and self-reliance on the part of the people in general, but they also provided lesser role differentiation according to sex in comparison to the plains ecology, although these patterns to a large extent seemed to be linked with other cultural features of the groups. For example, the Gurung people inhabiting the hills of Nepal constitute not only a less stratified society, but also one which provides lesser role differentiation according to sex. On the other hand, Brahmins who inhabit the same areas constitute a highly stratified society with clear sex role differentiation. The former represent a relatively "loose" society (Pelto, 1968), whereas the latter seem to represent a "tight" society (Pelto, 1968) despite occupying the same geographical terrain. Sex differences in cognitive style in relation to varying ecological and cultural features of the groups have not been systematically studied.

The present study, which is part of a larger research work, examines sex differences in the cognitive style of Brahmin and Gurung children inhabiting the hills and plains of Nepal. Drawing upon the predictions of the eco-cultural model (Berry, 1976) in terms of adaptive demands, it may be argued that sex differences in cognitive style would be significantly reflected in the samples of plains ecology and Brahmin culture. However, in view of the evidence about the patterning of sex differences according to differential socialisation experiences of boys and girls towards fulfilling role obligations, it was hypothesised that sex differences in cognitive style would be more evident in the Brahmin than the Gurung group irrespective of their hill or plains habitation.

METHOD

Sample and Design

The sample ($N = 176$) was drawn from two ecological habitats (hills and plains) and two cultural groups (Brahmin and Gurung). Boys and girls between 6 and 8 years of age were studied, using a 2 (ecology) × 2 (culture) × 2 (sex) factorial design. There were equal number of school going and nonschool going children in each group. Thus, the groups were fairly matched in terms of their overall school experiences.

The Setting of the Study

The study was conducted in Lamjung and Chitwan districts of Nepal which sharply differ in their topographical and cultural features. Lamjung is a hilly region stretching from the western Gandaki zone (approximately 490 mt high) to the south of the high peaks of Annapurna (7950 mt) and Manaslu (8160 mt). Topographically, the whole area may be divided into three regions: the *mountains* consisting of the Himalayas which are largely uninhabited; the *villages on the hills* (approximately 1070 mt high); and the *villages on the plateau* (approximately 1830 mt high). All these are characterised by rocky land and scanty populations. The hill sample was drawn from these villages.

Chitwan is located in the central region which has some hilly land to the north, but a greater part of the area consists of foothills and plains (called *Terai*). The fertile land has attracted a large number of people who have settled there in relatively large villages with agriculture as their main occupation.

Gurungs, who constitute approximately 26 per cent of the population of the Lamjung district (1971 Census), represent a dominant group of this region. Their origins can be traced back to the Mongolians (Allen, 1976) and their language is of a Tibetan–Burmese variety. Traditionally, they were mountain dwellers, leading a pastoral life, but over the years many of them have settled in the lower hilly regions and plains, engaging in agriculture and providing labour and military service to earn their livelihood. Those Gurungs who live on high lands have retained their traditional lifestyle, and have very little contact with the outside world.

Gurungs have a joint family system and do not attach much importance to privacy and personal possession (Allen, 1976). Both boys and girls mix freely with each other and choose their own marriage partners. As mentioned earlier, the Gurung society appears to be a "loose" (Pelto, 1968) one with little social stratification and sex role differentiation. The Gurungs constitute basically an egalitarian society (Messerschmidt, 1974), and encourage autonomy and self-reliance among children from an early age (Allen, 1976). On the other hand, the plains Gurungs with their wider contact with the Hindus have developed a caste hierarchy with defined roles and norms, representing more of a "tight" (Pelto, 1968) society.

The Brahmins differ sharply from the Gurungs in a number of ways. They have descended from the Indo-Aryans, and have a complex social system and status hierarchy based on membership of subcastes (determined by birth). Traditionally, they were priests, and they have not abandoned this profession even today. A large number of them have settled in the low lands of river valleys and plains, but some of them have moved to the hilly regions, serving as priests. Children are encouraged to conform to caste norms and religious rules from an early age. Deviation from these norms is generally not tolerated. As mentioned earlier, they represent a "tight" (Pelto, 1968) society. They live in large villages in exclusively demarcated areas. Contact with the outside world has led to a number of changes in their traditional lifestyle, but the influences are largely confined to villages which are situated on the road side, or are easily accessible. The Brahmins engage in agriculture, but they employ other people as labourers to cultivate the land. With the expansion of education many of them have also taken up government jobs.

The subjects were drawn from a number of randomly selected Brahmin and Gurung villages located in hilly and plain regions. If there was more than one child between 6 and 8 years of age in any family, only one child was selected randomly for the study. In the random selection of families some socio-economic differences did creep in, but these were not large enough to significantly influence the test performance of the subjects. Moreover, it has been observed in numerous studies that the performance on the SPEFT, the test used here, is not influenced by socio-economic factors (Mishra, 1990).

The Test Material

The subjects were administered the Story–Pictorial Embedded Figures Test (SPEFT), a test which was specifically designed for use with unsophisticated children who find the conventional EFT or CEFT less meaningful and uninvolving (Sinha, 1978, 1984). In the SPEFT drawings of common objects like birds, dogs, squirrels, snakes, and butterflies, are presented as stimuli and the child is asked to locate them in complex scenes depicting trees, forests, fields, flowers, etc., in which the stimulus objects are embedded. Each picture set is presented against the background of a story that provides the reason for doing the test, and makes the task interesting as well as challenging to the child. The split-half reliability of the test is. 80, and the validity coefficient (with CEFT) is .47. The test comprises 8 test sets and 2 practice sets. The scores range from 0 to 41, the higher score indicates greater field independence. The test has been found to be appropriate for Nepalese children (Sinha and Shrestha, 1992).

TABLE 12.1
Mean Scores of the Samples according to Treatment Levels

Samples	Mean	SD
Hill Ecology	25.58	7.26
Plain Ecology	18.16	4.96
Brahmin Culture	22.97	8.72
Gurung Culture	20.76	5.14
Boys	22.32	7.70
Girls	21.41	6.71

A $2 \times 2 \times 2$ ANOVA yielded significant main effects of ecology (F: 79.72, df: 1,168, $p < .01$) and culture (F: 7.11, df: 1,168, $p < .01$). The effect of sex (F: 1.23, df: 1,168, $p > .05$) was not significant. Analysis of interaction effects revealed ecology $\times$ culture effect to be significant (F: 40.04, df: 1,168, $p < .01$). In the hills the difference between Brahmin (M: 27.98) and Gurung (M: 23.18) children was greater than that noted in the plains (Brahmin M: 17.97, Gurung M: 18.38). Culture $\times$ sex effect was also significant (F: 3.91, df: 1,168, $p < .05$). There was significant sex difference in the Brahmin sample (Boys M: 24.09, Girls M: 21.86), but this difference was negligible in the

Gurung sample (Boys M: 20.57, Girls M: 20.95). Thus, differences due to ecology and sex were more pronounced among the Brahmins than among the Gurungs.

DISCUSSION

The findings of the study indicate that the general assumption regarding differences in the cognitive style of boys and girls (as measured by the SPEFT) did not seem to be valid. The overall comparison of the scores of boys and girls did not provide any evidence of significant differences between them. Hill or plains dwelling also did not reliably contribute to sex difference despite its potential influence on the SPEFT scores. Sex affected the pattern of scores only in the case of Brahmin children, a characteristic feature which was not exemplified in the Gurung culture.

These findings can largely be interpreted in terms of the "ecological" and "social conformity" models proposed by Witkin and Berry (1975). The ecological model (Berry, 1966, 1976) with its "adaptive selection" hypothesis argues that as cultures evolve over time from a nomadic to a sedentary form of life, the demands of closer and larger group living emphasise greater social conformity and sensitivity at the cost of individual independence. Barry, Child, and Bacon (1959) have shown that a sedentary (physically static) society permits greater role diversity in the community at large and greater role specialisation among individuals. Both lead to a high degree of preoccupation with specific activities, with women occupying more of "family care" roles. It is not at all adaptive for such cultures to develop individuals who have a strong sense of psychological separation from others. Adherence to authority, conformity and social sensitivity are inculcated more strongly in girls than boys in the course of socialisation during the childhood years in "tight" societies like the one of Brahmins of Nepal. Lower field independence among Brahmin girls than Brahmin boys compared to the Gurung sample may be attributed to these influences.

While greater field dependence among females has been a general finding of earlier studies, research with preschool children has reported greater field independence among girls than boys (Britain and Small, 1969; Chynn, Garrod, De Vos, and Demick, 1991). The findings reported here do not support either of the claims. The restricted age range of the subjects of this study(6–8 years)does not warrant any conclusions about the age at which such differences may first appear (if they do appear at all), however, the findings allow us to argue that sex differences are largely culturally conditioned, and that they appear somewhere in the course of sedentarisation of groups. As long as the groups have a nomadic lifestyle (as is the case with Gurungs), they are unlikely to exhibit sex differences in cognitive styles.

There are some methodological issues, however, that need to be addressed prior to drawing any definite conclusions about sex differences FI–FD cognitive styles. Reviewing the research on field independence–dependence among preschool children Kogan (1983) found evidence of greater field independence in the case of girls than boys. It was argued that this was not due to true gender differences, but due to a basic difference between the Witkin et al. (1971) EFT and the Coates' PEFT (1972) which have often been used in studies with preschool children. While the former requires decontextualisation of simple shapes from more complex geometrical designs, the latter requires disembedding of geometric shapes from meaningful pictures of objects and persons. This has led to the speculation that gender differences may be associated with the social context of the task such as the PEFT (confirmed by Kojima, 1978), or to the possibility that the EFT and the PEFT tap different psychological processes (Waber, 1979). The characteristic features of other tests (for example, RFT or Draw-a-Person-Test) deserve similar considerations. The SPEFT (used in this study) varies considerably from the EFT or the CEFT not only in terms of the use of familiar objects and scenes as stimuli instead of geometrical designs, but also in terms of providing a context of story with regard to the embedded objects. It is possible that these variations influenced the performance of boys and girls of the two cultural groups besides other cultural characteristics. It is necessary to examine this hypothesis in further studies of FI–FD cognitive style aimed at exploring sex differences.

REFERENCES

ALLEN, N.J. (1976). The Rodi: Female association among Gurungs of Nepal. Unpublished doctoral dissertation, Colombia University, New York.

BARRY, H., CHILD, I.L., and BACON, M.K. (1959). Relation of child training to subsistence economy. *American Anthropologist, 61*, 51–63.

BERRY, J.W. (1966). Temne and Eskimo perceptual skills. *International Journal of Psychology, 1*, 207–229.

BERRY, J.W. (1976). *Human ecology and cognitive style: Comparative studies in cultural and psychological adaptation.* New York: John Wiley.

BERRY, J.W. (1981). Developmental issues in comparative study of psychological differentiation. In R.H. Munroe, R.L. Munroe, and B.B. Whiting (Eds.), *Handbook of cross-cultural human development.* New York: Garland.

BRITAIN, S.D. and SMALL, B. (1969). The role of field independence in sex role identification in young children. Paper presented at the annual meeting of the Western Psychological Association, Toronto.

CHYNN, E.W., GARROD, A., DE VOS, E., and DEMICK, J. (1991). Relationship of sex, sex role stereotyping, age and I.Q. to field independence in preschool children. Unpublished manuscript.

COATES, S.W. (1972). *Preschool embedded figures test manual.* Palo Alto, CA: Consulting Psychologists Press.

DAWSON, J.L.M. (1967a). Cultural and psychological influences upon spatial-perceptual processes in West Africa, Part I. *International Journal of Psychology, 2*, 115–128.

DAWSON, J.L.M. (1967b). Cultural and psychological influences upon spatial-perceptual processes in West Africa, Part II. *International Journal of Psychology, 2*, 171–185.

KOGAN, N. (1983). Stylistic variation in childhood and adolescence: Creativity, metaphor, and cognitive style. In J. Flavell and E. Markman (Eds.), *Handbook of child psychology* (Vol. 4). New York: John Wiley.

KOJIMA, H. (1978). Assessment of field dependence in young children. *Perceptual and Motor Skills, 46*, 479–492.

MESSERSCHMIDT, D.A. (1974). Social status, conflicts and change in Gurung community of Nepal. Unpublished doctoral dissertation, University of Oregon.

MISHRA, R.C. (1990). Cognitive stimulation, training, and perceptual-cognitive task performance by socially deprived children. *Indian Journal of Current Psychological Research, 5*, 1–11.

PANDE, C.G. (1970a). Performance of a sample of Indian students on a test of field dependence. *Indian Journal of Experimental Psychology, 4*, 46–50.

PANDE, C.G. (1970b). Sex difference in field dependence: Confirmation with Indian sample. *Perceptual and Motor Skills, 31*, 70.

PARLEE, M.B. and RAJAGOPAL, J. (1974). Sex difference on the embedded figures test: A cross-cultural comparison of college students in India and in the United States. *Perceptual and Motor Skills, 39*, 1311–1314.

PELTO, P.J. (1968, April). The difference between "tight" and "loose" societies. *Transaction*, 37–40.

SINHA, D. (1978). Story–Pictorial E.F.T.: A culturally appropriate test for perceptual disembedding. *Indian Journal of Psychology, 53*, 160–171.

SINHA, D. (1980). Sex differences in psychological differentiation among different cultural groups. *International Journal of Behavior Development, 3*, 455–466.

SINHA, D. (1984). *Manual for Indo-African E.F.T. and Story–Pictorial E.F.T.* Varanasi: Rupa.

SINHA, D. and SHRESTHA, A.B. (1992). Eco-cultural factors in cognitive style among children from hills and plains of Nepal. *International Journal of Psychology, 27*, 49–59.

VAN LEEUWEN, M.S. (1978). A cross-cultural examination of psychological differentiation in males and females. *International Journal of Psychology, 13*, 87–122.

WABER, D.P. (1979). Cognitive abilities and sex related variation in the maturation of cerebral cortical functions. In M.A. Wittig and A.C. Paterson (Eds.), *Sex-related differences in cognitive functioning: Developmental issues.* New York: Academic.

WITKIN, H.A. and BERRY, J.W. (1975). Psychological differentiation in cross-cultural perspective. *Journal of Cross-Cultural Psychology, 6*, 4–87.

WITKIN, H.A. and GOODENOUGH, D.R. (1981). *Cognitive styles: Essence and origin.* New York: International University Press.

WITKIN, H.A., GOODENOUGH, D.R., and KARP, S.A. (1967). Stability of cognitive style from childhood to young adulthood. *Journal of Personality and Social Psychology, 7*, 291–300.

WITKIN, H.A., OLTMAN, P.K., RASKIN, E., and KARP, S.A. (1971). *Manual for embedded figures test, children's embedded figures test, and group embedded figures test.* Palo Alto, CA: Consulting Psychologists Press.

WITKIN, H.A., DYK, R.B., FATERSON, H.E., GOODENOUGH, D.R., and KARP, S.A. (1962). *Psychological differentiation: Studies in development.* New York: John Wiley.

Section 3

Dimensions of Self and Achievement Process

13

Introduction

This section includes six papers which deal with various aspects of self-concept and self-monitoring highlighting the implications of self-related variables in learning and achievement process. The section begins with Biggs' paper on approaches to learning of Asian students. Biggs has argued that the conditions of schooling and learning processes in China, Hong Kong, Korea, Japan, Taiwan, and Singapore are culturally rooted defying some of the assumptions of western research. Western observers have frequently noted that the Confucian heritage cultures place more emphasis on rote learning and low performance on tasks requiring high level cognitive activity. According to Biggs, however, compared to western students Asian students are more likely to use meaning-oriented approaches to learning, and they perform not only at a high cognitive level but also do better than western students.

The second paper by Feather and McKee reports the findings of a study on Australian and Japanese University students with regard to global self-esteem and their attitudes toward high achievers or "tall poppies". The authors have predicted that Japanese students would manifest lower levels of global self-esteem and that they would be more inclined to see high achievers cut to size when compared with Australian students. This prediction was based upon the assumption that construals of self tend to be more interdependent and less independent in the Japanese culture than in the Australian culture. The findings supported this prediction and also indicated a negative correlation between global self-esteem and the favour fall variable in the case of the Australian sample, a finding that was consistent with the theoretical expectation and with previous research. The study also revealed that Japanese and Australian students were similar in the extent to which they believed that high achievers should be rewarded.

Researchers have assumed all too often that the nature of a psychological construct identified in one culture is appropriate for another. This assumption is particularly erroneous where a variable such as self-esteem, prone to cultural influences, is involved. David Watkins has examined the etic properties of one of the best developed western models of self-esteem, the Shavelson model, and the cross-cultural validity of instruments based on this model in several developing countries such as Nepal, Hong Kong, Nigeria, and the Philippines. In another paper, Watkins and Regmi have attempted to determine the basis of self-esteem of male and female Nepalese children both from poor, traditional, rural and from rich, modernised, urban backgrounds. The subjects were asked to respond (either in Nepali or English) to the question "What are the most important areas of your life?" Content analysis of the subjects' responses revealed that as in western studies, "school", "reading", and "sport" were also important to the self-concept of many Nepalese children. However, in the case of the relatively underprivileged rural children basic life necessities such as "health", "food", and "money" were equally important. Gender and developmental differences were also noted. The authors have discussed the implications of these findings for the assessment of self-esteem of Nepalese children.

Cheng, in his paper, has argued for a culturally relevant model of self-concept. The construct of self has been found to be multidimensional in western research. The structure of self-concept may not remain consistent across different social and cultural contexts. Cheng has concluded that the construct be indigenously explicated and operationalised. He has identified the multidimensional model of the Chinese self-concept.

In the last paper of this section, Gudykunst, Gao, and Franklyn-Stokes have reported cross-cultural findings on self-monitoring and concern for social appropriateness in the collectivistic culture of China and in the individualistic culture of England. They have noted that the English reported greater ability to modify their self-presentations, tendency to avoid public performances, sensitivity to others' expressive behaviour, and self-monitoring than the Chinese. The Chinese, in contrast, paid greater attention to social comparison information and others' status characteristics than the English. The consistencies in the findings from the two studies have been discussed by the authors and general patterns of self-monitoring and concern for social appropriateness in individualistic and collectivistic cultures have been identified.

14

Approaches to Learning of Asian Students: A Multiple Paradox

JOHN B. BIGGS

SOME PARADOXES

The performance of Asian students from "Confucian heritage" cultures (Ho, 1991) poses several paradoxes to western observers. The basic problem is that the conditions of schooling that prevail in countries such as China, Hong Kong, Korea, Japan, Taiwan, and Singapore defy conventional wisdom derived from western research about what constitutes good and poor teaching/learning environments. Briefly, the kind of environment that prevails in Confucian heritage cultures would be predicted to lead to much rote learning, and low performance on tasks requiring high level cognitive engagement. Western observers have duly reported such a relationship, frequently on anecdotal evidence. When hard data are examined, however, Asian students are more likely than westerners to report that they use meaning-oriented approaches to learning, and they perform not only at a high cognitive level, but also better than western students. How to reconcile these conflicting sets of data?

First, the evidence needs to be examined.

THE TEACHING/LEARNING CONTEXT

Schools in Confucian heritage cultures typically use expository teaching methods, in highly authoritarian classrooms, with the main thrust of teaching and learning being sharply focused on preparation for external examinations, which themselves tend to address low level cognitive goals, and exert excessive pressure on teachers and exam stress on students (Beeby, 1966; Biggs, 1991; Ho, 1991; Morris, 1985).

Even in prosperous systems such as those in Hong Kong and Singapore, public funding per student capita is a fraction of what it is in the USA, Canada, Great Britain, or Australia; class sizes are correspondingly larger, and support services such as guidance and counselling much lower. Such conditions in western contexts have been associated empirically with low cognitive level learning strategies and with poor learning outcomes (Biggs, 1979, 1987a; Bourke, 1986; Crooks, 1988; Ramsden, 1985).

Reported Use of Rote Learning

Asian students, according to western observers, reliably use predominantly rote based, low level, cognitive strategies, both in their own culture (Hong Kong) (Murphy, 1987) and overseas in Australian tertiary institutions (Ballard and Clanchy, 1984; Bradley and Bradley, 1984; Samuelowicz, 1987). Murphy, a tertiary educator in Hong Kong, has noted

Hong Kong students display almost unquestioning acceptance of the knowledge of the teacher or lecturer. This may be explained in terms of an extension or transfer of the Confucian ethic of filial piety. Coupled with this is an emphasis on strictness of discipline and proper behavior, rather than an expression of opinion, independence, self-mastery, creativity and all-round personal development (1987, p. 43).

Asian students studying abroad are perceived as fitting a common stereotype:

In my discipline they all want to rote learn material rather than think. (Animal Science and Production)

Students from Malaysia, Singapore, Hong Kong appear to be much more inclined to rote learning. Such an approach does not help problem solving. (Dentistry)

... it can be difficult to cope, in small (graduate) classes, with overseas students who are reluctant to discuss, criticize reading and express an opinion. (Commerce) (Samuelowicz, 1987, pp. 123–125).

The picture is a coherent one to the western observer. Asian students are brought up in a restrictive teaching/learning environment, which commits them to a passive, uncritical, and reproductive mode of learning.

A scrutiny of the studies of approach to learning performance, however, reveals a different picture.

APPROACHES TO LEARNING

A concept that is useful in the present discussion is that of "approach to learning" and its operationalisation. Approaches were originally used to refer to the processes adopted while engaging in an academic task (Marton and Saljo, 1976). These authors identified "surface" and "deep" approaches in their studies of tertiary students studying text. A student using a surface approach would start with the intention of learning what the author *said*, and thus focus on reproducing the words used, while a student using a deep approach would focus on what the author *meant*, and focus on constructing the author's probable intended meaning.

Approaches may also refer to *predispositions* to adopt particular processes, which is what is meant when students are asked to describe how they usually go about learning in a questionnaire. Factor analysis of questionnaire responses has typically produced factors closely resembling the Marton and Saljo deep and surface approaches, and additionally a third, achieving approach (Biggs, 1979, 1987a; Entwistle and Ramsden, 1983; Watkins, 1983b). These approaches have two components: a motive, corresponding to Marton's intention, and a strategy, that enables that motive to be fulfilled.

The *surface approach* is based on extrinsic motivation, school learning being viewed as a means towards some other end, such as obtaining a qualification. The problem is to invest minimal time and effort but to avoid failure; the strategy is thus one of cutting corners, a common one in the academic context being to limit the target to essentials, reproducing them through rote learning.

The *deep approach* is based on interest in the subject matter of the task and thus to engage in the task appropriately; the strategy is to maximise understanding, with a focus on the underlying meaning. Precisely what that involves depends on the task in question, but in general it means using a well structured knowledge base, and an abstract conceptual framework. The student is likely to read widely, discuss with others, theorise and form hypotheses.

The *achieving approach* is based on the pride of visibly achieving, in particular through high grades; the strategy is to organise time, working space, and syllabus coverage in the most efficient way. A student adopting an achieving approach is self-disciplined and systematic in the use of study skills, planning, and allocating time according to task importance.

A student's preferred approach would be the one that has been found to be viable and personally comfortable in the day-to-day teaching/learning environment; if that environment is changed, in time that individual's approach will also change (Biggs, 1993). These approaches can be assessed by a questionnaire, responses to which thus reflect differences in context. The *Learning Process Questionnaire* (LPQ) (at the secondary level) (Biggs, 1987b) and the *Study Process Questionnaire* (SPQ) (at the tertiary level) (Biggs, 1987c), originally developed and normed for Australian samples, are examples of this kind of assessment of learning approaches.

As the LPQ and the SPQ have been translated into Chinese and adapted for use in Hong Kong, with local norms (Biggs, 1992), these instruments provide an opportunity for assessing the learning environments of Asian students.

Approaches to Learning in Asian Students

In the light of the typical Hong Kong teaching conditions and those prevailing in Australia, at both the secondary and tertiary levels, it is expected that, in comparing the norming samples from the two countries, Hong Kong students would be higher on surface, probably also on achieving approach, but Australian students would be higher on deep approach.

Expectations were confirmed with respect to the achieving approach, but the opposite was seen in the case of deep and surface approaches (Biggs, 1991). With minor exceptions, the majority of Chinese students, at middle and senior secondary levels, and in university and in polytechnics, reported to be higher on the achieving approach, as expected, but surprisingly they were higher on deep and lower on the surface approach, than comparable Australian students. The number of cases involved in each comparison were usually several hundred, and in the tertiary samples, nearly 2,000; statistical significance was mostly well beyond the .0001 level. Similar results were observed in comparisons of Singaporean and Australian students.

The only major exception to this pattern was a comparison between medical students, where the differences were even more pronounced in the opposite direction: Hong Kong students ($N = 200$) were much higher on surface, and lower on deep and achieving approaches, than Australian students ($N = 600$). These differences, however, fully supported the expectations based on the learning environment and previous research (Newble and Clarke, 1986), in that the Hong Kong students came from a highly traditional medical school, involving heavy workloads and memorising of content, while the Australian students came from a medical school using the problem based learning approach. This finding is important, because it would otherwise have been easy to explain the previous findings in terms of, say, response set—Chinese students tend to rate themselves in socially desirable ways (less surface, more deep).

Despite the (presumably) unpromising learning/teaching environments, Chinese students appear to rely *less* on rote learning than do western students, and more on a deep approach emphasising the underlying meaning. This is, of course, contrary to the stereotype discussed earlier. It is, however, entirely compatible with the evidence on levels of achievement.

Comparative Studies of Academic Achievement

Asian students, both at home and abroad, achieve significantly higher than western students particularly in the areas of mathematics and science (Sue and Okazaki, 1990; Stevenson, Stigler, Lee, Lucker, Kitamura, and Hsu, 1985). The International Association for the Evaluation of Educational Achievement (IEA) has been particularly involved in these international comparisons (Comber and Keeves, 1973; Garden, 1987; IEA, 1988). Medrich and Griffith (1992) critically scrutinised three IEA surveys conducted over the last 25 years in science and mathematics, and after allowing for retention rates and sampling error, and for different patterns at different age levels and in different subjects and subtests, Hong Kong, Korea, Japan, and Singapore were amongst the highest scoring countries, and nearly always higher than the US.

The general pattern is clear. The Asian countries mentioned are not only holding their own against better equipped western educational systems, but typically outperform them. It cannot reasonably be argued that such consistently good performances, and top "A" level results, first class honours in mathematics, and university medals (Biggs, 1990a), can be attributed to excessive rote learning, however skilful.

Conclusion

Each of the elements of the conumdrum is well founded: the facts of Asian schooling, western perceptions of rote learning, self-perceptions of deep learning, and academic performance of a high cognitive level. How can these be reassembled to form a coherent picture?

PRESAGE, PROCESS, AND PRODUCT IN CLASSROOM LEARNING: THE 3P MODEL

The relationships expressed in these inconsistencies are familiar. Research on student learning has for some time focused on establishing relationships between the teaching context, student learning processes, and learning outcomes. Such relationships are conceptualised in the so-called presage–process–product (hence "3P") model (Biggs, 1990b).

The model, first outlined by Dunkin and Biddle (1974) in the context of classroom interaction, represents in the present version an integrated system, in the sense outlined by Von Bertalanffy (1968). In the ecology of a system, a change in any one component will, depending on the state of equilibrium already achieved, either effect change throughout creating a new equilibrium and hence a new system, or the changed component will be absorbed and the system reverts to the *status quo*. A steady state is the norm; when a system is not in balance, something is amiss and change may be expected.

There are three main sets of components in the present system: presage, process, and product, with interaction between all the components (see Figure 14.1). But before discussing the systemic implications, the components should be explained.

Presage

Presage factors exist prior to learning. Student presage factors refer to relatively stable, learning related characteristics that students bring to the classroom, such as, prior knowledge, abilities, preferred ways of learning, language competence in the medium of instruction, and values and expectations concerning achievement. Teaching presage factors refer to the superstructure set by the teacher and the institution: the course structure, curriculum content, and methods of teaching and assessment. This context also generates a climate for learning, which could be "cold" or "warm", and it has important motivational consequences.

Process

The two sets of factors interact, and their interaction may be tracked from either the teacher's or the student's point of view. The latter will be considered here. Students, being immersed in this teaching context,

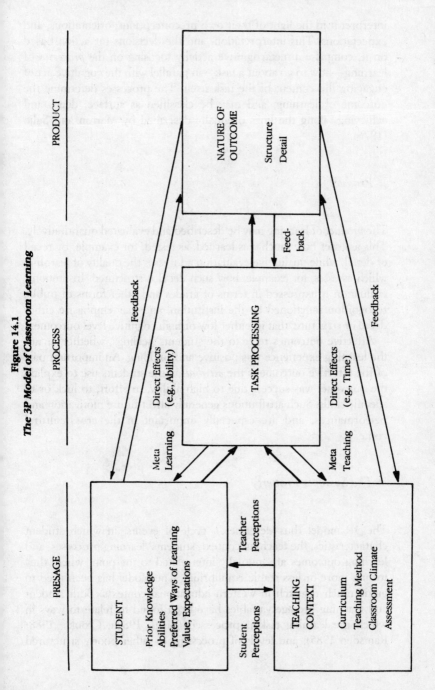

Figure 14.1
The 3P Model of Classroom Learning

interpret it in the light of their own preconceptions, orientations, and expectations. This interpretation, and the decisions for action based on it, comprise a metacognitive activity focusing on the *processes* of learning—how to go about a task—in parallel with the cognitive act of engaging the content of the task itself. The processes determine the outcome of learning, and may be classified as surface, deep, and achieving, along the lines originally described by Marton and Saljo (1976).

Product

The *product* of learning may be described and evaluated quantitatively. This assesses how much was learned, as tested, for example, by recall of detail, while qualitative evaluation addresses the quality of learning, which assesses, for example, how such detail is structured. Institutional evaluation is expressed in terms of grades and other forms of public recognition sanctioned by the institution, and may emphasise either detail or structure, that is, either low or high cognitive level outcomes.

Affective outcomes refer to the students' feelings, whether or not the learning experience was positive and fulfilling. An important part of the affective outcome is the *attribution* the students use to explain the outcome: was success due to high ability, to effort, to luck or to specific skills. Such attributions generally affect future motivation and performances, and are especially important in the cross-cultural context.

The Systems Property

The 3P model thus describes a cycle of events, in which student characteristics, the teaching context, students' learning processes, and learning outcomes are mutually interrelated to the point where they form a more or less stable equilibrium. The model has been used to guide much research in western educational contexts. Both student and teaching presage variables have been found to relate to ways in which the learning task is processed (Biggs, 1987a; Crooks, 1988; Ramsden 1985), and levels of processing to either poorly structured and low level outcomes, or to well structured, high level outcomes (Biggs, 1979, 1987a; Marton and Saljo, 1976; Watkins, 1983a).

Thus, rich teaching/learning contexts yield high level processes, which in turn lead to complex and appropriately integrated outcomes; rigid or impoverished teaching leads to low level learning, and fragmented, unsatisfactory outcomes. In the systemic approach, teaching, assessment, student perceptions, processes, and outcomes interact to strike a balance that supports a way of coping. As can be seen from Figure 14.1, this applies both to students and teachers. Students receive their own feedback, as indicated along the top of the figure, and adjust to the best of their ability; that adjustment becomes their predispositional approach to learning. Some students are predisposed to surface learning, others to deep learning. As for teachers, they too receive feedback, as indicated along the bottom of the figure, and make adjustments to their teaching. Eventually, allowing for day-to-day and subject-to-subject variation, an overall balance is struck. It is this systems property, by means of which the student achieves a more or less steady state with regard to motivation and strategy use in a given learning context, that results in a typical approach to learning that can be assessed by the use of a questionnaire (Biggs, 1993).

In the Asian context, the system seems to be out of balance: an unpromising teaching context, but a meaning-oriented approach to learning, and high level outcomes. As systems are not usually out of balance, it would follow that the appropriate components of the system are not being examined.

RECONCEPTUALISING PRESAGE–PROCESS RELATIONS

Sue and Okazaki (1990) have examined two main hypotheses relating to Asian students' superior learning: that Asians are genetically superior to Caucasians in learning ability, and that Asians value education more highly and thus provide a more supportive home environment. Neither hypothesis can be sustained on the basis of the evidence they have reviewed. On the last point, Stevenson and his associates have specifically located Asian superiority to schooled rather than unschooled performances. Sue and Okazaki have favoured a sociological "relative functionalism" hypothesis of upward mobility, relating the functional utility of schooling to second generation immigrants, which does not explain the performance of Asians in their own cultures.

In their comparative study of Japanese and US mothers, children, and teachers, Hess and Azuma (1991) observed that Japanese teachers used two teaching strategies not used by US teachers: "repetition as a route to understanding" (p. 6), and "sticky probing", that is, a single problem was discussed by students, with teacher adjudicating, for hours until a consensus acceptable to the teacher and group was reached. In both methods, students were required to be willing to persist in the face of boredom and lack of immediate feedback, hence to use a high degree of metacognition or awareness of one's own cognitive processes, and to accept rules governing group participation. Hess and Azuma have asserted that Japanese socialisation practices in the home probably produced such "internalised dispositions" to learn. Possibly, then, the components missing from the systems model to date refer to socialisation and schooling, as Figure 14.1 itself is classroom based. Nevertheless, classrooms, and the people who inhabit them, belong to cultures, into which they are socialised. The school, too, is a microcosm, a subsystem within the overall cultural system.

What other clues do we have from a cultural point of view? The teaching strategy of understanding through repetition certainly strikes a chord in Chinese culture. Marton, Tse, and dall'Alba, in phenomenographic studies of Mainland Chinese teachers' conceptions of learning and understanding, found a very similar structure of "understanding through memorising". Tang (1991a) observed in tertiary students in Hong Kong (taught in English in an English-style polytechnic) an approach to learning she labelled "deep memorising", which students adopted specifically as an exam-taking strategy. They first ensured that they understood the point or concept in focus, and then committed it to memory in order to ensure ready access. Kember and Gow (1989) also noted that tertiary students in Hong Kong used a "narrow approach", which comprised the sequence: "understand–memorise–understand–memorise . . . ".

Although "deep memorising" and "the narrow approach" may be occasioned by the perceived demands of the assessment tasks rather than by culture, the *focus* in all these cases is on understanding, memorising being only a means to that end. Thus, in rating themselves highly on the deep approach related items in the LPQ and the SPQ, the Chinese students were responding validly and appropriately. Likewise, western observers have correctly perceived a great deal of repetitive effort, with the emphasis on accuracy of recall; however, they have incorrectly termed it "rote learning", which according to them, replaces understanding. Memorisation and understanding are perceived by Asians to be mutually supportive, not incompatible, processes.

When presented with the prospect of endorsing surface (based on memorising) and deep (based on understanding) processes, Chinese students would rate the latter as more important: not that they do not memorise, but that they do not perceive memorising as part of a surface approach, rather as a means towards understanding.

Other culturally based factors distinguishing western and Confucian heritage learners include the following.

1. Attributions for success and failure. Numerous studies have drawn attention to the fact that Asian cultures attribute success to effort, and failure to lack of effort, rather than to ability, which is the first attribution westerners make for good or poor perform-ance (Hess and Azuma, 1991; Holloway, 1988). The top 5 attributions for success of Hong Kong secondary students were effort, interest in study, study skill, mood, and ability (Hau and Salili, 1991). Apart from ability all the others are more or less controllable; ability, which western students perceive as most important for success, is not controllable. In other words, Asian students tend to see ways in which they can improve their performance; western students tend to attribute past performance to things beyond their control.

2. Cue seeking. Attributions to effort and strategy rather than to ability would tend to make students diligent at cue seeking (Miller and Parlett, 1974). Examining tertiary students' adaptation to different modes of assessment, Tang (1991a) found in a path analysis that student presage variables exerted little effect, but contextual presage variables had strong linkages with process and product; the subjects were very sensitive to teacher cues. Most students saw test and assignment as assessing different things, broad coverage and study in depth respectively, and hence adapted their approach to the format.

3. Spontaneous collaboration. Asian students appear unusually ready to collaborate in their study behaviour. Tang (1991b) reported that 87 per cent of 38 students interviewed prepared for the assignment in spontaneously formed groups, in which they decided

principally to discuss the question and clarify possible interpretations, and to share readings. Students then wrote up their own assignment individually. Students who collaborated obtained higher marks (not statistically significant), and wrote better structured essays ($p < .05$). Cooperative groups seem to work surprisingly well in a system that is strongly expository and competitive. This is not surprising, given the collectivist orientation of Chinese culture (Ho, 1991). This case illustrates how the cultural supports for learning overtake the classroom structures.

4. Time on task. Asian students spend much more time on task than western students, both in formal or timetables hours and informal time spent on either homework, or voluntarily in studying. It was observed that for the same period of formal time, Asian teachers and students were more task-oriented, with more time actually spent on task (Stevenson and Stigler, 1992).

5. Language medium of instruction. Teaching through the medium of a foreign language is not a cultural factor so much as an executive decision, but it may be relevant for generating a deep approach. It is incorrect to assert that students being taught in a foreign language medium of instruction learn the surface strategy of focusing on key words, as many academic staff believe (Samuelowicz, 1987). In an attempt to understand the concepts taught, students may translate them from the second language (English) into the mother tongue, work on and elaborate them in the mother tongue, then translate them back into English. All this activity is meaning-oriented, and it is found that students taught in a foreign language, and who are surviving, adopt deep rather than surface approaches (Biggs, 1987a; 1990c).

Apart from the medium of instruction, these and other learning related factors are founded in the culture and transmitted through socialisation. They all appear to be highly adaptive for learning. For example, a western student in attributing failure to lack of ability is creating a self-fulfilling prophecy of further failure; a Chinese attributing failure to insufficient effort is (given other incentives, such as family expectations) pledged to further task engagement. Hess and Azuma (1991) have even suggested that Japanese socialisation practices produce "internalised dispositions" that create: "a sense of diligence and receptiveness (which) fit uncomfortably into the more familiar American concepts of intrinsic and extrinsic motivation" (p. 7). In other words, Japanese children have less *need* to be "motivated" to perform well in school; they are predisposed to do those things that are required of them by their teachers.

THE FIT BETWEEN SCHOOL AND CULTURE

Hess and Azuma (1991) have noted that western children are generally raised to be assertive, independent, curious, and to explore on their own terms. These are not, however, qualities that are rewarded in most western schools, which require obedience, conformity to group norms, persistence in the absence of feedback at essentially boring tasks, as is required in Japanese schools, or schools anywhere. The difference is that in Japanese schools the latter qualities are also built into the pre- and extra-school social environment.

There thus seems to be a mismatch in the western system. Children are socialised one way out of school, another way in school. They, therefore, need to be "motivated" in a way that Japanese children do not. Either classroom activities are made attractive or elaborate systems of negative reinforcement are created, all of which make western classrooms highly externally controlled (Hess and Azuma, 1991).

How "Unpromising" is the Asian Classroom in Fact?

These characteristics are perhaps more adaptive in Asian classrooms than appears at first sight. Or, to put it differently, Asian classrooms may not be unpromising environments, in their own context, that they would be in western contexts. One should take a more fine-grained look at what is going on in the Asian classroom.

The first clue that western observers may be misinterpreting Asian teaching comes from the matter of memorising which has already been discussed. Then, Hess and Azuma have raised issues about group participation and sticky probing, which do not occur in quite these forms in western classrooms. Stevenson and Stigler (1992) have noted that interaction between teachers and students tends to be different in the east and the west. Despite classes having up to 50 students,

Chinese and Japanese teachers find time to interact on one-to-one basis in their classroom rounds more frequently than do western teachers, thus spending more time with each student. Western teachers, on the other hand, see interaction more in terms of the whole class, with "quick and snappy" public questioning (Hess and Azuma, 1991), which probably contributes little to higher order cognitive engagement. Certainly, at the tertiary level, a western teacher teaching a class of Chinese students is likely to be disappointed at the apparent lack of interaction or responsiveness to public questioning (Biggs, 1990a; Murphy, 1987), but the number of students seeking one-to-one inter-action with the teacher as soon as class is over, and with each other (Tang, 1991b), may be higher than one would find with western students.

In short, there is likely to be greater harmony between student expectations, metacognitions, and teaching expectations and procedures in the east than in the west. This makes direct comparisons between similar classroom behaviours in different cultural contexts rather diffi-cult, the same behaviour, such as teacher criticism, taking on quite a different role. In the west criticism is frequently meant, and taken, punitively, yet in Japan criticism is part of the teaching process of "sticky probing", which is meant, and taken, as cognitive feedback.

EXTENDING THE 3P MODEL

All this implies that the original classroom based 3P model needs to be explicitly extended to take into account the cultural complex of which the classroom and school are a part. Such an extension is, of course, implicit in a systems model from the beginning, but by interpreting the components of the system in a pseudo-etic way (Triandis, 1972), generalisations from western research seem to throw up contradictions. To conclude, the model is redrawn to reinstate harmony, and the implications discussed.

Teacher and student are specifically shown in Figure 14.2 as sharing learning related beliefs and values that arise in the general social *milieu* and that produce docility. "Docility" literally means "teachability", and it may well be that some Asian groups are higher on characteristics relating to docility in this technical sense. Such "docility dispositions"

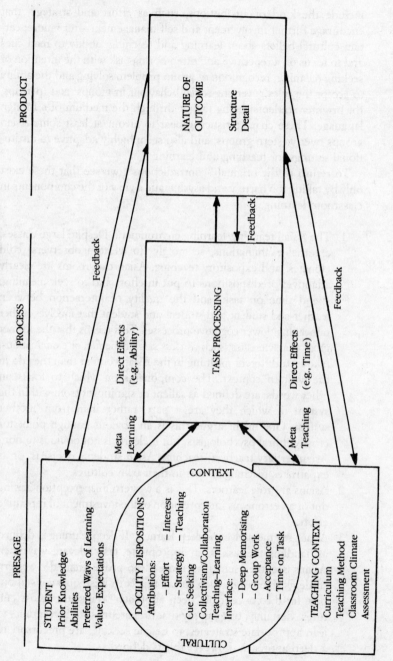

The 3P Model Modified for Cultural Effects

include the kind of attributions, such as effort and strategy, that encourage further involvement and self-management after failure; certain cultural beliefs about learning and teaching; ability to read cues and to focus on a repetitive and often boring task with the intention of seeking meaning; recognition of group problem solving and the ability to accept the rules governing social behaviour in groups; and (perhaps, for brighter students) being taught through the medium of a foreign language. These characteristics appear to favour at least some Asian groups over western groups, and also seem highly adaptive in institutional settings for teaching and learning.

To return to the original "contradictions", we see that these exist only by taking too narrow and asystematic a view of the components in classroom learning.

1. The Asian teaching/learning environment. Despite large classes, external examinations, seemingly (to western observers) cold climates, and expository teaching, Asian classrooms are clearly adaptive: predispositions to put in effort and to seek meaning, spend time on task, and the quality of interaction between teacher and student and student and student that involves higher rather than lower cognitive processes. This means that the former gross characteristics, such as class size or the *fact* of examinations, take on a different meaning in the Asian context than they do in the western context. The components on which to focus, in other words, are defined as salient or significant from within the system of which they are a part, rather than from another system. One might argue this is an obvious enough point for cross-cultural psychologists, but it clearly is not obvious to non-Asian tertiary teachers, teaching Asian students overseas, or as expatriates teaching Asians in their own cultures.

2. Asians are rote learners. This is a western misperception arising out of an erroneous interpretation of the investment of repetitive effort.

3. Asians see themselves as deep learners. If deep learning is defined as handling the task in an appropriate, task relevant way, then Asians see themselves as more deep-prone than do western students. However, even to say this is to raise questions about how far the concept of "deep approach" translates across cultures. Certainly, one can say that preparedness to invest time, to lean appropriate strategies, to be cue seeking, are precursors to a deep approach, however this is defined.

4. Asians perform at high cognitive levels in academic tasks. The evidence for this is very clear, and certainly gives support to component (3) in the present argument.

These elaborated statements are no longer in deep conflict, however much they need to be explored and developed in detail, such development is an obvious target for further research. More detailed definition and operationalisation of the "docility syndrome", and its manifestation in different cultural groups, would be an obvious step. Practically speaking, its genesis and linking with indigenous teaching contexts, eastern and western, could be important in enhancing teaching and learning anywhere. Thus, there are obvious lessons here for western schooling, where the "fit" between in-school and out-of-school learning environments seems to be poor (Resnick, 1987). In short, the lesson is that it is probably easier to change schools than to change society.

Finally, a systems approach to cross-cultural research seems valuable, at the very least in damage control brought about by indulging the pseudo-etic fallacy. Accepting our original contradictions at their face value would have led to erroneous conclusions about the nature of Asian schooling, and of the quality of learning of Asian students, errors based simply on western misperceptions of what was really going on. In terms of cross-cultural psychology that would be most unfortunate, and in the modern period of increasing international study, a costly mistake.

REFERENCES

BALLARD, B. and CLANCHY, J. (1984). *Study abroad: A manual for Asian students*. Kuala Lumpur: Longmans.

BEEBY, C. (1966). *The quality of education in developing countries*. Cambridge: Harvard University Press.

BIGGS, J.B. (1979). Individual differences in study processes and the quality of learning outcomes. *Higher Education, 8*, 381–394.

BIGGS, J.B. (1987a). *Student approaches to learning and studying*. Hawthorn, Vic: Australian Council for Educational Research.

BIGGS, J.B. (1987b). *The Learning Process Questionnaire (LPQ): Manual*. Hawthorn, Vic: Australian Council for Educational Research.

BIGGS, J.B. (1987c). *The Study Process Questionnaire (SPQ): Manual*. Hawthorn, Vic: Australian Council for Educational Research.

BIGGS, J.B. (1990a). Asian students' approaches to learning: Implications for teaching overseas students. In M. Kratzing (Ed.), *Eighth Australasian learning and language conference* (pp. 1–51). Queensland: University of Technology Counselling Services.

BIGGS, J.B. (1990b). Teaching for desired learning outcomes. In N.J. Entwistle (Ed.), *Handbook of educational ideas and practice* (pp. 681–693). Beckenham: Croom Helm.

BIGGS, J.B. (1990c) Effects of language medium of instruction on approaches to learning. *Educational Research Journal, 5,* 16–26.

BIGGS, J.B. (1991). Approaches to learning in secondary and tertiary students in Hong Kong: Some comparative studies. *Educational Research Journal, 6,* 27–39.

BIGGS, J.B. (1992). *Learning processes in Hong Kong students: Using the Learning and Study Process Questionnaires.* University of Hong Kong: Faculty of Education, Occasional Papers 14.

BIGGS, J.B. (1993). What do inventories of students' learning processes really measure? A theoretical review and clarification. *British Journal of Educational Psychology, 63,* 1–17.

BOURKE, S. (1986), How smaller is better: Some relationships between class size, teaching practices, and student achievement. *American Educational Research Journal, 23,* 558–571.

BRADLEY, D. and BRADLEY, M. (1984). *Problems of Asian students in Australia: Language, culture and education.* Canberra: AGPS.

COMBER, L.C. and KEEVES, J.P. (1973). *Science education in 19 countries.* Stockholm: Almquist & Niksell.

CROOKS, T.J. (1988). The impact of classroom evaluation practices on students. *Review of Educational Research, 58,* 438–481.

DUNKIN, M.J. and BIDDLE, B.J. (1974). *The study of teaching.* New York: Holt, Rinehart and Winston.

ENTWISTLE, N. and RAMSDEN, P. (1983). *Understanding student learning.* London: Croom Helm.

GARDEN, R. (1987). The second IEA mathematics study. *Comparative Education Review, 31,* 47–68.

HAU, K.T. and SALILI, F. (1991). Structure and semantic differential placement of specific causes: Academic causal attributions by Chinese students in Hong Kong. *International Journal of Psychology, 26,* 175–193.

HESS, R.D. and AZUMA, M. (1991). Cultural support for schooling: Contrasts between Japan and the United States. *Educational Researcher, 20* (9), 2–8.

HO, D.Y.F. (1991, June 29–July 2). Cognitive socialization in Confucian heritage cultures. Paper presented at the workshop on Continuities and Discontinuities in the Cognitive Socialization of Minority Children, US Department of Health and Human Services, Washington, DC.

HOLLOWAY, S.D. (1988). Concepts of ability and effort in Japan and the US. *Review of Educational Research, 58,* 327–345.

INTERNATIONAL ASSOCIATION FOR THE EVALUATION OF EDUCATIONAL ACHIEVEMENT. (1988). *Science achievement in seventeen countries: A preliminary report.* Oxford: Pergamon Press.

KEMBER, D. and GOW, L. (1989). Cultural specificity of approaches to study. *British Journal of Educational Psychology, 60,* 356–363.

MARTON, F. and SALJO, R. (1976). On qualitative differences in learning—I: Outcome and process. *British Journal of Educational Psychology, 46,* 4–11.

MEDRICH, E. and GRIFFITH, J. (1992). *International mathematics and science assessments: What have we learned?* Washington, DC: US Department of Education, National Center for Education Statistics.

MILLER, C.M.L. and PARLETT, M. (1974). *Up to the mark: A study of the examination game.* London: Society for Research into Higher Education.

MORRIS, P. (1985). Teachers' perceptions of the barriers to the implementation of a pedagogic innovation: A South East Asian case study. *International Review of Education, 31,* 3–18.

MURPHY, D. (1987). Offshore education: A Hong Kong perspective. *Australian Universities Review, 30* (2), 43–44.

NEWBLE, D. and CLARKE, R.M. (1986). The approaches to learning of students in a traditional and in an innovative problem-based medical school. *Medical Education, 20,* 267–273.

RAMSDEN, P. (1985). Student learning research: Retrospect and prospect. *Higher Education Research and Development, 5* (1), 51–70.

RESNICK, L.B. (1987). Learning in school and out. *Educational Researcher, 16* (9), 13–20.

SAMUELOWICZ, K. (1987). Learning problems of overseas students: Two sides of a story. *Higher Education Research & Development, 6,* 121–134.

STEVENSON, H.W., STIGLER, J., LEE, S., LUCKER, G., KITAMURA, S., and HSU, C. (1985). Cognitive performance and academic achievement of Japanese, Chinese and American children. *Child Development, 56,* 718–734.

STEVENSON, H.W. and STIGLER, J.W. (1992). *The learning gap: Why our schools are failing and what we can learn from Japanese and Chinese education.* New York: Summit Books.

SUE, S. and OKAZAKI, S. (1990). Asian–American educational achievements: A phenomenon in search of an explanation. *American Psychologist, 44,* 349–359.

TANG, K.C.C. (1991a). Effects of different assessment procedures on tertiary students' approaches to learning. Doctoral dissertation, University of Hong Kong, Hong Kong.

TANG, K.C.C. (1991b, August 24–28). Spontaneous collaborative learning: Its student characteristics, group dynamics, and effects on the learning process and the learning outcome. Paper presented at the 4th European Conference for Research in Learning and Instruction, Turku, Finland.

TRIANDIS, H.C. (1972). *The analysis of subjective culture.* New York: Wiley.

VON BERTALANFFY, L. (1968). *General systems theory.* New York: Braziller.

WATKINS, D.A. (1983a). Depth of processing and the quality of learning outcomes. *Instructional Science, 12,* 49–58.

WATKINS, D.A. (1983b). Assessing tertiary students' study processes. *Human Learning, 2,* 29–37.

15

Global Self-esteem and the Fall of High Achievers: Australian and Japanese Comparisons[1]

N.T. FEATHER •
I.R. McKEE

An important area of cross-cultural research concerns how people from different cultures regard achievement and how they construe the self. There is now a considerable amount of research literature on self-concept and its influence on thought and action (e.g., Greenwald and Pratkanis, 1984; Higgins, 1987; Markus and Kitayama, 1991; Markus and Wurf, 1987; Rosenberg, 1981; Wylie, 1979). There is also a large body of research on the expression of achievement needs and the personality characteristics of those who have been successful in various fields of endeavour (Atkinson and Feather, 1966; McClelland,

[1] A longer and more detailed account of this study may be found in Feather and McKee (1993).

1985; Spence, 1983). Much of this research has been western based and, therefore, culture bound. However, several authors have emphasised the need to move away from the restrictive lens of a particular culture and to adopt a cross-cultural perspective (Bond, 1986, 1988; Feather, 1975, 1986a, 1986b; Fiske, 1991; Hofstede, 1980; Maehr and Nicholls, 1980; Markus and Kitayama, 1991; Triandis, 1990; Triandis, Bontempo, Villareal, Asai, and Lucca, 1988).

For various reasons cross-cultural research concerned with achievement and self-concept is not easy to pursue. Questions involving the appropriateness of measures, the equivalence of concepts, and the sampling of subjects are difficult to deal with. Yet the topic is an important one because the concepts of self and achievement span different cultures. Our understanding of cross-cultural similarities and differences in attitudes, values, and behaviours should be enhanced by detailed research on how people from different cultures construe both the self and achievement.

Over the past few years Feather and his associates have conducted research in Australia on attitudes towards high achievers and how subjects react to the success or failure of high achievers (Feather, 1989a, 1989b, 1991a, 1992, 1993a, 1993b, in press; Feather, Volkmer, and McKee, 1991). It is commonly asserted that Australians experience a certain amount of satisfaction when "tall poppies" are cut down to size or suffer a major reverse in status. Tall poppies are people who are conspicuously successful or who have high status because of their achievements, rank, or wealth.[2] The dynamics of tall poppy attitudes have been investigated using different samples of Australian subjects. Some of the studies have involved scenarios or vignettes in which achievement status was varied and in which the hypothetical stimulus persons fell from grace (Feather, 1989a, 1989b, 1992). Other studies have investigated attitudes toward high achievers or tall poppies in general, and have examined relations between these attitudes and

[2] The 1982 supplement to the *Oxford English Dictionary* defines "tall poppy" in Australia as "an especially well-paid, privileged, or distinguished person". The 1988 edition of the *Australian national dictionary* defines a "tall poppy" as "a person who is conspicuously successful" and (frequently) as, "one whose distinction, rank, or wealth attracts envious notice or hostility" (Ramson, 1988). The origins of the term can be traced back to ancient times. The Roman historian, Livy, referred to the symbolic decapitation of the heads of the tallest poppies by the elder Tarquinius when walking in his garden. This message was conveyed to his son, Sextus Tarquinius, who then rid himself of the chief men of Gabii and thus delivered the state unresisting to the Roman king.

other variables such as global self-esteem and value priorities (Feather, 1989a, 1989b, 1991a). More recently, Feather and his associates have moved beyond the use of hypothetical scenarios to investigate how people react to the rise and possible fall of highly visible public figures in the Australian culture (Feather et al., 1991). The results of these studies have enhanced our understanding of attitudes towards high achievers and how these attitudes relate to other variables.

This study extends the investigation of attitudes towards high achievers and global self-esteem to another culture, Japan. A comparison was made between the responses of Japanese students and those of Australian students. The hypotheses that were tested were related to previous discussions of Japanese and Australian cultural differences and to the recent analysis of culture and the self provided by Markus and Kitayama (1991). These authors have compared an *independent* view of self with an *interdependent* view. These different views of self are conceptualised as schemata that a person uses to evaluate, organise, and regulate his or her experience and action.

What are the differences between an independent construal of self and an interdependent construal of self? According to Markus and Kitayama (1991), an *independent* construal of self involves viewing the self as separate from others and with a focus on one's unique internal attributes. This view of self as an autonomous, independent person is assumed to be more typical of individuals in western cultures when compared with non-western cultures, although people vary within cultures in the degree to which they construe self as an independent agent.

In contrast, Markus and Kitayama (1991) have proposed that an *interdependent* construal of self is more typical of many non-western cultures. An interdependent construal of self emphasises the connectedness of human beings to each other. A person's autonomy takes second place and the primary task is to fit in with the social context. As Markus and Kitayama (1991) have observed, " . . . the self-knowledge that guides behavior is of self-in-relation to specific others in particular contexts" (p. 227).

What are the implications of this distinction between different construals of self for the present study? Markus and Kitayama (1991) have provided evidence from anthropological, sociological, and social psychological sources that indicates that the Japanese culture emphasises an interdependent construal of self. For example, the anthropologist Lebra (1976) has defined the essence of Japanese culture as an "ethos of social relativism". Belongingness, occupying one's proper place, promoting other's goals, engaging in socially appropriate action, reliance, dependency, empathy, reciprocity, and humility are all important aspects of this ethos.

One implication of this analysis is that Japanese subjects would not be expected to assert the independent construal of self that is implied in western based scales designed to measure global self-esteem. In particular, one would expect them to obtain lower scores on the Rosenberg Self-Esteem Scale (Rosenberg, 1965) when compared with Australian subjects. This scale involves statements such as, "I feel that I am a person of worth, at least on an equal plane with others", and "I feel that I have a number of good qualities". Agreeing with these items implies an independent construal of self rather than an interdependent construal. These kinds of items would be more appropriate for Australian subjects where the construal of self would involve more emphasis on independence and autonomy. Outward expressions of personal worth would be constrained in Japan, however, because they conflict with an interdependent view of self that emphasises the interpersonal context, ingroup cohesion and harmony, and self-effacement. Hence, Japanese subjects should report lower levels of global self-esteem on the Rosenberg Self-Esteem Scale when compared with Australian subjects (Rosenberg, 1965).

There is some evidence to support this hypothesis (Bond and Cheung, 1983; Hama and Plutchnik, 1975; Lebra, 1976; Mahler, 1976). Evidence that responses to the Rosenberg Self-Esteem Scale (Rosenberg, 1965) reflect an independent construal of self has been obtained in Australian studies (Feather, 1985, 1991a, 1991b) that show that global self-esteem is positively related to values concerned with self-direction and achievement and with a personal record of competence.

It is also expected that Australian and Japanese subjects would differ in their attitudes towards high achievers. It has already been mentioned that Australians like to see tall poppies cut down to size. Feather (in press) has examined this belief in an extensive series of studies that investigated variables that influence tall poppy attitudes and how people react to a tall poppy's fall. What kinds of attitudes would the Japanese subjects express towards high achievers? There is a well-known Japanese proverb that "the nail that sticks out gets pounded down". This proverb could be interpreted as the Japanese equivalent of the belief that a tall poppy should be lopped. But it would be misleading to equate the two. Where the Australian phrase "bringing down the tall poppy" is directed at those who stand out by virtue of their eminent status, the Japanese proverb refers more to those who stand out from the group for whatever reason. The protruding nail may cause harm to others and should be levelled in the interests of the group. Thus, the emphasis in the Japanese proverb is more on the negative consequences that individuals may suffer when they deviate from the wishes of the group. The proverb is consistent with an interdependent construal of self because the nail that sticks out implies independent assertion and autonomy and conflicts with the norms for modest and self-effacing behaviour.

The tendency to want to level high achievers should be lower in cultures that emphasise independence, autonomy, and individual achievement. The Australian culture includes a combination of individualism and collectivism and, when compared with Japan, it may be assumed to be more independent and less interdependent insofar as the construal of self is concerned. Hence, it is hypothesised that Japanese subjects would be more likely to agree that tall poppies should fall and that the protruding nail should be levelled when compared with Australian subjects.

This hypothesis does not imply that achievement is not valued in cultures that are interdependent and collectivist in their orientation. The meaning of achievement differs across cultures (Fyans, Salili, Maehr, and Desai, 1983; Maehr and Nicholls, 1980). De Vos (1973) has indicated that the Japanese culture involves a high level of achievement concern but the emphasis is on achievement through the pursuit of group goals rather than via individual goals, although the latter may be attained within the group context. Other authors have described the relation of achievement to group role and status in Japan, the valued achievements being those that are the result of effort directed toward social or group goals rather than the pursuit of personal ambition (Christopher, 1983; Markus and Kitayama, 1991; Weisz, Rothbaum, and Blackburn, 1984).

Finally, this study also investigates relations between global self-esteem and attitudes towards high achievers. The results from previous studies with Australian samples have consistently indicated negative relations between global self-esteem and attitudes favouring the fall of tall poppies. Subjects low on global self-esteem were more likely to want to see tall poppies cut down to size when compared with subjects high on global self-esteem (Feather, 1989a, 1989b, 1991a; Feather et al., 1991). Less consistently, some of the previous studies also indicated positive relations between global self-esteem and favouring the reward of tall poppies for their achievements. These relations tended to be weak and were more likely to occur in student samples (Feather, 1991a; Feather et al., 1991). An attempt is made here to replicate the negative relation between global self-esteem and favouring the fall of tall poppies with the Australian student samples. One can interpret this negative relation as indicating that subjects with a more independent construal of self (higher global self-esteem) are less likely to want to see high achievers lose their high status and are less likely to be happy when they fall.

A similar negative relation between global self-esteem and favouring the fall of tall poppies may also be seen in the Japanese sample but for different reasons. In this case it could be argued that lower scores on the Rosenberg Self-Esteem Scale (Rosenberg, 1965) would probably reflect a more interdependent construal of self. Subjects obtaining low scores would tend to be more modest and self-effacing than those who are less interdependent, not wanting to push themselves forward, and they would be expected to express more negative attitudes towards tall poppies or high achievers who stand too far above the group. Thus, for the Japanese sample, a negative relation between global self-esteem and favouring the fall of tall poppies would reflect individual differences in self-effacement and humility, cultural norms that are linked with collectivist values and an interpersonal construal of self.

It could also be argued, however, that the Japanese subjects may construe some of the items on the Rosenberg Self-Esteem Scale (Rosenberg, 1965) as reflecting an interdependent construal of self, worth being assessed in terms of success in social relationships. If this were the case for many of the items, then higher global self-esteem scores may be associated with interdependence and a stronger desire to see high achievers cut down to size.

It should be clear, therefore, that it is difficult to make a firm prediction about the relationship between global self-esteem and attitudes toward high achievers for the Japanese sample. Such a prediction would depend upon how the scale items are interpreted.

METHOD

The sample comprised 127 Australian students (35 males, 89 females, 3 did not specify gender) who were enrolled in second year under-graduate psychology courses at The Flinders University of South

Australia in 1989. The Flinders University is a relatively small Australian university situated in metropolitan Adelaide. The mean age of the sample was 23.78 years (SD: 6.72).

The Japanese sample comprised 112 students (68 males, 44 females) who were enrolled in second year undergraduate courses in psychology at Keio University in Tokyo in 1989. Keio University is a large, private Japanese university. This university was selected for the study because a colleague worked there who made data collection possible. The mean age of the sample was 21.68 years (SD: 1.04).

Students in both samples completed a questionnaire comprising the Rosenberg Self-Esteem Scale (Rosenberg, 1965), the Tall Poppy Scale (Feather, 1989a), as well as other specially designed items. All sections of the questionnaire were translated into Japanese with the exception of the Rosenberg Self-Esteem Scale which had already been translated earlier. The translation was done by an experienced Japanese translator and it was followed by back-translation into English to ensure comparability and equivalence of meaning (Brislin, 1970). Three translators translated the Tall Poppy Scale so as to ensure that the Japanese translation did not omit colloquial expressions.[3]

The original 10-item version of the Rosenberg Self-Esteem Scale (Rosenberg, 1965) was used. Responses were scored 1 to 5 in the direction of increasing self-esteem and total self-esteem scores ranged from 10 to 50. The internal reliability of the scale was .90 for the Australian sample and .78 for the Japanese sample.

The Tall Poppy Scale (Feather, 1989a) consists of 20 items. Half of the items express positive attitudes towards tall poppies (e.g., "People who are very successful deserve all the rewards they get for their achievements") and the remaining 10 items express negative attitudes (e.g., "Very successful people sometimes need to be brought back a peg or two, even if they have done nothing wrong") (see Table 15.1).

Two scores were obtained based on the subscales of items. The first subscale included 10 items which expressed positive attitudes towards tall poppies. This variable was labelled *favour reward* and scores on it ranged from 10 to 70. The internal reliability of the subscale was .79 for the Australian sample and .80 for the Japanese sample. The second

[3] We are indebted to Hirotaka Mitsui of Keio University who made collection of the Japanese data possible and to Martin Holda, Shoko Yoneyama, and Mark Radford for their assistance in the translation of the questionnaire into Japanese.

subscale included 10 items which expressed negative attitudes towards tall poppies. This variable was labelled *favour fall* and scores on it also ranged from 10 to 70. The internal reliability of the subscale was .80 for the Australian sample and .59 for the Japanese sample.

TABLE 15.1
The Tall Poppy Scale

Item
1. People who are very successful deserve all the rewards they get for their achievements.
2. It's good to see very successful people fail occasionally.
3. Very successful people often get too big for their boots.
4. People who are very successful in what they do are usually friendly and helpful to others.
5. At school it's probably better for students to be near the middle of the class than the very top student.
6. People shouldn't criticise or knock the very successful.
7. Very successful people who fall from the top usually deserve their fall from grace.
8. Those who are very successful ought to come down off their pedestals and be like other people.
9. The very successful person should receive public recognition for his/her accomplishments.
10. People who are 'tall poppies' should be cut down to size.
11. One should always respect the person at the top.
12. One ought to be sympathetic to very successful people when they experience failure and fall from their very high positions.
13. Very successful people sometimes need to be brought back a peg or two, even if they have done nothing wrong.
14. Society needs a lot of very high achievers.
15. People who always do a lot better than others need to learn what it's like to fail.
16. People who are right at the top usually deserve their high position.
17. It's very important for society to support and encourage people who are very successful.
18. People who are very successful get too full of their own importance.
19. Very successful people usually succeed at the expense of other people.
20. Very successful people who are at the top of their field are usually fun to be with.

Note: Items 1, 4, 6, 9, 11, 12, 14, 16, 17 and 20 comprise the Favour Reward subscale; items 2, 3, 5, 7, 8, 10, 13, 15, 18 and 19 comprise the Favour Fall subscale.

RESULTS

The mean scores for global self-esteem, for the favour reward and the favour fall variables are presented in Table 15.2. Also presented in the table are the correlations between these variables.

TABLE 15.2

Mean Scores and Correlations between Global Self-esteem and Tall Poppy Attitudes for Japanese and Australian Samples

Variable	Japanese Sample		Correlations		
	Mean	SD	Global Self-esteem	Favour Reward	Favour Fall
Global Self-esteem	31.19	5.88	–	.11	−.15
Favour Reward	48.41	8.50	.09	–	−.12
Favour Fall	45.37	6.73	−.24**	−.33***	
	Australian Mean	39.32	47.58	34.17	
	Sample SD	6.36	8.55	9.09	

Notes: Ns varied from 108 to 109 for the Japanese sample and from 122 to 126 for the Australian sample due to missing cases. Correlations for the Japanese sample are above the diagonal; correlations for the Australian sample are below the diagonal. Tests of significance are two-tailed.

** $p<.01$; *** $p<.001$.

Comparison of mean scores of the Japanese and Australian students indicated that the Japanese students had a significantly higher mean score than the Australian students for the favour fall variable (means of 45.37 and 34.17 respectively, $t(233)$: 10.60, $p<.001$), but the difference in the mean favour reward scores of the two groups was not statistically significant (means of 48.41 and 47.58 respectively, $t(230)$: .75, ns). However, the mean global self-esteem score was significantly lower for the Japanese sample than for the Australian sample (means of 31.19 and 39.32 respectively, $t(233)$: −10.11, $p<.001$).

The statistically significant differences that were observed for global self-esteem and favour fall variables were consistent with the predictions of this study.

The correlations in Table 15.2 show that, as predicted, global self-esteem and favour fall variables were negatively correlated for the

Australian sample. There was also a negative correlation between favour fall and favour reward variables, thus confirming the results obtained with other Australian samples (Feather, 1989a, 1989b, 1991a; Feather et al., 1991). Both these correlations were statistically significant.

None of the correlations in Table 15.2 were statistically significant for the Japanese sample, although the correlations were in the same direction as the respective correlations for the Australian sample. However, when items 7 and 8 with low item/total correlations were deleted from the favour fall scale so as to improve the scale's internal reliability, the negative correlation between global self-esteem and favour fall variables for the Japanese sample increased in size and was statistically significant ($r(106)$: $-.25$, $p <$ .01). Following this item deletion, the correlation between the shorter 8-item favour fall scale and the 10-item favour reward scale was also statistically significant ($r(107)$: $-.24$, $p <$ .05).

DISCUSSION

The data in Table 15.2 indicate strong cultural differences in global self-esteem and in attitudes towards the fall of high achievers that were consistent with a theoretical analysis in which it was assumed that the Japanese culture involves a more interdependent construal of self and a less independent construal of self when compared with the Australian culture. The correlations between variables were also consistent with this theoretical analysis, but more so for the Australian sample. Overall, the evidence indicated that both groups valued achievement and were similar in their attitudes towards rewarding high achievers. But the Japanese students had lower global self-esteem and they were more in favour of seeing the high achiever or tall poppy cut down to size. For the Japanese, the high achiever or tall poppy could not stand apart from the group or collectivity. The protruding nail had to be pounded down in accordance with an interdependent construal of self. Moreover, the lower global self-esteem scores of the Japanese students implied that for them the self had to be presented in a modest and self-effacing way, in contrast to the more independent construal of self in many western societies.

This research could be expanded in a number of different ways. It would obviously be advantageous to use larger samples that are more representative of the general population in order to determine whether the observed differences could be generalised to the population at large and are not restricted to student samples. It would be useful to sample a range of cultures that vary in their construals of self and basic values. Some cultural comparisons may reveal even more dramatic differences than those reported here. It would also be of value to use more differentiated measures of self-esteem that, for example, enable one to distinguish between the academic self, the social self, the physical self, and the moral self (e.g., Byrne and Shavelson, 1987; Marsh and O'Neill, 1984).

Finally, it would be important to go beyond general attitudes towards high achievers and to investigate how people in different cultures react to high achievers in particular domains (for example, politics, sports, entertainment) and the kinds of variables that influence their attitudes. A fair amount of research on these issues has been conducted in Australia (Feather, 1989a, 1989b, 1991a, 1992, in press; Feather et al., 1991) but such research efforts need to be extended to other countries to test the generality of cultural similarities and differences. Studies that vary the particular conditions under which tall poppies achieve their success or suffer a fall are needed in order to identify the culture specific contextual variables that are important in the cultures that are being compared, as well as the variables that are important across all cultures (e.g., Feather and McKee, 1992). The results of studies with Australian samples have provided new information about how human values, causal attributions, perceptions of justice, deservingness, self-esteem, and personality characteristics affect attitudes towards high achievers and their possible fall.

On a more general level, the research programme illustrates how detailed analysis of what is thought to be a unique cultural characteristic ("cutting down tall poppies") can be expanded cross-culturally, providing new insights into a range of variables that have more general significance for attitudes towards high achievers. The strategy of identifying attitudes and beliefs that are commonly held to be unique to one's own culture, and then examining whether similar attitudes and beliefs are present in other cultures, is useful for determining what is unique in a culture and what it shares with other cultures. This kind of research also provides a context for investigating how values operate within cultures with regard to attitudes, beliefs, and the construal of self. The shared beliefs of a culture may be linked to a deeper functional base that includes values and the maintenance and enhancement of a culturally defined selfhood.

REFERENCES

ATKINSON, J.W. and FEATHER, N.T. (Eds.). (1966). *A theory of achievement motivation.* New York: Wiley.

BOND, M. (1986). *The psychology of the Chinese people.* New York: Oxford University Press.

BOND, M. (Ed.). (1988). *The cross-cultural challenge to social psychology.* Beverly Hills, CA: Sage.

BOND, M. and CHEUNG, T. (1983). College students' spontaneous self-concept. *Journal of Cross-Cultural Psychology, 14,* 153–171.

BRISLIN, R.W. (1970). Back-translation for cross-cultural research. *Journal of Cross-Cultural Psychology, 1,* 185–216.

BYRNE, B.M. and SHAVELSON, R.J. (1987). Adolescent self-concept: Testing the assumptions of equivalent structure across gender. *American Educational Research Journal, 24,* 365–385.

CHRISTOPHER, R.C. (1983). *The Japanese mind: The goliath explained.* New York: Linden Press.

DE VOS, G.A. (1973). *Socialization for achievement: Essays on the cultural psychology of the Japanese.* Berkeley, CA: University of California Press.

FEATHER, N.T. (1975). *Values in education and society.* New York: Free Press.

FEATHER, N.T. (1985). Masculinity, femininity, self-esteem, and subclinical depression. *Sex Roles, 12,* 491–500.

FEATHER, N.T. (1986a). Cross-cultural studies with the Rokeach Value Survey: The Flinders program of research on values. *Australian Journal of Psychology, 38,* 269–283.

FEATHER, N.T. (1986b). Value systems across cultures; Australia and China. *International Journal of Psychology, 21,* 697–715.

FEATHER, N.T (1989a). Attitudes towards the high achiever: The fall of the tall poppy. *Australian Journal of Psychology, 41,* 239–267.

FEATHER, N.T. (1989b). The fall of the high achiever: Research into attitudes toward the tall poppy. In J.P. Forgas and J.M. Innes (Eds.), *Recent advances in social psychology: An international perspective* (pp. 7–20). Amsterdam: Elsevier Science Publishers.

FEATHER, N.T. (1991a). Attitudes towards the high achiever: Effects of perceiver's own level of competence. *Australian Journal of Psychology, 43,* 121–124.

FEATHER, N.T. (1991b). Human values, global self-esteem, and belief in a just world. *Journal of Personality, 59,* 83–107.

FEATHER, N.T. (1992). An attributional and value analysis of deservingness in success and failure situations. *British Journal of Social Psychology, 31,* 125–145.

FEATHER, N.T. (1993a). Authoritarianism and attitudes toward high achievers. *Journal of Personality and Social Psychology, 65*, 152–164.

FEATHER, N.T. (1993b). The rise and fall of political leaders: Attributions, deservingness, personality, and affect. *Australian Journal of Psychology, 45*, 61–68.

FEATHER, N.T. (in press). Attitudes toward high achievers and reactions to their fall: Theory and research concerning tall poppies. (Forthcoming in *Advances in Experimental Social Psychology*, Vol. 26). Orlando, FL: Academic Press.

FEATHER, N.T., VOLKMER, R.E., and McKEE, I.R. (1991). Attitudes towards high achievers in public life: Attributions, deservingness, personality, and affect. *Australian Journal of Psychology, 43*, 85–91.

FEATHER, N.T. and McKEE, I.R. (1992). Australian and Japanese attitudes towards the fall of high achievers. *Australian Journal of Psychology, 44*, 87–93.

FEATHER, N.T. and McKEE, I.R. (1993). Global self-esteem and attitudes toward the high achiever for Australian and Japanese students. *Social Psychology Quarterly, 56*, 65–76.

FISKE, A.P. (1991). *Structures of social life: The four elementary forms of human relations.* New York: Free Press.

FYANS, L.J., SALILI, F., MAEHR, M.L., and DESAI, K.A. (1983). A cross-cultural exploration into the meaning of achievement. *Journal of Personality and Social Psychology, 44*, 1000–1013.

GREENWALD, A.G. and PRATKANIS, A.R. (1984). The self. In R.S. Wyer and T.K. Srull (Eds.), *Handbook of social cognition* (pp. 129–178). Hillsdale, NJ: Erlbaum.

HAMA, H. and PLUTCHNIK, R. (1975). Personality profile of Japanese college students: A normative study. *Japanese Psychological Research, 17*, 141–146.

HIGGINS, E.T. (1987). Self-discrepancy: A theory relating to self and affect. *Psychological Review, 94*, 319–340.

HOFSTEDE, G. (1980). *Culture's consequences: International differences in work-related values.* Beverly Hills, CA: Sage.

LEBRA, T.S. (1976). *Japanese patterns of behavior.* Honolulu: University of Hawaii Press.

McCLELLAND, D.C. (1985). *Human motivation.* Glenview, Il: Scott, Foresman and Co.

MAEHR, M.L. and NICHOLLS, J.G. (1980). Culture and achievement motivation: A second look. In N. Warren (Ed.), *Studies in cross-cultural psychology* (Vol. 2, pp. 221–267). London: Academic Press.

MAHLER, L. (1976). What is the self-concept in Japan? *Psychologia, 19*, 127–132.

MARKUS, H.R. and KITAYAMA, S. (1991). Culture and the self: Implications for cognition, emotion, and motivation. *Psychological Review, 98*, 224–253.

MARKUS, H.R. and WURF, E. (1987). The dynamic self-concept: A social psychological perspective. *Annual Review of Psychology, 38*, 299–337.

MARSH, H.W. and O'NEILL, R. (1984). Self-Description Questionnaire III (SDQ III): The construct validity of multidimensional self-concept ratings by late adolescents. *Journal of Educational Measurement, 21*, 153–174.

RAMSON, W.S. (1988). *Australian national dictionary.* Melbourne: Oxford University Press.

ROSENBERG, M. (1965). *Society and the adolescent self-image.* Princeton, NJ: Princeton University Press.

ROSENBERG, M. (1981). The self-concept: Social product and social force. In M. Rosenberg and R.H. Turner (Eds.), *Social psychology: Sociological perspectives* (pp. 593–624). New York: Basic Books.

Spence, J.T. (Ed.). (1983). *Achievement and achievement motives: Psychological and sociological approaches*. San Francisco: Freeman.

Triandis, H.L. (1990). Cross-cultural studies of individualism and collectivism. In J.J. Berman (Ed.), *Nebraska symposium on motivation 1989: Cross-cultural perspectives* (pp. 41–133). Lincoln: University of Nebraska Press.

Triandis, H.C., Bontempo, R., Villareal, M.J., Asai, M., and Lucca, N. (1988). Individualism and collectivism: Cross-cultural perspectives on self-ingroup relationships. *Journal of Personality and Social Psychology, 54*, 323–338.

Weisz, J.R., Rothbaum, F.M., and Blackburn, T.C. (1984). Standing out and standing in: The psychology of control in America and Japan. *American Psychologist, 39*, 955–969.

Wylie, R. (1979). *The self-concept: Vol. 2. Theory and research on selected topics*. Lincoln: University of Nebraska Press.

16

The Cross-Cultural Validity of the Shavelson Model of Self-esteem

DAVID WATKINS*

CROSS-CULTURAL MEASUREMENT OF SELF-ESTEEM

Personality measurement is a difficult task even within one's own culture. Bond and Tak-sing (1983) have criticised many early cross-cultural studies on self-esteem for basically involving the administration of an American developed test of self-esteem in a non-western country, after translation if necessary. The tests were then scored, the results compared to American norms, and a "conclusion" was drawn about the relative level of self-esteem in each society. Cross-cultural psychologists have consistently pointed out the drawbacks of such an approach. It assumes what Hui and Triandis (1985) have referred to as scalar equivalence, that is, that the construct of interest is measured on the

*The Nepalese and Nigerian investigations were supported by funds from the Committee on Research and Conference Grants, University of Hong Kong.

same metric in different cultures. Such a level of equivalence is very hard to establish and involves demonstrating conceptual, construct operational, and item equivalence. It certainly cannot be assumed unquestioningly (Poortinga, 1989). However, for many research purposes all that needs to be demonstrated is that the instruments measure equivalent concepts and that the relationships between variables are comparable. If it can be shown that a western measure of self-esteem is embedded in the same network of constructs in both countries then one can be fairly confident that the measure is conceptually, functionally, and operationally equivalent in both cultures and one is also in a much stronger position to claim scalar equivalence (Hui and Triandis, 1985). As Shavelson, Hubner, and Stanton (1976) have pointed out, this involves testing both within-construct and between-construct portions of the nomological network.

MEASUREMENT FROM EMIC AND ETIC PERSPECTIVES

For years Third World psychologists have been questioning the appropriateness of western psychological concepts in cross-cultural settings (Enriquez, 1977). Bond and Tak-sing (1983) have pointed out that there has been relatively little self-concept research in non-western cultures. According to them, one reason for this is that western societies tend to have an ideological bias towards individualism. Cultures high on collectivism tend to downplay the role of self in determining behaviour (Markus and Kitayama, 1991; Triandis, 1989). Hence, there is doubt about the relevance of models of self-esteem developed in western, individualist cultures.

Before one can make cross-cultural comparisons one needs to clarify the meaning of the constructs which are of interest in each culture. Berry (1989) has indicated two fundamentally different approaches to deciding what to measure—the "emic" and the "etic". The former approach utilises only concepts that emerge from within a particular culture and is associated with the traditions of anthropology. The latter approach seeks to compare different cultures on what are thought to be universal categories. The danger with the "etic" approach is that it is all too easy to administer a test developed in one culture and add up the results without demonstrating the relevance of the construct or the validity of the instrument for the new culture—"pseudo etic" research (Triandis, 1972).

It is contended that progress can be made by adopting either perspective and that full understanding requires a combination of both. In this paper the validity of one of the few well developed western self-concept models is investigated for a range of cultures.

THE CROSS-CULTURAL VALIDITY OF THE SHAVELSON MODEL: AN ETIC APPROACH

Self-concept has long been regarded by many psychologists as a fundamental personality variable. Consequently, a considerable amount of research has focused on how self-concept develops and can be enhanced. Unfortunately, as reviews in this area by Wylie (1974, 1979) have highlighted, these research findings are seldom clear cut. Wylie attributed much of the blame for this situation to the poor quality of instruments measuring self-concept available at that time.

The proposal by Shavelson, Hubner, and Stanton (1976) of a hierarchical model of self-concept has been recognised as heralding a major advance in this area of research (Briggs and Cheek, 1986; Hattie, 1992). Shavelson's model has been operationalised in a number of instruments with excellent psychometric properties, which is certainly not typical of the area (Wylie, 1974). These include the Self Description Questionnaire (SDQ; Marsh, Barnes, Cairns, and Tidman, 1984), the Self Rating Scale (Fleming and Courtney, 1984), the About Myself Scale (Song and Hattie, 1984), the Academic Self-Concept Scale (Reynolds, 1988), and the Personal and Academic Self-Concept Inventory (PASCI; Fleming and Whalen, 1990). The use of such scales has helped to clarify not only the nomological network into which self-concept is entwined (Byrne, 1986) but also the influence of age and gender on self-concept (Byrne and Shavelson, 1986; Marsh et al., 1984). The purpose of this paper is to review recent evidence regarding the cross-cultural validity of this model.

The Shavelson Model

Shavelson and associates have argued that an ideal definition of self concept would involve both within-construct specifications (what the features of the construct are and how they are linked together) and between-construct specifications (how these features of self-concept are related to other constructs). They went on to identify seven critical aspects of the definition of self-concept and, in particular, to formulate a hierarchical and multifaceted model (HMFM) of self-concept. According to the HMFM, general self-concept is at the apex of the hierarchy, supporting increasingly more specific aspects (facets) as one moves down the hierarchy. The lowest levels represent evaluation of behaviours in specific situations, whereas intermediate levels represent more general constructs (factors, in the factor analytic sense). Higher levels (e.g., social or physical self) are potentially higher order factors, though some existing scales are aimed at the direct measurement of these levels.

These researchers have utilised factor analysis to demonstrate that a hierarchical, multifaceted structure underlies responses to these instruments. These studies have strengthened the construct validity both of the HMFM and of the instruments used to measure it. However, some investigations have indicated that revisions to the original formulation may be necessary. For example, physical appearance is more highly correlated with social self-esteem than with physical abilities (Fleming and Courtney, 1984; Marsh and Shavelson, 1985), calling into question the notion of a second order physical self-esteem factor, and suggesting instead a second order "self-presentational" factor. Also, research has shown verbal and math self-esteem to be nearly uncorreleated, even though support for a second order academic factor still exists (Byrne and Shavelson, 1986). At this point it seems fair to say that the major facets (factors) beyond the very lowest level can be measured and are useful, but that the structure of the hierarchy is still fuzzy in certain places.

Cross-Cultural Validity

Although the research evidence supporting at least the within-construct validity of these instruments based on the Shavelson model is quite impressive the great bulk of these investigations has been conducted in the USA, Canada, or Australia—all developed countries with similar cultural heritages. This paper reviews recent evidence from several Asian countries using both high school and college students and a variety of self-esteem questionnaires all based on the Shavelson model (see Table 16.1).

All these investigations with only one possible exception supported the factor structure intended by the test designers and consequently the self-concept model on which they were based. The odd case out is that of Watkins, Fleming, and Regmi (1990) utilising PASCI with Nepalese college students. In their study exploratory factor analysis was encouraging but the fit of the responses to the underlying factor model predicted by the SDQ was not strong enough to satisfy the goodness-of-fit tests of confirmatory factor analysis. The results of one of the other studies (Watkins and Gutierrez, 1989) will be described in some detail.

WATKINS AND GUTIERREZ (1989)

Method

Subjects

The subjects were 194 students (64 per cent female) who were in their first year of study at a large public high school in Manila. This school generally had students from lower to middle class families, which represent the great bulk of Filipinos. The subjects were between 11 to 12 years of age and fluent in speaking and reading English.

Self-Description Questionnaire (SDQ)

The version of the SDQ adopted for this study consisted of 76 items designed to measure 7 factors based on Shavelson's hierarchical model of self-concept and a general self-scale derived from the Rosenberg (1965) Self-Esteem Scale (see Marsh, 1988 for further details and for

TABLE 16.1

Summary of Cross-Cultural Factor Analytic Research on the Shavelson Model of Self-esteem

Country	Researchers	Subjects	Instruments	Factor Analytic Approach
Philippines	Watkins, Fleming, and Alfon	198 psychology undergraduates	Self-Rating Scale	Confirmatory
Philippines	Watkins and Gutierrez	194 public high school students	Self-Description Questionnaire	Exploratory
Philippines	Watkins and Astilla*	184 elite private high school students	About Myself Scale	Exploratory
Korea	Song and Hattie	2,297 high school students	About Myself Scale	Confirmatory
Hong Kong	Lo	582 high school students	Expanded Chinese version of SDQ	Confirmatory
Hong Kong	Chung	146 high school students	SDQ (Chinese translation)	Exploratory
Nepal	Watkins, Hattie, and Regmi*	398 elite high school students	About Myself Scale	Exploratory
Nepal	Watkins, Fleming, and Regmi*	302 university students	Personal and Academic Self-Concept Inventory	Exploratory
Nepal	Watkins, Lam, and Regmi	404 elite high school students	Self-Description Questionnaire	Exploratory
Nigeria	Watkins and Akande	462 public high school students	Self-Description Questionnaire	Exploratory

* Unpublished research.

evidence of the reliability and validity of the SDQ scales). The subjects responded to each of the items, some of them negatively worded, along a 5-point response scale: false; mostly false; sometimes false sometimes true; mostly true; true. A brief description of the 8 SDQ scales is as follows:

1. Physical Abilities/Sports (Phys)—student ratings of their ability and enjoyment of physical activities, sports and games (9 items);
2. Physical Appearance (Appr)—student ratings of their own attractiveness, how their appearance compares with others, and how others think they look (9 items);
3. Peer Relations (Peer)—student ratings of how easily they make friends, their popularity, and whether others want them as a friend (9 items);
4. Parent Relations (Prnt)—student ratings of how well they get along with their parents and whether they like their parents (9 items);
5. Reading (Read)—student ratings of their ability in and their enjoyment/interest in reading (10 items);
6. Mathematics (Math)—student ratings of their ability in and their enjoyment/interest in mathematics (10 items);
7. General-School (Schl)—student ratings of their ability in and their enjoyment/interest in "all school subjects" (10 items);
8. General-Self (Genr)—student ratings of themselves as effective, capable individuals, who are proud and satisfied with the way they are (10 items).

The items of the SDQ had previously been read by two Filipino educators who judged the level of English involved, which was found suitable for students at the high school level.

Procedure

The SDQ was administered to the subjects during normal class periods. Their most recent school grades in English, Maths and Science were obtained from school records. The subject's gender was also recorded (and coded M = 1, F = 2) to allow investigation of gender differences in responding to the SDQ.

Analysis

The SPSS[x] computer programme (Hull and Nie, 1984) was utilised to calculate variable intercorrelations and scale reliabilities and to conduct item analyses and exploratory factor analysis. The latter involved using iterated communality estimates, a Kaiser normalisation, and an oblique rotation.

Due to the small number of variables (items) per subject (194:76, far less than the recommended 5:1 or large ratio) responses to trios of items from the scale were summed to form a new variable, which was used as a basis of the factor analysis (responses to the negatively worded items were reversed so that a higher scale score indicated higher self-esteem). Marsh, Barnes, Cairns, and Tidman (1984) have argued that this item summing procedure is preferable to factoring responses to individual items for the reason cited earlier (to increase the subject: variable ratio). In addition, the new variables would be more reliable than individual items and the factor loadings would be less affected by the unique variance of individual items.

Results and Discussion

Item and Scale Analysis

The internal consistency reliability coefficients $\propto$'s for the 8 SDQ scales ranged from 0.61 (Genr) to 0.85 (Math) with a mean r_{tt}: of 0.71. Each of the 3 total scores is based on more items than the specific scales hence their reliabilities are higher (mean r_{tt}: 0.86). While not as high as the figures reported by Marsh (1988) for Australian students these $\propto$'s are quite encouraging considering the Filipino context, where English is not the first language, and the relatively short scales of the SDQ.

Item analyses of the SDQ scales indicated some weak items (4 items had corrected item-scale correlations below 0.20) but the majority were quite reasonable (the median corrected item-scale correlations for the 8 SDQ scales ranged from 0.30 to 0.59, the mean of the median r's: 0.43). While negatively worded items tended to have lower item-scale correlations, it was not considered that this trend was strong enough to justify omitting these items from the SDQ scales as Marsh and associates (1984) have argued should be done for young children.

Factor Analysis

Factor analysis of the responses to the SDQ item trios generally supported the factors the SDQ was designed to measure. Both the eigen values greater than 1.00 and the Scree test criteria indicated that a 6 factor solution would be most appropriate. The factor pattern matrix for the 6 factor oblique solution (which accounted for 51 per cent of the variance) is shown in Table 16.2.

Factor loadings for each variable were consistently high on the factor that it was designed to measure (most exceeded 0.60 and only 1 out of 18 was less than 0.30) and low on other factors. The exceptions were the School scale variables which tended to be split on the Reading and Maths factors (Factors V and VI, respectively). When the General Self-scale (not strictly a Shavelson factor) was included in the factor analysis it tended to load on the Peer scale.

Factor analysis of responses to the first 7 SDQ scales again provided strong support for an underlying general factor as predicted by Shavelson's model. The size of the eigen values clearly indicated a single factor which each of the SDQ scales loaded significantly upon (the range of factor loadings was 0.37 to 0.84 and the mean loading was 0.56).

Between-Construct Validity

To date the main support for the Shavelson model has been provided by factor analytic evidence. Thus the focus has been on within-construct aspects of this model. More evidence is needed of between-construct validity both in western and non-western countries. Some support for discriminant validity has been provided by studies which have shown that maths grades of Filipino pupils correlated most highly with their scores on the Maths self-esteem rather than other SDQ subscales (Watkins and Gutierrez, 1989); that Nepalese and Filipino college students' estimates of the quality of their family relationships correlated most highly with the "About Myself" family self-esteem scale (Watkins, Hattie, and Regmi, 1993); and that Hong Kong

TABLE 16.2
Factor Pattern Matrix of Responses to the Self-Description Questionnaire (SDQ)

Self-concept Areas	I	II	III	IV	V	VI
Physical Abilities						
1	.74	−.07	−.03	.02	.01	−.01
2	.72	.05	−.08	.02	.10	.03
3	.74	.00	.08	.04	−.08	.05
Physical Appearance						
1	.02	.64	.05	.03	.04	−.07
2	.03	.62	.07	.08	.10	.00
3	.25	.42	.40	.04	.12	−.03
Relationship with Peers						
1	.00	−.05	.34	.16	.19	−.06
2	.06	.15	.23	.20	.19	.03
3	.10	.24	.60	.07	−.08	.07
Relationship with Parents						
1	.08	.07	.02	.41	−.09	.19
2	.03	.18	−.10	.66	−.06	.01
3	.04	−.12	.09	.69	.04	−.08
Reading						
1	.04	.19	.00	−.17	.65	.06
2	.05	.05	−.13	.02	.80	−.10
3	.06	−.07	.20	−.01	.65	.11
Mathematics						
1	.11	−.08	−.03	.09	.02	.71
2	.03	−.05	.05	−.04	−.05	.88
3	.00	.03	−.03	−.06	.02	.85
School						
1	.00	.37	−.06	.14	.24	.25
2	.14	.16	.01	.25	.23	.32
3	−.03	−.03	.25	.15	.46	.33

secondary school students' scores on peer and social self subscales were the PASCI scales which correlated most highly with assessment of their social skills and were the scales which most strongly revealed the benefit of a social skills training programme (Chung, 1991).

CONCLUSIONS

The research reviewed in this paper is based on responses of subjects from several Asian cultures to a range of different self-esteem questionnaires. The samples include students from both high school and college level and from both privileged and average family backgrounds. The great majority of these studies support the within-construct validity both of the particular measuring instruments and the underlying Shavelson model of self-esteem. Evidence based on both exploratory and confirmatory factor analysis generally confirmed both the expected lower order self-esteem facets and a higher order underlying general self factor. Moreover, this paper provides some evidence of the between-construct validity of the model.

While the research evidence presented here is promising, further research is required to demonstrate the validity of the Shavelson model cross-culturally. As with western research, it is not yet possible to determine how appropriate the model is with non-student samples. However, it is clear that very different facets of self-esteem will be required for non-student populations irrespective of their cultural background. Such different facets can only emerge if subjects are allowed a free response format where they can volunteer the aspects of self which are important to them. Such a format would also permit an exploration of indigenous notions of the self. Questionnaires developed by indigenous methods can then be administered together with current western instruments. Factor analysis of items from the two questionnaires together should indicate the degree of overlap between the "indigenous" and "imported" instruments and the models of self on which they are based.

REFERENCES

BERRY, J. (1989). Imposed etics-emics-derived etics: The operationalization of a compelling idea. *International Journal of Psychology, 24,* 721–735.

BOND, M.H. and TAK-SING, C. (1983). College student's spontaneous self-concept. *Journal of Cross-Cultural Psychology, 14,* 153–171.

BRIGGS, S.R. and CHEEK, J.M. (1986). The role of factor analysis in the development and evaluation of personality scales. *Journal of Personality, 54,* 106–147.

BYRNE, B.M. (1986). Self-concept/academic achievement relations: An investigation of dimensionality, stability, and causality. *Canadian Journal of Behavioural Science, 18*, 173–186.

BYRNE, B.M. and SHAVELSON, R.J. (1986). On the structure of adolescent self-concept. *Journal of Educational Psychology, 78*, 474–481.

CHUNG, C.H. (1991). An empirical investigation of the effects of social skills training on a group of F2 students. Unpublished M.Ed. dissertation, University of Hong Kong, Hong Kong.

ENRIQUEZ, V.G. (1977). Filipino psychology in the Third World. *Philippine Journal of Psychology, 10*, 3–17.

FLEMING, J.S. and COURTNEY, B.E. (1984). The dimensionality of self-esteem: II. Hierarchical facet model for revised measurement scales. *Journal of Personality and Social Psychology, 46*, 404–421.

FLEMING, J.S. and WHALEN, D.J. (1990). The personal and academic self concept inventory. *Educational and Psychological Measurement, 50*, 197–204.

HATTIE, J. (1992). *The self-concept.* Hillsdale, NJ: Lawrence Erlbaum.

HUI, C.H. and TRIANDIS, H. (1985). Measurement in cross-cultural psychology: A review and comparison of strategies. *Journal of Cross-Cultural Psychology, 16*, 131–152.

HULL, C.H. and NIE, N.H. (1984). *SPSS-X.* New York: McGraw-Hill.

LO, M.F. (1989). Self-concept: Interpretations as a psychological construct and relations with sex and achievement. In S. Winter (Ed.), *The Hong Kong adolescent.* University of Hong Kong: Education Department.

MARKUS, H.R. and KITAYAMA, S. (1991). Cultural variation in the self-concept. In J. Strauss and G.R. Goethals (Eds.), *The self: Interdisciplinary approaches.* New York: Springer-Verlag.

MARSH, H.W. (1988). *The Self-Description Questionnaire I: SDQ Manual and Research Monograph.* San Antonio: The Psychological Corporation.

MARSH, H.W., BARNES, J., CAIRNS, L., and TIDMAN, M. (1984). Self-Description Questionnaire: Age and sex effects in the structure and level of self-concept for preadolescent children. *Journal of Educational Psychology, 76*, 940–956.

MARSH, H.W. and SHAVELSON, R.J. (1985). Self-concept: Its multifaceted, hierarchical structure. *Educational Psychologist, 20*, 107–123.

POORTINGA, Y.H. (1989). Equivalence of cross-cultural data: An overview of basic issues. *International Journal of Psychology, 24*, 737–756.

REYNOLDS, D. (1988). Academic Self-Concept Scale. *Journal of Personality Assessment, 52*, 223–240.

SHAVELSON, R.J., HUBNER, J.R., and STANTON, G.C. (1976). Self-concept: Validation of construct interpretation. *Review of Educational Research, 46*, 407–441.

SONG, I.S. and HATTIE, J. (1984). Home environment, self-concept, and academic achievement: A causal modeling approach. *Journal of Educational Psychology, 76*, 1269–1281.

TRIANDIS, H.C. (1972). *The analysis of subjective culture.* New York: Wiley.

TRIANDIS, H.C. (1989). The self and social behavior in differing cultural contexts. *Psychological Review, 96*, 506–520.

WATKINS, D. and AKANDE, D. (1992). The internal structure of the Self-Description Questionnaire: A Nigerian investigation. (Forthcoming in *British Journal of Educational Psychology*.)

WATKINS, D., FLEMING, J.S., and ALFON, M.C.A. (1989). A test of Shavelson's hierarchical multifaceted self-concept model in a Filipino college sámple. *International Journal of Psychology, 24*, 367–379.

WATKINS, D., FLEMING, J., and REGMI, M. (1990). The factor structure of PASCI with Nepalese students. Unpublished study.

WATKINS, D. and GUTIERREZ, M. (1989). The structure of self-concept: Some Filipino evidence. *Australian Psychologist, 24*, 401–410.

WATKINS, D., HATTIE, J., and REGMI, M. (1993). Internal structure of "About Myself" questionnaire for Nepalese students. Unpublished research, University of Hong Kong.

WATKINS, D., LAM, M.K., and REGMI, M. (1991). Cross-cultural assessment of self-esteem: A Nepalese investigation. *Psychologia, 34*, 98–108.

WYLIE, R.C. (1974). *The self-concept: Vol 1*. Nebraska: University of Nebraska Press.

WYLIE, R.C. (1979). *The self-concept: Vol 2*. Nebraska: University of Nebraska Press.

17

Exploring the Basis of Self-esteem of Urban and Rural Nepalese Children

DAVID WATKINS •
MURARI P. REGMI

Self-esteem research has long been plagued by problems of inadequate theoretical conceptualisation and poor questionnaire development and evaluation (Wylie, 1974). Wylie pointed out that it may be best to treat self-esteem as a multidimensional construct rather than measure an individual's self-esteem as if it were global or as a simple total score. Fortunately, the situation has improved following the development of a multifaceted, hierarchical model of the self by Shavelson, Hubner, and Stanton (1976). This model has served as the basis for the development of several questionnaires validated with the aid of the latest techniques of causal modelling (Fleming, 1986; Marsh and Shavelson, 1985; Song and Hattie, 1984). These instruments and the underlying model have been shown to be valid for student samples in a number of developing countries (Watkins, 1992).

However, these instruments, like most other well known measures of self-esteem assume that individuals share the same components of self—typically covering areas like school, family, friends, and personal appearance (see Table 17.1). The major drawback of questions preset by the researcher is that they may focus on aspects of life which are not salient for an individual subject (McGuire and Padawer-Singer, 1976). Alternatively, some aspect salient for that subject may be omitted. Self-esteem questionnaires also typically fail to allow for developmental and cultural, let alone individual, differences in value systems (Juhasz, 1985; Watkins, 1978). Of course, even if the dimensions of self are salient for an individual this does not necessarily mean that they are of equal importance to the subject as these questionnaires assume. Theorists since the time of William James have argued to the contrary that an individual's self-esteem should weight each aspect of the self according to its subjective importance to that subject (James, 1890; Marsh, 1986; Wylie, 1974).

While previous research indicates that the multidimensional Shavelson model of self and the questionnaires based on it are appropriate for Nepalese students (Watkins and Regmi, 1991), the question may still be asked if a country like Nepal with its strong Hindu traditions and relative isolation from western influences may well have indigenous dimensions of self not tapped by these questionnaires. In addition, there may be differences between the basic components of self of relatively affluent and modernised urban children and poorer more traditional rural children. The possibility of developmental and gender differences also needs to be explored. Depending on the findings of this study it may be possible to develop culturally appropriate self-esteem instruments, separately if need be for age, gender, and rural/urban subgroups. Or, it may be that little agreement about the salience of life areas even for subgroups of Nepalese children is found. It may then be necessary to develop self-esteem instruments which allow individual Nepalese to choose their own individual life areas. This would be of particular importance if the instruments are to be used for other than research purposes where the emphasis is on group rather than individual trends.

TABLE 17.1
Subscales of 5 Well Known Children's Self-Esteem Questionnaires

Self-Esteem Inventory (Coopersmith, 1959)	Piers-Harris Children's Self-Concept Scale (Piers and Harris, 1969)	Perceived Competence Scale for Children (Harter, 1982)	Self-Description Questionnaire 1 (Marsh, 1988)	Self-Concept Inventory (Sears, 1963)
Self and Peers	Popularity	Social	Peer Relations	Social Relations/Virtues
Academic	Intellectual and School Status	Cognitive	Academic	School Subjects
Home and Parents	Physical Appearance and Attributes	Physical	Parent Relations	Mental Ability
	Anxiety		Physical Appearance	Relations with Parents
	Happiness and Satisfaction		Physical Abilities	Relations with Teachers
				Work Habits
				Happy Qualities

Research Questions

The aims of this research were to answer the following questions:

1. What life areas are important to the majority of Nepalese children?
2. Are these the areas covered by typical western self-esteem questionnaires for children?
3. Are these areas equally salient for these children?
4. Are there rural/urban, developmental, and gender differences in the above?

METHOD

Subjects

The sample included 746 Nepalese secondary school children. The breakdown of the sample according to location (urban/rural), grade level and sex is shown in Table 17.2. The average ages of the children were around 12, 14, and 16 years for Grades VI, VIII, and X, respectively. The urban sample was drawn from two well-known schools in Kathmandu while the rural subjects were attending schools in the southern *terai*.

Instruments

The subjects were administered the "How I See Myself" questionnaire (Juhasz, 1985) which seeks answers to the following open-ended questions: "What are the most important areas of your life?" "Which of these usually make you feel good?" "Which of these usually make you feel bad?" This instrument has been used previously to explore the self-concepts of American (Juhasz, 1985), Filipino (Watkins, 1988), and New Zealand adolescents (Watkins, Alabaster, and Freemantle, 1988). The questions were explained in both English and Nepalese

TABLE 17.2

Percentages of Subjects Endorsing the Importance of Self-esteem Components according to Location, Sex, and School Grade

| | Urban | | | | | | Rural | | | | | | Average Percentage |
| | Males | | | Females | | | Males | | | Females | | | |
	VI (n=69)	VIII (n=61)	X (n=56)	VI (n=82)	VIII (n=87)	X (n=62)	VI (n=82)	VIII (n=90)	X (n=82)	VI (n=15)	VIII (n=39)	X (n=21)	
School	30.4	27.9	71.4	85.4	73.6	87.1	48.8	25.6	97.6	53.3	30.8	71.4	59.5
Reading	68.1	73.8	37.5	18.3	41.4	12.9	39.0	56.7	29.3	66.7	51.3	14.3	42.9
Sport	20.3	67.2	64.3	68.3	54.0	48.4	30.5	31.1	24.4	20.0	48.7	4.8	41.8
Play	75.4	42.6	30.4	24.4	50.6	17.7	0.0	28.9	37.8	13.3	25.6	52.4	33.5
Food	43.5	23.0	5.4	20.7	25.3	1.6	23.2	36.7	12.2	13.3	71.8	4.8	24.1
Dancing	8.7	14.8	17.9	30.5	55.2	27.4	1.2	26.7	4.9	0.0	38.5	19.0	21.8
Singing	31.9	14.8	37.5	15.9	62.1	40.3	0.0	7.8	4.9	0.0	0.0	0.0	20.8
Health	0.0	1.6	3.6	0.0	0.0	6.5	18.3	62.2	22.0	0.0	76.9	81.0	19.2
Clothes	1.4	0.0	0.0	2.4	1.1	1.6	4.9	42.2	4.9	13.3	79.5	0.0	11.3
Friends	1.4	11.5	8.9	1.2	20.7	22.6	3.7	0.0	1.2	0.0	12.8	14.3	12.9
Home/Family	17.4	8.2	1.8	14.6	6.9	6.5	15.9	4.4	13.4	20.0	2.6	0.0	9.7
Cinema/TV	29.3	31.1	19.6	1.2	16.1	9.7	0.0	0.0	0.0	0.0	0.0	0.0	8.7
Money	0.0	0.0	5.4	1.2	0.0	0.0	3.7	10.0	3.7	0.0	41.0	0.0	4.7

and the subjects were allowed to respond in either language. Most of
the respondents chose to answer in English while the Nepalese
responses were translated into English. All responses were then content
analysed.

RESULTS

An average of about 3 life areas were listed as important for every
subject. The majority of these could be classified into one of 13
categories. These life areas together with the percentage of subjects
reporting that area by "location", gender, and school grade are shown
in Table 17.2.

It can be seen that "school" was the only life area considered
important by the majority of the Nepalese subjects. However, "reading", "sport", and "play" were considered important by at least one-
third of the sample. Evidence of grade differences was provided by the
increased salience of school for the more senior students (probably
reflecting their promixity to major external exams). "School" was also
particularly salient to most of the urban girls regardless of grade.
Further, grade and gender differences were observed in "reading" (of
less importance to the more senior) and "play" (particularly salient to
the younger boys). When the importance ratings of urban and rural
children were placed in rank order, a nonsignificant rank order correlation of 0.47 (11df; $p > 0.05$) was found. "Health", "money",
and "clothes" were particularly salient to the rural children. Further
analysis revealed that deficiencies in these areas made these subjects
feel "bad". While "food" was of importance to both rural and urban
subjects there was a fundamental difference: lack of food made the
former feel "bad" and its availability made the latter feel "good".
"School" and "reading" were areas which made a large percentage of
all subgroups feel "good". "Sport" and "play" tended to make majority
of the children feel "bad" (presumably because they got into trouble
for not studying).

DISCUSSION

In previous research, using the same instrument as used in this study, it was found that the majority of middle class New Zealand children reported life areas such as "family", "friends", "sport", and (to a lesser extent) "school" to be important (Watkins et al., 1988). Thus it was concluded that while there were individual differences, the focus of self-esteem instruments such as those described in Table 17.1 seemed appropriate. Similarly, in a study with children from a deprived area of the Philippines (Watkins, 1988), "family", "friends", and "school" were considered to be salient by over half of the subjects. These were aspects of their lives that usually made these children feel happy. However, the majority of the Filipino children also considered "food", "money", and "clothes" to be important aspects of their lives but these areas are generally omitted in typical western self-esteem instruments. As these were areas that these relatively poor Filipinos were unhappy about it may well be that such instruments would overestimate their self-esteem.

The Nepalese subjects in this study showed less internal agreement than the subjects in the Filipino and New Zealand studies described earlier. "School" being the only life area that was reported by over half the students. Dimensions of self commonly tapped by western self-esteem instruments such as "friends", "family", and "physical appearance" did not seem to be of importance to the Nepalese subjects. Thus, the appropriateness of western self-esteem instruments must be questioned. Evidence also indicated that there were significant differences between the salient life areas of urban and rural Nepalese children. The latter, like the poor Filipinos, reported that lack in areas such as "food", "health", and "money" made them unhappy. In contrast, the more privileged and westernised urban children enjoyed themselves at the cinema, watching TV, or singing. There was also some evidence of gender and age differences in salient life areas.

Overall this research raises doubts about the appropriateness of the dimensions tapped in typical western self-esteem questionnaires for use with Nepalese children. It is doubtful if the Nepalese children share sufficiently similar salient self-dimensions to warrant the development of a separate Nepali self-instrument. At the least separate forms may be needed for the more privileged urban and the more deprived rural children. Given these findings, in societies like Nepal it may be worth focusing more attention on the development of self-esteem instruments which allow individual subjects to choose their own self-dimensions and to weight and rate themselves on them according to their own feelings. In an earlier study (Watkins, 1978) it was shown that this is possible.

REFERENCES

COOPERSMITH, S. (1959). *The antecedents of self-esteem.* San Francisco: Freeman.

FLEMING, J.S. (1986). Academic influences on self-esteem in college students. Paper presented at the Annual Conference of the American Educational Research Association, San Francisco.

HARTER, S. (1982). The perceived competence scale for children. *Child Development, 53,* 87–97.

JAMES, W. (1890). *The principles of psychology.* New York: Holt.

JUHASZ, A. (1985). Measuring self-esteem in early adolescents. *Adolescence, 20,* 877–887.

McGUIRE, W.J. and PADAWER-SINGER, A. (1976). Trait salience in the spontaneous self-concept. *Journal of Personality and Social Psychology, 33,* 743–754.

MARSH, H.W. (1986). Global self-esteem: Its relation to specific facets of self-concept and their importance. *Journal of Personality and Social Psychology, 51,* 1224–1236.

MARSH, H.W. (1988). *The Self-Description Questionnaire I: SDQ manual and research monograph.* San Antonio: The Psychological Corporation.

MARSH, H.W. and SHAVELSON, R.J. (1985). Self-concept: Its multifaceted, hierarchical structure. *Educational Psychologist, 20,* 107–125.

PIERS, E.V. and HARRIS, D. (1969). *The Piers-Harris Children's Self-Concept Scale.* Nashville, Tennessee: Counsellor Recordings and Tests.

SHAVELSON, R.J., HUBNER, J.J., and STANTON, G.C. (1976). Self-concept: Validation of construct interpretations. *Review of Educational Research, 46,* 407–441.

SONG, I.S. and HATTIE, J.A. (1984). Home environment, self-concept, and academic achievement: A causal modeling approach. *Journal of Educational Psychology, 76,* 1269–1281.

WATKINS, D. (1978). The development and evaluation of self-esteem measuring instruments. *Journal of Personality Assessment, 42,* 171–182.

WATKINS, D. (1988). Components of self-esteem of children from a deprived cross-cultural background. *Social Behavior and Personality, 16,* 1–3.

WATKINS, D. (1992, January 3–7). The cross-cultural validity of the Shavelson model of self-esteem. Paper presented at the Asian Regional Congress of the International Association for Cross-Cultural Psychology, Kathmandu.

WATKINS, D., ALABASTER, M., and FREEMANTLE, S. (1988). Assessing the self-esteem of New Zealand adolescents. *New Zealand Journal of Psychology, 17,* 32–35.

WATKINS, D. and REGMI, M. (1991). Cross-cultural assessment of self-esteem: A Nepalese investigation. *Psychologia, 34,* 98–108.

WYLIE, R.C. (1974). *The self-concept: Volume 1.* Lincoln: University of Nebraska Press.

18

Towards a Culturally Relevant Model of Self-concept for the Hong Kong Chinese

CHRISTOPHER H.K. CHENG*

Self-concept has been a central issue for decades in the area of personality and social psychology. The configuration of the phenomenology of self has long been of interest to psychologists. Early in the late nineteenth century, William James (1892) conceived of a hierarchical model of the self by commenting that "the consequent different orders of his self-regard (may be arranged) in an hierarchical scale, with the bodily me at the bottom, the spiritual me at the top, and the

* The author wishes to express his gratitude to David Watkins for his helpful comments and review. The generous assistance and cooperation provided by the participating students, school teachers, and principals is also gratefully acknowledged. The conducting of this research and presentation of this paper were partly supported by the Research Grant Committee (Grant No. 903076) and the Department of Applied Social Studies of the City Polytechnic of Hong Kong.

extra-corporeal material selves and the various social selves between" (p. 190).

Self-concept research has been more fruitful than ever before in the western arena of psychology. The proposition that self-concept should be a multidimensional construct with its constituent parts hierarchically and differentially organised was made in the last decade. Rosenberg (1979) believed that "self-concept is a structure whose elements are arranged in a complex hierarchical order" and "that the global attitude (of self-concept) is the product of an enormously complex synthesis of elements" (p. 21). While Rosenberg (1979) realised the intrinsic complexities of the combinations of different elements of the self, he was content to assess the global evaluation believing that it was almost impossible to delineate the process and structure of the "complex synthesis".

Having reviewed the self-concept instruments and research, Shavelson, Hubner, and Stanton (1976) proposed a hierarchical multifaceted model of self-concept, in which general self appears at the apex and is divided into higher order academic and nonacademic self-concepts at the next level. The academic self-concept is subdivided into specific academic subject areas (for example, Mathematics and English), and the nonacademic self-concept is subdivided into social, emotional, and physical self-concepts. Social self-concept is again divided into two lower order areas: relations with peers and with significant others; and physical self-concept is broken down into two lower order categories: physical abilities and physical appearance. The lower the hierarchical level, the more specific the self-concept is (that is, the more closely related to actual behaviour). The hierarchical multifaceted model of self-concept posited by Shavelson and associates (1976) was empirically examined and operationalised through the construction of the Self-Description Questionnaire 1 (SDQ 1) (Marsh, 1988). For the sake of convenience, the hierarchical multifaceted model posited by Shavelson and associates (1976) and revised by Marsh (Marsh, 1986; Marsh, Byrne, and Shavelson, 1988) will be referred to as the Shavelson/Marsh model hereafter.

CROSS-CULTURAL EVIDENCE FOR MULTIDIMENSIONAL MODEL

Generally, very high validity (both within and between constructs) has been reported for the Shavelson/Marsh model and its instrument (SDQ) in different cultural backgrounds, including Australia, the Philippines, Hong Kong, Nepal, and Nigeria (see Watkins, 1992). For example, using the Fleming–Courtney Self-Rating Scales, Watkins, Fleming, and Alfon (1989) have found "impressive evidence" of cross-cultural validity of Shavelson's model among Filipino college students. To further examine the cross-cultural generalisability of the Shavelson/Marsh model and the SDQ to other Asian cultures, Watkins, Lam, and Regmi (1991) administered the Self-Description Questionnaire (Marsh, 1988) to Nepalese children and found strong evid ce of cross-cultural validity of both the SDQ I and the conceptual model.

Based on the Shavelson's model, Lo (1988) adapted the Self-Description Questionnaire (Marsh, Cairns, Relich, and Barnes, 1984) into Chinese for Hong Kong students, and added two domains to the academic self-concepts: Chinese Language and Social Studies. Lo (1988) found that the construct of self may be hierarchically organised but may not be arranged exactly the same way as Shavelson and associates (1976) have suggested. Though the hierarchical and multi-faceted nature of the self construct is supported, Lo speculated that the self-concept categorisation system among the Chinese may not be exactly the same as that suggested by the Shavelson/Marsh model in the west.

Skaalvik and Rankin (1990) tested Marsh's (1986) Internal/External (I/E) frame of reference model using Norwegian students and noted strong correlations between verbal and math self-concepts. Having found results contradictory to Marsh's (1986) postulation (which is based on weak correlations between verbal and math self-concept), Skaalvik and Rankin (1990) pointed to the need for further cross-cultural research on the model which explains verbal and math self-concept in an I/E frame of reference.

In general, there is evidence supporting the position that the construct of self is multifaceted in nature, with its lower order concepts supporting the higher ones in a hierarchical manner, and an underlying general self-concept factor at the apex of the hierarchy. However, there is no strong consensus as to which specific content dimensions are universally valid and how these dimensions are structured. It is possible that the content areas of the higher order self-concepts may not be the same as Shavelson and associates (1976) and Marsh (1986, 1988) have postulated. In other words, under the general self-concept there may be some cultural significant domains other than academic, social, emotional, and physical self-concepts, and under each of the higher order domains there may also exist specific self-concepts in different subareas which are significant to the particular culture. Further empirical evidence is necessary to investigate the cross-cultural generalisability of the Shavelson/Marsh model.

THE IMPOSED ETIC ISSUE

A common method to assess the cross-cultural validity is to administer a western developed test for the construct in a non-western country, and it was a common practice to translate these western developed instruments into the native language to make them legible to the local people. This transplanting of scientific theory is not problematic all the time especially when the phenomenon explained by that theory is less vulnerable to cultural influence. The phenomenology of self, however, is rather sensitive to the social environment. Cross-cultural studies adopting this approach could be termed "imposed-etic"—"the importation or exportation of a theory of human behaviour which has been developed in one culture (typically U.S.) to be tested in another cultural context" (Segall, Dasen, Berry, and Poortinga, 1990, p. 57). This paper does not discount the value of the etic approach, as comparative studies using this approach could provide valuable information regarding cross-cultural equivalence of certain psychological systems of peoples from different cultural backgrounds.

The imposed etic method, however, has its inherent problems. By definition, the imposed etic approach assumes the universal nature of the underlying construct developed in one culture and applies it in other cultures. The problems of this approach have been pointed out by a number of cross-cultural psychologists in the last decade (Bond and Cheung, 1983; Hui and Triandis, 1985; Yang and Bond, 1990; Segall et al., 1990). Yang and Bond (1990) have voiced their concern over this issue and asked whether imposed etics are "in fact tapping cultural general processes as hoped, or pasting one culture's emic or particular processes over another's checkerboard of constructs as feared" (p. 1088).

Some cross-cultural evidence found by imposed etics could be the effects of "scalar equivalence" (Hui and Triandis, 1985). In other words, the seeming equivalence is simply produced by measuring the construct with the same metric in different cultures on the basis of the assumption that the construct in question is semantically and connotatively equivalent across cultures. This method, however, is insufficient to test whether such an assumption is true or not.

SELF-CONCEPT RESEARCH IN THE EAST

One of the major difficulties facing self-concept research in the east is the problem of compatibility of conceptual paradigms encompassing the self between the east and the west. Unlike perceptual abilities, personality constructs like concepts of self are particularly vulnerable to cultural influences. The compatibility could be twofold: first, on the level of scale translation which refers to equivalent cognitive and perceptual representation of people talking (and thinking) about self, and second, on the level of construct conceptualisation which has implications for the theoretical construct. Yang and Bond (1990) have questioned the compatibility of the perceptual frames of people using different languages. The semantic repertoire of the vocabulary of a language may represent different pictures from the "translational equivalents".

In an emic–etic comparative study of values, 40 ethnocentrically produced items of Chinese values were factor analysed into 4 orthogonal factors, namely, Integration, Confucian Work Dynamism, Human-Heartedness, and Moral Discipline (The Chinese Culture Connection, 1987). Moral Discipline, Integration, and Human-Heartedness were found to correlate significantly and negatively with Hofstede's Individualism, Power Distance, and Masculinity. These three Chinese value dimensions were labelled "collectivism", which denotes a balance between self-seeking and the maintenance of harmony with the community, as relative to the individualism of western cultures. However, Confucian Work Dynamism was not correlated with any of the western value dimensions. On the contrary, it was particularly salient in some Asian societies, such as Hong Kong, Taiwan, Japan, South Korea, India, Thailand, and Singapore. It seems that this dimension is highly oriental.

It was observed that cultures which value collectivism (such as the Chinese culture) may provide a rather different perceptual frame when they talk about concepts of self (Yang and Bond, 1990; Triandis, 1989; Hsu, 1985). As self-perceptions and self-evaluations largely depend on how an individual views the importance of things related to oneself and the achievements one attains or perceives in those aspects, premature assumptions of construct equivalence could be dangerous and thus hamper the advance of cross-cultural research.

Discussing indigenous research on self of the Chinese people, Yang (1988) has pointed out the potential problems of investigating the "Chinese self" and has suggested that Chinese psychologists should address the issue taking into account the following considerations: (a) the configuration and characteristics of the Chinese self; (b) the "boundary" of self as the Chinese self is often extended to the "social self" or the "collective self"; (c) the self-presentation versus self-restraint issue (self-restraint is often regarded as a positive presentation of the self rather than a manifestation of low self-esteem); and (d) the relationship between "public self" and "private self" in a social environment which reinforces self-restraint.

In spite of the lack of conceptual and scalar equivalence for the construct of self of the Hong Kong Chinese, it is rare to find this construct indigenously explicated and empirically tested before it is operationalised for the local people. Some adaptation or validation procedures may have been undertaken to safeguard the construct validity during the construction of an instrument of self-concept, however the fundamental question of conceptual equivalence of the underlying construct remains unanswered. For example, the 4 domains and 5 perspectives[1] used by Lau and Cheung (1990) in the construction of their Chinese Self-concept Scale resulted from a careful analysis of western research findings, but it is unfortunate that they did not indigenously explicate the construct before it was operationalised.

The present study aims to delineate the phenomenology of self-conception and self-evaluation in the Hong Kong Chinese school

[1] The 4 domains are: Academic, Appearance, Social, and General self-concepts. The 5 perspectives are perceived feedback from parent, school, social comparison (impression), social comparison (concrete), and global evaluation.

students. It aims to uncover the construct of self as held in the perceptual space of the local young people. In order to capture any possible semantic differences associated with age and gender, both school boys and girls from 1 to 7 were included in the study. While it is almost impossible not to impose any theoretical framework during the process of research, care has been taken to minimise such effect and to retain as far as possible the original information given by the subjects. Responses recorded from the interview and the written forms were used as raw data for content analysis, which formed the basis of the conceptualisation of the self-concept. It is expected that this emic study of self-concept will provide a culturally relevant explication of the construct, and the findings of this study will form an integral part of the conceptual foundation of the self-concept research for the Chinese (or even Asian) people.

METHOD

Subjects

A total of 112 students from 6 secondary schools participated in the study. Efforts were made to ensure representativeness of the sample. The sample was fairly representative as the participating schools covered the majority of the school types in Hong Kong and ability levels. Consent was requested from the students (since they either had to stay after school or come back during the weekend) and notification was given to parents in written form.

Materials

The materials used included a tape recorder, 2 sheets of printed form (Form A and Form B) for each subject, and some pencils.

Form A

Form A is a sentence completion exercise which reflects the kind of things and people the subjects care most about. Each subject was expected to complete 10 sentences. Subjects had to answer questions relating to when they felt happiest and saddest, what they thought they were best at and worst in, what they most preferred and hated to hear from others and from whom, and what things about themselves they were most eager to and most reluctant to share with others.

Form B

Unlike Form A, Form B is divided into two parts. Part 1 is similar to the classic "Who am I" 20-statement test (Kuhn and McPartland, 1954) with some modifications. Subjects were asked to describe themselves briefly in 10 statements. It is designed to reflect the self-descriptions and self-evaluations of the subjects. In Part 2, the subjects were asked to list 5 life areas most important to them.

Procedures

Subjects were divided into small groups of 5 or 6 for small group discussion. Discussion was held in a quiet and friendly atmosphere to enable the participants to freely express their ideas of "who they think they are" and their feelings of being themselves. Subjects were seated in a circle along with the researcher (group leader) and a group assistant. The group assistant was expected to note the subjects' responses and behaviour. At the beginning of the discussion, the group leader introduced himself, this was followed by a warm-up session of casual self-introduction. Subjects were assured of confidentiality about all information they would give including the audio recordings. At the end of the warm-up session, Form A was distributed and subjects were requested to fill in the form individually. Subjects were allowed free movement while filling in the form. After they completed the form, they were asked to take their seats for a sharing session. The sharing session was audio-recorded. At the end of the sharing session, Form B was distributed and the subjects were requested to complete it individually. Again, there was no time limit. After they had completed the task (about 10 minutes), they were again grouped for the second sharing session. The same procedure was followed for the second sharing session. The whole process took between 45 to 90 minutes.

Data Analysis

Data collected by means of written forms and oral discussion was content analysed. The audio recordings were transcribed into written forms for data analysis. From the responses recorded on Form B ("Who am I?") phrases or statements describing oneself were drawn as "descriptors". Statements denoting the same meaning were treated as one descriptor. A descriptor denoting exactly the opposite meaning of another one was also treated as the same descriptor (for example, hardworking and lazy). In the case of predicates which could not be expressed in a single noun/adjective/adverbial phrase the whole clause was noted on the card and was treated as one descriptor. Each descriptor was then noted on a card in the subjects' own language (usually Chinese). A second independent judge (a social scientist) content analysed the data.

RESULTS

There were 727 meaningful responses to the "Who am I" question in Form B. A total of 173 different descriptors were drawn from these written responses. Following certain iterative procedures of identification and comparison, the descriptors were clustered into 19 categories, including the Nominal Self and the Unclassified (Table 18.1). It should be mentioned that there was some overlapping. (For example, descriptors like "easily annoyed" could be grouped into both Social Skills and Self-Controlling.)

Following the classification of the descriptors, the categories were then compared with each other in terms of their semantic and contextual similarities and differences. Descriptors were checked again for their semantic and connotative representations. Recordings from

TABLE 18.1

Examples of Self-Descriptors in Categories

Nominal Self Name, Sex, Student	**Social Skills** Verbal Skills, Taciturn Humorous, Telling Jokes Smiling Face, Disclosing Self
General Self Confident, Have Own Ideas, I am Useless	
	Social Personality Optimistic, Open, Cheerful (*hoi-long, song-long*)
Physical Appearance Look Pretty/Ugly Strong/Slim Body Built	Lively, Lovely (*wood-pood,* *hall-oi, tin-tsun*) Extroversive, Stubborn
Physical Skills/Other Abilities Good at Sports, Swimming Good at Cooking, Music, etc.	**Family Relations** Care/Love Family, Love to Stay with Family
Academic Abilities Good/Bad School Performance Competent in Studying	**Filial Piety** Respect the Elderly, Filial Pious (*hau shun*),
Academic Orientation Hardworking/Lazy, Diligent (not) Serious in Studies Playful	Misuse My Parents' Money **Virtues** Honest, Cheating Loving Heart, Sympathetic
Intellectual Abilities Poor Analytical Ability, Knowledgeable, Creative Intelligent, Smart	Kind/Good Heart, Selfish, Greedy, Unpretending **Social Responsibilities** Serving People, Helping Others
Intellectual Orientation Investigative, Curiosity Persistent in Knowing, Love Thinking	**Self-controlling** Emotional, Unstable Perseverence, Lack Endurance,
Peer Relations Care about Friends, Code of Brotherhood (*yee hay*) Sociable, Love to Communicate	Patient Sense of Responsibility **Rule-abiding** Rebellious, Act Aimlessly
Social Manner Generous Manners (*leung-do,* *dai-fong, siu-hay*) Cool, Hospitable Quiet and Gentle (*mun-jing*), Rough Manner (*tso-lo*)	Have Principles Punctual, Following Rules

* For words which do not have close translations in English their Cantonese pronunciations are given in parentheses.

oral discussion and written forms were consulted occasionally for clarifications. Categories which belonged to the same definitional or relational paradigm were grouped to form one higher order category. As a result, excluding the Nominal Self and the Unclassified categories the remaining 17 categories were grouped into 4 major areas and 1 general area (General Self) on the basis of their common attributes and concerns. These 4 main categories are Physical Self, Social Self, Moral Self, and Intellectual Self. They may be termed as higher order self-concepts (see Figure 18.1).

Figure 18.1
The Four Higher Order Self-concepts

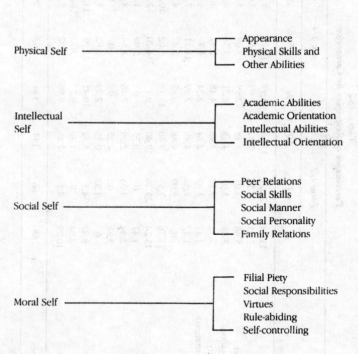

Physical Self — Appearance / Physical Skills and Other Abilities

Intellectual Self — Academic Abilities / Academic Orientation / Intellectual Abilities / Intellectual Orientation

Social Self — Peer Relations / Social Skills / Social Manner / Social Personality / Family Relations

Moral Self — Filial Piety / Social Responsibilities / Virtues / Rule-abiding / Self-controlling

The percentages of responses in different categories by form and gender are shown in Table 18.2. Apparently, students of junior forms (1 and 2) gave less responses than the older students. While the statistical significance of rank ordering, gender and age differences

TABLE 18.2

Percentages of Responses by Categories

	Form 1/2			Form 3/4			Form 5/6			Total
	M	F	All	M	F	All	M	F	All	
AP (Appearance)	13.24	21.21	17.16	5.97	11.73	9.12	3.42	3.0	3.25	8.58
AB (Ability)	7.35	4.5	5.97	2.99	0.62	1.69	1.37	3.0	2.03	2.66
AA (Academic Ability)	5.88	3.03	4.48	2.99	3.09	3.04	2.74	0	1.63	2.81
AO (Academic Orientation)	5.88	3.03	4.48	8.21	5.56	6.76	6.16	9.0	7.32	6.51
GA (Intellectual Ability)	7.35	1.52	4.48	4.48	2.47	3.38	8.9	0	5.28	4.29
GO (Intellectual Orientation)	1.47	3.03	2.24	2.24	3.7	3.04	2.05	3.0	2.44	2.66
PR (Peer Relation)	1.47	7.58	4.48	2.99	11.11	7.43	6.16	11.0	8.13	7.10
MN (Manner)	0	9.09	4.48	6.72	2.47	4.39	6.16	7.0	6.5	5.18
SK (Social Skills)	11.76	7.58	9.70	14.18	8.02	10.81	12.33	10.0	11.38	10.80
PE (Personality)	13.24	25.76	19.40	9.7	14.20	12.16	11.64	12.0	11.79	13.46
FR (Family Relation)	1.47	0	0.75	0	3.09	1.69	0	2.0	0.81	1.18
VR (Virtues)	2.94	3.03	2.99	7.46	8.64	8.11	9.59	13.0	10.98	8.14
FP (Filial Piety)	5.88	0	2.99	2.99	0	0	5.48	2.0	4.07	2.07
SR (Responsibility)	0	1.52	0.75	2.99	0.62	1.69	1.37	3.0	2.03	1.63
DP (Self-control)	8.82	4.5	6.72	10.45	12.97	11.82	10.27	14.0	11.79	10.80
RU (Rule-abiding)	2.94	0	1.49	9.7	3.7	6.42	4.11	2.0	3.25	4.29
G (General)	10.29	4.5	7.46	8.96	8.02	8.44	8.22	6.0	7.32	7.84
Frequency of Responses	68	66	134	134	162	296	146	100	246	676

was not calculated, Social Personality, Self-Control, Social Skills, Physical Appearance and Virtues emerged as the 5 most salient categories (in rank order). When higher order dimensions were considered, Social Self had the highest response rate (37.72 per cent), followed by Moral Self (26.93 per cent). Surprisingly, Intellectual Self and Physical Self were less frequently mentioned than expected, accounting for only 16.27 per cent and 11. 24 per cent respectively.

Apart from the self-descriptors, the important areas of life recorded on Part 2 of Form B could be grouped into 18 categories (Table 18.3). The descriptors of these important life areas were more direct and general than the descriptors used to describe oneself. The list of life areas possibly reflected the subjective value system, which theoretically had a broader perceptual frame than the specific evaluations of self. The 5 most salient life areas were (in order): Family (19.3 per cent), Friends (16.84 per cent), Money and Possessions (11.29 per cent), Lover and Gut-level Friends (8.83 per cent), and Health (7.60 per cent). These salient life areas could be grouped similarly into the 4 higher order domains as for the self perceptions. Among the 4 types of salient life areas, those pertaining to the Social Self were mentioned most frequently (51.74 per cent) and hence should be most significant to the phenomenal world of the students. Furthermore, life areas related to the Social Self could be differentiated in two fields, one in the field of interpersonal relations (friends, family, lovers, etc.), and the other in the field of achievements and status.

A comparative analysis of the self-descriptors and the salient life areas, however, revealed an interesting picture. Family relations and love between family members were deemed the most important life areas but they did not have the same weightings in self-conception and self-esteem (only 1.18 per cent on Family Relations and 2.07 per cent on Filial Piety). Second, Social Relations emerged as the second most important life area, whereas the Social Self appeared to be more differentially organised (yet the most salient) in the phenomenology of self. Among the different dimensions of Social Self, Social Skills and Social Personality appeared to have a great impact on self-esteem while Peer Relations and Social Manner were less attributed. Therefore, a model which allows multidimensional analysis would be more informative and suggestive.

An interesting aspect which deserves attention is the emphasis on virtues and moral values. Both in the individual written forms and in group discussions the students emphasised moral values. Among the

TABLE 18.3
Most Important Things in Life (%)

	Form 1/2			Form 3/4			Form 5/6			Total
	M	F	All	M	F	All	M	F	All	Total
Friends, Friendship	9.38	11.86	10.57	20.24	18.85	19.42	16.30	21.54	18.47	16.84
Parents, Family Love (chun ching)	20.31	20.34	20.33	20.24	19.67	19.90	16.30	20.00	17.83	19.30
Lovers, Gut-level Friends	6.25	10.17	8.13	9.50	10.66	10.19	8.70	6.15	7.64	8.83
Achievements, Career	3.13	10.17	6.50	3.57	2.46	2.91	4.35	10.77	7.00	5.13
Social Status, Reputation, Honour	1.56	0.00	0.81	2.38	0.82	1.46	4.35	0.00	0.00	1.64
Life, Basic Needs	10.94	5.09	8.13	5.95	1.64	3.40	4.35	4.62	4.46	4.93
Health, Strong Body	6.25	5.09	5.69	4.76	9.84	7.77	9.78	7.69	8.92	7.60
Sense of Security (on-ding)	1.56	1.69	1.63	0.00	1.64	0.49	0.00	0.00	0.00	0.82
Money, Possessions and Properties	10.94	13.56	17.20	9.52	13.10	11.65	11.96	7.69	10.19	11.29
Activities	4.69	0.00	2.44	4.76	0.00	1.94	1.09	0.00	0.64	1.64
Studying, Educational Qualifications	9.38	11.86	10.57	2.38	2.46	2.43	1.09	9.23	4.46	5.13
Knowledge, Wisdom	6.25	3.39	4.88	5.95	9.02	7.77	5.43	1.54	3.82	5.75
Ideals	4.69	3.39	4.07	2.38	0.82	1.46	3.26	1.54	2.55	2.46
Freedom	0.00	0.00	0.00	3.57	3.28	3.40	4.35	3.08	3.82	2.67
Dignity	0.00	0.00	0.00	0.00	2.46	1.46	1.09	0.00	0.64	0.82
Faith	1.56	0.00	0.81	2.38	0.00	0.97	0.00	0.00	0.00	0.62
Peace	0.00	0.00	0.00	0.00	0.82	0.49	1.09	3.08	1.91	0.82
Other Virtues	3.13	3.39	3.25	2.38	3.28	2.91	6.52	3.08	5.10	3.70

different categories of the Moral Self, Self-Control (or self-discipline) had the highest response rate consistently across different age groups and between genders. It should be noted that Self-Control is different from Rule-Abiding both in its semantic and connotative represent-ations, where the former refers to self-awared discipline and self-initiatives. Age difference was observed in the emphasis on moral values, students of higher forms tended to place more emphasis on moral values than the lower form students.

The criteria of virtues, however, tended to become blurred when the students were asked to clearly define their moral aspirations orally. A common resolution suggested by the students was to consider one's conscience as behavioural principles. In one particular case there has been a hot debate on whether not expressing oneself is hypocritical. Though the delineation of the moral self still awaits further clarification, it seems that the moral self played an important role in the configur-ation of self in the case of Hong Kong students and it should be appropriately represented in a model which claims to be conceptualising the self construct of the Chinese people.

Several dimensions have emerged under Intellectual Self. A differ-entiation between formal academic and general intellectual activities was noted. Descriptors in these areas focused on two aspects, one on competence and abilities, and the other on attitudinal orientation. Information obtained from Form A and interviews also indicated that the students were rather anxious about their performance in school and their image of being intelligent and smart in their teachers' and peers' eyes. It was found that the students (especially males) were concerned about how others thought of them more in terms of general intellectual competence (4.29 per cent) than their actual formal academic performance (2.81 per cent). Conversely, they expressed greater concern about their attitude and orientation towards formal academic activities than towards general intellectual activities, as indicated by the response rates (6.51 per cent and 2.66 per cent respectively). Surprisingly, higher form students were less concerned about their academic abilities than the lower form students. The reasons for this interesting finding are as yet not known and await further investigation.

The specific academic self-concepts about which the students expressed great concern included Chinese language, English language, Chinese history, science subjects (physics, chemistry, biology), and mathematics. This finding extended Lo's (1988) research in which he included social studies but excluded Chinese history from the academic portion. It appeared that the students were not concerned about how well they did in social studies but were quite anxious about (or proud of) their performance in Chinese history. Whether this is a result of the changed university admission policy[2] and the reaffirmation of the Chinese identity because of the June Fourth incident in 1989[3] is not known. This shift of interest deserves more attention in the coming years. Thus, the academic self-concept model postulated by Shavelson and associates (1976) and Marsh (1990) was partially supported by the findings of this study.

Generally speaking, most students wished to "look" intelligent and capable, especially in their teachers' eyes. Some even mentioned their school names or residential address when asked about things they were most anxious about. It is, however, not clear whether these concerns (such as looking intelligent, studying in a prestigious school, living in a respected district) belong to the Chinese "face" concept, in which case they are related more to the Social Self than the Intellectual Self.

Physical Self is the last of the higher order self-concepts to be discussed. In general, Appearance (including body built, figure, and looks) was a more salient factor than Physical Abilities across forms and between genders; however, girls (especially those in the lower forms) were more aware of their Physical Appearance than boys. It should be noted that the responses pertaining to Physical Abilities were rather diverse and included abilities and skills in different domains, such as sports, arts, and domestic areas.

DISCUSSION

Using an emic and non-directive approach, an attempt has been made to investigate the phenomenology of self-concept and self-esteem among the Hong Kong Chinese students. Four salient factors, namely,

[2] The two universities and the polytechnics have waived the requirement of a pass in social studies at the A-level exam as an entry criterion.

[3] There were cases where students mentioned the names of some student leaders of the June Fourth Movement as their heroic figures, and some were proud to claim themselves "Chinese" but not "communist", while others expressed their admiration of "freedom" and "democracy" (the two terms are usually associated with the Democratic Movement in China in general, and the June Fourth Incident in 1989 in particular).

physical, social, moral, and intellectual, emerged as higher order concepts of self. Within each higher order factor certain dimensions were identified, and within each dimension there could be some lower order (or specific) concepts (see Figure 18.2). While the Shavelson/Marsh model was found to be partially valid, some cultural differences were also found in the dimensions of the tentative model that emerged. Among these dimensions some may be culturally significant, such as those of the Moral Self (i.e., virtues and self-control) and the constituent parts of the Social Self, others may be cross-culturally universal (such as those of the Physical Self).

As a matter of fact, it is not uncommon to find Moral Self (or the like) in western self-concept research and development. James (1892)

Figure 18.2
A Tentative Hierarchical Tree of the Self-concept

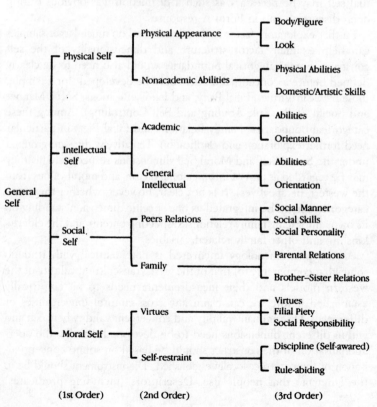

(1st Order)   (2nd Order)   (3rd Order)

incorporated the "Moral and Religious Aspirations" in the composition of the Spiritual Me. Various self-concept scales have also included virtues (or other similar concepts) as a subscale or factor (such as the Tennessee Self-Concept Scale, Fitts, 1965). Only in later models and instruments of self has this factor been diminished. The data presented here, however, revealed that this concept has been sustained and is still salient in Hong Kong. It seems that the inclusion of this factor in the construct of self is appropriate.

Academic self-concept was found to be as highly relevant in Hong Kong as in the west, though the content areas (i.e., the specific academic subjects) were apparently different from those in the west. The inclusion of Chinese language in addition to the English language in the Hong Kong curriculum makes it more complicated to apply Marsh's model of verbal/maths self-concepts to the Hong Kong setting. Moreover, a differentiation between academic self and general intellectual self may be necessary as such a distinction was obvious during open discussion and in Form A responses.

Further exploratory factor analysis conducted on much larger samples can help examine factor structure and dimensionality of the self construct. Some categorical boundaries would also need to be clearly defined before a conceptual model could be developed (for example, those between Virtues, Filial Piety, and Family Relations; Social Manner and Social Skills; Rule-Abiding and Self-Controlling). Among these categorical boundaries, Family Relations and Filial Piety in particular need further exploration and clarification. Tentatively, they are grouped under the Social Self and Moral Self dimensions respectively (as they may be regarded as part of interpersonal factors and moral values from the western perspectives). It is not clear, however, whether these two categories should be integrated as one specific dimension standing on its own, embracing family relations, respecting parents and the elderly, kinship, and other family related variables.

As the phenomenology uncovered is not identical with (though somewhat comparable to) that of the west, transcultural validity of the western models and their measurements needs to be empirically established before we can claim any cross-cultural universalities or differences. Discriminant validity and convergent validity between and within different dimensions need to be developed. Ideally, the operationalisation of the construct should be based on sound conceptualisation of the construct locally established. The instrument should be in the language that people use. Descriptors (including predicates) extracted in this study may serve as a bank for the item pool in test construction. More emic–etic comparative studies should be deployed, instead of importing scales developed in the west and being content to adapt them to fit the people of another culture.

REFERENCES

Bond, M.H. and Cheung, T.S. (1983). College students' spontaneous self-concept. *Journal of Cross-Cultural Psychology, 14,* 153–171.

The Chinese Culture Connection. (1987). Chinese values and the search for culture-free dimensions of culture. *Journal of Cross-Cultural Psychology, 18,* 142–164.

Fitts, W.H. (1965). *Tennessee Self-Concept Scale: Manual.* San Francisco: Freeman.

Hsu, F.L.K. (1985). The self in cross-cultural perspective. In A.J. Marsella, G. DeVos, and F.L.K. Hsu (Eds.), *Cultural and self* (pp. 24–55). London: Tavistock.

Hui, and Triandis, H.C. (1985). Measurement in cross-cultural psychology. *Journal of Cross-Cultural Psychology, 16,* 131–152.

James, W. (1892). *Psychology.* London: MacMillan.

Kuhn, M.H. and McPartland, T.C. (1954). An empirical investigation of self-attitudes. *American Sociological Review, 19,* 68–76.

Lau, S. and Cheung, P.C. (1990). The self-concept of primary school students in Hong Kong. Paper presented at the 7th Annual Conference of the Hong Kong Educational Research Association, Hong Kong.

Lo, M.F. (1988). Self-concept: Interpretation as a psychological construct and relations with sex and achievement. In S.J. Winter (Ed.), *The Hong Kong adolescent: Selected papers of education papers.* Hong Kong: University of Hong Kong.

Marsh, H.W. (1986). Verbal and math self-concepts: An internal/external frame of reference model. *American Educational Research Journal, 23,* 129–149.

Marsh, H.W. (1988). *The Self-Description Questionnaire 1: SDQ manual and research monograph.* San Antonio: The Psychological Corporation.

Marsh, H.W. (1990). *Self-Description Questionnaire 2.* N.S.W.: University of Western Sydney.

Marsh, H.W., Byrne, B.M., and Shavelson, R.J. (1988). A multi-faceted academic self-concept: Its hierarchical structure and its relation to academic achievement. *Journal of Educational Psychology, 80* (3), 366–380.

Marsh, H.W., Cairns, L., Relich, J., and Barnes, J. (1984). The relationship between dimensions of self-attributions and dimensions of self-concept. *Journal of Educational Psychology, 76,* 3–32.

Rosenberg, M. (1979). *Conceiving the self.* New York: Basic Books.

Segall, M.H., Dasen, P.R., Berry, J.W., and Poortinga, Y.H. (1990). *Human behavior in global perspective: An introduction to cross-cultural psychology.* New York: Pergamon.

Shavelson, R.J., Hubner, J.J., and Stanton, G.C. (1976). Self-concept: Validation of construct interpretation. *Review of Educational Research, 46,* 407–441.

SKAALVIK, E.M. and RANKIN, R.J. (1990). Math, verbal, and general academic self-concept: The internal/external frame of reference model and gender differences in self-concept structure. *Journal of Educational Psychology, 82* (3), 546–554.

TRIANDIS, H.C. (1989). The self and social behavior in differing cultural contexts. *Psychological Review, 96,* 506–520.

WATKINS, D., FLEMING, J.S., and ALFON, M.C.A. (1989). A test of Shavelson's hierarchical multifaceted self-concept model in a Filipino college sample. *International Journal of Psychology, 24,* 367–379.

WATKINS, D., LAM, M.K., and REGMI, M. (1991). Cross-cultural assessment of self-esteem: A Nepalese investigation. *Psychologia, 34* (2), 98–108.

YANG, C.F. (1988). What questions should Chinese research of self address? Paper presented at the Social Psychology Conference of China, Tsingdao.

YANG, K.S. and BOND, M.H. (1990). Exploring implicit personality theories with indigenous or imported constructs: The Chinese case. *Journal of Personality and Social Psychology, 58* (6), 1087–1095.

19

Self-monitoring and Concern for Social Appropriateness in China and England

WILLIAM B. GUDYKUNST •
GE GAO •
ARLENE FRANKLYN-STOKES

Self-monitoring is one of the most widely used constructs in social psychology. The vast majority of the research conducted on self-monitoring has been undertaken in the United States. Little cross-cultural or intercultural research has been conducted using the construct. One reason self-monitoring has not been used in cross-cultural and/or intercultural research is the individualistic bias of the conceptualisation and measurement of the construct. To incorporate self-monitoring into cross-cultural and intercultural theory and research, a conceptualisation and measure of the construct that is not individualistically biased is needed.

Most cross-cultural studies using Snyder's (1974) self-monitoring scale (e.g., Gudykunst, Gao, Nishida, Bond, Leung, Wang, and Barraclough, 1989; Gudykunst, Yang and Nishida, 1987) and Lennox and Wolfe's (1984) revised self-monitoring scale (Schumaker and Barraclough, 1989) have used "pseudoetic" or "imposed etic" analyses (Berry, 1969; Triandis, Malpass, and Davidson, 1973). Snyder's and Lennox and Wolfe's scales were developed in the individualistic culture of the United States and do not appear to tap factors important to self-monitoring in collectivistic cultures like Japan (e.g., the importance of others' group memberships and status characteristics in influencing individuals' behaviour). Gudykunst, Gao, Nishida, Nadamitsu, and Sakai (1992) developed a "derived etic" measure of self-monitoring (i.e., a measure that incorporated aspects of self-monitoring that is common to individualistic and collectivistic cultures and aspects that are unique to each) using data from Japan and the United States. The purpose of this study is to determine if the patterns obtained in Japan and the United States extend to the collectivistic and individualistic cultures of China and England.

SELF-MONITORING

Snyder (1974) characterised self-monitoring as "self-observations and self-control guided by situational cues to social appropriateness" (p. 526). He went on to argue that "the self-monitoring individual is one who, out of a concern for social appropriateness, is particularly sensitive to the expression and self-presentation of others in social situations and uses those cues as guidelines for monitoring his [or her] own self-presentation" (p. 528). Snyder (1974) developed a 25-item (true-false statements) instrument to assess self-monitoring arguing that the measure is unidimensional. Snyder's assumption that the self-monitoring scale is unidimensional has been called into question by several scholars (Briggs, Cheek, and Buss, 1980; Gabrenya and Arkin, 1980; Iwabuchi, Tanaka, and Nakazato, 1982).

Previous cross-cultural research using Snyder's (1974) self-monitoring scale have used translated versions of the scale (i.e., imposed etic measures). Some researchers, however, have taken the individualistic bias of the scale into consideration when making their predictions. Gudykunst, Yang, and Nishida (1987) have argued that individualism–collectivism should influence self-monitoring behaviour. On the surface, it appears that individualistic cultures would reinforce low self-monitoring and collectivistic cultures would reinforce high self-monitoring. And this is indeed the position that Snyder (1987) advocated. The rationale for this argument is that members of collectivistic cultures are under great pressure to conform in social situations and, therefore, they must monitor their behaviour more than people in individualistic cultures. If Snyder's conceptualisation and measurement of self-monitoring is taken into consideration, however, this is not a plausible prediction.

Snyder (1979) concluded that high self-monitors imagine what the prototypic person would be in a situation and try to be that person, while low self-monitors "draw upon an enduring self-image or self-conception that represents knowledge of her or his characteristic actions in the behavioral domains most relevant to the situation" (p. 103). The behaviour of members of collectivistic̄ cultures in a particular situation is based, at least in part, on their relationship to others present in the situation (Triandis, 1988). People in collectivistic cultures must take the group/status relationships to others in the situation into consideration when deciding how to behave. This suggests that they cannot base their behaviour on how a "prototypic" person would behave in the situation; that is, members of collectivistic cultures would *not* be high self-monitors using Snyder's conceptualisation. Research by Gudykunst, Yang, and Nishida (1987) and Gudykunst, Gao, Nishida, Bond, Leung, Wang, and Barraclough (1989) support the argument outlined here. Gudykunst and his associates (1989) argued that these results are due, at least in part, to the measurement scale used (that is, Snyder's scale).

The only alternative to Snyder's (1974) scale to measure self-monitoring is Lennox and Wolfe's (1984) revised self-monitoring scale. They argued that self-monitoring should refer only to the ability to modify self-presentations (they developed a 7-item subscale) and to the sensitivity to the expressive behaviour of others (they presented a 6-item subscale). Lennox and Wolfe also proposed that the tendency to conform to others' behaviour (that is, concern for social appropriateness; part of Snyder's conceptualisation of self-monitoring) is separate from self-monitoring and can be measured through two subscales: cross-situational variability (they developed a 7-item subscale) and attention to social comparison information (they prepared a 13-item subscale).

Two studies provide insight regarding the use of the concern for appropriateness scale cross-culturally. Lennox and Wolfe (1984) found that the total concern score correlated negatively with individuation (reported in Wolfe et al., 1986). Cutler, Lennox, and Wolfe (1984) also observed that the greater the importance individuals attach to their social identities, the greater their concern for social appropriateness. The importance of personal identity, however, was not correlated with concern for appropriateness. Given that people focus on individuation and personal identity in individualistic cultures and on social identity in collectivistic cultures (Gudykunst and Ting-Toomey, 1988), it is expected that there would be greater concern for social appropriateness in collectivistic cultures than in individualistic cultures.

To the best of our knowledge, there is only one cross-cultural study that has used part of Lennox and Wolfe's scale. Schumaker and Barraclough (1989) examined differences in the concern for social appropriateness between Australians and Malaysians. They predicted that Malaysians would be more motivated toward "appropriateness" than Australians. They found that Australians scored higher on the total scale and both subscales than the Malaysians. The authors indicated that the "western" bias in the items used to construct the concern for social appropriateness scale may account for the differences.

Given the previous cross-cultural research using Snyder's (1974) self-monitoring scale and Lennox and Wolfe's (1984) concern for social appropriateness scale, it appears thàt aspects of self-monitoring important in collectivistic cultures are not being tapped in current measurements. Gudykunst, Gao, Nishida, Nadamitsu, and Sakai (1992), therefore, constructed a "derived etic" measure (Triandis et al., 1973) of self-monitoring that incorporates factors important in individualistic and collectivistic cultures.

Gudykunst and associates (1992) developed a derived etic measure of self-monitoring using data from the United States and Japan. Their study was carried out in two stages. Initially, items that tapped aspects of self-monitoring in collectivistic cultures were generated through open-ended interviews conducted with Japanese and Chinese students in their native languages. The items generated from the interviews were written in Japanese and Chinese and then translated into English. These items were then combined with Snyder and Gangestad's (1986) 18-item scale and Lennox and Wolfe's (1984) revised self-monitoring and concern for social appropriateness scales in a questionnaire. The English questionnaire was translated into Japanese. The questionnaires were administered to samples in Japan and the United States. The 62 self-monitoring items were decultured (i.e., by subtracting the mean for the item in each culture; Bond, 1988) and factor analysed. Seven factors emerged in Gudykunst et al.'s (1992) study. The factors and the items that loaded on each factor are summarised in Table 19.1.

TABLE 19.1
Items in Gudykunst et al.'s (1992) Derived Etic Measure

Factor 1: Ability to Modify Self-Presentations

1. In social situations, I have the ability to alter my behavior if I think something else is called for.
2. I have the ability to control the way I come across to people, depending on the impression I wish to give them.
3. When I feel the image I'm portraying isn't working, I can readily change it to something that does.
4. I have trouble changing my behavior to suit different people and different situations. (negative loading).
5. I have found that I can change my behavior to meet the demands of the situation I find myself in.
6. Once I know what the situation calls for, it's easy for me to regulate my actions accordingly.

Factor 2: Cross-Situational Variability

1. In different situations and with different people, I often act like very different persons.
2. I am not always the person I appear to be.
3. I tend to show different sides of myself to different people.
4. Although I know myself, I find others do not know me.
5. Different situations make me behave like very different persons.
6. Different people tend to have very different impressions about the type of person I am.
7. I sometimes have the feeling that people don't know who I really am.

Factor 3: Attention to Others' Behavior

1. In social situations when I am not sure how to behave, I look to the behavior of my friends for cues.
2. In social situations when I am not sure how to behave, I look to the behavior of people I respect for cues.
3. When I am unsure how to act in a social situation, I look to the behavior of others for cues.
4. If I am the least bit uncertain as to how to act in a social situation, I look to the behavior of others for cues.

Factor 4: Tendency to Avoid Public Performances

1. I find it hard to imitate the behavior of other people.
2. I am not particularly good at making other people like me.
3. At a party, I let others keep the jokes and stories going.
4. I feel a bit awkward in company and do not show up as well as I should.
5. I have never been good at games like charades and improvisational acting.

Table 19.1 (Continued)

Factor 5: Sensitivity to Others' Expressive Behavior
1. I am often able to read people's true emotions correctly through their eyes.
2. In conversations, I am sensitive to even the slightest change in the facial expression of the person I am conversing with.
3. My powers of intuition are quite good when it comes to understanding others' emotions and motives.
4. I can usually tell when others consider a joke in bad taste, even though they may laugh convincingly.
5. I can usually tell when I've said something inappropriate by reading the listener's eyes.
6. If someone is lying to me, I usually know at once from the person's manner of expression.

Factor 6: Social Comparison Information
1. It is my feeling that if everyone else in a group is behaving in a certain manner, this must be the proper way to behave.
2. I find that I tend to pick up slang expressions from others and use them as part of my vocabulary.
3. The slightest look of disapproval in the eyes of the person with whom I'm interacting is enough to make me change my approach.
4. My behavior often depends on how I feel others wish me to behave.

Factor 7: Attention to Others' Status Characteristics
1. I pay attention to my behavior in new situations.
2. I pay attention to my behavior to maintain harmony with others.
3. I pay attention to my behavior when I am with people of higher social status than I am.
4. It is important to pay attention to one's behavior.
5. I pay attention to my behavior when I am with someone older than I am.

Given that the 7 factors might combine into higher order scales, Gudykunst et al. (1992) did a secondary factor analysis (Hunter and Gerbing, 1982). Two factors emerged in the second order factor analysis. The first factor included four indices: cross-situational variability, attention to others' behaviour, attention to social comparison information, and attention to others' status characteristics. Following Lennox and Wolfe (1984), this second order factor was labelled concern for social appropriateness. The remaining three indices loaded on the second factor: ability to modify self-presentations, sensitivity to others' expressive behaviour, and tendency to avoid public performances (negative loading). Again, following Lennox and Wolfe, this factor was labelled self-monitoring.

The results of Gudykunst et al.'s (1992) multivariate analysis of variance revealed that the means in the United States sample were greater on two first order factors and one second order factor: ability to modify self-presentations, sensitivity to others' expressive behaviour, and self-monitoring. The means in the Japanese sample were greater than the means in the United States sample on three first order and one second order factors: attention to others' behaviour, tendency to avoid public performances, attention to others' status characteristics, and concern for social appropriateness. No significant differences emerged on the cross-situational variability and attention to social comparison information.

Gudykunst and associates (1992) also correlated scores on the 7 first order and two second order factors with a measure of idiocentrism (separation from ingroups; Triandis et al., 1986). In the United States, idiocentrics were less sensitive to others' expressive behaviour than allocentrics. In Japan, idiocentrics paid less attention to group based information than allocentrics.

The purpose of this study was to determine if the patterns obtained in Gudykunst et al.'s (1992) study in Japan and the United States can be extended to other individualistic and collective cultures. To accomplish this, the questionnaire used in Gudykunst et al.'s study was administered to samples in China and England.

METHODS

Respondents

The sample included 317 students in China and England: 198 (145 males and 48 females, 5 did not identify sex) from a large university in China and 119 (57 males and 62 females) from a university in England. The average age of the Chinese sample was 20.76, while the average age of the English sample was 19.50.

Measurement

A list of 62 self-monitoring items was presented in the first part of a questionnaire on "self-conceptions". The questionnaire was prepared in English and translated into Chinese with back translation to ensure equivalency. Snyder and Gangestad's (1986) 18 items were intermixed with the 11 collectivistic items in the first part of this section. These items were followed by Lennox and Wolfe's (1984) revised self-monitoring and concern for social appropriateness scales. Following Lennox and Wolfe, a 6-point response scale was used (0: certainly always false; 1: generally false; 2: somewhat false; 3: somewhat true; 4: generally true; 5: certainly always true).

The items used to define each of the factors are specified in Table 19.1. Reliabilities for the scales were as follows: ability to modify self-presentations: China: .68, England: .70; cross-situational variability: China: .65, England: .80; attention the others' behaviour: China: .78, England: .86; tendency to avoid public performances: China: .32, England: .51; sensitivity to others' expressive behaviour: China: .75, England: .77; attention to social comparison information: China: .49, England: .56; and attention to status characteristics: China: .72, England: .60.

Also included in the questionnaire was Triandis et al.'s (1986) measure of separation from ingroups, a scale designed to assess idiocentrism–allocentrism (personality level equivalents of individualism–collectivism, respectively). In order to increase reliabilities on this scale it was necessary to drop one item ("In most cases, to cooperate with someone whose ability is lower than yours is not as desirable as doing the thing on your own"). The final reliabilities (Cronbach's alpha) were .39 for the Chinese sample and .69 for the English sample. While not high, these reliabilities are compatible with those obtained by Triandis (personal communication, 30 March 1990). The higher the score on the separation from ingroups scale, the greater the level of idiocentrism.

RESULTS

The mean separation from ingroups score was 1.52 in the Chinese sample and 4.82 in the English sample. These scores yielded a t value of 17.23 (p < .001). The respondents in the English sample, therefore, were more idiocentric than those in the Chinese sample.

A 2 (China, England) × 2 (male, female) multivariate analysis of variance was conducted using the 7 factors as dependent variables. Bartletts' test of sphericity indicated that multivariate analysis was warranted (211.52, 21df, p < .001). The two-way multivariate interaction effects were not significant (Wilks' lambda: .98, F[7,273] < 1, p: ns). The multivariate main effect for sex was also not significant (Wilks' lambda: .96, F[7,273]: 1.47, p: ns). The multivariate main effect for culture was significant (Wilks' lambda: .82, F[7,273]: 8.46, p < .001).

Given that the multivariate main effect for culture was significant, the univariate tests were examined. Five of the 7 univariate tests were significant: tendency to avoid public performances (F[1,279]: 16.03, p < .001, eta^2: .05), sensitivity to others' expressive behaviour (F[1,279]: 12.67, p < .001, eta^2: .04), attention to others' status characteristics (F[1,279]: 6.87, p < .01, eta^2: .02), attention to social comparison information (F[1,279]: 6.77, p < .01, eta^2: .02), and ability to modify self-presentations (F[1,279]: 5.41, p < .05, eta^2: .02). Only cross-situational variability (F[1,279]: 5.41, p: ns) and attention to others' behaviour (F[1,279] < 1, p: ns) were not significant. An examination of the mean scores reveals that the English means were higher than the Chinese means on ability to modify self-presentations (E: 2.82, C: 2.60), tendency to avoid public performances (E: 3.11, C: 2.78), and sensitivity to others' expressive behaviour (E: 3.35, C: 3.00). The Chinese means were higher than the English means for attention to social comparison information (C: 2.78, E: 2.51) and attention to others' status characteristics (C: 3.21, E: 2.51). The means and standard deviations are presented in Table 19.2.

A 2 (China, England) × 2 (male, female) multivariate analysis of variance was applied to the second order factors. The Bartletts' test of sphericity indicated that multivariate analysis was warranted (42.19, 1df, p < .001). The two-way multivariate interaction effect was not significant (Wilks' lambda: .99, F[2,278]: 1.23, p: ns) and the multivariate main effect for sex was not significant (Wilks' lambda: .99, F[2,278] < 1, p: ns). The multivariate main effect for culture was significant (Wilks' lambda: .89, F[2,278]: 16.72, p < .001).

The univariate test for self-monitoring was significant (F[1,279]: 26.80, p < .001, eta^2: .09), while the univariate test for concern for social appropriateness was not significant (F[1,279] <1, p: ns). The

TABLE 19.2
Means and Standard Deviations by Culture

Factors	England		China	
	Mean	SD	Mean	SD
First Order Factors				
1. Ability to modify self-presentations	2.82	.42	2.60	.71
2. Cross-situational variability	2.81	.63	2.96	.74
3. Attention to others' behaviour	2.96	.82	2.80	.89
4. Tendency to avoid public performances	3.11	.66	2.78	.63
5. Sensitivity to others' expressive behaviour	3.34	.64	3.00	.75
6. Attention to social comparison information	2.58	.60	2.59	.72
7. Attention to others' status characteristics	3.01	.67	3.21	.74
Second Order Factors				
1. Concern for social appropriateness	2.84	.47	2.89	.48
2. Self-monitoring	2.63	.30	2.61	.51

English mean (3. 09) for self-monitoring was higher than the Chinese mean (2.76).

In the Chinese sample, separation from ingroups correlated with one first order factor and both second order factors: attention to others' status characteristics (r: −.19, p < .01), concern for social appropriateness (r: −.16, p < .05), and self-monitoring (r: .14, p < .05). In the English sample, separation from ingroups correlated with four first order factors and both second order factors: ability to modify self-presentations (r: .27, p < .001), sensitivity to others' expressive behaviour (r: .27, p < .001), attention to others' status characteristics (r: .23, p < .01), attention to others' behaviour (r: .18, p < .05), self-monitoring (r: .30, p < .001), and concern for social appropriateness (r: .18, p < .05).

DISCUSSION

The data suggest that the Chinese and English differed in their self-monitoring tendencies and their concern for social appropriateness.

The English respondents reported greater ability to modify their self-presentations, tendency to avoid public performances, and sensitivity to others' expressive behaviour than the Chinese respondents. The Chinese, in contrast, reported that they paid more attention to social comparison information and to others' status characteristics than the English.

These findings are generally compatible with predictions based on individualism–collectivism. The patterns based on individualism–collectivism become clear when these findings are compared with Gudykunst et al.'s (1992) study in Japan and the United States. There are several similarities between these findings and those of the earlier study. It appears that people in individualistic (England and the United States) cultures have greater ability to modify their self-presentations and greater sensitivity to others' expressive behaviour than people in collectivistic cultures (China and Japan). Members of collectivistic cultures, in contrast, pay greater attention to others' status characteristics than people in individualistic cultures. Further, there did not appear to be any significant differences between people in individualistic and collectivistic cultures in terms of the self-reported cross-situational variability of their behaviour.

The results for three factors in this study are inconsistent with those in Gudykunst ct al.'s (1992) study. In Gudykunst et al.'s study, the mean for tendency to avoid public performances was higher in Japan than in the United States. In the present study, the mean was higher in the English sample than in the Chinese sample. Further, Gudykunst et al. reported that the Japanese paid more attention to others' behaviour than the North Americans, while in the present study no significant differences were observed between the Chinese and English samples. Finally, Gudykunst et al. did not observe significant differences between Japan and the United States with respect to the use of social comparison information. The present data, however, revealed that the Chinese paid more attention to social comparison information than the English. These findings suggest that the tendency to avoid public performances, attention to others' behaviour, and attention to social comparison information may not be related directly to individualism–collectivism.

The findings of the two studies combined suggest that members of individualistic and collectivistic cultures have different concerns when it comes to self-monitoring. Members of individualistic cultures appear to focus on how they can change their behaviour to meet generalised expectations of others in a social situation (for instance, how a proto-typic person is expected to behave in the situation). Members of collectivistic cultures, in contrast, appear to focus on how they can behave appropriately given their relationship to specific people in a social situation. Both aspects of self-monitoring, however, exist in individualistic *and* collectivistic cultures.

Only two of the correlations between separation from ingroups and the dimensions of self-monitoring and concern for social appropriate-ness were consistent in the Chinese data and Gudykunst et al.'s (1992) study in Japan. Specifically, separation from ingroups correlated negatively with the first order factor attention to others' status char-acteristics and the second order factor concern for social appropriate-ness in China and Japan. It, therefore, appears that the more idiocentric individuals are in collectivistic cultures, the less they pay attention to others' status and the less concerned they are with behaving in a socially appropriate fashion.

There were no correlations between separation from ingroups and the dimensions of self-monitoring and concern for social appropriate-ness in the English data and Gudykunst et al.'s (1992) study in the United States. Since England and the United States are individualistic cultures, personality variations in idiocentrism do not appear to have a consistent influence on self-monitoring processes. If a personality level measure of collectivism (that is, allocentrism) had been included, differences may have emerged. Sinha (cited in Triandis et al., 1986), for example, has argued that allocentrics in individualistic cultures yield to ingroup norms (such as, concern for social appropriateness) more than idiocentrics in collectivistic cultures.

REFERENCES

Arkin, R.M. (1981). Self-presentation styles. In J. Tedeschi (Ed.), *Impression manage-ment and social psychological research* (pp. 311–333). New York: Academic Press.

Berry, J. (1969). On cross-cultural comparability. *International Journal of Psychology, 4*, 119–128.

Bond, M.H. (1988). Individual variation in multicultural studies of values. *Journal of Personality and Social Psychology, 55*, 1006–1015.

Briggs, S.R. and Cheek, J.M. (1988). On the nature of self-monitoring: Problems with assessment, problems with validity. *Journal of Personality and Social Psychology, 54*, 664–678.

BRIGGS, S.R., CHEEK, J.M., and BUSS, A. (1980). An analysis of the self-monitoring scale. *Journal of Personality and Social Psychology, 38*, 679–686.

CUTLER, B.L., LENNOX, R.D., and WOLFE, R.N. (1984). Reliability and validity of the aspects of identity questionnaire. Paper presented at the American Psychological Association Convention, Toronto.

GABRENYA, W and ARKIN, R. (1980). Factor structure and four correlates of self-monitoring. *Personality and Social Psychology Bulletin, 6*, 13–22.

GUDYKUNST, W.B., GAO, G., NISHIDA, T., BOND, M.H., LEUNG, K., WANG, G., and BARRACLOUGH, R. (1989). A cross-cultural comparison of self-monitoring. *Communication Research Reports, 6* (1), 7–12.

GUDYKUNST, W.B., GAO, G., NISHIDA, T., NADAMITSU, Y., and SAKAI, J. (1992). Self-monitoring in Japan and the United States. In S. Iwaki, Y. Kashima, and K. Leung (Eds.), *Innovations in cross-cultural psychology* (pp. 185–198). Amsterdam: Swets and Zeitlinger.

GUDYKUNST, W.B. and TING-TOOMEY, S. (1988). *Culture and interpersonal communication*. Newbury Park, CA: Sage.

GUDYKUNST, W.B., YANG, S.M., and NISHIDA, T. (1987). Cultural differences in self-consciousness and self-monitoring. *Communication Research, 14*, 7–36.

HUNTER, J.E. and GERBING, D.W. (1982). Unidimensional measurement, second order factor analysis, and causal models. *Research in Organizational Behavior, 4*, 267–320.

IWABUCHI, C., TANAKA, K., and NAKAZATO, H. (1982). A study of the self-monitoring scale. *Japanese Journal of Psychology, 1*, 54–57 (in Japanese with English abstract).

LENNOX, R. and WOLFE, R. (1984). Revision of the self-monitoring scale. *Journal of Personality and Social Psychology, 46*, 1349–1364.

SCHUMAKER, J.F. and BARRACLOUGH, R. (1989). Protective self-presentation in Malaysian and Australian individuals. *Journal of Cross-Cultural Psychology, 20*, 54–63.

SNYDER, M. (1974). Self-monitoring of expressive behavior. *Journal of Personality and Social Psychology, 30*, 526–537.

SNYDER, M. (1979). Self-monitoring processes. In L. Berkowitz (Ed.), *Advances in experimental social psychology* (Vol. 12, pp. 85–128). New York: Academic Press.

SNYDER, M. (1987). *Public appearances/private realities*. San Francisco: Freeman.

SNYDER, M. and GANGESTAD, S. (1986). On the nature of self-monitoring. *Journal of Personality and Social Psychology, 45*, 1061-1072.

TRIANDIS, H.C. (1988). Collectivism vs. individualism: A reconceptualization of a basic concept in cross-cultural psychology. In C. Bagley and G. Verma (Eds.), *Cross-cultural studies of personality, attitudes, and cognition* (pp. 60–95). London: Macmillan.

TRIANDIS, H.C., BONTEMPO, R., BETANCOURT., H, BOND, M.H., LEUNG, K., BRENES, A., GEORGAS, J., HUI, C.H., MARIN, G., SETIADI, B., SINHA, J., VERMA, J., SPANGEN-BERG, J., TOUZARD, H., and DE MONTMOLLIN, G. (1986). The measurement of etic aspects of individualism and collectivism across cultures. *Australian Journal of Psychology, 38*, 257–267.

TRIANDIS, H.C., MALPASS, R., and DAVIDSON, A. (1973). Cross-cultural psychology. *Biennial Review of Anthropology, 24*, 1–84.

WOLFE, R.N., LENNOX, R.D., and CUTLER, B.L. (1986). Getting along and getting ahead: Empirical support for a theory of protective and acquisitive self-presentation. *Journal of Personality and Social Psychology, 50*, 356–361.

Section 4

Social Values and Problems of Developing Societies

20

Introduction

The first paper of this section by Best and Williams makes a cross-cultural examination of young adults' views of growing old. With the elderly constituting an increasing proportion of the population in both developing and developed countries, young adults' views of older persons and the aging process have important social policy implications. The authors have examined the perception and views of respondents from 19 countries regarding the definition of old age and middle age, predicted life expectancies, most productive time of life, feelings about growing old, etc. The authors have discussed the similarities and differences across cultural groups.

Ward and Kennedy, in their paper, have reported the findings of three studies exploring the relationships between the psychological and socio-cultural dimensions of adjustment during cross-cultural transitions. The level of psychological and socio-cultural adjustment, and the variations in psychological and socio-cultural adjustment over time have been examined in various sojourning and sedentary groups. Study one compared sojourners who made a large vs small cross-cultural transition (Malaysian and Singaporean students in New Zealand and Malaysian students in Singapore). Study two contrasted a sojourning (New Zealand AFS students) and a sedentary group (New

Zealand students at home). The third study was a longitudinal investigation of psychological and socio-cultural adaptation. The results of the studies revealed that socio-cultural adjustment problems were greater in sojourning compared to sedentary groups, and in sojourners who made a large cross-cultural transition. There were no significant differences, however, in psychological adjustment in these groups. In line with the hypotheses, significantly higher correlations were found in sojourning groups that made small as opposed to large transitions. Higher correlations were also observed in the sedentary compared to the sojourning groups. The longitudinal study of newly arrived Malaysian and Singaporean students in New Zealand revealed that socio-cultural adaptation problems decreased over time while the pattern of psychological adjustment problems assumed a V shape, initially decreasing and then subsequently increasing over a one year period.

Bhawuk and Udas have reported the findings of their study on Nepalese entrepreneurs. Using the INDCOL Scale developed by Triandis et al. (1986), the attitude of Nepalese entrepreneurs was measured to determine whether they are individualistic like entrepreneurs in the west. Results indicated that Nepalese entrepreneurs have: (a) the spirit of competition, a drive to be on their own, and a sense of internal control, and (b) commitment to aging parents, friends, and relatives in need. A factor analysis of the data yielded 7 factors of which 4 are etic and 3 emic. The findings imply that entrepreneurs can be both individualist and collectivist depending on the situation (work or family). The authors have added that further research is necessary to fully understand the relationship between entrepreneurship and individualism and collectivism.

Unemployment in developing countries is of special significance because of the population pressure. Mala Sinha and R.C. Tripathi have reported their findings about motivational states and stress–strain perceptions of unemployed youth in India. The authors have observed both cross-cultural similarities and differences in the psychological attributes of Indian and Euro–American unemployed. For example, *niskama karma*, an indigenous concept, was found to be a better predictor of fit and well being than internal control. *Niskama karma* focuses on effort without being concerned about outcomes and internal control assumes effort–outcome contingency.

In their paper, Gupta and Pandey discuss the socio-cultural causes of non-reporting of crimes in India. Interdimensional correlations provide additional relevant information to understand the dynamics of non-reporting of crimes. They observed that fatalism, ignorance of people, and alternative judicial methods were positively correlated. People's belief that God would punish the culprit inhibit their motivation to report crime. Sometimes, people prefer to use the local judicial system like the Panchayat for the settlement of criminal related disputes.

In his paper, Anthony has strongly argued for the establishment of international networks to facilitate development of mechanisms for culturally viable development. To achieve this goal, membership of professional organisations could provide the base to form alliances or networks across countries.

21

Anticipation of Aging: A Cross-Cultural Examination of Young Adults' Views of Growing Old*

DEBORAH L. BEST • JOHN E. WILLIAMS

In 1790 when the USA was just 14 years old, the official census began and has been conducted every 10 years ever since. At the time of the first census barely 2 per cent of the population of the USA was over the age of 65, and that number had grown to only 4 per cent by 1900 (Kalish, 1982). As of 1990 more than 35 million persons, or almost 16 per cent of the population of the USA was 65 years of age or older

* Cooperating researchers: Marja Ahokas, Finland; Hasan Bacanli, Turkey; Tore Bjerke, Norway; Kai Sook Chung, Korea; John Edwards, Canada; Ann Edworthy, Wales; Abdul Haque, Pakistan; Stanislawa Lis, Poland; Ann Levett, South Africa; John McMaster, Zimbabwe; Alegria Majluf, Peru; Felix Neto, Portugal; Janak Pandey, India; Esteban Roa, Venezuela; José Saiz, Chile; Shripathi Upadhyaya, Malaysia; Hans-Georg Voss, Germany; and Colleen Ward, New Zealand.

(Hoffman, 1991). Similar figures are seen in the population distributions of other developing and developed countries (United Nations, 1980). A large proportion of the increase in life expectancy has resulted from medical advances that have eliminated many health conditions causing death at early ages, thus increasing life expectancies around the world.

Growing older is a process experienced by everyone. In the short time taken to read the preceding paragraph, we have all aged, whether we are in our teens, 20s, 30s, or older. Interest in the field of gerontology has grown greatly in the past decade, spurred by increases in the aging populations around the world. Courses in aging or older adulthood are now taught regularly in many universities, and younger adults are being asked to learn more about older people and what it means to age. Along with factual knowledge, another kind of awareness is growing among these younger adults. Students are sometimes asked to consider whether certain physical losses will apply to them and how they will cope with the inevitable changes that accompany the aging process. Will they become lonely, depressed, or will they experience greater contentment and happiness in their older years? It is this anticipation of aging that is the focus of this paper. The data presented here are part of a larger cross-cultural study of young adults' stereotypes of the elderly and attitudes toward the aging process. Findings concerning three components of aging addressed in the larger study will be presented here: questions about age definitions, predictions of life expectancy, and perceptions of future life satisfaction.

Asking younger adults about the elderly is somewhat unique when compared with other outgroup stereotype and attitude research. By asking young adults to describe older adults, they are being asked to describe a group of which they will some day be a part. That is not the case for other stereotypes, such as those concerning gender, race, or ethnic groups. Hence, the task is a bit unusual for the subjects. The context of looking forward at "themselves" may influence the attitudes they disclose about aging when asked to define age categories, estimate their life expectancies, or predict their own satisfaction with life when they are older.

METHOD

Subjects

Subjects were university students from 19 countries representing 6 continents: Africa (South Africa, Zimbabwe), Asia (India, Korea, Malaysia, Pakistan, Turkey), Europe (Finland, Germany, Norway, Poland, Portugal, Wales), North America (Canada, the USA), Oceania (New Zealand) and South America (Chile, Peru, Venezuela). In each country, the sample consisted of approximately 100 students, evenly distributed by gender. Each subject group was selected to represent a relatively general group of university students, rather than a specialised curricular group.

Materials

The questionnaire used in the study is presented in Table 21.1. In order to determine the ages associated with labels for two adult age categories (old, middle aged), two age definition questions were developed. To evaluate life expectancy, two questions concerning life expectancies, one for the subjects themselves and the other for the average person in the subject's country, were devised (see Table 21.1.) It was assumed that life expectancy would be influenced by the actual life expectancy in each country, and these data were collected from the United Nations census records.

Life satisfaction was evaluated in three ways (see Table 21.1). First, subjects were asked to indicate the decade of their lives that they thought was/would be the most satisfying and productive. Second, the Life Satisfaction Index (Neugarten, Havighurst, and Tobin, 1961), one of the most frequently used scales for measuring subjective well-being in the elderly, was modified to be appropriate for use with young adults. Since 11 of the 20 items of the scale could not be altered to suit young adults, the final scale comprised 9 items, with 5 representing positive feelings about being older and 4 representing negative feelings. Using only half of the original items was not considered a problem since other researchers have used as few as 13 items reliably

TABLE 21.1
Age Definition and Attitudes toward Aging Questions

Age Definition Questions

1. When you hear someone described as being "old," what age do you think of? At least _____ years.
2. When you hear someone described as being "middle aged," what age do you think of? At least _____ years.

Life Expectancy

1. Assuming that you die of natural causes, at what age would you expect this to happen? _____ years.
2. What is your estimate of the number of years the average person in our country lives? _____ years.

Life Satisfaction

Which decade of your life (e.g., your teens, 30s, 70s) do you think will be your most satisfying and productive years?

0–9 years	50–59 years
10–19 years	60–69 years
20–29 years	70–79 years
30–39 years	80–89 years
40–49 years	90–99 years

Please indicate your degree of agreement or disagreement with each of the following statements by putting one of the following numbers in the blank.

(1) Agree Strongly
(2) Agree
(3) Agree Somewhat
(4) Disagree Somewhat
(5) Disagree
(6) Disagree Strongly

_____1. When I am old, it will be the saddest time of my life.
_____2. When I am old, I will be just as happy as now when I am younger.
_____3. My older years will be the best years of my life.
_____4. When I am old, most of the things I do will be boring or monotonous.
_____5. When I am old, I will feel old and tired.
_____6. When I am old, I know I will feel my age, but it won't bother me.
_____7. When I am old, I will look back on my life and will feel fairly well satisfied.
_____8. By the time I am old, I will have made many foolish decisions.
_____9. By the time I am old, I will have gotten pretty much what I expected out of life.

Overall, how do you feel about growing older? (Please circle to indicate your answer.)

Very negatively _____ Very positively

1   2   3   4   5   6

with the elderly (Kane and Kane, 1981; Wood, Wylie, and Sheafor, 1969). Subjects were asked to indicate their agreement with each statement using a 6-point scale ranging from (1) strongly agree to (6) strongly disagree. Responses to positive items were reversed such that high scores represent positive attitudes toward aging. Third, subjects were asked to indicate overall how they felt about growing older using a 6-point scale ranging from (1) very negative to (6) very positive.

In addition to collecting data from individual subjects in each country, cultural comparison indices were compiled for each country. These indices were selected because they reflect the diversity of the cultures and because reliable data were available for the group of countries under study. The comparison variables were grouped into 8 areas: general demographics (e.g., per cent of population urban, latitude), indices of development (e.g., GNP, average size of household), work related values (Hofstede, 1980), religious indices (per cent of population with Protestant affiliation, Muslim affiliation), status of women (e.g., per cent of women employed outside the home, in the university enrolment), educational indices (e.g., per cent of school age population in school, literacy rate), health indices (e.g., infant mortality, life expectancy), and public expenditures (e.g., health, education). A more useful summary comparative indices, economic and social status ranking (Sivard, 1986), is a composite index on which countries are ranked in terms of overall economic–social development based on three equally weighted factors: GNP per capita, education (a summary of 5 indicators), and health (a summary of 5 indicators).

Procedure

In each country, the questionnaires were administered in English where appropriate or translated when necessary by our cooperating researcher or students working under his or her supervision. Subjects were simply asked to respond to the questions.

RESULTS AND DISCUSSION

In each country the responses to each item were tabulated for males and females separately. Comparisons between gender groups and across countries were made using univariate and multivariate analyses of variance. Correlations among variables were also calculated.

Age Definitions

The subjects' responses concerning old and middle age are summarised in Table 21.2 which shows the mean minimum age for "old" and "middle age" for both sexes in each country. Across all 19 countries, males defined old as being at least 60 years of age, significantly younger than females' definition of 62 years of age. A similar significant difference was found in the definitions of middle age, with males defining it as at least 39 years of age and females defining it as at least 41 years of age (see Table 21.2). Despite these differences, age definitions of males and females were significantly correlated for both old (r: .73, $p < .0001$), and middle age (r: .79, $p < .0001$), indicating similar patterns across countries for the two gender groups.

TABLE 21.2

Mean Minimum Ages Associated with Old and Middle Age by Male and Female Subjects in 19 Countries

Country	Age Defining Old		Age Defining Middle Age	
	Male Ss	Female Ss	Male Ss	Female Ss
Canada	61.9	66.4	40.3	44.0
Chile	61.4	67.2	38.3	40.5
Finland	61.7	65.6	40.0	40.4
Germany	59.1	62.7	40.4	41.8
India	57.3	59.3	38.9	40.1
Korea	58.2	54.2	40.0	39.9
Malaysia	55.0	53.9	35.1	35.9
New Zealand	58.9	63.1	41.2	41.2
Norway	65.2	65.8	42.7	45.3
Pakistan	59.7	64.1	40.2	41.1
Peru	58.7	61.2	36.9	38.8
Poland	58.0	63.1	37.5	43.9
Portugal	63.2	67.9	43.0	47.8
South Africa	61.9	60.7	40.5	42.0
Turkey	55.7	58.4	36.9	37.5
United States	61.1	62.9	40.7	41.1
Venezuela	65.4	64.7	38.6	39.6
Wales	61.7	60.4	40.2	40.7
Zimbabwe	57.6	60.2	38.2	38.7
Total	60.1	62.2	39.5	41.1

The lowest ages for defining old and middle age were found in Malaysia (55 years and 40 years) and Turkey (57 years and 37 years), and the highest were observed in Portugal (66 years and 45 years). When these age definitions were correlated with actual life expectancy in each country, neither reached significance (.42 for old, .37 for middle age). However, age definitions of old were significantly correlated with several measures of development, such as economic social standing rank (males, r: $-.47$, $p < .04$), percentage of the population that is Christian (males, r: .68, $p < .002$; females, r: .66, $p < .002$), and living space as measured by persons per room density (males, r: $-.67$, $p < .002$; females, r: $-.61$, $p < .005$). These finding suggest that the ages used to define these categories were somewhat higher in more developed countries and those with a larger Christian population.

Life Expectancy

As can be seen in Table 21.3, male and female subjects differed slightly in their predictions of their own life expectancies. Men predicted that they would live 73 years and women predicted that they would live 72 years. These predictions are extremely interesting in the light of the fact that, in every country, actual life expectancies and mortality at each age of adulthood favoured women. Compared with women, men perceived aging as occurring earlier but they expected to live longer.

Subjects' self-predictions of life expectancy were significantly correlated for both men and women (r: .92, $p < .0001$). Males' predictions were correlated with actual life expectancy (r: .73, $p < .0001$), with self-definitions of age (r: .47, $p < .045$), and with a number of cultural comparison variables, such as population growth (r: $-.53$, $p < .019$), living space (r: $-.77$, $p < .0001$), economic social standing rank (r: $-.74$, $p < .0001$), and individually with other measures that compose the ranking. Females' self life expectancies were also correlated with a number of comparison variables, such as economic social standing (r: $-.83$, $p < .0001$), individually with many of the measures composing the ranking, and with two religious variables, percentage of Protestants (r: .52, $p < .047$), and percentage of Christians (r: .81, $p < .0001$). These data suggest that the predictions of one's own life expectancy is influenced by socio-economic development, but in the case of women, religious values also seem to play an important role.

TABLE 21.3
*Subjects' Predicted Life Expectancies for Self and Average Person
in their Own Country and Actual Life Expectancies in 19 Countries*

Country	Self Life Expectancy		Average Person Life Expectancy		Actual Life Expectancy at Birth (1989)	
	Male Ss	Female Ss	Male Ss	Female Ss	Men	Women
Canada	78.4	76.8	71.9	72.3	73	80
Chile	73.0	71.6	67.2	67.8	68	75
Finland	74.1	76.3	72.3	74.1	71	79
Germany	73.2	72.7	70.6	69.3	72	78
India	68.4	63.1	56.2	59.9	57	58
Korea	71.3	69.6	66.9	68.0	66	73
Malaysia	74.5	67.2	71.8	64.8	65	70
New Zealand	76.6	79.2	70.5	64.8	72	78
Norway	76.9	80.7	74.7	74.9	73	80
Pakistan	53.3	52.4	52.8	62.4	54	55
Peru	71.0	71.7	62.7	65.6	61	66
Poland	75.0	70.9	67.4	66.5	66	74
Portugal	82.1	79.9	65.5	67.7	71	78
South Africa	76.2	76.2	67.5	68.8	58	64
Turkey	61.0	62.8	62.8	61.5	63	66
United States	81.0	82.3	74.6	75.9	72	79
Venezuela	75.7	71.8	65.0	67.4	67	73
Wales	78.8	77.1	72.2	72.5	72	78
Zimbabwe	71.8	69.2	63.3	67.1	59	63
Total	73.3	72.2	67.2	68.0	66	72

Predictions for the average person did not differ for male and female subjects (see Table 21.3), with males predicting that the average person would live 67 years and females predicting 68.5 years. Interestingly, these predictions were not correlated with actual life expectancies nor with many of the cultural comparison variables. However, self and average person life expectancies were significantly correlated for both male (r: .77, p < .001) and female subjects (r: .85, p < .0001), indicating that the subjects made similar predictions for themselves and for others. For both life expectancy predictions, the lowest age predictions were observed in Pakistan, Turkey, and India, and the highest in the USA, Norway, and Finland. It should be noted that the lowest actual life expectancies were in Pakistan and India, and the highest in Canada and Norway.

Life Satisfaction

Best Decade

The findings concerning the most satisfying and productive decade of life are presented in Table 21.4. Across the 19 countries, both males and females indicated that the 20s and the 30s would be the best period of their lives. While the differences between male and female

TABLE 21.4
Most Satisfying and Productive Decade of Life in 19 Countries

Country	Male Ss	Female Ss
Canada	3.63	3.60
Chile	3.78	3.47
Finland	3.89	3.60
Germany	3.48	3.40
India	3.16	3.18
Korea	3.62	3.18
Malaysia	3.53	3.44
New Zealand	3.52	3.48
Norway	3.70	3.80
Pakistan	3.74	2.65
Peru	3.38	3.49
Poland	3.58	3.81
Portugal	3.46	3.61
South Africa	3.43	3.41
Turkey	3.80	3.58
United States	3.59	3.75
Venezuela	3.72	3.52
Wales	3.52	3.42
Zimbabwe	3.94	3.72
Total	3.61	3.48

Decade 3: 20–29 Years of Age; Decade 4: 30–39 Years of Age.

subjects were not significant, correlations with other variables varied for men and women. Men's most productive decade scores were not correlated with any of the comparison variables examined in the larger study, while women's scores were correlated with a number of variables, such as economic social standing rank (r: $-.83$, $p < .0001$), percentage of women in universities (r: $.57$, $p < .007$), literacy rate (r: $.68$, $p < .001$), percentage of women working outside the home (r: $.78$, $p <$

.0001), actual life expectancies for women (r: .61, $p <$ .006), and percentage of Christians (r: .59, $p <$ .008). These correlations suggest that in the more developed countries where women were afforded more opportunities, women mentioned slightly older ages as being the most productive, satisfying time of their lives. Perhaps in these countries the emphasis upon societal functions, such as child bearing and child rearing, that are closely associated with younger ages in a woman's life cycle is not so strong.

Younger ages were mentioned as the most productive time of life in India, Germany, and Peru while somewhat older ages were mentioned in Finland, Zimbabwe, and New Zealand. These observations are interesting since socio-economic development alone cannot account for these differences.

Life Satisfaction Index

The Life Satisfaction Index scores shown in Table 21.5 indicate that across all 19 countries, with mean scores generally between 3 and 4, subjects' responses varied from neutral to slightly positive about getting older. An examination of the individual item means across all subjects shown in Table 21.6, revealed that on the positive side, subjects reported that when they were old it would not be the saddest time of life and they would not be bored, thereby indicating that they had optimistic views of growing old. However, subjects did express that they would not be as happy as when they were younger, they would not look back and feel satisfied with life, and they would not have gotten what they wanted out of life. This negative attitude indicates that the subjects were concerned with how they would feel about the success of their life course when they were older. This same concern was noted in a study in the USA where older adults were more positive about the life cycle than younger adults (Harris, 1975). Across all items, the most negative responses were to the item—when they were older, they would feel their age and that would bother them a great deal.

In the case of female subjects, life satisfaction scores were correlated with self life expectancy (r: .71, $p <$ .001), literacy rates (r: .59; $p <$ .008), percentage of the labour force that is agricultural (r: $-$.48, $p <$ .04), and with percentage of Christians (r: .55, $p <$ .016). None of

TABLE 21.5
Life Satisfaction Index Scores in 19 Countries

Country	Male Ss	Female Ss
Canada	3.82	3.90
Chile	4.31	4.46
Finland	3.99	4.18
Germany	3.96	4.11
India	3.92	3.78
Korea	4.01	4.05
Malaysia	3.95	3.98
New Zealand	4.03	3.82
Norway	3.86	4.18
Pakistan	3.39	3.14
Peru	4.23	4.56
Poland	3.76	3.63
Portugal	3.76	3.63
South Africa	3.86	4.07
Turkey	3.85	3.64
United States	4.00	4.16
Venezuela	4.58	4.40
Wales	4.01	3.94
Zimbabwe	3.60	3.67
Total	3.95	3.97

9 items with 1–6 scale; high scores: positive attitude toward aging.

TABLE 21.6
Mean Life Satisfaction Index Items across All Subjects in 19 Countries

Mean Score	
4.39	1. When I am old, it will be the saddest time of my life.
2.30	2. When I am old, I will be just as happy as now when I am younger. (P)
3.12	3. My older years will be the best years of my life. (P)
4.37	4. When I am old, most of the things I do will be boring or monotonous.
3.97	5. When I am old, I will feel old and tired.
1.83	6. When I am old, I know I will feel my age, but it won't bother me. (P)
1.52	7. When I am old, I will look back on my life and will feel fairly well satisfied. (P)
3.13	8. By the time I am old, I will have made many foolish decisions.
1.78	9. By the time I am old, I will have gotten pretty much what I expected out of life. (P)

6-point scale, 1: agree strongly and 6: disagree strongly; high scores: positive attitude toward aging.

these correlations were significant in the case of male subjects. However, both male and female scores were correlated with each other (r: .85, $p < .0001$), and with the percentage of urban population (males, r: .59, $p < .008$; females, r: .60, $p < .007$). Female subjects reported more positive feelings about growing older in countries that are no longer dependent upon agriculture and are more urbanised and emphasise education, i.e., variables that represent development.

Returning to Table 21.5, the lowest satisfaction with life was noted in Pakistan and Zimbabwe, and the highest in Venezuela, Chile, and Peru. Again, as with the most productive decade data, development alone does not predict life satisfaction scores.

Overall Rating of Aging

For both males and females in all 19 countries, the overall rating of growing older was neutral, 3.72 on a 1–6 scale. Males and females did not differ on this dimension, and their scores were correlated significantly with each other (r: .69, $p < .001$). As expected, these scores were correlated with life satisfaction scores for both males (r: .91, $p < .0001$) and females (r: .68, $p < .001$). Males' scores were also correlated with percentage of Catholics (r: .46, $p < .05$).

The most positive ratings for feelings about growing older were noted in Venezuela and Chile, and the most negative in Pakistan, Canada, and Zimbabwe; the pattern being similar to the Life Satisfaction Index scores. Obviously, predictions of the quality of life in older adulthood are not clearly related to indices of development or to actual life expectancies. They seem to be more reflective of young adults' psychological perceptions of the subjective well-being of older individuals in their culture.

Consistent with other research conducted mostly in the United States, these cross-cultural findings reflect the inconsistent nature of attitudes toward aging. Some studies have reported negative attitudes toward the elderly and aging (Eisdorfer and Altrocchi, 1961; Wernick and Manaster, 1984) while others have found no differences or more positive attitudes toward the elderly (Drefenstedt, 1981; Puckett, Petty, Cacioppo, and Fisher, 1983). The results presented here indicate that younger adults were somewhat ambivalent about their own eventual aging. While they did not perceive it as a time of gloom and doom, they did not see it as the most satisfying and productive time of life

TABLE 21.7
Overall Rating of Feelings about Growing Older

Country	Male Ss	Female Ss
Canada	3.33	3.47
Chile	4.05	4.12
Finland	3.65	3.65
Germany	3.89	4.11
India	3.67	3.55
Korea	3.66	3.51
Malaysia	4.00	4.03
New Zealand	3.81	3.54
Norway	3.80	4.10
Pakistan	3.08	3.41
Peru	4.10	3.71
Poland	3.60	3.50
Portugal	3.60	3.50
South Africa	3.59	3.57
Turkey	3.78	3.50
United States	3.64	4.02
Venezuela	4.49	4.08
Wales	3.70	3.71
Zimbabwe	3.24	3.48
Total	3.72	3.72

1–6 scale, 1: very negative, 6: very positive.

either. Moreover, their predictions about their own life span and their projections of their satisfaction with growing older were coloured not by the actual facts concerning aging in their society, such as actual life expectancies, but more by cultural factors, such as development and religion.

CONCLUSIONS

The data reported in this paper represent only a part of a larger cross-cultural study of age stereotypes and attitudes toward aging. A report of the larger project (Williams, Best, and Saiz, 1991) focused on the stereotyped characteristics that young adult subjects associated with younger and older adults. Preliminary analyses of the stereotype data indicated that in some countries the young and old were seen as more dissimilar than in other countries. Surprisingly, across all the 19 countries, adjectives associated with old persons were somewhat more favourable than those associated with young persons. The stereotype data reported previously and the data concerning attitudes toward aging reported in this paper are consistent and indicate that young adults were generally more positive about aging and the elderly than might have been expected. In spite of the generally positive views expressed by young adults towards older adults and the aging process, clear cultural variations existed in the perceptions of aging and the elderly. These findings, in turn, have social policy implications as all modern societies seek to deal with the challenges and problems associated with the increasing proportion of elderly persons in their respective populations.

REFERENCES

DREFENSTEDT, J. (1981). Age bias in evaluation of achievement: What determines? *Journal of Gerontology, 36*, 453–454.

EISDORFER, C. and ALTROCCHI, J. (1961). A comparison of attitudes toward old age and mental illness. *Journal of Gerontology, 16*, 340–343.

HARRIS, L. (1975). *The myth and reality of aging in America.* Washington, D.C.: National Council on Aging.

HOFFMAN, M.S. (1991). *The world almanac and book of facts.* New York: Pharos Books.

HOFSTEDE, G. (1980). *Culture's consequences: International differences in work-related values.* Beverly Hills, CA: Sage.

KALISH, R.A. (1982). *Late adulthood: Perspectives on human development* (2nd ed.). Monterey, CA: Brooks/Cole.

KANE, R.A. and KANE, R.L. (1981). *Assessing the elderly: A practical guide to measurement.* Lexington, MA: Lexington Books.

NEUGARTEN, B., HAVIGHURST, R., and TOBIN, S. (1961). The measure of life satisfaction. *Journal of Gerontology, 16*, 134–143.

PUCKETT, J.M., PETTY, R.E., CACIOPPO, J.T., and FISHER, D.L. (1983). The relative impact of age and attractiveness stereotypes on persuasion. *Journal of Gerontology, 18*, 340–343.

SIVARD, R.L. (1986). *World military and social expenditures.* Leesburg, VA: World Military and Social Expenditures Publications.

UNITED NATIONS. (1980). *Selected demographic indicators by country, 1950–2000: Demographic estimates and projections as assessed in 1978*, Ser. R138.

WERNICK, M. and MANASTER, G.J. (1984). Age and perception of age and attractiveness. *The Gerontologist, 24*, 408–414.

WILLIAMS, J.E., BEST, D.L., and SAIZ, J.L. (1991, July). Age stereotypes viewed cross-culturally: A first report. Paper presented at the regional meeting of the International Association for Cross-Cultural Psychology, Debrecen, Hungary.

WOOD, V., WYLIE, M., and SHEAFOR, B. (1969). An analysis of a short self-report measure of life satisfaction: Correlation with rater judgments. *The Gerontologist, 6*, 31.

22

Crossing Cultures: The Relationship between Psychological and Socio-cultural Dimensions of Cross-Cultural Adjustment*

COLLEEN A. WARD • ANTONY KENNEDY

Although the processes and consequences of culture contact and culture change have attracted considerable attention in recent years, theory and research in this area have remained largely unsynthesised. The empirical literature has been derived from quite separate domains, e.g., research on sojourners, refugees, immigrants and native peoples; systematic comparisons between groups in transition have been comparatively rare. Theoretical diversity, including varying emphases on

* The research was supported by a grant (No. 8914) from the Foundation for Research, Science and Technology (formerly known as the New Zealand Social Science Research Fund Committee).

clinical, cognitive and behavioural factors in the transition process, has also complicated comparative analyses. While the exceptional work by Berry and colleagues on acculturative stress (e.g., Berry and Kim, 1988; Berry, Kim, Minde, and Mok, 1987; Berry, Kim, Power, Young, and Bujaki, 1989) and studies on culture learning by Furnham and Bochner (Furnham, 1983; Furnham and Bochner, 1982, 1986) represent more substantive and systematic research on culture contact and change, a single overarching framework has yet to emerge as a major integrative force in the study of cross-cultural transition.

Although acculturation literature has concentrated primarily on the prediction of adjustment during cross-cultural transition, a major problem has emerged with the definition and operationalisation of outcome variables (Church, 1982). Acculturation, adaptation, and adjustment have been used interchangeably, and numerous variables have been utilised as indices of adjustive outcomes: attitudes toward the host culture (Ibrahim, 1970), feelings of acceptance and satisfaction (Brislin, 1981), mood states (Stone Feinstein and Ward, 1990), acquisition of culturally appropriate behaviour and skills (Bochner, McLeod, and Lin, 1977), nature and extent of interactions with hosts (Sewell and Davidsen, 1961), health indicators (Babiker, Cox, and Miller, 1980), academic and job performance (Harris, 1972; Perkins, Perkins, Guglielmino, and Rieff, 1977), and premature termination of an overseas assignment (Black and Gregersen, 1990). Given this assortment of outcome indicators it has been problematic for researchers to draw firm conclusions about what precisely facilitates competent coping in a cross-cultural milieu.

In their attempts to integrate acculturation literature and sojourner research Ward and colleagues have proposed the distinction of psychological and socio-cultural adaptation during cross-cultural transitions (Searle and Ward, 1990; Ward and Kennedy, 1992, in press a, in press b; Ward and Searle, 1991). The former refers to feelings of satisfaction and well-being while the latter relates to the ability to "fit in" or negotiate interactive aspects of the host culture. Theorising by Ward and associates has borrowed heavily from two divergent traditions in the "culture shock" field. The first derives from the psychology of adjustment. It is underpinned by the work of Lazarus and Folkman (1984) on stress and coping and is exemplified by research by Berry and colleagues on acculturation and adaptation (Berry and Kim, 1988; Chataway and Berry, 1989). The second tradition is based on Argyle's

(1980) social skills model which has been popularised by Furnham and Bochner (1986) in their culture learning approach to cross-cultural transition.

Combining features of both stress and coping and social skills models in their investigations of cross-cultural transition and adjustment, Ward and colleagues have reported that the two adjustment domains are interrelated but are predicted by different types of variables. Psychological adjustment, defined in terms of well-being or mood states (e.g., depression, anxiety, tension, and fatigue), is predicted by personality, life changes, and social support variables. More specifically, psychological adjustment is associated with variables such as extraversion, locus of control, loneliness, life change units as measured by readjustment rating scales, and a range of relationship satisfaction measures (Armes and Ward, 1989; Searle and Ward, 1990; Stone Feinstein and Ward, 1990; Ward and Kennedy, 1992, in press a, in press b; Ward and Searle, 1991). In contrast, socio-cultural adaptation, measured by the amount of difficulty experienced in the management of everyday social situations in the host culture, is predicted by variables which are related more strongly to cognitive factors and social skills acquisition; these include cultural knowledge, language ability, expectations, cultural distance, and cultural identity.

Extending the distinction between psychological and socio-cultural adjustment during cross-cultural transitions, the researchers have made three additional points: (a) the level of psychological and socio-cultural adjustment varies over groups; (b) the magnitude of the relationship between psychological and socio-cultural adaptation varies according to groups and contexts; and (c) psychological and socio-cultural dimensions of adjustment follow different patterns over time.

Level of Psychological and Socio-cultural Adjustment

Much of the cross-cultural transition literature has been based on the implicit assumption that relocations to unfamiliar cultures are more difficult than relocations to familiar ones. Indeed, Oberg's (1960) early work on culture shock highlighted the impact of loss of familiar cues on sojourners' emotional reactions to transition. Although cultural similarity–dissimilarity has long been regarded as an important factor in adjustment to culture change, the credit goes to Babiker, Cox, and

Miller (1980) for devising a means of measuring cultural distance and for demonstrating its relationship to physical and mental health. Cultural distance has also been associated with socio-cultural adaptation. Furnham and Bochner (1982), for example, reported that cultural distance was related to the level of social difficulty experienced by European, Middle Eastern and Asian students in the United Kingdom; cultural distance has emerged as a robust predictor of socio-cultural adaptation in studies by Ward and associates (Searle and Ward, 1990; Ward and Kennedy, 1992, in press a, in press b).

The concept of cultural distance underpins both stress and coping models of adjustment which maintain that life changes are linked to the development of physical and mental illness and social skills approaches to cross-cultural transition which suggest that greater cultural distance is associated with the availability of fewer culturally appropriate skills. Against this theoretical and empirical background, two hypotheses are advanced about cultural distance:

1. Psychological and socio-cultural adjustment problems will be greater in sojourners who make a large, compared to a small, cross-cultural transition.
2. Psychological and socio-cultural adjustment problems are greater in a sojourning group compared to a sedentary group.

The Relationship between Psychological and Socio-cultural Adjustment

Ward and colleagues have argued that the magnitude of the relationship between psychological and socio-cultural adjustment varies according to the context (Ward and Kennedy, in press a, in press b). More specifically, it has been suggested that the association between psychological and socio-cultural adaptation will fluctuate in relationship to the sojourner's need, capacity or opportunity for integration into the host culture. The greater the reliance on the host culture as the primary environment for interaction, the stronger the relationship between the two adjustment dimensions. For example, if sojourners choose to inhabit an "expatriate bubble" and have minimum interaction with nationals of the host culture, it is unlikely that there will be a strong relationship between psychological well-being and culture specific competence. On the other hand, for sojourners who are well integrated into the host culture, the relationship between culture specific social skills and psychological adjustment in the new culture is likely to be much stronger. As such, two hypotheses follow:

3. The magnitude of the relationship between psychological and socio-cultural adaptation will be greater in a sojourning group who makes a small, compared to a large, cross-cultural transition.
4. The magnitude of the relationship between psychological and socio-cultural adjustment will be greater in a sedentary group compared to a sojourning group.

The Pattern of Adjustment over Time

While many researchers have acknowledged variations in cross-cultural adaptation over time, there is some disagreement as to the precise pattern of change. The most popular stage theory of adjustment, advanced by Lysgaard (1955) and expanded by Gullahorn and Gullahorn (1963), suggests that psychological adjustment follows a U-curve with an initial stage of euphoria, followed by a downward stress related mood swing and eventual recovery and restabilisation. Ward and associates have been critical of the U-curve hypothesis (Searle and Ward, 1990; Ward and Searle, 1991), failing to document evidence of the early euphoria, and, indeed, reviews by both Church (1982) and Furnham and Bochner (1986) have suggested that the empirical evidence for the U-curve is limited. As most cross-cultural transition research has been cross-sectional, rather than longitudinal, disputes about psychological adjustment and the U-curve have not been resolved.

The differentiation of socio-cultural and psychological adaptation further undermines the utility of the U-curve hypothesis. As the former is based on the acquisition of culturally appropriate skills, it would be expected that socio-cultural adaptation would increase over time, either following a linear pattern or approximating a learning curve. Indeed, a number of studies have indicated that length of residence in the host culture is associated with increased local knowledge and skills (Armes and Ward, 1989; Zaidi, 1975). With respect to the two dimensions of adjustment, then, the following hypotheses are advanced:

5. The level of socio-cultural difficulties is highest in the initial stage of transition and decreases over time.

6. The level of psychological adjustment problems (mood disturbance) is high (as opposed to low) at the initial stage of transition;
however, no hypothesis is made about the consequential changing pattern over time.

METHOD

The data presented here are taken from three larger studies in a
research programme on cross-cultural transition and adjustment. The
first study compared sojourners who made a large vs small cross-
cultural transition, the sample included Malaysian and Singaporean
students in New Zealand and Malaysian students in Singapore. The
second study examined psychological and socio-cultural adjustment in
a sojourning group with a comparative home based sample, i.e., New
Zealand American Field Service (AFS) students abroad and secondary
school students at home. The third study was a longitudinal investigation
of psychological and socio-cultural adjustment in a newly arrived
sojourning group, the subjects were Malaysian and Singaporean
students during the first year of residence in New Zealand.

Subject

A sample of 145 Malaysian and Singaporean university students (76
males and 69 females) participated in the first study. Of the total, 90
per cent of the subjects were Chinese, 5 per cent Malay, 2 per cent
Indian and 3 per cent other. Ages ranged from 19 to 29 years with a
mean age of 21.93 years (SD: 1.79). The length of residence in New
Zealand varied from 2 months to 8 years (M: 33.4 months, SD: 18.6).

The comparative group included a sample of 156 (110 males and 46
females) Malaysian university students in Singapore. Of these 94.2 per
cent were Chinese and 4.5 per cent Indian (the remaining 1.3 per cent
Malay and Eurasian). Subjects' ages ranged from 18 years to 25 years
with a mean age of 20.91 years (SD: 1.29). The length of residence in

Singapore varied from 1 week to 9 years and 5 months (*M*: 32.6 months, *SD*: 31.1).

A group of 178 New Zealand secondary school students (135 females and 43 males) who were participating in the AFS programme served as subjects in the second study. The mean age was 17.4 years (*SD*: 0.75). The majority of the subjects were white New Zealanders (94 per cent), with 2 per cent Maori, 0.6 per cent Asian and 4 per cent unknown. Subjects were placed in 23 countries in North America (such as the United States and Canada), South America (for example, Argentina and Brazil), Eastern Europe (for example, Hungary and Czechoslovakia) and Western Europe (for example, Germany and Sweden) and Asia (such as, Hong Kong and Malaysia). The average length of residence in the host culture was 10.88 weeks (*SD*: 11.83).

The comparative sample was 141 (49 females and 92 males) state and private secondary school students in Christchurch, New Zealand. The mean age of the sample was 17.5 years (*SD*: 0.53). Of the total, 90 per cent of the subjects were white New Zealanders, 3.5 per cent Maori, 2.8 per cent Pacific Islanders, 1.4 per cent Asian, and 2 per cent unknown.

A sample of 14 Malaysian (*N*: 12) and Singaporean (*N*: 2) secondary and tertiary students participated in the third study. The sample included 8 males and 6 females; and the mean age of the subjects was 19.07 years (*SD*: 1.54). All subjects were Chinese with the exception of one Eurasian participant.

Materials

Questionnaires were utilised for the measurement of psychological and socio-cultural adjustment in the three studies. Psychological adjustment was assessed by McNair, Lorr, and Droppleman's (1971) Profile of Mood States (POMS), a 65-item adjective rating scale which measures symptoms of tension, depression, anger, vigour, confusion and fatigue (characteristics commonly ascribed to sojourners experiencing "culture shock") in the first and second studies. Subjects rated the intensity of their emotional experiences in the last week on 5-point rating scales. Scores ranged from 0–260 with higher scores indicating greater mood disturbance. The POMS has proven reliable and valid in previous research with multi-national sojourning samples (Ward and Searle, 1991).

In the third study the longitudinal sample completed a measure of depression, a slightly modified version of the Zung (1965) Self-rating Depression Scale (ZSDS), for the assessment of psychological adjustment. Subjects used 4-point frequency scales to respond to 19 statements which examined the affective, physiological, and psychological components of depression. Scores ranged from 0–57 with higher scores indicative of greater depression. Chang and Ward (1990) have provided evidence of the scale's reliability and validity with Chinese students in Singapore, and its reliability has also been established in previous research by Searle and Ward (1990) with Malaysian and Singaporean students in New Zealand.

Socio-cultural adjustment was assessed by a 20-item scale relating to the skills required to manage everyday social situations and aspects of living in a new culture. The instrument resembled the Social Situations Questionnaire used by Furnham and Bochner (1982), and it has been used extensively in research by Ward and colleagues with various sojourning groups. Subjects were required to rate the amount of difficulty they experienced in dealing with everyday social situations (for example, making yourself understood, making friends). Scores ranged from 0–80 with higher scores indicating greater difficulty in social interactions. The original 20-item questionnaire was shortened to 16 items in the second study as 4 items were irrelevant to the sedentary secondary school sample.

Procedure

Participation in the research was anonymous and voluntary. The first study relied on questionnaire distribution through research assistants; the return rate for Malaysian and Singaporean students in New Zealand was 76 per cent and for Malaysian students in Singapore the return rate was 74.4 per cent. The second study used postal questionnaires for AFS students and secured a 51 per cent return rate. Questionnaires for local secondary students were administered during classes for voluntary participation without calculating the return rate.

The final sample relied upon both research assistant distribution and postal questionnaires. Students were contacted within a month of arrival in New Zealand, then were contacted again 6 and 12 months later. Of the original group of 22 students, 14 (63.6 per cent) completed the psychological and socio-cultural adjustment questionnaires over a 12-month period.

RESULTS

Preliminary analyses included reliability checks on the psychological and socio-cultural adjustment measures. Cronbach alphas confirmed the internal consistency of the instruments. For the POMS coefficient alphas were .95 (Malaysian and Singaporean students in New Zealand and Malaysian students in Singapore) and .96 (AFS students and the secondary school sample in New Zealand).[1] For the socio-cultural adjustment measurement the alphas were .86 (Malaysian and Singaporean students in New Zealand), .84 (Malaysian students in Singapore), 85 (AFS students), and .83 (secondary school students in New Zealand). Due to the small sample size a reliability analysis was not done on the longitudinal sample of Malaysian and Singaporean students in New Zealand; however, Searle and Ward (1990) reported a coefficient of .79 on the ZSDS for Malaysian and Singaporean students in their earlier research. After the initial reliability checks the six hypotheses were tested.

Level of Psychological and Socio-cultural Adjustment

Due to the unequal proportion of male and female subjects, analysis of variance with sex as a covariate was done on the adjustment measures in the first two studies. As predicted, the sojourning sample who made a large, compared to a small, transition experienced greater socio-cultural adjustment problems; F (1,290): 4.95, $p < .03$. Malaysian and Singaporean students in New Zealand (M: 17.05) had significantly higher social difficulty scores than Malaysian students in Singapore (M: 14.77). There were no significant differences, however, in the level of psychological adjustment between these groups; F (1,290): 1.63,

---

[1] The POMS was reduced to 55 items in the Asian samples to achieve sound internal reliability.

ns. The same pattern held for comparisons between a sojourning and a sedentary group. AFS students who resided abroad experienced greater social difficulty (M: 18.3) than students who remained at home (M: 13.3); F (1,317): 16.0, $p<.001$. In a parallel analysis no significant differences were observed between the groups on the measurement of psychological adjustment; F (1,317): 0.93, ns. As such, hypotheses one and two were confirmed for socio-cultural adaptation, but not for psychological adjustment.

The Relationship between Psychological and Socio-cultural Adjustment

Zero order correlations were undertaken separately on the psychological and socio-cultural adjustment measures for the four samples in the first two studies, and this was followed by tests to determine the significant difference between the independent correlations. Analysis revealed that the magnitude of the relationship between psychological and socio-cultural adjustment in the case of Malaysian students in Singapore (r: .49) was significantly greater than the magnitude of the relationship between these variables in the sample of Malaysian and Singaporean students in New Zealand (r: .28); z: 2.02, $p<.05$. In addition, the relationship between the adjustment dimensions was significantly stronger in a non-relocating secondary school sample (r: .66) than in the sojourning AFS sample (r: .23); z: 4.92, $p<.0001$. As such, hypotheses three and four were confirmed.

The Pattern of Adjustment over Time

One way analysis of variance was used to examine the pattern of adjustment over time. As predicted, social difficulty was high during the initial stage of transition, dropped sharply during the first 6 months and continued in a slightly downward direction; F (2,26): 12.76, $p<.0001$ (see Figure 22.1). As predicted, depression was highest initially; it decreased during the first 6 months, but increased again 6 months later F (2, 26): 3.55, $p<.04$ (see Figure 22.2). The data support the differentiation of psychological and socio-cultural adjustment patterns over time. The results also undermine the U-curve proposition, as there is no evidence of euphoria during the early stages of transition. Indeed, the V pattern revealed by these data is opposed

Figure 22.1
Mean Social Difficulty Scale Scores over Time of Malaysian and Singaporean Students in New Zealand

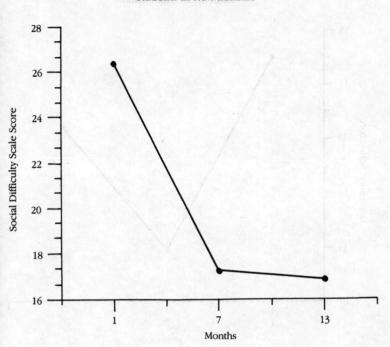

to Lysgaard's (1955) and Gullahorn and Gullahorn's (1963) propositions. The results indicate that hypotheses five and six were confirmed.

DISCUSSION

The research examined psychological and socio-cultural dimensions of adjustment during cross-cultural transitions. The findings supported the hypotheses that socio-cultural adaptation problems are greater in: (*a*) sojourning compared to sedentary groups, and (*b*) sojourning groups who make large, compared to small, cross-cultural transitions.

Figure 22.2
***Mean Depression Scale Scores over Time of Malaysian and Singaporean
Students in New Zealand***

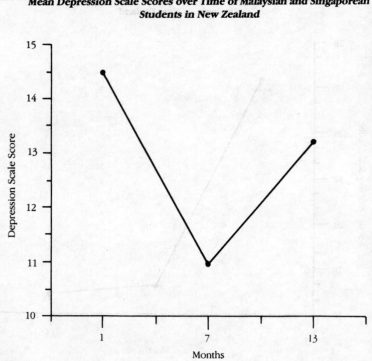

There was no evidence, however, to distinguish these groups in terms
of psychological adjustment. The results further demonstrated that the
relationship between psychological and socio-cultural adaptation varies
across groups and socio-cultural settings. More specifically, the magnitude of the relationship between psychological and socio-cultural
dimensions of adjustment was greater in: (*a*) sedentary compared to
sojourning groups, and (*b*) sojourning groups who make small, compared to large, transitions. Finally, the findings revealed that the
pattern of psychological and socio-cultural adaptation varied over
time. Although psychological and socio-cultural adjustment problems
were greatest during the early stages of transition, they diminished
rapidly; psychological disturbances, however, were more variable, and

unlike socio-cultural difficulties, did not show a downward trend over a 12-month period.

Earlier research by Ward and colleagues, based on the construction of predictive models of adjustive outcomes, has also highlighted the distinction between psychological and socio-cultural elements in the cross-cultural adjustment process. These studies have suggested that psychological adjustment is largely dependent upon personality, life changes and social support factors and that socio-cultural adaptation, by contrast, is primarily affected by culture specific elements such as cultural knowledge, cultural identity, cultural distance and amount of host culture contact (Searle and Ward, 1990; Stone Feinstein and Ward, 1990; Ward and Kennedy, 1992, in press a, in press b; Ward and Searle, 1991). In this context Ward and associates have argued that the empirical findings on the two adjustment dimensions reflect two popular, but divergent, theoretical approaches to acculturation: stress and coping models and culture learning perspectives. The findings reported here pertaining to the level of relationship between, and temporal variations in the adjustment domains are consistent with the earlier theoretical and empirical work and further support the differentiation and construct validity of psychological and socio-cultural dimensions of adjustment. They also suggest that psychological adjustment may be more appropriately interpreted in terms of a stress and coping model while socio-cultural adaptation may be viewed from a social learning perspective.

Stress and coping models are based on the notion that both positive and negative life events are stress inducing; in short, life changes present adjustive demands. The level of stress experienced and the adjustive consequences, however, may be affected by mediating variables such as personality resources or social support networks. Viewing cross-cultural transition within this framework has the effect of demystifying "culture shock". In this context it can be persuasively argued that factors which affect psychological well-being during cross-cultural transitions are the ones which affect psychological adaptation during other life changes.

If a stress and coping model is adopted for the analysis of psychological adjustment during cross-cultural transitions, why did the findings fail to differentiate various sojourning and sedentary groups on the adjustive outcome? The characteristics of the samples and the measurement of adjustment may have influenced the results. On the first

count, the developmental stage of the research subjects may be important. In the study the subjects were late adolescents and young adults.
Students in this age range are likely to be experiencing a wide range of
life changes, including emotional and social maturation, which may
impact on psychological stability. The specific effects of cultural transition, compared to other life changes, on mood disturbance in these
groups have not been clarified. Second, the duration of relocation may
be significant. It is worth noting that with respect to the comparable
Asian samples in Singapore and in New Zealand, cross-cultural transitions were not recent events; the mean length of residence abroad was
32–33 months. Therefore, the negative impact on psychological well-
being, whether from a large or small cross-cultural transition, may
have been ameliorated during this period. Finally, the psychological
characteristics of sedentary and sojourning groups should be considered.
It may be that students who choose to study abroad are self-selected
and more psychologically robust. Certainly, the AFS scholars are
chosen in competition, and in addition to their intellectual resources,
may possess other personality traits which are conducive to successful
coping. This may give them a psychological advantage over a comparable sample of non-relocating students.

The failure to distinguish sedentary and sojourning groups in terms
of psychological adjustment may also be attributed to the assessment
instrument. In this research, mood disturbance was measured with
particular emphasis on feelings during the previous week. While this
measurement was used successfully in the construction of predictive
models of psychological well-being in earlier research, the Profile of
Mood States may not have been the best choice for comparisons of
psychological adaptation across groups. Mood may be affected by
such a large number and diverse range of factors, that any differences
specifically dependent upon cultural distance or life changes may have
been lost across groups.

The variation in psychological adjustment over time also deserves
attention. As predicted, mood disturbance was high in the earliest
stages of transition. It decreased at 6 months, but then rose again over
a 12-month period. There is a possibility that the longitudinal data
reflected a time of year effect as postulated by Selby and Woods
(1966) and Golden (1973) in their research with foreign students. As
the 12-month testing was undertaken at the beginning of the academic
year, it is also possible that overseas students had returned home

during the summer vacation and were again re-entering the cross-cultural milieu. Unfortunately, data on the international movement during the summer break were not available.

In contrast to the findings on psychological adjustment, the research results on socio-cultural adaptation are rather straightforward and in line with the original hypotheses. Socio-cultural adaptation can be understood within a culture learning framework and appears to be influenced more directly by culture specific variables. In earlier research, social difficulty in a new cultural environment was predicted by factors such as cultural distance, language ability, cultural knowledge and cultural identity (Searle and Ward, 1990; Ward and Kennedy, in press a, in press b). In this research, the cultural distance variable retained its significance. More specifically, socio-cultural adjustment problems were greater for those who undertook cross-cultural transitions compared to those who remained at home and for those who made large, compared to small, transitions. As expected, people required time and practice to acquire skills appropriate for a new cultural setting, and social difficulty decreased over time in a predictable fashion.

The association between social skills and psychological well-being has been noted in clinical literature (Haley, 1985); in addition to the studies by Ward and colleagues, Klineberg and Hull (1979) have reported an association between social difficulty and depression in foreign university students. While a significant relationship is typically expected between the two adjustment domains, Ward and Kennedy (in press a, in press b) have argued that the extent of the relationship varies according to the socio-cultural context. Speculations about the precise nature of the variation are considered preliminary, but it is generally expected that the greater the sojourner's ability and opportunity for integration into the host culture, the stronger the association between psychological and socio-cultural adaptation. These findings support that contention. Correlations between the two adjustment domains were greater in groups that made small, compared to large, transitions and in non-relocating, compared to sojourning, groups. These represent groups who are more likely to rely on the host culture as the primary context for social interaction. This theme, however, requires further investigation, as the relationship between the adjustment domains is expected to be affected not only by sojourners' desire, ability or opportunity for integration, but also by the host culture's reception of foreigners. At present research is being done to assess psychological and socio-cultural adjustment in relation to the host culture's perceptions of foreigners and in relation to Berry's (1980, 1990) model of acculturation strategies.

In conclusion, Ward and associates have argued for the differentiation of psychological and socio-cultural dimensions of adaptation in their review of the literature on cross-cultural transition. These outcome indicators, along with their theoretical underpinnings, reflect two dominant approaches to the study of culture contact and change—stress and coping and social learning perspectives. In previous research Ward and associates emphasised that much of the literature on cross-cultural transition can be interpreted within these theoretical frameworks, and in their own research they offered evidence for the empirical distinction of the adjustive domains. This research has further explored the utility of the distinction, and findings support the hypotheses that patterns of psychological and socio-cultural adjustment vary across groups and over time. It is hoped that the conceptual and empirical differentiation of psychological and socio-cultural dimensions of adaptation offers an avenue for the synthesis of past and future research on cross-cultural transition and adjustment.

REFERENCES

ARGYLE, M. (1980). Interaction skills and social competence. In P. Feldman and J. Orford (Eds.), *Psychological problems: The social context*. Chichester: Wiley.

ARMES, K. and WARD, C. (1989). Cross-cultural transitions and sojourner adjustment in Singapore. *Journal of Social Psychology, 129*, 273–275.

BABIKER, I.E., COX, J.L., and MILLER, P. McG. (1980). The measurement of cultural distance and its relationship to medical consultations, symptomatology and examination of performance of overseas students at Edinburgh University. *Social Psychiatry, 15*, 109–116.

BERRY, J.W. (1980). Acculturation as varieties of adaptation. In A. Padilla (Ed.), *Acculturation: Theory, models and some new findings*. Washington: AAAS.

BERRY, J.W. (1990). Psychology of acculturation. In J. Berman (Ed.), *Cross-cultural perspectives: Nebraska symposium on motivation*. Lincoln: University of Nebraska Press.

BERRY, J.W. and KIM, U. (1988). Acculturation and mental health. In P. Dasen, J.W. Berry, and N. Sartorius (Eds.), *Health and cross-cultural psychology: Toward applications*. London: Sage.

BERRY, J.W., KIM, U., MINDE, T., and MOK, D. (1987). Comparative studies of acculturative stress. *International Migration Review, 21*, 490–511.

BERRY, J.W., KIM, U., POWERS, S., YOUNG, M., and BUJAKI, M. (1989). Acculturation attitudes in plural societies. *Applied Psychology: An International Review, 38*, 185–206.

BLACK, J.S. and GREGERSEN, H.B. (1990). Expectations, satisfaction, and intention to leave of American expatriate managers in Japan. *International Journal of Intercultural Relations, 14*, 485–506.

BOCHNER, S., MCLEOD, B.M., and LIN, A. (1977). Friendship patterns of overseas students: A functional model. *International Journal of Psychology, 12*, 277–297.

BRISLIN, R.W. (1981). *Cross-cultural encounters*. New York: Pergamon.

CHANG, W.C. and WARD, C. (1990, July). Depressive symptomatology of Singaporean Chinese students. Paper presented at the X International Congress of the International Association for Cross-Cultural Psychology, Nara, Japan.

CHATAWAY, C.J. and BERRY, J.W. (1989). Acculturation experiences, appraisal, coping and adaptation: A comparison of Hong Kong Chinese, French and English students in Canada. *Canadian Journal of Behavioral Science, 21*, 295–309.

CHURCH, A.T. (1982). Sojourner adjustment. *Psychological Bulletin, 76*, 215–230.

FURNHAM, A. (1983). Social difficulty in three cultures. *International Journal of Psychology, 18*, 215–218.

FURNHAM, A. and BOCHNER, S. (1982). Social difficulty in a foreign culture: An empirical analysis of culture shock. In S. Bochner (Ed.), *Cultures in contact*. Oxford: Pergamon.

FURNHAM, A. and BOCHNER, S. (1986). *Culture shock: Psychological reactions to unfamiliar environments*. London: Methuen.

GOLDEN, J.S. (1973). Student adjustment abroad: A psychiatrist's view. *International Educational and Cultural Exchange, 8*, 28–36.

GULLAHORN, J.T. and GULLAHORN, J.E. (1963). An extension of the U-curve hypothesis. *Journal of Social Issues, 19*, 33–47.

HALEY, W.D. (1985). Social skills deficit and self-evaluation among depressed and non-depressed psychiatric patients. *Journal of Clinical Psychology, 41*, 162–168.

HARRIS, J.G. (1972). Prediction of success on a distant Pacific Island: Peace Corps style. *Journal of Consulting and Clinical Psychology, 38*, 181–190.

IBRAHIM, S.E.M. (1970). Interaction, perception and attitudes of Arab students toward Americans. *Sociology and Social Research, 55*, 29–46.

KLINEBERG, O. and HULL, W.F. (1979). *At a foreign university: An international study of adaptation and coping*. New York: Praeger.

LAZARUS, R.S. and FOLKMAN, S. (1984). *Stress, appraisal and coping*. New York: Springer.

LYSGAARD, S. (1955). Adjustment in a foreign society: Norwegian Fulbright grantees visiting the United States. *International Social Science Bulletin, 7*, 45–51.

MCNAIR, D., LORR, M., and DROPPLEMAN, L. (1971). *Profile of Mood States*. San Diego: Educational and Industrial Testing Service.

OBERG, K. (1960). Cultural shock: Adjustment to new cultural environments. *Practical Anthropology, 7*, 177–182.

PERKINS, C.S., PERKINS, M.L., GUGLIELMINO, L.M., and RIEFF, R.F. (1977). A comparison of adjustment problems of three international student groups. *Journal of College Student Personnel, 18*, 382–388.

SEARLE, W. and WARD, C. (1990). The prediction of psychological and socio-cultural adjustment during cross-cultural transitions. *International Journal of Intercultural Relations, 14*, 449–464.

SELBY, H.A. and WOODS, C.M. (1966). Foreign students at a high pressure university. *Sociology of Education, 39*, 138–154.

SEWELL, W.H. and DAVIDSEN, O.M. (1961). *Scandinavian students on an American campus*. Minneapolis: University of Minnesota Press.

STONE FEINSTEIN, B.E. and WARD, C. (1990). Loneliness and psychological adjustment of sojourners: New perspectives on culture shock. In D.M. Keats, D. Munro, and L. Mann (Eds.), *Heterogeneity in cross-cultural psychology*. Lisse: Swets and Zeitlinger.

WARD, C. and KENNEDY, A. (1992). Locus of control, mood disturbance and social difficulty during cross-cultural transitions. *International Journal of Intercultural Relations, 16*, 175–194.

WARD, C. and KENNEDY, A. (in press, a). Psychological and socio-cultural adjustment during cross-cultural transitions: A comparison of secondary students overseas and at home. *International Journal of Psychology*.

WARD, C. and KENNEDY, A. (in press, b). Where's the culture in cross-cultural transition? Comparative studies of sojourner adjustment. *Journal of Cross-Cultural Psychology*.

WARD, C. and SEARLE, W. (1991). The impact of value discrepancies and cultural identity on psychological and socio-cultural adjustment of sojourners. *International Journal of Intercultural Relations, 15*, 209–225.

ZAIDI, S.M.H. (1975). Adjustment problems of foreign Muslim students in Pakistan. In R.W. Brislin, S. Bochner, and W. Lonner (Eds.), *Cross-cultural perspectives on learning*. New York: Wiley.

ZUNG, W.W.K. (1965). A self-rating depression scale. *Archives of General Psychiatry, 12*, 63–70.

23

Entrepreneurship and Collectivism: A Study of Nepalese Entrepreneurs

DHARM P.S. BHAWUK • ARJUN UDAS*

Research in entrepreneurship has gradually shifted from studying entrepreneurial traits to entrepreneurial processes. The most recent shift in the study of entrepreneurship is the inclusion of culture as a variable in explaining entrepreneurial attitudes and behaviours, and researchers increasingly agree that entrepreneurship should be studied in the context of culture (Fleming, 1979; Fairbairn, 1988; Peterson, 1988). This paper reports some of the findings of a research (Bhawuk and Udas, 1991) that was carried out to study entrepreneurship in the cultural context of Nepal. Literature on entrepreneurship and individualism and collectivism is briefly reviewed before describing the purpose of the research.

* The authors are grateful to Professors Harry Triandis and Janak Pandey for their assistance in improving the first draft of this paper. The authors also appreciate the encouragement provided by Mr. Rudolph Guthier and Kapil Ghimire of the Small Business Promotion Project.

Entrepreneurship

According to Schumpeter (1934), an entrepreneur is an innovator, a person driven by the will to found a private kingdom, the will to conquer, and a person who is propelled by satisfaction derived from achievement. Would a Nepalese entrepreneur fit Schumpeter's description? Or, are they what Broehl (1970) has termed "A less developed entrepreneur"—conservative in ideology, believing strongly in family solidarity, and promoting their sons irrespective of talent or motivation?

McClelland (1961) suggested that entrepreneurship was related to a particular human motive—the need to achieve, or nAch. Are Nepalese entrepreneurs McClelland's archetypical entrepreneur, and place high value on success, personal initiative, curiosity and rational and practical approach to problem solving? Or, are there other needs that are more important to them?

Fairbairn (1988), based on his research in the Pacific, argued that Schumpeter's concept of the innovating entrepreneur appeared to have a limited value in understanding entrepreneurship in many developing countries where the entrepreneurial task lay in applying, modifying, and adapting existing knowledge, rather than in implementing ideas based on new discoveries. He further noted that large, closely integrated families or kinship groups continue to persist in many developing countries which means that the focus should be on the family as the entrepreneurial unit rather than on the individual.

Peterson (1988) stated that "entrepreneurship's true believers often fail to appreciate the degree to which effective entrepreneurship is enmeshed with culture" and that "gradually it is becoming clear that each country/culture must develop its own brand of entrepreneurship and raise its own champions to promote entrepreneurial behavior that fits the prevailing societal mores".

Studying entrepreneurship in the cultural context demands defining and operationalising culture in some measurable way. Hofstede (1980) operationalised culture in terms of four constructs: Individualism and Collectivism, Power Distance, Masculinity and Femininity, and Uncertainty Avoidance. Of these four, Individualism and Collectivism are the most researched constructs (Triandis, 1990; Triandis et al., 1990; Triandis et al., 1988; Triandis et al., 1985; Hui, 1988; Hui and Triandis, 1986) that show potential for both explaining and predicting cultural similarities and differences. Therefore, the instrument developed by Triandis and associates (1986) to measure attitudinal differences in individualistic and collectivist cultures was used to measure the attitude of Nepalese entrepreneurs.

Individualism and Collectivism

Hui and Triandis (1986) carried out a study to define the construct of individualism and collectivism, and asked a group of psychologists and anthropologists from all over the world to respond to a questionnaire in the way an individualist or a collectivist would respond. They found collectivism to be a cluster of a wide variety of beliefs and behaviours which could be categorised into the following 7 categories: (a) people's concern about how their decisions would affect others in their collectivity; (b) sharing of material resources; (c) sharing of non-material resource like time, affection, fun, or sacrificing some interesting activities for a member of the collective; (d) willingness of people to accept the opinions and views of others, or in other words, willingness to conform; (e) concern about face saving or gaining the approval of the collective; (f) belief in the correspondence of own outcomes, both positive and negative, with the outcomes of others; and (g) feeling of involvement in others' lives. According to these researchers, collectivism requires the subordination of individual goals to the goals of a collective. Underlying these characteristics is the term "concern". Concern does not refer to affection and worry only, rather it is "a sense of oneness with other people, a perception of complex ties and relationships, and a tendency to keep other people in mind." They argued that collectivism is not equivalent to altruism. Collectivism recognises the *group*, and not the *individual*, as the basic unit of survival. The researchers participating in the research showed a high level of consensus in recognising collectivism as an etic or universal concept.

In a study of 200 Americans by Bellah, Madsen, Sullivan, Swindler, and Tipton (1985), it was found that individualism consists of the following aspects: (a) self-reliance, independence and separation from family, religion, and community; (b) hedonism, utilitarianism, and emphasis on exchange (helping the community only if the individual gets something); (c) competition; (d) equity and fairness in the distribution of rewards; (e) trust in others; (f) emphasis on competence; (g) involvement in community life; (h) equality of people and the rejection of arbitrary authority; and (i) the self as the only source of reality. Involvement in community life may seem out of place, but the interpretation is that in an individualistic culture people can choose from a number of community activities and switch from one to another when the particular activity does not benefit the individual.

At a higher level of abstraction, Triandis et al. (1986) found that the construct of individualism and collectivism consists of "separation from ingroups" and "self-reliance with hedonism" for individualism, and "family integration" and "interdependence with sociability" for collectivism. They suggested that individualism and collectivism are not opposite poles of a bipolar construct, but two independent factors.

It should be noted that Triandis and colleagues (1985) emphasised individual differences and used the terms idiocentrism and allocentrism as personality attributes corresponding to individualism and collectivism respectively. Thus, it is possible to find idiocentrics as well as allocentrics in both individualistic and collectivist cultures.

Triandis (1990) speculated that collectivism is best described by family integrity and individualism by emotional detachment; allocentrism is best described by interdependence and sociability, and idiocentrism by self-reliance.

The purpose of this study was twofold. First, the factor structure of the INDCOL Scale developed by Triandis and associates (1986) was examined to see if it could be meaningfully used in Nepal. Second, to examine if Nepalese entrepreneurs are individualistic like the prototypical western entrepreneurs.

METHOD

Data Collection and Measures

Data was collected by using an omnibus questionnaire in the Nepali language that had four sections: items tapping biographical and business information, Rotter's Internal–External Control Scale (Rotter, 1966), the INDCOL Scale (Triandis et al., 1986), and Personal Entrepreneurship Characteristic Scale (Mansfield et al., 1968). All the instruments were translated into Nepali using the back-translation method (Brislin,

1986). The instrument was administered to the respondents. It took about an hour to fill out the questionnaire. In this paper only the findings of the INDCOL Scale are reported.[1]

Sample

The sample consisted of 239 small business owners from 7 urban centres in Nepal. Of these, 151 had attended a training programme organised by the Small Business Promotion Project[2] (SBPP) before starting their business, whereas 88 of them had started their enterprise on their own, without any initial training.

RESULTS

The sample comprised young entrepreneurs (85 per cent of them under 40 years of age). About 93 per cent of them were male, 81 per cent married, 82 per cent did not have more than three children, and 77 per cent lived in a joint family (with their parents and siblings). Nearly 55 per cent of the respondents had 10 to 12 years of formal school education, while 24 per cent had a college degree. The remaining had less than 10 years of formal education.

The mean response of the 17 items varied between 2.36 for item number 8 to 5.21 for item number 16. Standard deviation ranged from 0.92 to 1.45. The participants used the full range of the scale for all the items.

Cronbach's alpha (Cronbach, 1951) for the whole scale was 0.58. However, the alphas for 13 individualism and 4 collectivism items were 0.53 and 0.52 respectively.

Principal component factor analysis with varimax rotation extracted 7 factors that explained 61 per cent of the common variance. A scree

[1] The results for the other scales can be obtained from Dharm P.S. Bhawuk.

[2] The Small Business Promotion Project (SBPP) is a German cooperation project between His Majesty's Government of Nepal and the German government. This organisation conducts numerous practical training programmes in new business creation and management. It also provides consultancy services to small business owners.

test indicated that all 7 factors should be retained. These 7 factors, the percentage of total variance explained by each factor, and items and their loadings on each of the factors are given in Table 23.1.

TABLE 23.1
Summary of Factor Analysis

Factor 1: Competition vs Responsibility (Per cent Var: 16.1)

12. It is important to me that I perform better than others on a task. 0.75
13. Ageing parents should live at home with their children. 0.65
16. I like to live close to my friends. 0.61
15. I would help within my means, if a relative told me that (s)he is in financial difficulty. 0.55

Note: Items 12 and 13 also loaded on Factor VI (0.31 and 0.34 respectively).

Factor II: Self-Reliance and Independence (Per cent Var: 10.1)

5. When faced with difficult personal problem, it is better to decide what to do yourself than follow the advice of others. 0.67
4. One does better work working alone than in a group. 0.63
3. I tend to do my own thing, and others in my family do the same. 0.61

Note: Items 4 and 3 also loaded on Factors V (0.42) and VI (0.4) respectively.

Factor III: Separation from Ingroup (Per cent Var: 8.7)

8. If the child won the Nobel Prize, the parents should not feel honored in any way. 0.84
9. Children should not feel honored even if the father were highly praised and given an award by a government official for his contribution and services to the community. 0.83

Factor IV: Doing Your Own Thing (Per cent Var: 7.2)

10. In most cases, to cooperate with someone whose ability is lower than yours is not as desirable as doing the thing on your own. 0.74
17. Individuals should be judged on their own merits, not by the company they keep. 0.55
1. I would rather struggle through a personal problem by myself than discuss it with my friends. 0.51
7. If the group is slowing me down, it is better to leave it and work alone. 0.44

Note: Item 17 also loaded on Factor VII (0.38) and item 1 on Factor II (0.48).

Factor V: Hedonism (Per cent Var: 6.5)

2. The most important thing in my life is to make myself happy. 0.73
11. One should live one's life independently of others as much as possible. 0.47

Factor VI: Family Integrity (Per cent Var: 6.5)

14. Children should live at home with their parents until they get married. 0.81

Table 23.1 (Continued)

Note: Items 3, 13 and 12 had loadings of 0.40, 0.34, and 0.31 respectively on this factor.

Factor VII: Internal Control (Per cent Var: 6.1)
  6. What happens to me is my own doing.   0.87

Note: Item 17 also loaded (0.38) on this factor.

A second order factor analysis was done by treating these 7 factors as variables. For each factor the score was computed by adding the score on the items that loaded on the factor. Principal component factor analysis with varimax rotation extracted two second order factors which explained 43.0 per cent of the common variance.

The first second order factor which explained 27.1 per cent of the common variance is labelled Individualism since the factors of self-reliance and independence, doing your own thing, and hedonism loaded on this factor (.77, .70, and .66 respectively). The other factor explained 15.9 per cent of the common variance and is labelled Collectivism since competition vs responsibility, separation from ingroup, and family integrity loaded (.67, −.66, and .65 respectively) on this factor. The 7th factor loaded on both the factors (Collectivism −.24; Individualism −.17).

DISCUSSION

Of the 13 individualistic items, 8 items (items 1, 2, 3, 6, 7, 11, 12, and 17) had mean values greater than 4 which indicates that these items tap individualistic attitudes. Item 12, which taps competition, had the highest mean score (5.16), this clearly shows that the entrepreneurs considered competition to be important. They also consider independence (items 11, 7, 3, and 1; mean: 2.74, 4.16, 4.12, and 3.95 respectively), individual merit (item 17, mean: 4.23), internal control (item 6, mean: 4.18), and hedonism (item 2, mean: 4.13) important. The other 5 items had mean values of about 3.0 and hence did not tap individualistic attitudes.

An examination of the means of the 4 collectivism items reveals that the Nepalese entrepreneurs manifested a collective inclination in that they liked to live near their close friends (item 16, mean: 5.21), they believed that aging parents should live at home with their children (item 13, mean: 4.87), and they would help their relatives (item 15, mean: 4.45). Further, a low mean of 3.5 was obtained for item 14, i.e., children should live at home with their parents until they get married. Often school or college going children have to live away from their parents, and for this reason the respondents may have disagreed with this statement. They believed that parents should take pride in their children's success and expressed their disagreement with item 8 (mean: 2.36) and also that children should take pride in their parents' success (item 9, mean: 3.05).

The mean scores clearly indicated that Nepalese entrepreneurs manifested a spirit of competition, a drive to be on their own, and a sense of internal control; in short, they were idiocentric. But it is also clear that their commitment to aging parents, friends, and relatives in need was equally pronounced; in other words, they were allocentric. Thus, Nepalese entrepreneurs were individualistic in their work but collectivistic in their social–family relationships.

This finding is also confirmed by factor analysis. Factor I, competition vs responsibility, is intriguing since it includes two conflicting ideas: competition and responsibility towards family and friends, the former is an idiocentric attitude and the latter is an allocentric one. A plot of competition vs responsibility (item 12 along the X-axis and items 13, 15, and 16 along the Y-axis) shows that the respondents were high on both competition and responsibility. It may be concluded that Nepalese entrepreneurs were "collectivist entrepreneurs", a finding borne out by the fact that 77 per cent of all the entrepreneurs surveyed live in a joint family.

Items 5, 4, and 3, load on Factor II. These items tap the idea of self-reliance and independence, which are idiocentric attitudes (individualism) and, accordingly, the factor is labelled self-reliance and independence. Self-reliance and independence are considered entrepreneurial characteristics in the west, and since Nepalese entrepreneurs considered these values important, it is likely that these are universal entrepreneurial attributes.

Factor III, separation from ingroups, should not lead one to conclude that Nepalese entrepreneurs are alienated from their ingroups. The means of the two items (2.35 and 3.05) indicated that the respondents agreed with the idea that parents should be proud of their children's achievement, and children should feel honoured if their parents are successful. This factor captures an aspect of collectivism. The mean values of these items show an asymmetry in favour of "parents should be proud of children's success" compared to "children should be proud of their parents' success". It appears that since parents contribute to the growth of their children they have a right to feel proud of their children's success whereas children do not contribute to their parents' success, and hence should not be proud of their success.

Factor IV, doing your own thing, indicates that the respondents were task-oriented. Items 10 (cooperating with people of inferior ability is not desirable), 17 (individuals should be evaluated on own merit), 1 (struggle through personal problem by oneself), and 7 (it is better to leave the group if it slows one down) load on Factor IV, and since these items tap idiocentric attitude, this factor captures individualism.

Factors V (hedonism) and VII (internal control) tap idiocentric attitudes, and Factor VI (family integrity) taps allocentric attitude.

It is important to note that whereas self-reliance and independence, separation from ingroup, hedonism, and family integrity are etic factors because they were also observed in the study by Triandis and associates (1986) which included data from several cultures; competition vs responsibility, internal control, and doing your own thing are clearly emic factors. However, these emic factors could be sample specific and may not describe the Nepalese people in general.

The second order factor analysis revealed that Factors I, III, and VI are collectivist factors whereas Factors II, IV, and V are individualist factors. This not only further validates the factor structure of the instrument but also indicates that Nepalese entrepreneurs are both collectivists and individualists depending on the situation (family or work).

In conclusion, the findings of this study clearly indicate that Nepalese entrepreneurs are both individualists (idiocentric) and collectivists (allocentric). The findings further support the notion that entrepreneurship must be studied in the cultural context because it is not merely an individualistic phenomenon as indicated in the entrepreneurship literature. The most interesting observation is the conflicting ideas captured in Factor I which shows that the respondents had an overriding need to be both competitive (a Euro-western entrepreneurial characteristic) and responsible to ingroup (perhaps an Asian entrepreneurial characteristic). This observation indicates that entrepreneurs can be both individualists and collectivists depending on the situation (work or family) which is in agreement with the suggestion made by Triandis (1990) that people in general are both individualists and collectivists. The finding that Nepalese entrepreneurs are collectivists supports the idea of Fairbairn (1988) that family should be the unit of analysis in the study of entrepreneurship in collectivist cultures.

Further research is necessary to fully understand the relationship between entrepreneurship and collectivism. It is believed that the study of entrepreneurs in collectivist cultures would provide valuable insights in understanding the compatibility of allocentrism and idiocentrism.

REFERENCES

BELLAH, R.N., MADSEN, R., SULLIVAN, W.M., SWINDLER, A., and TIPTON, S.M. (1985). *Habits of the heart: Individualism and commitment in American life*. Berkeley: University of California Press.

BHAWUK, D.P.S. and UDAS, A. (1991). *The biographical and psychographical profile of Nepalese entrepreneurs: A study of entrepreneurship in Nepal*. Technical report submitted to Small Business Promotion Project, Kathmandu, Nepal.

BRISLIN, R.W. (1986). The wording and translation of research instruments. In Walter J. Lonner and John W. Berry (Eds.), *Field methods in cross-cultural psychology*. California: Sage.

BROEHL JR., W.G. (1970). A less developed entrepreneur. *Columbia Journal of World Business, 5* (2), 26–34.

CRONBACH, LEE J. (1951). Coefficient alpha and the internal structures of tests. *Psychometrica, 16*, 297–334.

FAIRBAIRN, T.I.J. (Ed.). (1988). *Island entrepreneurs: Problems and performances in the Pacific*. Honolulu: The East-West Center.

FLEMING, W.J. (1979). The cultural determinants of entrepreneurship and economic development: A case study of Mendoza Province, Argentina. *Journal of Economic History, 34* (1), 211–224.

HOFSTEDE, G. (1980). *Culture's consequences*. Beverly Hills, CA: Sage.

HUI, C.H. (1988). Measurement of individualism–collectivism. *Journal of Research in Personality, 22*, 17–36.

HUI, C.H. and TRIANDIS, H.C. (1986). Individualism–collectivism: A study of cross-cultural researchers. *Journal of Cross-Cultural Psychology, 17*, 225–248.

McCLELLAND, D. (1961). Methods of measuring human motivation. In J.W. Atkinson (Ed.), *Motives in fantasy, action, and society*. Princeton: D. Van Nostrand.

MANSFIELD, R.S., McCLELLAND, D., SPENCER, L.M., and SANTIAGO, J. (1968). *The identification and assessment of competencies and other personal characteristics of entrepreneurs in developing countries*. Final Report. Massachusetts: McBer and Company.

PETERSON, R. (1988). Understanding and encouraging entrepreneurship internationally. *Journal of Small Business Management, 26,* 1–7.

ROTTER, J.B. (1966). Generalized expectancies for internal versus external control of reinforcement. *Psychological Monographs, 80* (1, Whole No. 609).

SCHUMPETER, J.A. (1934). *The theory of economic development.* Massachusetts: Harvard University Press.

TRIANDIS, H.C. (1990). Cross-cultural studies of individualism and collectivism. In J. Berman (Ed.), *Nebraska symposium on motivation.* Lincoln: University of Nebraska Press.

TRIANDIS, H.C., BONTEMPO, R., BETANCOURT, H., BOND, M., LEUNG, K., BRENES, A., GEORGAS, J., HUI, C.H., MARIN, G., SETIADI, B., SINHA, J.B.P., VERMA, J., SPANGENBERG, J., TOUZARD, H., and DE MONTOMOLLIN, G. (1986). The measurement of etic aspects of individualism and collectivism across cultures. *Australian Journal of Psychology, 38,* 257–267.

TRIANDIS, H.C., BONTEMPO, R., VILLAREAL, M.J., ASAI, M., and LUCAS, N. (1988). Individualism and collectivism: Cross-cultural perspectives on self–ingroup relationships. *Journal of Personality and Social Psychology, 54,* 323–338.

TRIANDIS, H.C., LEUNG, K., VILLAREAL, M., and CLARK, F.L. (1985). Allocentric vs. idiocentric tendencies: Convergent and discriminant validation. *Journal of Research in Personality, 19,* 395–415.

TRIANDIS, H.C., McCUSKER, C., and HUI, C.H. (1990). Multimethod probes of individualism and collectivism. *Journal of Personality and Social Psychology, 59* (5), 1006–1020.

24

Motivational States and Stress–Strain Perception of Unemployed Youth in India

MALA SINHA •
R.C. TRIPATHI

Unemployment in India, as in any other developing society, assumes special significance because it is a resource scarce society with an enormous population. Labour participation projections indicate that the Indian government will have to generate 65 million jobs if the backlog and future unemployment is to be eliminated by 1995 (Ghosh, 1991). A growing trend among social scientists is to view unemployment as a highly subjective phenomenon strongly influenced by the attitudes, norms, customs, traditions, taboos, and inhibitions prevailing in a society. Psychologists are in a position to study and understand psychological principles underlying labour participation behaviour. However, Indian psychologists have ignored the issue of unemployment. Only six studies have been conducted during the period between 1961 and 1988 (Mitra, 1972; Pareek, 1981; Pandey, 1988). Most of the documented psychological research on unemployment has come from

Euro–American countries. Easy generalisations of the Euro–American studies to the Indian conditions cannot be made due to socio-cultural and economic differences.

Studies in the Euro–American cultural context are largely centred on the unemployed who have lost their jobs after working for a certain number of years. As such these unemployed suffered from losses in finances, social network and stimulation but not so much from work identity (Warr, 1984). In India, on the other hand, most of the unemployed have still to find even their first job, and yet to establish a work identity. Lack of a consistent role provided by a job leads to loss of identity and emotional problems (Kakkar and Chaudhary, 1970).

Further, a number of Euro–American studies that have investigated stages of unemployment have reported that the unemployed faced serious well-being problems within a span of 2 years of unemployment (Hill, 1978). In India, the negative effects of unemployment are not expected to occur as early as this due to the role played by the unemployed person's family. For various biological, social, religious, and economic reasons Indian families are extremely supportive towards male offsprings (Stork, 1980). Thus, the cutting edge of unemployment is eliminated by the unquestioning social support provided by the family (Visaria, 1988).

Family socialisation patterns in India are quite different from those in the Euro–American societies. As a result, Indian males develop a strong sense of duty towards their family (Gore, 1965), regarding it to be the most important ingroup (Sinha and Verma, 1987). It plays a significant role in shaping the needs, work attitudes, and job choice of young males (Mehta, 1971).

The traditional Indian work attitudes are also quite different from those prevalent in the Euro–American societies. In India jobseekers, even with a small measure of education, consider manual work plebian. Strict observance of caste proscriptions renders interjob mobility invalid (Nair, 1961). These attitudes are reminiscent of the *Karma–Varna* concept of work which has its roots in the Indian cultural past. Although in modern India this traditional work attitude is weakening (Khan, 1989), jobseekers still prefer to remain unemployed rather than take up work not permitted by their caste or class. In contrast, work is central to life in the Euro–American societies. Social values are attached to people not so much in terms of religious belief or geneological descent, but in terms of the type of work performed now.

CONCEPTUAL FRAMEWORK OF THE STUDY

This study assumes that unemployment is a stressful experience and leads to psychological and physical ill health (Warr and Jackson, 1983). The unemployed are governed by certain motivational and cognitive states like needs, aspirations, causal beliefs, control perceptions or attributions. These psychological factors mobilise energy for some instrumental behaviour that leads to goal attainment and have consequences for the individual's well-being.

Needs and job aspirations are like Schlenker's (1987) "desired identity images", that indicate what the unemployed person wants to be at a particular juncture of his/her life. They are a compromise between values, needs, goals and the existing reality, being based on consensual validation of significant others like family or peer group. They lead to goal directed behaviour involving standards of goal completion through cognitive and behavioural acts (Langer, 1978).

Control perceptions and causal beliefs of the unemployed indicate whether the response at their disposal will affect or change the negative outcomes of an event. These psychological processes have their roots in the unemployed persons' cultural background and they predispose them to certain mental states which govern behaviour (Brim, 1974). Euro–American studies have shown that the unemployed individuals exhibit greater external control when compared to the employed (Gurney, 1981). A longer duration of unemployment, and lower socio-economic status are also associated with external control (Payne, Warr, and Hartley, 1984; Feather and O'Brien, 1987). Younger and higher educated unemployed have greater internal control in comparison to older or less educated unemployed (Bright and Wilkes, 1980). Most of these studies have compared individuals at some stage of employment or unemployment. As such, there are a few studies that have attempted to establish the links between control perceptions and stress–strain perceptions of the unemployed.

Causal attributions are important aspects of the unemployed persons' motivational state. In a failure situation they reveal how an individual constructs reality and how this influences his/her future expectations, self-esteem and well-being. Attributional analysis in unemployment studies have led to confusing results. For instance, it has been observed that the unemployment status determines the nature of attributions. Those who found employment after a period of being unemployed tended to blame the youth for their unemployment. However, those who remained unemployed for long gave up their earlier external stance and adopted an internal stance (Feather and O'Brien, 1986). With an increase in the duration of unemployment, stable attributions for unemployment were associated with reduced job seeking and expectations of success (Feather and Barber, 1983).

Thus, motivational states are important precursors of job seeking, stress and strain in the unemployed. Also, there are cultural differences in the work settings of Indian and Euro–American unemployed persons. In view of this, an attempt is made in this paper:

1. To understand needs, aspirations, control perceptions, causal beliefs, and attributions of Indian unemployed youth.
2. To see how these variables predict job seeking behaviour, duration of unemployment and stress–strain perceptions of the un-employed.

An attempt is made here to highlight the cross-cultural implications of the findings by exploring the similarities and differences in motivational and other psychological characteristics of Indian and Euro–American unemployed persons.

METHOD AND PROCEDURE

Questionnaire data were collected from 325 male unemployed youth (mean age: 24.32 years). The subjects were interviewed in the employment exchange, university campus and rural areas. An individual was considered unemployed if he: (a) was actively looking for a job, (b) was currently not employed anywhere, and (c) was financially dependent on his family or others. The age of the respondents ranged from 19 to 35 years, more than half were married and were Arts graduates. About two-thirds of the respondents had been unemployed for more than 2 years.

MEASURES

In-depth interviews and a pilot study were conducted before formalising the questionnaire. The final questionnaire comprised 5 scales measuring the different aspects of motivational states. In addition to these 5 scales, another 2 scales measured stress perception and psychological strain resulting from unemployment. Some of the scales were subjected to the principal component factor analysis with varimax rotation to derive measures, while correllograms (Andrews and Withey, 1976) were used for others to form indices. A measure was formed by combining items subsumed in a factor or cluster, provided all items which loaded highly on it made theoretical sense.[1] Coefficient alphas were calculated for each measure (Cronbach, 1951). All the scales were 5-point rating scales.(Henceforth, the names of derived measures will have their first letters capitalised.)

Measures of Motivational States

Three types of needs were derived from the scale that measured reasons for seeking employment: (a) *Material Well-being and Social Need* (α: .68) comprised 6 items like need to earn wealth, build social contacts, and old age security, (b) *Self Growth Need* (α: .68) had 4 items representing mental development, constructive use of time, and finding roots in society through a job, (c) *Family Duty and Honour Need* (α: .22) included 2 items dealing with a need to fulfil family responsibility and to contribute to the social prestige and honour of the family.

The job attitude scale measured the nature of jobs the unemployed were willing to or not willing to perform. Two measures were derived: (a) *Selective Job Aspiration* (α: .50) had 3 items that measured a need to do only those jobs that matched the status, interest pattern, and ability of the jobseeker., (b) *Job Need* (α: .68) comprised 3 items that measured a need to do *any* available job.

The scale measuring perceptions of control regarding job attainment comprised 6 items. Principal component factor analysis yielded 3

---

[1] Details of scale construction can be obtained from the authors.

factors: (a) *Internal Control* (α: .57) a 2-item measure which emphasised the role of ability and effort in finding a job, (b) *External Control—Influence* (α: .50) also included 2 items which measured the degree to which helpful personal contacts were considered important in finding a job, (c) *External Control—Luck* (α: .30), comprised 2 items which emphasised God's will and luck as important factors in finding a job.

To measure the causal belief systems 8 commonly understood Hindu proverbs were used. The principal component factor analysis yielded 2 factors: (a) *External Causation—Belief* (α: .63) included 4 proverbs which relegated responsibility of life events to external agencies like God, *Karma*, powerful others, and money; and (b) *Niskama Karma* (α: .42) which also included 4 proverbs. Of these, 2 dealt with individual effort as the determinant of outcomes while the remaining focused on individual effort, but without having any concern for the outcomes. This notion is preached by the *Bhagvad Gita*, and is considered to be part of the Hindu cultural tradition. Briefly stated, this concept means effort orientation on the part of the individual with detachment towards its outcomes and this being an ideal state of being.

The causal attributions scale asked the respondents to endorse 8 reasons for not finding a job. On correllogram construction, 2 clear clusters emerged which were used to form 2 measures: (a) *Attribution to Lack of Power* (α: .40) included 2 items, under this measure lack of money and influential contacts were perceived as causes of one's unemployment, (b) *Attribution to Deficiencies in Self* (α: .63) comprised 3 items, lack of good education, ability and perseverence were perceived as causes of one's unemployment, and (c) *Attribution to Bad Fate*, which was a single item measure.

Measures of Stress

The scale measuring unemployment stress was derived from the P-E Fit theory (Caplan, Tripathi, and Naidu, 1985). The respondent answered questions keeping in view the demands of the job he was aspiring for. "Fit" referred to the degree of effort made, abilities owned, academic grades obtained, money and contacts possessed, and they were commensurate with the demands of the aspired job. High score indicated high Fit which meant low perceived stress. The scale was factor analysed and 2 measures of Fit emerged: (a) *Current Internal Fit* (α: .77) included 6 items measuring Fit regarding resources possessed by the jobseeker (e.g., effort, ability, and interview taking skill), (b) *Current Resource Fit* (α: .34), a 3-item measure that dealt with Fit vis-à-vis money, influential contacts owned by the jobseeker to meet the job market demands.

Measures of Strain

Strain was measured by a 19-item scale describing both positive and negative feelings arising from unemployment. Positive items were reverse coded so that a high score meant greater strain. Factor analysis revealed 6 factors, but only 3 were used to form measures: (a) *Low Self Worth* (α: .78) comprised 7 items measuring a general state of guilt, worthlessness, feelings of failure, and deteriorating social relations, (b) *Threatened Role Identity* (α: .55) consisted of 3 items and measured guilt for being a burden on the family and not fulfilling the role of a bread winner, and (c) *Low Future Success Orientations* (α: .48) included 4 items measuring the person's lack of confidence about succeeding in future. It is noteworthy that Low Future Success Orientations had a negative correlation with Low Self Worth (r: $-.13$, $p<.001$) and Threatened Role Identity (r: $-.24$, $p<.001$).

An index of *Socio-Economic* class was developed by combining parents' education and economic level with the caste of the unemployed. Job Seeking Behaviour was assessed by the number of job applications currently sent out and visits made to the employment exchange.

RESULTS

Job Linked Needs of the Unemployed

Indian unemployed youth looking for their first job considered Family Duty and Honour (M: 3.93) as the most important need for seeking employment. Material Well-being and Social Need (M: 3.30) was the least important and between these two needs was the Self Growth Need (M: 3.60). Euro–American studies have highlighted the saliency of needs like personal autonomy, status and independence outside the family among the unemployed youth (Maitland-Edwards, McMullen, Welbers, and Woolthius, 1981). In the case of older unemployed workers, regaining material benefits, social contacts and activity levels were more important reasons for seeking re-employment (Jahoda, 1981; Warr, 1984). Cross-cultural differences in the reasons for seeking employment are apparent.

Product-moment correlations of job linked needs with other variables have cross-cultural relevance. Family Duty and Honour Need had a positive and significant correlation with Internal Control (r: .20, p<.001), Niskama Karma (r: .13, p<.001), and Current Internal Fit (r: .25, p<.001). Regression analysis further revealed that as a predictor, this need increased Current Internal Fit and reduced strain like Low Future Success Orientations (Table 24.1). Thus, concern with the family is associated with Fit and well-being.

Self Growth Need was positively correlated with External Causation Belief (r: .21, p < .001), Attributions to Deficiencies in Self (r: .17, p < .001), and Job Need (r: .20, p < .001). However, as a predictor Self Growth Need decreased Threatened Role Identity (Table 24.1).

Work Related Attitudes of the Unemployed

Unemployed youth had a higher mean for Selective Job Aspiration (M: 3.00) than for Job Need (M: 2.70). Both were negatively correlated (r: −.13, p < .01), thus indicating that a tendency towards selective job aspiration was associated with a low desire to do any available job. Despite being positively correlated with Current Resource Fit (r: .14, p < .001), Selective Job Aspiration as a predictor increased Low Self Worth (Table 24.1). Thus, a selective attitude towards jobs was associated with financial and social resourcefulness, but it did not reduce strain.

Job Need was positively correlated with External Causation Belief (r: .20, p < .001), Attributions to Bad Fate (r: .24, p < .001), Current Resource Fit (r: −.23, p < .001), and Low Self Worth (r: .31, p < .001). However, despite its linkages with low motivational states, Job

Table 24.1

Regression Coefficients of Significant Predictors of Job Seeking Behaviour, Duration of Unemployment, Fit, and Strain Variables

	Job Seeking Behaviour	Duration of Unemployment	Current Internal Fit	Current Resource Fit	Low Self-worth	Threatened Role Identity	Low Future Success Orientations
Age	—	.46**	—	—	—	—	—
Education	-.16**	-.13**	—	.12**	—	.31**	—
Socio-economic Class	—	—	—	—	—	-.16**	—
Material and Social Need	—	—	.12*	.12**	—	—	—
Self Growth Need	—	—	.17**	—	—	—	-.21**
Family Duty and Honour Need	—	—	—	—	.18**	—	—
Selective Job Aspiration	—	—	—	—	—	—	—
Job Need	.21**	—	—	-.16**	—	—	-.20**
Job Aspiration Level	—	-.13**	—	.20**	-.16**	—	—
Internal Control	.17**	—	—	—	—	.27**	—
External Control—Influence	—	.18**	—	—	.23**	—	-.15**
External Control—Luck	—	.16**	—	—	—	—	—
External Causation Belief	—	—	.14**	—	—	—	—
Niskama Karma	—	—	—	—	—	—	-.13*
Attribution to Lack of Power	—	—	—	—	.17**	—	—
Attribution to Deficiencies in Self	—	—	—	—	.17**	—	—
Attribution to Bad Fate	—	—	—	—	—	—	—
Job Seeking Behaviour	—	.18**	—	—	.16**	—	—
Duration of Unemployment	—	—	—	—	—	.17**	—
Current Internal Fit	—	—	—	—	—	—	—
Current Resource Fit	—	—	—	—	—	—	-.17**
R^2	.15	.44	.09	.14	.31	.23	.21
dF	3,302	6,290	3,290	4,293	6,203	4,205	5,204

* $p < .05$; ** $p < .01$.

Need as a predictor increased Job Seeking Behaviour, thereby indicating that it had an energising influence on the unemployed. Feather and O'Brien (1987) have reported a contrary finding: Job Need was negatively correlated with external control and depressive affect. This difference could be due to the manner in which job need has been conceptualised in the two studies. According to Feather and O'Brien, job need is immediate motivation for job, perhaps representing a highly motivated state. In the present study, the relationship between Job Need and external control and low resource fit indicated that it could be a result of a deprived socio-economic background.

Of all the measures of job attitudes, the Level of Job Aspiration alone was instrumental in increasing Current Resource Fit and reducing Low Self Worth (Table 24.1). Thus, high job aspirations, material and social resources and well-being are associated with each other.

Control Perceptions and Causal Beliefs of the Unemployed

The unemployed ranked Internal Control (M: 3.90) and *Niskama Karma* (M: 3.92) higher than External Control—Influence (M: 3.05), External Control—Luck (M: 3.05), and External Causation Belief (M: 2.90). Both *Niskama Karma* and Internal Control were positively correlated with Current Internal Fit (r: .21, p < .001 and r: .19, p < .001 respectively). Both were negatively correlated with Low Future Success Orientations (r: −.17, p < .001 and r: −.24, p < .001 respectively). Regression analysis further revealed that *Niskama Karma* increased Current Internal Fit and lowered pessimistic concerns of future. Internal Control as a predictor was associated with a reduction in the duration of unemployment (Table 24.1). A similar finding has been reported by Feather and O'Brien (1987), in their study control-optimism was negatively related to the duration of unemployment.

Regression results also indicated that measures relating to external control predicted an increase in the duration of unemployment and strain. A noteworthy observation was that External Control—Influence increased job seeking behaviour.

Causal Attributions for Unemployment

Attributing blame to external factors like lack of money and influential contacts was the most important reason for unemployment (Lack of Power,M: 3.04). On the other hand, internal attributions like deficiencies in self had a lower mean (M: 2.57). Feather and Davenport (1981) have reported similar findings. They have also observed a negative correlation between internal attributions and depressive affect. A finding not replicated in the present study. Attributions to Deficiencies in Self were not only positively correlated with Low Self Worth (r: .16, p < .001) but they also predicted Low Self Worth (Table 24.1). Recent studies on the unemployed have reported similar linkages (Winefield, Tiggeman, and Winefield, 1992).

DISCUSSION AND CONCLUSIONS

The results have highlighted cross-cultural similarities as well as differences in the psychological attributes of Indian and Euro–American unemployed. The most important differences were in the reasons cited for seeking employment. For the Indian unemployed youth, family duty had high saliency. Individualistic needs like material gains, self-improvement, and social network development were more frequently reported reasons for working in Euro–American studies (Jahoda, 1981; Warr, 1984). As a motivational variable, Family Duty and Honour Need was associated with high Fit, well-being, and internal control. This is contrary to the assumption that concern for ingroup (a collectivist value) would de-emphasise internal control in individuals (Triandis, 1988). The centrality of the family in the unemployed person's schema reflected that he was rooted in the social system. In all probability this system provided the person with social support which kept him motivated and in good health.

Self Growth Need as conceptualised in the study is similar to Maslow's (1970) self-actualisation need. Self Growth was instrumental in lowering stress and strain. However, its linkages with external control variables indicated this was not a higher order need that unlike Maslow's self-actualisation need. The implications of this are that the meaning of any psychological construct depends to a large extent on the cultural context in which it is used. In developed Euro–American societies self-growth or actualisation may be a higher order need, arising after basic needs have been fulfilled. In resource scarce societies like India, Self Growth could be due to a deprived socio-economic environment.

Work related attitudes of the unemployed reflected traditional Indian attitude towards work. That is, there was a greater tendency to be selective about work even in the face of continued unemployment. It has also been established that this attitude led to problems of well-being in the unemployed. The desire to do any job was associated with high job seeking behaviour as well as ill-being. Sending out too many job applications and making frequent visits to the employment exchange indicated diffused job goals. This attitude is found to be associated with motivational deficits (Rath, 1983). Goal specificity, as measured by the Level of Job Aspiration, increased fit and reduced strain. These findings support the theoretical formulation that energisation towards a goal is a function of knowledge of task requirements and willingness to expend energy (Ford and Brehm, 1987). Thus, higher the level of job aspirations, greater would be the awareness of task difficulties and confidence to overcome them. This explains how the Level of Job Aspiration increased Fit and well-being.

Niskama Karma, an indigenous concept, was a better predictor of Fit and well-being than Internal Control. *Niskama Karma* focuses on effort without being concerned about the outcomes (Pande and Naidu, 1986), and Internal Control assumes effort–outcome contingency (Rotter, 1966). The Indian labour market is complex and a contingency between effort and outcomes is not readily discernible by the unemployed. The concept of *Niskama Karma* is effective in reducing stress and strain because it helps absorb failures without making the unemployed lose the will to make efforts towards a goal.

It is also believed that in difficult environments where attempts at primary control (internal control) have failed, people adopt external control (Rothbaum, Weisz, and Snyder, 1982). In line with this, the present study found that external control was associated with high job seeking behaviour, indicating that "externals" were motivated and were not lacking in control. Job seeking behaviour was also positively associated with the duration of unemployment, thereby indicating that the skill of job seeking was perhaps faulty and not the attitude of external control.

The study was unable to replicate the negative correlation between internal attributions and negative affect (Feather and Davenport, 1981). An explanation is offered: for societies which value challenge and confrontation, blaming the self for failure may not be too damaging (Lazarus, 1981). Indian society, on the other hand, is perceived to be religion-oriented, values harmony, safety and there is an absence of extreme disappointments. Thus, attributing blame for unemployment to self related causes is damaging to the self-esteem causing strain. It is noteworthy that a recent Euro–American study on the unemployed obtained a positive correlation between internal attributions and negative affect (Winefield, Tiggeman, and Winefield, 1992).

In conclusion, the study established the relevance of the cultural context in psychological studies. It has highlighted that indigenous concepts like *Niskama Karma* and duty to family play a vital role in shaping the unemployment experience. The study also identified those motivational variables which were effective in reducing stress and strain and those which were not. Finally, a number of cross-cultural similarities between the Indian and Euro–American unemployed have been pointed out. Higher socio-economic class was negatively associated but negative affect and job seeking behaviour were positively associated with the duration of unemployment (Feather and O'Brien, 1987; Warr, 1984). Thus, societies which differ with respect to their cultural milieu may be similar with respect to some psychological attributes.

REFERENCES

ANDREWS, F.M. and WITHEY, S.B. (1976). *Social indicators of well being: Americans' perception of life quality*. New York: Plenum Press.

BRIGHT, R. and WILKES, R. (1980). An analysis of views on work and unemployment among school leavers in Brisbane. Paper presented at the annual conference of the Australian Association for Research in Education, Sydney.

BRIM, O.G. (1974, September). The sense of personal control over one's life. Invited address to Divisions 7 and 8 of the American Psychological Association, New Orleans, LA.

CAPLAN, R.D., TRIPATHI, R.C., and NAIDU, R.K. (1985). Subjective past, present and future fit: Effects on anxiety, depression and other indicators of wellbeing. *Journal of Personality and Social Psychology, 48* (1), 180–197.

CRONBACH, L.J. (1951). Coefficient alpha and the internal structure of tests. *Psychometrika, 16*, 297–234.

FEATHER, N.T. and BARBER, J.G. (1983). Depressive reactions and unemployment. *Journal of Abnormal Psychology, 92*, 185–195.

FEATHER, N.T. and DAVENPORT, P.R. (1981). Unemployment and depressive affect: A motivational and attributional analysis. *Journal of Personality and Social Psychology, 41*(3), 422–436.

FEATHER, N.T. and O'BRIEN, G.E. (1986). A longitudinal analysis of the effects of different patterns of employment and unemployment on school leavers. *British Journal of Psychology, 77*, 459–479.

FEATHER, N.T. and O'BRIEN, G.E. (1987). Looking for employment: An expectancy, valence analysis of jobseeking behaviour among young people. *British Journal of Psychology, 78*, 251–272.

FORD, C.E. and BREHM, J.W. (1987). Effort expenditure following failure. In C.R. Snyder and C.E. Ford (Eds.), *Coping with negative life events: Clinical and social psychological perspctives* (pp. 81–99). New York/London: Plenum Press.

GHOSH, A. (1991). Eighth Plan: Challenges and possibilities—III, employment core of the plan. *Economic and Political Weekly, XXVI* (5).

GORE, M.S. (1965). The traditional Indian family. In M.F. Nemkoff (Ed.), *Comparative family systems*. Boston: Houghton Mifflin.

GURNEY, R.M. (1981). Leaving school, facing unemployment and making attributions about causes of unemployment. *Journal of Vocational Behaviour, 18*, 79–91.

HILL, J.M.M. (1978). The psychological impact of unemployment. *New Society, 43* (798), 118–120.

JAHODA, M. (1981). Work, employment and unemployment: Values, theories and approaches in social research. *American Psychologist, 36* (2), 184–191.

KAKKAR, S. and CHAUDHARY, K. (1970). *Conflict and choice: Indian youth in a changing society*. Bombay: Somaiya Publications.

KHAN, R. (1989). The total state: The concept and its manifestation in the Indian political system. In Z. Hasan, S.N. Jha, and R. Khan (Eds.), *The state, political processes and identity* (pp. 33–72). New Delhi: Sage.

LANGER, E.J. (1978). Rethinking the role of thought in social interactions. In J.H. Harvey, W. Ickes, and R.F. Kidd (Eds.), *New directions in attributions research* (Vol. 2, pp. 35–38). Hillsdale, NJ: Erlbaum.

LAZARUS, R.S. (1981). Costs and benefits of denial. In S. Breznetz (Ed.), *Denial of stress* (pp. 1–30). New York: International Universities Press.

MAITLAND-EDWARDS, J., MCMULLEN, T., WELBERS, G., and WOOLTHIUS, T. (1981). Transition from education to working life: Pointers from European communities action plan. *Journal of Adolescence, 4*, 27–46.

MASLOW, A.M. (1970). *Motivation and personality* (2nd ed.). New York: Harper and Row.

MEHTA, P. (Ed.). (1971). *The Indian youth: Emerging problems and issues*. Bombay: Somaiya Publications.

MITRA, S.K. (Ed.). (1972). *A survey of research in psychology*. Bombay: Popular Prakashan.

NAIR, K. (1961). *Blossoms in the dust*. London: Gerald, Duckworth & Co. Ltd.

PANDE, N. and NAIDU, R.K. (1986). Effort and outcome orientations as moderators of stress–strain relationship. *Psychological Studies, 31*, 207–214.

PANDEY, J. (Ed.). (1988). *Psychology in India: The state-of-the -art* (3 vols.). New Delhi: Sage.

PAREEK, U. (Ed.). (1981). *A survey of research in psychology, 1971–76* (Vols. I & II). Bombay: Popular Prakashan.

PAYNE, R., WARR, P., and HARTLEY, J. (1984). Social class and psychological illhealth during unemployment. *Sociology of Health and Illness, 6* (2), 152–174.

RATH, R. (1983). Cognitive growth and classroom learning of culturally deprived children in the primary schools. In M.G. Hussain (Ed.), *Psycho-ecological dimensions of poverty.* Delhi: Manohar.

ROTHBAUM, F., WEISZ, J.R., and SNYDER, S. (1982). Attitudes and social cognition. *Journal of Personality and Social Psychology, 42* (1), 5–37.

ROTTER, J.B. (1966). Generalized expectancies for internal versus external control of reinforcement. *Psychological Monographs, 80,* 1–28.

SCHLENKER, B.R. (1987). Threats to identity: Self identification and social stress. In C.R. Snyder and C.E. Ford (Eds.), *Coping with negative life events: Clinical and sociological psychological perspectives* (pp. 273–313). New York/London: Plenum Press.

SINHA, J.B.P. and VERMA, J. (1987). Structure of collectivism. In Ç. Kağitçibaşi (Ed.), *Growth and progress in cross-cultural psychology* (pp. 123–129). Lisse: Swets and Zeitlinger.

STORK, H. (1980). La raissance d'un fils dans la tradition religieuse de'Inde(The birth of a son in the religious traditions of India). *Journal de Psychologie Normale at Pathologique, 77* (2–3), 151–186.

TRIANDIS, H.C. (1988). Collectivism and development. In D. Sinha and H.S.R. Kao (Eds.), *Social values and development: Asian perspectives* (pp. 285–303). New Delhi: Sage.

VISARIA, P. (1988). Unemployment among the Asian youth: Its incidence, causes and consequences. In Association of Asian Social Science Research Councils, *Youth in Asia: Viewpoints for the future* (pp. 209–283). New Delhi: New Statesman Publishing Company.

WARR, P. (1984). Economic recession and mental health: A review of research. *Tijdschrift Voor Sociale Gezondheidszorg, 62* (8).

WARR, P. and JACKSON, P. (1983). Self esteem and unemployment among young workers. *La Travail Humain Tome, 46* (2), 355–366.

WINEFIELD, A.H., TIGGEMAN, M., and WINEFIELD, H.R. (1992). Unemployment distress, reasons for job loss and causal attributions for unemployment in young people. *Journal of Occupational and Organizational Psychology, 65,* 213–218.

25

Perceived Socio-cultural Causes of Non-reporting of Crimes in India

ARCHANA GUPTA •
JANAK PANDEY

There is a general consensus regarding the alarming increase in crimes in recent years. Although statistics relating to crime are inadequate in India, overwhelming evidence shows a faster rate of growth in crimes as compared to the population growth. The reported figure was 6,25,000 for a population of 342 million in the year following independence (i.e., 1948). Thirty years later, in 1978, the total number of reported crimes was 13,13,564 while the population rose to 635.8 million (Rao, 1980). By the end of the century, it is estimated that the population of India will cross the one billion mark. If the prevailing situation continues, about two million crimes will be reported under the Indian Penal Code and about five million offences under special and local laws.

Reported crimes account for approximately one-fifth of all crimes in India since a large number of crimes are committed against the weaker sections, children, and against women in particular, which do not get reported (Abdulali, 1988; Flavia, 1988). India has one of the lowest rates of reported crimes in the world—187.9 per 100,000 citizens—less than 4 per cent of the United States (Kurian, 1984). Non-reporting of crimes is fairly prevalent both in developing and in developed countries. According to the Bureau of Justice Statistics (National Crime Survey, 1983), only one-third of all crimes are reported to the police even in a developed country like the USA.

A number of factors may determine non-reporting of crimes. These factors, however, may vary because of differences in the socio-cultural and legal systems. In India, the general public impression of the police is one of dissatisfaction and disenchantment because the vast majority of reported cases do not lead to any positive action against the offenders. This is partly due to the apathy of the police or their inefficiency to produce convincing evidence (Rao, 1985). According to the Bureau of Justice Statistics (National Crime Survey, 1983), in the USA, many violent crimes were unreported because they were "private matters" and many crimes of theft were considered "not important enough to report". Lack of proof and fear of reprisal were also considered as the major factors responsible for non-reporting of crimes.

There are only a few cross-cultural studies on the phenomenon of non-reporting of crimes in various societies. For example, a survey done in India, Indonesia, Iran, Italy, erstwhile Yugoslavia, and the USA (Newman, 1974) to assess people's reactions to a robbery involving $50 and injury to the victim so as to require hospitalisation revealed that the number of people who said that they would report the crime to the police varied from 50 per cent in Italy to 95 per cent in the USA as compared to 84 per cent in India. Another cross-cultural investigation of calling the police was conducted by Greenberg and Ruback (1989) in India, the USA, Thailand, and Nigeria. Subjects rated 49 crimes on a scale ranging from 10 (very strongly approve of dealing with the matter privately) to 1 (very strongly approve of calling the police). The mean value was lowest in India followed by Nigeria, Thailand, and the United States.

Generally, a crime is reported by the victim or by his relatives or friends. In some cases a bystander may also report the crime. Studies reveal that crime reporting behaviour is greatly influenced by the advice given by the bystanders. Victims are more willing to accept judgments which are consistent with their prior attitudes. Other factors which effectively predict reporting behaviour are perceived outcomes, social expectations, and certain situational factors (Ruback, Greenberg, and Westcott, 1984; Bickman and Rosenbaum, 1977; Summers and Norris, 1984).

In a developing society like India, a number of reasons are frequently mentioned for non-reporting of crimes. In general, people perceive the police as not helpful and responsible for crimes and victimisations. There are informal social institutions in Indian society such as the caste or community, *Panchayat* (committee), which intervene and settle the matter. Most of the crimes related to female members of the family do not get reported due to fear of reprisal and to save the reputation of women. There is lack of psychological research, however, on the various possible causes of non-reporting of crimes in India. People's perception of attribution of causality for non-reporting of crimes may differ as a result of various personal and situational factors. This study is an attempt to examine the perception of the causes of non-reporting of crimes by males and females when they are a bystander and when they are not a bystander of a crime.

METHOD

Design

A 2 × 2 mixed ANOVA design was used in this study. The perception of causes of non-reporting of crimes was a within subjects measure and gender of respondents was a between subjects measure.

Sample

The respondents were 50 male and 50 female undergraduates of a North Indian University with the average age of 20.07 years. They volunteered to participate in the study.

Measures

A 23-item questionnaire to assess the respondents' perception of causes for non-reporting of crimes was used. Each item was rated on a 5-point response scale. Item analysis was done to prepare the final questionnaire. For example, 5 independent judges rated the suitability (face validity) of each item and also arranged the items into 7 broad dimensions related to the causes for non-reporting of crimes. The number of items finally selected for each dimension with scores range and Cronbach alpha values are presented in Table 25.1.

TABLE 25.1

Dimensions of the Causes of Non-reporting of Crimes, Number of Items, Scores Range, and Cronbach Alphas

Dimensions	No. of Items	Scores Range	Cronbach Alpha Value (α)
Police	5	5–25	.64
Legal System	3	3–15	.75
Personal Reasons	5	5–25	.52
Interpersonal Reasons	2	2–10	.63
Ignorance of People	3	3–15	.62
Alternative Judicial Methods	3	3–15	.57
Fatalism	2	2–10	.47

Procedure

The respondents were approached individually and were asked to complete the questionnaire. They were encouraged to ask questions if they had any difficulty in understanding the questionnaire. In the first part of the questionnaire, the instructions required the respondents to think about non-reporting of crimes. The respondents, therefore, rated each item to answer the question "why people generally do not report a crime?" In the second part of the questionnaire, the respondents were asked to think of a situation involving crime, which they witnessed as a bystander but did not report to the police. Thus, in the second part of the questionnaire, the respondents again rated the same items of the questionnaire.

RESULTS

The results revealed significant differences in the respondents' perception of the causes when they rated them as a general observer and when they rated them as a bystander of a crime, on all dimensions with the exception of court system and interpersonal reasons. The means and F values summarised in Table 25.2 reveal that means of the general observer condition are significantly higher than the bystander condition.

TABLE 25.2

Means and F Ratios of Dimensions as a Function of Main Effects and General as well as Bystander Conditions

Dimensions	General Condition Means	Bystander Condition Means	F (1,98)	Males Means	Females Means	F (1,98)
Police	13.54	12.73	12.96**	13.73	12.53	3.25
Court System	10.77	10.35	1.44	10.77	10.29	.78
Personal Reasons	15.64	14.40	8.69**	15.25	14.53	.67
Interpersonal Reasons	4.74	4.87	.35	4.70	4.81	.45
Ignorance of People	8.15	6.40	60.61**	7.29	7.26	.005
Alternative Judicial Methods	6.32	5.94	4.78*	5.72	6.42	2.63
Fatalism	4.52	3.92	33.09**	4.07	4.34	1.18

* p < .05; ** p < .01.

The main effect of gender did not reach significant level for any of the dimensions. The trend of differences between the means of males and females, however, revealed that males showed a higher degree of agreement to the causes of non-reporting as compared to the females. None of the interaction effects were found to be significant.

The correlation coefficients presented in Table 25.3 show two broad clustering of the measures. In the first group, the closely related

TABLE 25.3

Interdimensional Correlations among the Perceptions of the Causes of Non-reporting

	x1	x2	x3	x4	x5	x6	x7
x1	1.00						
Police	1.00						
x2	.44**	1.00					
Court System	.54**	1.00					
x3	.59**	.68**	1.00				
Personal Reasons	.43**	.65**	1.00				
x4	.42**	.42**	.49**	1.00			
Interpersonal Reasons	.43**	.49**	.49**	1.00			
x5	.14	.37**	.29**	.11	1.00		
Ignorance of People	.23*	.29**	.17	.18	1.00		
x6	.14	.10	.07	.12	.05	1.00	
Alternative Judicial Methods	.22*	.08	−.003	.13	.40**	1.00	
x7	.13	.09	.14	.07	.08	.25**	1.00
Fatalism	−.06	.14	.22*	.14	.24*	.45**	1.00

Note: Upper correlations are for general condition and lower are for bystander condition. * p < .05 (N =100); ** p < .001.

dimensions are the police, the court system, personal and interpersonal reasons. In the second cluster, the positively correlated dimensions are ignorance of the people, fatalism and alternative judicial methods.

A close examination of the obtained means of each item on a 5-point scale shows the highest mean value of 4.02 for the item, "cases prolonged for many years in the courts", and the lowest mean of 1.75 for the item "case is settled in *Panchayat*".

DISCUSSION

The objective of this study was to understand the perceived causes of non-reporting of crimes in India. The results revealed that factors related to the police and the court system were perceived as the major causes of non-reporting of crimes. Issues related to the court system were considered to be the most important determinants of non-reporting indicating the difficulties involved in the process of seeking justice from the existing legal system and, therefore, people avoided reporting crimes. Respondents also perceived the police department as corrupt and, therefore, they hesitated in reporting crimes. Personal reasons, such as involvement of female members of the family as victims, also prevented people from reporting in order to protect the reputation of the family.

Mean ratings of various causes for the bystander condition were lower compared to the ratings given for the general observer condition. This could be explained by the fact that the respondents were fairly young, educated and belonged to urban, middle class background. They, therefore, perceived themselves as more responsible in reporting a crime when they were present as bystanders. On the other hand, the respondents considered the general population as less educated, poor, residing in rural areas and generally harassed by the police and the legal system. The marked differences in perception of ignorance of the people and fatalism also support this finding.

Results show that males and females did not differ in their perceptions of the causes of non-reporting. This may be due to the fact that both male and female respondents were from urban background, and had similar educational and socio-economic status.

Inter-dimensional correlations provide additional information to understand the dynamics of non-reporting of crimes. Fatalism, ignorance of the people, and alternative judicial methods are positively correlated. It is generally observed that Indians have fatalistic values. Therefore, their belief that God will punish the culprit, may inhibit them to report the crime. If, however, the settlement of a case is crucial, then existing alternative judicial systems such as *Panchayats* may be approached.

The findings of this study imply that for increasing the reporting rate of crimes, steps should be taken to speed up the disposal of cases at all levels by simplifying the procedures, establishing special courts, improving the skills of the judicial staff, modernisation of court management systems, and ensuring availability of up-to-date law reports to judges, lawyers, and clients. The cost of litigation should be reduced. The police–public relationship needs to be strengthened. The training of police personnel to orient them towards the service of the people may be helpful. There is also a need to organise campaigns to make people aware of their legal rights. Public participation and vigilance is extremely important for increasing the reporting rate of crimes. This study has some limitations because of the selective nature of the sample: the respondents were young and many of them may not have had any experience of crime. It would be interesting to study those who have been victims of crimes and who did report or did not report the crime to the police.

REFERENCES

ABDULALI, S. (1988). Rape in India: An empirical picture. In R. Ghadially (Ed.), *Women in Indian society: A reader* (pp. 196–206). New Delhi: Sage.

BICKMAN, L. and ROSENBAUM, D.P. (1977). Crime reporting as a function of bystander encouragement, surveillance and credibility. *Journal of Personality and Social Psychology, 35,* 577–586.

BUREAU OF JUSTICE STATISTICS. (1983). Report to the nation on crime and justice. *The Data* (Washington, D.C., US Department of Justice), 6–13, 24–25.

FLAVIA. (1988). Violence in the family: Wife beating. In R. Ghadially (Ed.), *Women in Indian society: A reader* (pp. 151–166). New Delhi: Sage.

GREENBERG, M.S. and RUBACK, R.B. (1989). *After the crime: Decision making by crime victims*. New York: Plenum.

KURIAN, G.T. (1984). *The new book of world rankings*. New York: Facts on File Publications.

NEWMAN, D.J. (1974). Role and process in the criminal court. In D. Glaser (Ed.), *Handbook of criminology*. Chicago: Rand McNally.

RAO, S.V. (1980). Criminal justice administration: Planning for their policy implications. *The Indian Journal of Public Administration, 26* (3), 618–630.

RAO, S.V. (1985). Law and order administration: Some emerging trends. *The Indian Journal of Public Administration, 31* (3), 767–777.

RUBACK, R.B., GREENBERG, M.S., and WESTCOTT, D.R. (1984). Social influence and crime victim decision making. *Journal of Social Issues, 40,* 51–76.

SUMMERS, S.F. and NORRIS, J. (1984). Differences between rape victims who report and those who do not report to public-agency. *Journal of Applied Social Psychology, 14* (6), 562–573.

26

International Networks: Mechanisms for Culturally Viable Development

BOBBIE M. ANTHONY

Worldwide cooperative endeavours between professionals could significantly bolster structural development efforts of countries desirous of progress in culturally congruent ways. There is at present an extremely large number of professional associations, many with sizeable memberships, from which professionals could be recruited to form alliances or networks, across countries. The recruitment would be for the specific purpose of assisting in the development of culturally viable development structures as requested by professionals from developing countries. Yet, there is a high probability that professionals across countries would experience serious difficulties were their development assistance attempts to be orchestrated by themselves. This is so, in large part, for several reasons.

PROFESSIONAL PITFALLS

Professional Scarcity

First, in proportion to population sizes, there is a relative scarcity of professionals within some developing countries (see, Bunge, 1983a, 1983b; Regmi, 1992; Ross, 1990). This means that the professionals most suitable for serving as liaisons within developing countries are numerically inadequate for large numbers of countrywide interactive endeavours.

Socio-cultural Complexities

Second, it is unlikely that the complexity of socio-cultural characteristics possessed by all the various groups within a developing country would be thoroughly understood and appropriately included in development strategies of professionals. Hence, the probability of repeating past failures, such as those cited in the literature (see, Laboratory of Comparative Human Cognition, 1986; Sinha, 1985), would be increased.

Collectivism Influences

Third, collectivism is a common characteristic of developing countries in Asia, Africa, and elsewhere (Brislin, 1993), and though the sharpness of ingroup and outgroup distinctions vary with cultures, in collectivist cultures, psychological involvement with other people depends significantly upon acquaintanceship, kinship, friendship, and geographical proximity (Hui, 1990).

The likelihood of indigenous professionals being included in these categories to any significant degree is low, if for no other reason than that their numbers are relatively small. Obviously, professionals in developed countries would be even less likely to be included. Thus, at the local or "grass roots" levels, professionals would have some difficulty in promoting psychological involvement of intended development beneficiaries, especially where the boundaries between ingroups and outgroups are stringently narrow. As a case in point, Sinha (1985) has noted that in India, collectives and social groups are very close-knit and that "professional groups have yet to compete" with the ingroups of families, close relatives, friends, neighbours, and caste men, in that order (p. 113).

Development Requisites

Fourth, and finally, there are questions related to development objectives and development needs. Whose needs are to be satisfied? Who decides the goals and the strategies for goal attainment? A study by UNESCO concluded that full development requires that the beneficiaries of development establish their own development aims (UNESCO, 1977). This conclusion, which implies that development should be "from the ground up" and not from the level of professionals external to the beneficiary groups, has been echoed by a growing number of professionals interested in appropriate growth and development within developing countries.

In order to clarify endogenous development, the type of development intended for international networks of professionals to assist, a discussion of this type of development and of previous development attempts follows. An example from education will further clarify the issue.

ENDOGENOUS AND EXTERNAL DEVELOPMENT

For nearly two decades, the emphasis of development effort within developing countries has been on societal development grounded in individual and group development, such that development beneficiaries develop, enhance, and utilise their own competencies to strategise about and to implement self-determined needs and goals. The impetus for such emphasis has been motivated by conceptions that internally controlled development would result in independence from the tried-and-failed externally designed and/or externally introduced ideas and strategies. The need to escape from the tried-and-failed external models of growth and development arose because the externally derived organisational structures for economic development created not only economic, but also psychological problems (Sinha, 1985). The escape method emphasised was a unified model encompassing the multiplicity of development areas or dimensions, and patterned around the people perceived to be, at once, "the source, the resources", and the beneficiaries of development (Sinha, 1985). In other words, development in developing countries was to be endogenous in the true sense of the word. The newer conceptualisation of development in developing countries is analogous to the social–psychological approach to the study of organisations described by Katz (1986). This approach links psychological processes to structural variables. "It recognizes the social context in which people operate but it also recognizes that it is people who are the causal agency and not the organization as an overperson" (p. 18).

An analogy within the area of education to the societal model of developing and using competencies of indigenous people to establish independence from external control of development is the model proposed by Sinha (1990) for intervention programmes designed to improve the performance of "disadvantaged" students. He has advocated that the objectives of such programmes should include reducing dependency attitudes toward external agencies, and instillation of a sense of control and feelings of self-worth within the students.

Conceptualisation Validity

That the conceptualisation of "from the bottom up" development is not a fantasy, but operationally valid is evident from the success stories reported in the literature (Singh, 1992; Sinha, 1985). It is noteworthy that voluntary efforts, even in the midst of scarcity, have been especially lauded for development achievements and that credit for the successes has been accorded to grass-roots resource mobilisation and flexibility of organisational structure (Singh, 1992). Sinha (1990) has also described success stories of local level people, in both cities and villages of India, who have made a dramatic impact on schooling through the provision of health related services.

An Illustration: Education

The problems, concerns, and thrust towards indigenous autonomy with respect to development in developing countries are all apparent in the area of education. From 1945 to 1960, "the methods of educational practitioners and cross-cultural psychologists from the United States and Europe were applied wholesale to Third World countries" because education was considered to be the "crucial" stepping stone for lesser developed countries to participate economically and politically at the international level in new ways (Laboratory of Comparative Human Cognition, 1986, p. 1049). The efforts generally resulted in "very high drop-out rates and uncertain economic benefits" as well as "an impact on students' values and their desire to leave their villages". Subsequently, the necessity for taking the socio-cultural context of the community in which schooling occurs into account has been recognised (Laboratory of Comparative Human Cognition, 1986).

The importance of the need for relating educational development to total development has been emphasised by some scholars in developing countries (Indiresan and Ghatak, 1983; Marimuthu, 1983; Sinha, 1985). A success story of implementation of this has been reported for Malaysia. Subsequent to its independence in 1957, the educational system was unified and restructured to not only satisfy economic needs through the creation of skilled manpower, but also to create "a unified and just Malaysia". It is noteworthy that the educational system developed from social demands within that multicultural society (Marimuthu, 1983).

In summary, it is highly improbable that professionals across countries seeking culturally viable development involvement are likely to succeed if they fail to be cognisant of the problems and concerns discussed here. Rather, their assistance endeavours should be incorporated into a system of networks which respect the initiatives, competencies, and cultures of indigenous peoples at all levels in developing countries.

INTERNATIONAL NETWORKS

An Analogy

The systems of culturally viable development networks within which networks of cross-cultural professionals could be integrated may be visualised as spider web structures. These structures extend outwards in a multitude of directions and consist of interlaced or interwoven strands, interdependent though separated. The destruction of a single strand impacts upon the entire web of which it is a part, but strands can be repaired as seen fit. Each web is expansible, the expanse depending upon the supports needed to anchor the outward extensions of the web. There are many different colours and sizes of webs, differences being determined by a multiplicity of environmental factors. Similarly, the patterns of webs are affected by physical and other environmental factors.

It is important to note that webs are functional and are initiated and woven by spiders whose sizes, energies, and other characteristics determine how the webs are spun. The webs are used at times as incubators for future generations of spiders, as well as to promote survival through containment of other insects in the environment. The young, in turn, become weavers of their own webs in time.

In the spider web analogy and in accordance with the earlier discussion of the true meaning of development, the spiders correspond to indigenous peoples, who constitute the vast majority of populations in developing countries. The local people must initiate development in the sense that true development must reflect their needs, desires, aspirations, and efforts. The spider web analogy accommodates a multiplicity of webs at the local level within developing countries, even within the same geographical area. In some—perhaps, many—cases, the spider may be the counterpart of the local level "key individual(s)", described by Sinha (1985), who organise(s) and enthuse(s) others in the group for endogenous development. These local level key people and/or local level traditional institutions representing the local people would seem to be the logical contacts with others in development strands beyond the local level.

Strands beyond Local Levels

The number and type of other development strands within developing countries necessarily depend upon the structural particularities of specific developing countries. National governments in these countries are certainly part of development webs. International and regional organisations, as well as national governments and voluntary associations in other more developed countries could be part of the web at the outer strands, but only if the dictates of the local population in the developing country guide development efforts. Further, cross-cultural professional networks could make important contributions at certain strands.

Existing Programmes

Governments of many developing countries and some professionals from these countries have been cooperating with international organisations and national associations or agencies in order to assist developing countries in various ways. This is clear from a study of the two volume *Encyclopedia of associations*, which lists more than 9,700 entries in its 1991 edition of *International organizations* (Burek, 1991). The organisations included are nonprofit and international in scope, membership, and/or interest. The entries include multinational and binational groups and national organisations with headquarters outside the United States of America. Entries are arranged by broad fields, such as business and commerce, science, medicine, education, agriculture, and public affairs. There is another volume, *National organizations of the U.S.* (Burek, 1991), which lists more than 22,000 entries in three parts, also arranged by broad fields.

The national volume, alone, lists many associations whose goals are to assist developing countries. These include private, public, as well as voluntary organisations. Some are explicitly supportive of the cultures of developing countries. For example, The International Foundation, based at the Physiology Department of the State University of New York, supports cultural and other projects, including preservation of resources, "throughout the Third World" (p. 1234). The Self Help Foundation in Iowa, dedicated to supporting "self-sufficiency in developing countries" and which works with international development organisations, among other groups, requires "the use of appropriate technology compatible with the technical, economic, and social environment of the users" (p. 1236).

The national volume provides evidence that many developing countries in Asia are already involved in international assistance efforts. Examples are the Nepal Blindness Program and the Aravind Eye Hospital in India, both assisted by the SEVA Foundation (p. 1236). Children's Aid International operates a primary health care clinic in Malaysia (p. 1166). India, Thailand, and the Philippines have autonomous programmes supported by the International Institute of Rural Reconstruction, which provides high level leadership training to stimulate the national leaders to implement programmes in their countries (p. 1278).

There are organisations in Bangladesh, Nepal, Thailand, and Indonesia which work with private agencies collaborating together. In addition to promoting a network of private–voluntary organisation financial managers, the aim is to strengthen the capabilities of development agencies (p. 1235). The Centre for Development and Population Activities is another organisation providing training and other support to Third World development professionals. Health, community development, and income generating activities are included in management topics (p. 1233). Technical assistance in the areas of water, energy, construction, agriculture, food processing, soil, foliage, and business is available to organisations in developing countries through volunteers in Technical Assistance, which places emphasis on technologies "appropriate to given situations" (p. 1236).

Many more organisations, agencies, associations, foundations, etc. offer assistance to developing countries in Africa, Asia, South America and island chains.

Forms of Networks

Many of the associations listed in the national volume of the *Encyclopedia of associations* (Burek, 1991) are forms of networks. Descriptions of these forms of networks and illustrative examples of listed associations which have these forms, will be discussed in the following.

Form 1: Non-indigenous persons train indigenous persons. The emphasis of this form is on training indigenous personnel, including professionals, of developing countries to develop needed structures within their countries. This is sometimes done through the recruitment of well qualified specialists from outside of a country to volunteer short-term assistance within the developing country. An example of this form of network is the "Farmer-to-Farmer" programme sponsored by Volunteers in Overseas Cooperative Assistance to address specific problems of cooperatives or producers (p. 1236).

This form of network appears to correspond to the type of relationship among the Chinese which Hwang (1987) has labelled "instrumental". The relationship, expected to be short-term, is for the sole purpose of achieving a particular goal.

Form 2: Non-indigenous persons assist, but do not train indigenous persons. In some cases, a network of external helpers volunteer their expertise through the direct application of their skills to tasks, but do not train indigenous personnel in the developing countries. An example of this type of network is Volunteer Optometric Services to Humanity, which recruits vision care workers to travel to developing countries at their own expense and attend to the visual problems of needy persons, rather than to train or assist local persons to establish clinics and provide services (p. 1245).

This form is likely to lead to dependency attitudes and relationships within developing countries if it were to be continued on a long-term basis without attempts to work with indigenous persons at appropriate strands to engender awareness of vision issues and, if requested, to help train local level or other indigenous level vision personnel. This is an example of giving developing countries fish, rather than the tools to enable them to fish for themselves on a continual basis.

Form 3: Indigenous people abroad to indigenous country networks. A third type of network enables people of an indigenous country living in another part of the world to come together to support the country in ways that seem needed. An example is the presently inactive Friends of India Society International. The participants are primarily persons of Asian Indian ancestry living outside of India who "function as a people's channel" of communication between India and their countries of residence. One goal is to support development projects in India (p. 1850).

This is a broader form of networking than the collectivist variant described by Sinha (1985, p. 114), characterised by "social networks of friends and relatives who are located at distant places, but keep in touch with each other and safeguard each other's interests". Both these types of networks are likely to take into account indigenous factors. Since the majority of the indigenous population of a developing country does not have friends and relatives abroad, the broader type of network is more likely to advance endogenous development within developing countries.

Form 4: Organisation-to-organisation networks. Another type of network, and one closer to the professional type of network presently proposed for assisting the creation of culturally viable development structures within developing countries, is exemplified by the International Association of Family Sociology. One of the objectives is to enable professional family organisations, among others, around the world to be in contact with each other and to address family issues in relation to societal problems (p. 1208).

This type of organisational interaction could contribute to culturally viable development in developing countries only to the extent that the issues addressed are those of concern to developing countries and to the extent that developing country participants operate at the appropriate development strands within their countries to uncover those aspects of issues which local level indigenous individuals and groups wish to explore.

Proposed New International Networks

As evidenced by the examples cited here, some international associations have experts in a single discipline or area, helping developing countries in certain ways. Some of these associations aim to support personnel in developing countries to establish and maintain the needed structures. But there seems to be a dearth of associations devoted to a single profession and established solely to work with their developing country members for the purpose of assisting them in their effort to strengthen the institution and/or improvement of development structures within their countries in accordance with the plans established by local level groups or their representative traditional institutions. This void needs to be filled.

Roles of Cross-cultural Professionals

In discussing endogenous development from the Indian perspective, Sinha (1985) has indicated that even if there is a consensus on development priorities among the local people and they are mobilised by key persons to work on problems of concern to them and to plan develop-ment, certain prerequisite conditions must be created. The require-ments for the creation of these conditions are appropriate amount of coordination, guidance, resources, and support. These requirements are needed to spur local level planning and participation in most, if not all, developing countries. Helping to meet such requirements is a role that cross-country professionals, that is, professionals from developed countries and their counterparts in developing countries, can assume without infringing upon truly endogenous development.

Culture Knowledgeable Professionals and Development Needs

Professionals who are citizens and/or culture knowledgeable residents of developing countries are most suitable for serving as liaisons between certain development strands within their own countries and their professional counterparts in developed countries. Professionals in developing countries are knowledgeable about their own profession, have, or can easily obtain, knowledge about their counterparts' countries, and are aware of the complexities of governmental and social strands in their own countries. They, themselves, are part of certain strands.

Indigenous professionals are in a unique and strategic position to contact key persons or institutions at lower development strands to ensure that the development needs as perceived from particular governmental perspectives are congruent with the needs expressed at the lower levels. For example, what may appear to be a suitable site for a development project related to energy production, a bridge, may be totally unsuitable from the point of view of a person familiar with the culture at the lower levels. To illustrate, native Americans, or American Indians, in the United States of America, considered to be a more developed country, have been protesting against industrial develop-ment in several areas where they live. The reason being that the process of development would destroy their ancestral burial mounds as well as other lands considered sacred and which are culturally valued, therefore, by the native Americans. Thus, their needs do not include development at these sites, as development is in contradiction to their cultural needs.

Professionals learn more about a country when they have had extensive first-hand experience of it. Knowledge of cultural factors such as customs, values, attitudes, beliefs, motivations, and other psychological characteristics which influence education, training, and other development related endeavours requiring interactions between people within a country is higher among professionals most familiar with the country. Professionals are more aware about cultural variations and the consequent ramifications in their own countries. These professionals are at an advantage to have more knowledge of population dispersions, topography, climatic variations, political and other social structures, societal systems, and social conflicts—factors related to the creation of culturally viable development structures.

They are also better equipped to become aware of the types and extent of development needed at the national government strand of the development web. Compared to other professionals, they have acquired more extensive knowledge, formally and informally, about their countries as a result of their day-to-day life in their country. In addition, because of their greater command of indigenous languages and/or dialects and because of the facilitative effects of cultural identification, these indigenous professionals are likely to be more effective than non-indigenous professionals in promoting utilisation of culturally viable development structures, once they have been established.

The importance of cultural knowledge for optimal interactions, whatever the goals might be, has been made clear by many cross-cultural professionals (see Pederson, 1987). Disregard for or violation of the psycho-social characteristics of the culture of a developing country in an attempt to satisfy the apparent needs of the country could impede development endeavours. Such potential conflicts are easily recognised by professionals in developing countries.

An example is the case of Indonesia in the area of health. Traditional beliefs about the causes of discomfort, illness, and disease and healing and practices have been blended into modern medicine. Recognising the improbability of abolishing or prohibiting traditional medical practices of the "dukun" or folk healer, the Department of Health instituted guidelines and programmes for these practices while, at the same time, concentrating on altering traditional attitudes toward health related behaviours through education (Bunge, 1983a, p. 114). This is a variation of "culture-care repatterning" whereby the best folk and professional lifeways are meaningfully integrated (Leininger, 1987, p. 110).

Variations of the concept of cultural preservation—whereby desirable factors are retained without any form of modification in development efforts—and the concept of cultural accommodation—whereby existing cultural factors are used as well as desirable new factors to achieve development goals—have been illustrated in the case of persons of Vietnamese and Filipino ancestry, among others (Leininger, 1987).

Roles of Professional Organisations

Many professions have regional, national, and/or international organisations which could develop networks for the purpose of assisting indigenous development in developing countries. In the case of international organisations, networking would be a question of recruiting members from both more developed countries and less developed countries to form a subcommittee or division of the international association for the specified purpose. Regional and/or national associations in developing countries could approach regional and/or national associations in other countries for the purpose of forming alliances with an emphasis on facilitating endogenous development in developing countries.

Thus, there could be psychologists-to-psychologists, engineers-to-engineers, architects-to-architects, etc., contacts at various levels.

The basic aspect of such networks would be to assist in the formation of development structures for the operationalisation or implementation of needs satisfaction. Thus, optometrists would not simply volunteer to examine eyes, fit glasses, or treat certain eye ailments, but would also help develop institutes for training indigenous personnel to grind lenses, use the Snellen Chart to determine normality of vision, provide other diagnostic and therapeutic treatments and services, and to manufacture and/or develop procedures for eye glasses and other vision related products. Psychologists from more developed countries could, depending upon their area of specialisation, share concepts and methods (to be accepted or not by their developing country counterparts in accordance with appropriate development). Psychologists from developed countries could also contribute materials, equipment, funds, and/or knowledge of available fund sources.

RECOMMENDATIONS

Considering that endogenous development begins from within a country, the following general recommendations are made for the initiation and continuation of an international developing country development network.

One or more members of a particular profession who are indigenous citizens of a developing country could contact international associations of their profession to request the formation of an association across countries the main objective of which would be to facilitate endogenous development within the country. To maximise the number of association contacts, developing country professionals could utilise literature and/or computerised data bases to learn more about existing agencies and/or associations of professionals willing and able to assist development efforts. Requests could also be made for pertinent publicity in the literature of professional associations. Associations could be made aware at the time of contact that development goals, plans, and strategies would be instituted in the developing country and that indigenous professionals would be the contacts requesting assistance as needed.

Developing country professionals could consult local key people and/or their representative institutions as well as government officials in their country to evolve ways in which the professionals could contribute to development through guidance, resources, coordination, and/or support. Once needs have been identified, whether related to new plans or old projects, these professionals could network with their non-indigenous counterparts to secure funding, information, personnel, materials, etc., as required to meet those needs. If developed country professional associations have ongoing programmes for developing countries, but a particular country is not a participant, indigenous professionals from that country could request participation if the programme fits in with endogenous development plans. Developing country professionals could compile a list of professional contacts in developed countries to help, in certain circumstances, to expedite, support, and/or inquire about help sought in the contact's country.

International networks for endogenous development within developing countries should include indigenous local level groups and their institutions, government agencies and indigenous professionals in developing countries, and the latter's counterparts in developed countries, recruited through professional associations and other groups. Professionals from developed countries could contribute to endogenous development in developing countries by responding to calls for assistance from their partners in developing countries, who are most suited for liaison between external professionals and indigenous persons or institutions at various development strands. Professionals in developing countries should initiate requests to professional associations to establish subcommittees, divisions, or new associations for the express purpose of assisting endogenous development in their countries.

REFERENCES

BRISLIN, R.W. (1993). *Understanding culture's influence on behavior*. Fort Worth, TX: Harcourt Brace Jovanovich.

BUNGE, E.M. (1983a). *Indonesia: A country study*. Washington, D.C.: US Government Printing Office.

BUNGE, E.M. (1983b). *Burma: A country study*. Washington, D.C.: US Government Printing Office.

BUREK, D.M. (1991). *Encyclopedia of associations* (Vol. 1, Part 2). Detroit: Gale Research.

HUI, C.H. (1990). Work attitudes, leadership styles, and managerial behaviors in different cultures. In R.W. Brislin (Ed.), *Applied cross-cultural psychology* (pp. 186–208). Newbury Park, CA: Sage.

HWANG, K.K. (1987). Face and favor: The Chinese power game. *American Journal of Sociology, 92*, 944–974.

INDIRESAN, J. and GHATAK, R. (1983). Society and the educational system in India. *International Review of Applied Psychology, 32*(4), 381–405.

KATZ, D. (1986). The social psychological approach to the study of organizations. *International Review of Applied Psychology, 35*(1), 17–37.

LABORATORY OF COMPARATIVE HUMAN COGNITION. (1986). Contributions of cross-cultural research to educational practice. *American Psychologist, 41*(10), 1049–1058.

LEININGER, N.M. (1987). Transcultural caring: A different way to help people. In P. Pederson (Ed.), *Handbook of cross-cultural counseling and therapy* (pp. 107–115). New York: Praeger.

MARIMUTHU, T. (1983). Education and occupation in Peninsular Malaysia. *International Review of Applied Psychology, 32*(4), 361–380.

PEDERSON, P. (1987). *Handbook of cross-cultural counseling and therapy*. New York: Praeger.

REGMI, M.P. (1992). History of psychological researches in Nepal. Abstract in the programme book for the Fourth Asian Regional Conference of the International Association for Cross-Cultural Psychology, Kathmandu.

ROSS, R.E. (1990). *Cambodia: A country study*. Washington, D.C.: US Government Printing Office.

SINGH, S.K. (1992). Management of scarce resources: Role of non-governmental organizations. Abstract in the programme book for the Fourth Asian Regional Conference of the International Association for Cross-Cultural Psychology, Kathmandu.

SINHA, D. (1990). Intervention for development out of poverty. In R.W. Brislin (Ed.), *Applied cross-cultural psychology* (pp. 77–97). Newbury Park, CA: Sage.

SINHA, J.B.P. (1985). Collectivism, social energy, and development in India. In I.R. Lagunes and Y.H. Poortinga (Eds.), *From a different perspective: Studies of behavior across cultures* (pp. 109–119). Lisse: Swets and Zeitlinger.

UNESCO. (1977). *Medium term plan* (1977–1982), Document 19c/4, Paris, 305–307. Cited by J.B.P. Sinha. (1985). Collectivism, social energy, and development in India. In I.R. Lagunes and Y.H. Poortinga (Eds.), *From a different perspective: Studies of behavior across cultures* (pp. 109–119). Lisse: Swets and Zeitlinger.

27

Coda

JANAK PANDEY

This section is not a summary or integration of the contents of papers
included in this volume. It is a "Coda", a closing section, attempting to
briefly share the contemporary ongoing important debates on the
nature and directions of cross-cultural psychology. In the 1990s, some
of these debates have moved to the centre stage shaping the course of
the discipline and, therefore, a brief discussion is in order.

The issue related to cross-cultural psychology versus cultural psychology (Shweder, 1990) acquired such prominence that Walt Lonner
(1992) made a proposal to rename the International Association for
Cross-Cultural Psychology. Of course, this provocative suggestion
evoked mixed reactions (Cole, 1990; Dasen, 1993; Davidson, 1994;
Poortinga and van de Vijver, 1994; Segall, 1993). The debate has,
however, demonstrated beyond doubt the importance of culture in the
understanding of human nature and psychological processes.

To some extent, the concepts of cross-cultural and cultural psychology
are sources of confusion. The two are more like approaches to link
culture with behaviour and psychological processes. Cross-cultural
psychology has its own long historical roots and background but it was
given a momentum and formal recognition as a discipline only in the
early 1970s. In the paradigm of cross-cultural psychology, culture is

generally treated as an independent variable. It is known as an approach of comparative studies involving more than one culture (Triandis, 1980). Under this tradition, some may treat culture and behaviour as independent of each other. Culture may be seen something outside of the individual. Thus, traditionally, cross-cultural psychology is more of a methodological approach.

The cross-culturalists argue strongly that without a study of the psychological phenomena across cultures the claim of universality of psychological laws and theories is a fraud. The major impetus for the development of cross-cultural psychology has been the "culture blind" and "culture bound" approach of general psychology (Lonner and Malpass, 1994). General psychology has remained heavily dependent upon theories and data of the western (Euro–American) world (Moghaddam, 1987).

Research and publication activities of cross-cultural psychology succeeded to some extent in challenging the claims of general psychology such as the universality of psychological phenomena without empirical support. For example, in the last two decades, the international and regional Congresses of the IACCP, publications of the proceedings, the *Journal of Cross-Cultural Psychology, Cross-Cultural Psychology Bulletin*, the Sage series of cross-cultural psychology monographs and many other efforts have influenced psychologists in general to realise the importance of a comparative study of psychological phenomena across cultures. Thus, in a short span of two decades cross-cultural psychology has emerged as a major force.

Recently, the cross-cultural approach paradigm has been challenged by an active group of scholars who call their approach cultural psychology (Cole, 1990; Shweder, 1990; Shweder and Sullivan, 1993). They do not see culture and behaviour like "cross-culturalists" as distinguishable. In cultural psychology, culture and behaviour are not separable. Cultural psychology studies psychological processes associated with culture. Culture is within the individual and it is a way of knowing, experiencing, and interacting in the world. Thus, culture is defined as a process.

The status of culture as an independent variable has been questioned. Jahoda (1992) has argued that culture and mind are inseparable. The advocates of cultural psychology take the position that all behaviour is in one sense or another cultural. According to Shweder and Sullivan (1993), cultural psychology is a ". . . study of the way culture and psyche make each other up" (p. 498). They have proposed "psychological pluralism" as the goal of cultural psychology. According to them, ". . . the goal of theory in cultural psychology is to develop a conception of psychological pluralism or group differences psychology that might be described as 'universalism without the uniformity'" (Shweder and Sullivan, 1993, p. 517). Thus, cultural psychology, as Shweder calls it, is a re-emergent discipline, which has yet to develop and convince psychologists about the viability of its assumptions and assertions.

In anthropology and psychology, the conceptualisation and meaning of "culture" have shown some major shifts encouraging the debate of cross-cultural versus cultural psychology. Berry (1994) has noted that the earlier conceptions of culture as a "given", "out there" and as a "separate entity" had an impact on cross-cultural psychology. He has argued that the recent cognitive revolution in various areas of psychology has influenced the meaning of culture and the present trend is not to view culture merely as an independent variable. The cognitive orientation implies that the individual experiences, analyses, and interprets culture in his own ways. On the other hand, social constructionists and cultural psychologists argue that culture is not "given", and "out there" but individuals create it. For example, Misra and Gergen (1973) have proposed the adoption of "interpretive modes of knowing", treating "culture as a resource" and the development of a "pluralistic social science" (p. 239).

In the 1980s, another approach called indigenous psychology received momentum. Kim and Berry (1993) in their edited volume entitled *Indigenous psychologies* have listed chapters contributed by psychologists from different parts of the world. They have preferred to call it the "indigenous psychologies approach" implying that there have to be many such psychologies emerging and developing in different cultures. They have noted, "The indigenous psychologies approach attempts to document, organize, and interpret the understanding people have about themselves and their world" (Kim and Berry, 1993, p. 3). It is not merely a study of exotic cultures and their people. It is essential for all developed, developing, and underdeveloped world. It is not a non-scientific tradition, it emphasises methodological pluralism.

The ecological, historical, religio-philosophical, political, and overall cultural contexts vary widely in different societies and determine the world-view of the people. The scientific study of psychological processes and behaviour of people necessitates an understanding of the various aspects of the context to which they belong. Many others, for example, Mexican psychologists prefer to use the term "ethnopsychology" (Diaz-Guerrero, 1993). Diaz-Guerrero (1993) and his colleagues have been consistently working to develop an ethnopsychology for Mexican culture by using systematic procedures, establishing historic socio-cultural premises and statements defined operationally as held by majority of the subjects. Another term which has been occasionally used is "societal psychology" (Berry, 1994). Thus, approaches which emphasise understanding "human behaviour in local cultural context but not (at least initially) in comparison with others; . . . include the 'ethnopsychology', 'indigenous psychology', 'societal psychology' . . . in non-contact situations, and the 'ethnic psychology' approach in culture-contact situations" (Berry, 1994, p. 12). Sinha (1994) has rightly pointed out that these approaches are ". . . reactions to the ethnocentric trends of modern psychology in which psychological tenets that have a monocultural base are considered universal, which is more frequently assumed rather than proved" (p. 2). These approaches also emphasise a comparative study of behaviour involving more than one culture. For example, cultural psychology's goal of "universalism without uniformity" does imply a comparative study of culture and behaviour. In the indigenous psychology approach, universal generalisations involve comparisons of results from one indigenous psychology with others (Enriquez, 1993). Thus, these approaches (indigenous, cultural, ethnic, societal) emphasise the development of a culturally relative knowledge base leading to sound comparative studies without the dominance of theories and epistemological tradition of a particular culture in search of universals. In terms of cross-cultural psychology, such an approach may not lead to pseudo-etic. Thus, various approaches are complementary and unity of approaches is required for recognising the role of culture in psychology, which it deserves.

The Asian–Pacific region has provided fertile soil for the growth of the approaches for the study of culture and behaviour. For example, specifically in the Philippines, India, and in the Chinese-speaking countries like Hong Kong and Taiwan, the indigenous approach has acquired prominence. Some of the best research in cultural psychology has been conducted in varied cultural settings in India (Shweder and Sullivan, 1993). The present volume also testifies the Asian contributions to the role of culture in the study of human nature.

REFERENCES

BERRY, J.W. (1994, July). Variations and commonalities in understanding human behaviour in cultural context. Paper presented at the symposium on Early and Recent Developments in Ethnopsychology at the 23rd International Congress of Applied Psychology, Madrid.

COLE, M. (1990). Cultural psychology: A once and future discipline. In J.J. Berman (Ed.), *Nebraska symposium on motivation 1989: Cross-cultural perspectives*. Lincoln: University of Nebraska Press.

DASEN, P.R. (1993). What is in a name? In response to W. Lonner's "Does the Association need a name change?". *Cross-Cultural Psychology Bulletin, 27* (2), 1–2.

DAVIDSON, G. (1994). Cultural, cross-cultural or intellectual? Comments on Lonner, Dasen and Segall. *Cross-Cultural Psychology Bulletin, 28* (1), 1–2.

DIAZ-GUERRERO, R. (1993). Mexican ethnopsychology. In U. Kim and J.W. Berry (Eds.), *Indigenous psychologies: Research and experience in cultural context*. Newbury Park, CA: Sage.

ENRIQUEZ, V.G. (1993). Developing Filipino psychology. In U. Kim and J.W. Berry (Eds.), *Indigenous psychologies: Research and experience in cultural context*. Newbury Park, CA: Sage.

GERGEN, K.J., LOCK, A., GULERCE, A., and MISRA, G. (in press). Psychological science in cultural context. *American Psychologist*.

JAHODA, G. (1992). *Crossroads between culture and mind: Continuities and change in theories of human nature*. London: Harvester Wheatsheaf.

KIM, U. and BERRY, J.W. (Eds.). (1993). *Indigenous psychologies: Research and experience in cultural context*. Newbury Park, CA: Sage.

LONNER, W.J. (1992). Does the Association need a name change? *Cross-Cultural Psychology Bulletin, 26* (3), 1.

LONNER, W.J. and MALPASS, R. (1994). *Psychology and culture*. Boston: Allyn & Bacon.

MISRA, G. and GERGEN, K.J. (1993). On the place of culture in the psychological sciences. *International Journal of Psychology, 28*, 225–243.

MOGHADDAM, F.M. (1987). Psychology in the three worlds. As reflected by the crisis in social psychology and the move toward indigenous Third-World psychology. *American Psychologist, 42*, 912–920.

POORTINGA, Y.H. and VAN DE VIJVER, FONS J.R. (1994). IACCP or IACP? *Cross-Cultural Psychology Bulletin, 28* (2), 3–4.

SEGALL, M.H. (1993). Cultural psychology: Reactions to some claims and assertions of dubious validity. *Cross-Cultural Psychology Bulletin, 27* (2), 2–4.

SHWEDER, R.A. (1990). Cultural psychology: What is it? In J.W. Stigler, R.A. Shweder, and G. Herdt (Eds.), *Cultural psychology: Essays on comparative human development*. Cambridge: Cambridge University Press.

SHWEDER, R.A. and SULLIVAN, M.A. (1993). Cultural psychology: Who needs it? *Annual Review of Psychology, 44*, 497–523.

SINHA, D. (1994, July). Culturally-rooted psychology in India: Dangers and developments. Paper presented at the symposium on Early and Recent Developments in Ethnopsychology at the 23rd International Congress of Applied Psychology, Madrid.

TRIANDIS, H.C. (1980). Introduction. In H.C. Triandis and W.W. Lambert (Eds.), *Handbook of cross-cultural psychology: Perspectives*. Boston: Allyn & Bacon.

Notes on Contributors

John G. Adair is Professor of Psychology at the University of Manitoba, Winnipeg. He is the former President of the Canadian Psychological Association, and is on the Executive Committee of the International Association of Applied Psychology. Prof. Adair has been involved in empirical research on the social psychology of behavioural sciences and education. He has published extensively and is the author of *The Human Subject*. His current research interests include cross-national studies of discipline development and indigenisation in developing countries.

Bobbie M. Anthony is Professor of Psychology and Coordinator for Black Studies at the Chicago State University. She is a member of several local, national, regional and international associations of mathematics, psychology, education. She is also a member of special groups concerned with ethnicity and gender. She has published and lectured in these areas extensively.

J.W. Berry is Professor of Psychology at Queen's University, Kingston, and is Past President of the International Association for Cross-Cultural Psychology. He is the author of *Human Abilities in Cultural Context*, co-editor of *Field Method of Cross-cultural Psychology*, and co-author of *Cross-Cultural Psychology: Research and Applications*, and *Human Behaviour in Global Perspective: An Introduction to Cross-cultural Psychology*.

Deborah L. Best is Professor in the Department of Psychology, Wake Forest University, Winston-Salem. She is Treasurer of the International Association for Cross-Cultural Psychology. Prof. Best has written extensively in the area of cross-cultural psychology and has contributed to numerous journals and edited volumes including *Measuring Sex Stereotypes: A Multinational Study* and *Sex and Psyche: Gender and Self Viewed Cross-culturally* (co-author).

Dharm P.S. Bhawuk has a degree in mechanical engineering from the Indian Institute of Technology, Kharagpur, and MBA from the University of Hawaii. He has specialised in cross-cultural and management training. At present he is working for his doctoral degree in organisational behaviour and management at the University of Illinois.

John B. Biggs is on the Faculty of the Department of Education, University of Hong Kong. His interests include comparative study of learning and teaching processes. He has contributed to reputed journals and edited volumes.

Klaus Boehnke received his doctoral degree from the University of Technology, Berlin. He has served as Assistant Visiting and Associate Professor at the Free University of West Berlin, the Australian National University, Canberra, and Humboldt-University, East Berlin. Dr. Boehnke is engaged in interdisciplinary research on youth and adolescence with a focus on cultural variations in socialisation and values.

Christopher H.K. Cheng is University Assistant Lecturer in Psychology at the City Polytechnic of Hong Kong, and Visiting Lecturer in Adolescent Psychology at the University of Hong Kong. He is actively engaged in research on Hong Kong adolescents' value systems, and cross-cultural study of self-concepts and self-esteem.

Lutz H. Eckensberger has been Professor of Psychology (Development and Culture) at the University of Saarland since 1976. In the mid-1960s, within the context of applied research in Afghanistan and Siam, he evinced a keen interest in cross-cultural psychology. In recent years, he has been working primarily on methods of psychology, moral development, and on the relation between cognition and affects. He was Fellow of the Centre for Advanced Studies, Berlin in 1985. He has been advisory editor for the *Journal of Cross-Cultural Psychology, Human Development* and *Psychologie in Erziehung und Unterricht*. He has edited several books.

N.T. Feather is Foundation Professor of Psychology in the School of Psychology at the Flinders University of South Australia, Adelaide. He is Past President of the Australian Psychological Society. He has written extensively on achievement motivation, expectancy-value theory, attribution theory, gender role, psychology of values, and the psychological impact of unemployment. Prof. Feather has authored or edited several books, including *Expectations and Actions: Expectancy-Value Models in Psychology* and *The Psychological Impact of Unemployment*.

Arlene Franklyn-Stokes is Lecturer in Psychology at the University of Plymouth, Devon. Her research interests include intergroup behaviour.

Ge Gao is Assistant Professor of Communication at San Jose State University. Her research interests include communication in China and the United States as well as intercultural communication.

Aydan Gülerce is Associate Professor of Clinical Psychology at Bogazici University, Istanbul. She pursued her doctoral training as a Fulbright scholar first at the University of Denver and then at CUNY. She has meta-theoretical interests in psychology, and has adopted an integrative approach to interpersonal, family system/structure, and socio-cultural issues.

William B. Gudykunst is Professor of Speech Communication at California State University, Fullerton. He is working on a theory of effective interpersonal and intergroup communication.

Archana Gupta is a doctoral research fellow at the Department of Psychology, University of Allahabad. She is interested in the social psychology of legal decision-making.

Çiğdem Kağitçibaşi is Professor at Bogazici University, Istanbul, and Past President of the International Association for Cross-Cultural Psychology. She was involved in a nine-country cross-cultural study on the value of children. She has several publications to her credit including *Sex Role, Family and Community in Turkey*, and *Growth and Progress in Cross-cultural Psychology*.

Antony Kennedy is a graduate student at the University of Canterbury, Christchurch. He has co-authored several papers on sojourners' adjustment. He is primarily interested in cross-cultural psychology, particularly the role of personality and psychology of women.

I.R. McKee is a graduate student and researcher at the School of Psychology, Flinders University of South Australia. He has collaborated in recent investigations of attitudes towards high achievers. His current research interests include models of retributive justice and revenge motive.

R.C. Mishra is Reader in Psychology at Banaras Hindu University. After obtaining his doctoral degree from the University of Allahabad, he worked at the Queen's University as a National Fellow, and later as Shastri Fellow. He has written extensively in the areas of perception, cognition, schooling and acculturation, and has contributed to prestigious journals and books.

Janak Pandey is Professor at the Centre of Advanced Study in Psychology, University of Allahabad, and President of the International Association for Cross-Cultural Psychology. He has published extensively on social influence processes and on contemporary social and environmental issues that are relevant to socio-economic change in developing societies. He has edited *Psychology in India: The State-of-the-Art* (3 volumes).

Ype H. Poortinga is senior Lecturer in the Department of Psychology at the Tilburg University. He is President of the European Federation of Professional Psychologists Associations and is the co-editor of *Basic Problems in Cross-cultural Psychology, Crosscultural Contributions to Psychology,* and *From a Different Perspective: Studies of Behaviour across Cultures.* He is the co-author of *Cross-cultural Psychology: Research and Applications,* and *Human Behaviour in Global Perspectives: An Introduction to Cross-cultural Psychology.*

Murari P. Regmi is Reader in Psychology, Tribhuvan University, Kathmandu. He has authored several books and journal articles on psychology and is a reputed literary critic. At present he is President of the Nepalese Psychological Association.

Ruth Scott has collaborated with her husband, William A. Scott, in research projects since 1957. During the last two decades she has focused on cross-cultural research. She is Research Assistant at the Social Psychiatry Unit of the Australian National University, Canberra.

William A. Scott was Professor of Psychology at the Australian National University, Canberra, since 1977. Prior to this, he was Professor at the James Cook University, Townsville, and at the University of Colorado. His research interests included values, attitudes, cognitive structure, social structure, and human adaptation. Prof. Scott passed away on 8 November 1991.

Ayan Bahadur Shrestha recently retired as Professor and Head, Central Department of Psychology, Tribhuvan University, Kathmandu. He obtained his doctoral degree from Patna University. He is primarily interested in the effect of cultural factors on cognitive development and the health behaviour of the people of Nepal. At present, he is working on acculturation and its psychological consequences.

Durganand Sinha was the founding Head and Professor of Psychology, Department of Psychology at the University of Allahabad. He has been the President of the International Association for Cross-Cultural Psychology, as also its Fellow. He has published extensively and has contributed to various national and international journals and is the author of several books including *Indian Villages in Transition: A Motivational Analysis, Motivation and Rural Development, Psychology in the Third World Country: The Indian Experience, Social Values and Development: Asian Perspectives* and *Effective Organizations and Social Values* (co-edited). His research interests include psychological dimensions of poverty and deprivation, cross-cultural psychology, psychology in developing countries and indigenisation in psychology.

Mala Sinha received her doctoral degree from the University of Allahabad. At present she is a Fellow at the Management Development Institute, New Delhi. She is interested in the psychological study of unemployed youth.

Nishamani Tripathi is a consulting psychologist in a child guidance centre at Allahabad. She obtained her doctoral degree from Banaras Hindu University. Her current research interests include issues related to perceptual–cognitive development of children from socio-culturally deprived communities.

R.C. Tripathi is Professor and Head, Centre of Advanced Study in Psychology, Allahabad University. He was a Fulbright Fellow at the Institute for Social Research, University of Michigan. His research interests include intergroup relations, processes in organisations and human behaviour in resource scarce environments. He has co-edited a book entitled *Norms Violations and Intergroup Relations*.

Arjun Udas is lecturer in Tribhuvan University, Kathmandu. He is interested in the psychological aspects of development and change.

Colleen A. Ward received her doctoral degree from the University of Durham. She has held teaching and research positions at the University of West Indies, Trinidad, the Science University of Malaysia, the National University of Singapore and the University of Canterbury, New Zealand. Her major research interests include cross-cultural psychology and psychology of women.

David Watkins is Reader in Education at the University of Hong Kong. He obtained his doctoral degree from the Australian National University. Dr. Watkins has contributed to numerous journals and edited volumes.

John E. Williams is Professor, Psychology Department at Wake Forest University. He is the co-author of *Race, Color and the Young Child; Measuring Sex Stereotypes: A Multidimensional Study*; and *Sex and Psyche: Gender and Self Viewed Cross-culturally*. He was the editor of the *Journal of Cross-Cultural Psychology*.